LIMITLESS

LIMITLESS

*The Federal Reserve Takes on
a New Age of Crisis*

JEANNA SMIALEK

Alfred A. Knopf   New York 2023

THIS IS A BORZOI BOOK
PUBLISHED BY ALFRED A. KNOPF

Copyright © 2023 by Jeanna Smialek

www.aaknopf.com

Knopf, Borzoi Books, and the colophon are registered
trademarks of Penguin Random House LLC.

Library of Congress Cataloging-in-Publication Data
Names: Smialek, Jeanna, 1991– author.
Title: Limitless : the Federal Reserve takes on a new age of crisis / Jeanna Smialek.
Description: First edition. | New York : Alfred A. Knopf,
[2023] | Includes bibliographical references.
Identifiers: LCCN 2022024145 | ISBN 9780593320235
(hardcover) | ISBN 9780593320242 (ebook)
Subjects: LCSH: Board of Governors of the Federal Reserve System (U.S.) | Federal
Reserve banks—United States. | Banks and banking, Central—United States. |
Monetary policy—United States. | United States—Economic policy—2009–
Classification: LCC HG2563 .S595 2023 | DDC 332.1/10973—dc23/eng/20220526
LC record available at https://lccn.loc.gov/2022024145

Jacket photograph by Ed Freeman/Stone/Getty Images
Jacket design by Oliver Munday

Manufactured in the United States of America
First Edition

For Pete

The average person's security is no greater than the stability of the economy in which he is a participant.

—*Marriner S. Eccles*

CONTENTS

LIMITLESS

INTRODUCTION

THE INTERVIEWER ON THE April 9, 2020, webcast had a simple question for the chair of the Federal Reserve: How much support could the central bank provide to businesses and households using its emergency powers? Markets were flailing and people were suddenly losing their jobs as the coronavirus pandemic swept the nation and the world. America was looking to Jerome Powell for help.

"There is no limit on how much of that we can do," Powell sternly explained, dark eyebrows knitted below his silver hair. "Other than that it must meet the test under the law."

Central banking doesn't offer a lot of mic-drop moments, but that was one. Powell's assertion came about a month and a half after the pandemic had begun to batter global asset prices and a few hours after the Federal Reserve had unveiled a rescue program unlike any it had previously attempted, one that would stretch the central bank's abilities further than they had ever extended before.

The Fed had once been definitively limited. Upon its creation in 1913, some of its founders didn't even want to call it a "central bank." It was supposed to monitor commercial banks to prevent risky business and to keep cash flowing around the financial system, so that it didn't get stuck in Memphis when it was needed in Montgomery. It was set up to help banks function smoothly in times of trouble, an ability that was curbed by strict rules. But as of Powell's tenure, decades of crises and a few pivotal characters had fundamentally changed the Fed's purpose and function in America's economy. By the time we all learned the term "social distancing" and became armchair experts on mRNA in 2020, the Fed had become central banker to the world, the most important economic policy setter in history,

and the enabler of modern finance. And the following year, as inflation took off in the wake of the government's sweeping response to
the pandemic, it was the Fed that America would look to as its first
line of defense.

In the modern era, the central bank's most basic job is—as it has
been for decades—to keep the economy humming along at a steady
but sustainable pace. The goal is to foster maximum employment
but also slow and stable inflation. The Fed attempts to achieve those
targets by guiding the cost of money—interest rates—in a way that
encourages people to save during good times and spend during bad
ones. Doing so can help to heat up a tepid economy, like the one that
followed the Great Recession of 2008, or slow down an overheating
economy, like the one that followed the onset of the pandemic.

But the Fed's twenty-first-century role goes far beyond economic
management, especially during moments of financial crisis. Central
banks around the world have long played the role of "lender of last
resort," keeping credit flowing through the plumbing of financial markets in moments of panic. The Fed began to stretch its backstop role
notably during the 2008 financial meltdown, helping to save large
banks and a wide variety of other financial companies from disaster.
In 2020, it took those emergency powers to new lengths. As the coronavirus caused a society-wide scramble for cash, the Fed leveraged its
ability to create money to promise to keep credit flowing to big corporations, state and local governments, and midsize businesses on Main
Street. In doing so, it redefined itself as a potential last-ditch financing
provider to the entire economy, rather than simply to Wall Street.

The Fed's modern footprint has also expanded in other ways. Perhaps most controversially, the Fed purchased government-backed
debt in massive sums in response to both the 2008 meltdown and
2020 Covid-related events. The goal each time was to soothe markets
and help to pull a flagging economy back from the brink by lowering interest rates on all kinds of debt, from business loans to mortgages, in hopes of prodding companies and consumers to borrow
and spend. But the effects and side effects of the policy remain hotly
debated. While fans of the post-2008 program have credited it with
supporting an economy in need at a time when Congress was failing

to pass legislation to jump-start growth, critics have blamed bond buying, often called quantitative easing, or QE, for fueling excess on Wall Street and worsening wealth inequality. Even so, when 2020 threatened a repeat disaster, the Fed rolled out bond buying again on an even bigger—for a brief time, literally unbounded—scale. The Fed under Jerome Powell was not just a powerful force in markets and society. It was limitless.

The Fed's towering role in modern America has been enabled by its most special authority: It can create money from nothing. While that ability works through the banking system and has been constrained by strict rules since the central bank's founding, more than a century of necessity, invention, and evolution has brought us to a moment in which the Fed's limits are fuzzy and its capabilities vast.

Now lawmakers, economists, and the public have begun to grapple with the potential consequences of the Fed's huge sway. Some of the questions are diagnostic. Have the Fed's bond purchases really widened the gap between the rich and the poor? Did the most recent round contribute to the post-2020 inflation? Others are fundamental. Is it healthy for our democracy to have a Fed this powerful?

The Fed itself is grappling with its role. It has tried to become more transparent and publicly accountable as it has grown more important, and that openness has helped to pull it into society-wide conversations about fairness, equality, and opportunity. In the time that I have covered the Fed for Bloomberg and *The New York Times,* it has gone from insisting that social issues are not its domain to flying Pride flags and shaping conversations about racial, gender, and geographic inequity with research and expert advice. Now central bankers are hurtling toward a future in which they could play a more critical role in policing climate risk and digital transactions. Fed officials often talk about "staying in their lane," but that lane has been expanding into an avenue.

Limitless is a book about a central bank that is wrestling to define its place in a changing world. It traces the period surrounding 2020, because the pandemic years distilled and put on display the challenges confronting the Fed. It is an institution that needs political independence to function well, but it is operating against a highly partisan backdrop. It wants to help Main Street, but it is best suited to supporting Wall Street. Its officials increasingly recognize the need to serve a diverse constituency, but they themselves tend to have elite backgrounds. And while the Fed is constantly battling cutting-edge problems, its ability to anticipate them can be hampered by an at times myopic focus on avoiding past mistakes.

At the time of this book's publishing, in early 2023, the Fed has spent months waging battle on what has been the fastest inflation since the early 1980s, slowing the economy and the job market in the process. From today's vantage point, what central bankers did and thought in the years around 2020 may seem almost quaint. Nevertheless, they laid the groundwork for this moment. The debates that happened before and amid the early pandemic, together with the Fed's longer history, are the key to understanding how we got here. And while inflation has captured the attention of central bankers and the world, it is essential to revisit the Fed's broader response to 2020 before it fades from memory. The central bank's actions both underlined weaknesses in our financial system and set out precedents that could shape the not-too-distant future.

The chapters ahead jump around chronologically. They will start at an event in late 2019, which I will use to explain the economic context—both in terms of employment and inflation—that the Fed faced coming into the tumultuous period that started in 2020. They will then move to mid-March 2020, detailing one particularly important day in the Fed's coronavirus rescue to show just how high the stakes were as it scrambled to blunt the financial and economic impact of the pandemic.

After setting the stage for the modern discussion, the book will jump back in time in Chapter 3, providing an overview of the history that brought us to this moment in American central banking. It will explain the Fed's early years partly through the eyes of Marriner Eccles—perhaps the most important person in the central bank's early development and almost certainly the funniest. As the chapters work their way back up to 2019, 2020, and 2021, they will track a wide cast of characters but focus on a few key ones. Those include Powell, the Fed chair at the time of the events in question; Lael Brainard, a governor who would go on to become vice-chair; Randal Quarles, the vice-chair for supervision for much of our story; and Neel Kashkari, the Federal Reserve Bank of Minneapolis president. Kashkari was less central to the main action in 2020, but he offers an interesting perspective, partly because of his position at the Treasury Department in the 2008 crisis and the way it haunted him, and partly because of his own considerable shift in thinking over the course of the pandemic and the inflation that followed.

As the modern part of this book tries to answer a deceivingly simple question—What does it mean to be the twenty-first-century Fed?—it will also take you to an oatmeal café in Manhattan's West Village, an elementary school in postindustrial Connecticut, an Orlando nightclub, Pittsburgh's airwaves, and the offices of Capitol Hill. The Fed's tale is, at its core, a story about all of America.

While *Limitless* is mainly a fact-based account of politics, economics, and public figures meant to show how American central banking works in the twenty-first century, it does make one big point. The argument is straightforward, but, I think, important: The Fed has fundamentally changed since its founding, a slow-burning evolution that sped up in 2008 and came fully to bear in 2020. Now it is essential for our democracy that the public understands just how far the Fed's authorities stretch.

America has placed a huge amount of power into just a few pairs of hands at its central bank. Many of the Washington-based Board's most important emergency tools are exercised without buy-in from the rest of the institution, giving the seven presidentially appointed Fed officials enormous license. In 2020, a handful of Fed Board members worked with the Treasury secretary to make critical choices about which businesses would receive potentially make-or-break financial help. And the Fed chair alone wields vast capabilities. During the 2008 financial crisis, for instance, chair Ben Bernanke unilaterally approved a $600 billion bond-buying program to shore up crumbling markets.* Checks and balances, meanwhile, are sparse.

---

* Bernanke notes in his 2022 book, *21st Century Monetary Policy,* that he first authorized the bond-buying program by relying on a rule that allows the Fed chair, based on economic or financial developments between meetings, to order the purchase of securities with the goal of adding reserves to the banking system and adjusting the Fed's main policy interest rate. The committee ultimately voted on the policy before purchases started.

The Fed answers to Congress, but Congress can change it only if lawmakers reach a political compromise, which is often a slow and unsure process. Presidents cannot easily remove Fed chairs.

The Fed is purposefully insulated from politics so that it has room to make hard decisions. Most important, it sometimes needs to harm the economy to contain inflation, a difficult short-term decision that leaves society better off in the longer run. That freedom to maneuver is critical to the Fed's mission and worth protecting. But because the central bank is only distantly accountable to voters, and because its role in our economy has expanded so much, society needs to pay attention to the Fed's abilities—and experts, the media, interest groups, and the broader public must keep pressure on lawmakers to appoint and confirm apolitical central bankers. Fed independence has always been important, but it now matters to more than just price stability. If elected officials were to place partisan loyalists on the Fed Board, the unconventional and emergency tools that the central bank used in 2020 to help stabilize markets and the economy could instead be leveraged to quietly circumvent the democratic process. Favored constituencies or even a handful of favored companies could be given cheap credit through the Fed even if it proves too hard to pass funding for those entities through Congress. The Fed's mass bond buying could also be wielded for political ends, for instance driving the value of the dollar to give the United States an advantage during trade wars. Much like the Supreme Court has sweeping authorities that can be wielded in partisan battles, the Fed's control over money could be used to quietly achieve political goals that are too divisive to accomplish with legislation. That risk is not entirely hypothetical, as this book will show, including through previously unreported details about the political wrangling that helped to shape the Fed's 2020 actions.

Since at least the 1980s, Fed officials have typically believed that the central bank should operate free of politics. Elected politicians have in recent decades mainly respected that independence, appointing officials with expertise to offer and technocratic rather than partisan views on the world. That could change. President Donald Trump carried out a pressure campaign on the Fed in 2019, and in 2020 nearly succeeded at appointing a nominee to the Fed Board who praised him lavishly in published writings and interviews. Likewise, prominent Democrats in 2020 considered trying to use one of the market rescue programs the Fed had established to funnel cheap money to state and local governments in lieu of passing legislation.

These issues are unlikely to go away. While the Fed's actions in 2020 came in response to an unprecedented global pandemic, the pages ahead will make clear that the financial vulnerabilities that necessitated huge Fed action were kindling waiting for a spark. They were known weaknesses, and many of them still exist. It is somewhere between possible and likely that Fed market interventions like the ones that took place during the pandemic will be required again in the future. A widespread understanding of what the Fed is capable of—one that keeps its emergency actions in particular under the scrutiny of the public eye—may be the best way to ensure that the institution is never transformed into a partisan instrument.

Limitless is the product of years of reporting and hundreds of interviews. To protect my sources and allow a narrative format, I generally do not cite people directly unless I'm referencing another journalist's reporting that I did not independently confirm. The endnotes provide details on publicly available material. Quotations from meetings do not always come from the speaker, but they do come from someone with firsthand knowledge. My descriptions of events draw on my own attendance, first-person accounts, public information, or records requests filed under the Freedom of Information Act.

I should offer a word of warning before you get started. Many people who write about the Fed (a) suggest that its officials have saved the world, (b) suggest that they have ruined the world, or (c) suggest that they're some sort of secret cult trying to take over the world. If that is what you're looking for, this is not the book for you. This is the tale of a mighty but fallible institution at a moment of intense soul-searching.

Central banking is one big experiment, and people who claim to have it all figured out are oversimplifying. On the other hand, writers have at times treated Fed policy makers as modern oracles who know something the rest of us do not. That also invites trouble, because the Fed's existence has been one extended parable on the perils of overconfidence.

If these chapters do convince you of something, I hope it is that Fed officials are ordinary people who control increasingly potent tools. Power like that doesn't necessarily make its holders good or bad, and it certainly doesn't make them priests or prophets. It does make them uncommonly interesting.

Chapter 1

THE BEFORE TIMES

"Normal" may vary from time to time.

—*Daniel Tarullo, then a Fed governor, December 2014*
Federal Open Market Committee meeting transcript

THE SCHOOL GYMNASIUM IN East Hartford, Connecticut, did not share much in common with the swanky Washington, D.C., dining establishment that Jerome Powell had frequented before becoming chair of America's Federal Reserve.

At the Metropolitan Club in D.C., which he had once visited regularly for work lunches, gentlemen were expected to wear ties. Real ones. String ties, ascots, and turtlenecks were "not acceptable," the bylaws of the members-only institution sniffed. If a gentleman were to make the faux pas of arriving without appropriate neckwear, something fitting would be loaned to him.

At Silver Lane Elementary School, where Powell had traveled on a late November morning in 2019, it was obvious that many of the jacket-wearing attendees had donned them for the chairman's benefit. Schoolchildren wore purple polo shirts, and at least one person had on blue jeans. The guest list, too, couldn't have been more different. He had usually held one-on-one meetings at the Club, joining high-ranking government officials—generally white men—for American fare served beneath chandeliers.[1] Nearby diners were often known figures from exclusive backgrounds. Women, banned for the bulk of the club's 150-year history, remained relatively scarce.

That gray autumn day in Connecticut, a diverse set of manufacturing workers, teachers, and community advocates sat around a horse-shoe of cafeteria tables hidden underneath black tablecloths. They spooned Mexican rice and roasted chicken from a local grocery store out of buffet-style aluminum steamers. Powell went back for seconds.

The chair of the Federal Reserve was the son of a D.C. lawyer, had been a private equity power player in his middle age, and was perhaps the mightiest economic policy maker in the world at sixty-six. That he had chosen to forsake Washington's more sumptuous halls for a squeaky-floored gym, where the waxy scent of crayons lingered in the air and industrial bulbs cast a cold white light on the proceedings, said something important about his priorities at the central bank he was quietly reshaping.

The Fed had ascended to become the nation's most important economic institution by the early twenty-first century. It guided the economy by setting interest rates, the price of money. It lowered rates to encourage lending and spending when the economy was weak or raised them to slow it down when consumption and hiring were running hot. It was a technocratic job, but an important one with big consequences for the American population. The Fed used its policy to achieve the two main goals Congress had assigned it: keeping inflation low and fostering full employment. Prosperity turned on whether it succeeded.

The Fed's role in society didn't stop there. As of 2019, it also regulated and supervised the nation's largest bank holding companies, monitored financial stability, managed the nation's cash supply and core payments system, and performed extensive economic research. Its officials often gave lawmakers advice, typically vague and nonpartisan, about the national debt or the importance of an unfolding labor force trend. It was, effectively, the government's largest economic and financial think tank. It also served as Wall Street's insurance policy. The central bank had the power to backstop troubled markets in times of extreme stress by lending money and smoothing over trading in hard-to-sell financial assets, a role it had filled most dramatically during the financial crisis that had rocked the world in 2008.

It was a big job, but the Fed was a big institution. It consisted of twelve regional banks scattered across the country and a Board of Governors in Washington, D.C. The regional Fed branches kept commercial banks in their districts supplied with cash, supervised those banks, and employed economic researchers. Regional bank presidents took turns voting on monetary policy—five had a vote at any given time, and one of those was always New York—and held a seat at every policy-setting Fed meeting. The presidents were selected by reserve bank boards, which consisted of local business-people and nonprofit representatives, and were confirmed to their posts by Washington-based officials. They typically stayed in their jobs for as long as they wanted, with some serving for decades. The reserve branches were set up like private corporations, though they functioned in the public's interest.

If the semiprivate regional banks were the Fed's limbs, the Washington-based board was the beating heart of the system. It was fully public, with its seven governors appointed by the president and confirmed by the Senate. The Fed's chairperson, vice-chair, and vice-chair for supervision were all governors, and board members had authorities that presidents lacked. They held constant votes on monetary policy, and they alone regulated the nation's largest banks and voted to create financial rescue programs in times of crisis. They also had very long terms: fourteen years if served from start to finish, though people rarely stayed for full stints. Thanks to how powerful the positions were and how long they could last, the White House typically treated appointments to the Fed Board with gravity, carefully vetting candidates and floating names in the press to make sure they didn't stir up too much controversy.[*]

Powell had first come to the Fed Board in 2012, when President Barack Obama appointed him as one of its seven governors. He was chosen, funnily enough, partly for his Republican politics. The president's latest nominee had failed to pass the Senate Banking Committee, his chances tanked by a Republican senator, and the Democratic administration felt it needed to make a bipartisan offering to the Senate to get a candidate confirmed. As Obama officials searched for qualified candidates to appoint to two open Fed seats, they landed on Jeremy Stein, a financial regulation expert and Harvard University academic who would bring needed expertise to the Board. Other

---

[*] For those following the arithmetic here, that made for nineteen central banking officials in total (twelve presidents and seven governors), but only twelve with a vote at any given time (five presidents and all seven governors).

economists insisted that Stein was a Republican, but when it turned out that he was actually a registered Democrat, the administration decided it wanted him anyway. Officials briefly contemplated pairing Stein with Richard Clarida, a genuine Republican who was a professor at Columbia and adviser at the asset management behemoth Pacific Investment Management Company, or Pimco. Clarida, unfortunately for them, decided that he didn't want to leave his job. They homed in on Powell.

The lawyer and financier had cut a low profile in the Washington policy scene until then, but he was an attractive pick for the political horse trade. He was a moderate Republican, and he was working at a think tank called the Bipartisan Policy Center when the administration came calling, earning $1 per year for his efforts, something unheard of at the institution. He had wanted to get a toehold in the Washington policy discussion, and he had already made tens of millions of dollars in his private-sector career. The debt ceiling crisis of 2011 had given him a major project. That year, congressional conservatives threatened not to raise the nation's borrowing limit, which would have prevented the country from continuing to pay its bills. As a former Treasury official and a clear public speaker, Powell had been able to wage a sober informational campaign detailing exactly when the debt limit would be breached and what that would mean.

Powell had compiled spreadsheets that allowed him to guess the "X Date" when the government would no longer be able to make payments. The government did not produce its own projection, so journalists began to regularly reference the estimate. In a seemingly endless string of meetings, Powell, a trim man with tidy suits and side-combed hair, explained the timeline to senators without hyperbole or judgment, using the same no-nonsense tone that had served him well through long years of private equity dealmaking. The national debt was on an unsustainable path, he agreed, but there was no real choice. Defaulting would pose a huge risk to markets, the economy, and America's standing in the world order.[2]

Republicans got the message, and though it came late in the game, the ceiling was lifted. Powell had been just one voice urging lawmakers to make that evidence-based choice, but the episode had left him looking savvy and, compared to some of his party colleagues, sane.

"Secretary Geithner and Treasury staff got to know Powell well during the debt limit debate when he was one of the most helpful Republican validators for their views," White House economic officials wrote in a memo to President Obama suggesting his potential nomination to the Fed. Still, Powell was not a credentialed academic economist or a storied monetary thinker.

"Perhaps the biggest downside of Powell is that he would bring less thought leadership and creativity to the Federal Reserve than some other candidates might," the memo went on. "Nevertheless, he brings many other strengths" and "is well above average compared to previous Fed governors."

People seek out big government jobs for different reasons, and Jerome Powell seemed to be driven to the higher reaches of American bureaucracy by some combination of a do-gooder attitude and genuine curiosity. The big questions plaguing the world had always piqued his interest. As a Princeton undergraduate in 1975, he had written a thesis on what could spur societal change in South Africa, then enforcing a gruesome apartheid segregation that discriminated against Black people. He had long seen public service as a high calling and a goal, inspired by lessons from the nuns of his Catholic school youth and by familial example. His father, a Washington-based lawyer, had been unable to take a job in the Nixon administration because of financial constraints. The Powell clan was rich by any reasonable standard, but the family of eight didn't feel they could bear the pay cut.[3]

The younger Powell had set out to make a fortune large enough to permit a career that flitted between the private sector and government, and he had succeeded.

After attending Georgetown's law school and beginning his professional life as a Wall Street lawyer at Davis Polk & Wardwell and the firm Werbel & McMillen, Powell in 1984 became an investment banker at the elite firm Dillon, Read & Co., focusing on financing and mergers and acquisitions.[4] The following year, he married Elissa Leonard, a Harvard graduate from Rockville, Maryland, who was then writing a science program for PBS.[5] Like Powell, Leonard was the daughter of socially engaged parents: Her father, a public health administrator and science fiction writer, had marched from Selma with Martin Luther King, Jr., in 1965, and her mother was a public school librarian and later a volunteer art museum docent.[6] Powell and Leonard were known by friends and acquaintances as lovely, charming, active in the world around them. They were the kind of people who seemed destined for higher things.

When George H. W. Bush was elected president, Powell's boss at Dillon, Read & Co., Nicholas F. Brady, became secretary of the Treasury Department. Powell, by then in his late thirties, decided to follow Brady to Washington in 1990. He became assistant secretary at the Treasury, and, at thirty-nine, moved up to become undersecretary for finance. Powell's various positions put him at the center of government debt issuance, giving him a bird's-eye view of the backbone of global bond markets. They also earned him a reputation as a master consensus forger.

As assistant secretary for domestic finance in 1991, Powell had helped to orchestrate a solution when it became clear that the bank Salomon Brothers had been rigging part of the Treasury market. Salomon was then a primary dealer, one of the few select institutions that could buy bonds directly from the government, and it was one of the largest financial firms of its time. If the government punished Salomon for its misdeeds by revoking its primary dealer status, it risked toppling the firm and causing it to dump assets on the market in a rush, which would have been dangerous for the broader system. Over a frantic weekend, officials had wheeled and dealed to keep Salomon in the fold, with some restrictions, while replacing its leadership with Warren Buffett, the famous investor who was then one of its major shareholders. The thorny decisions he was involved in forced officials to exercise one of the principles that would define Powell's later career as a policy maker: relentless pragmatism. If Treasury had made an example of Salomon, it could have sparked wider economic damage. Keeping it alive looked bad, but it was less painful.

"It still gives me nightmares," Powell would say of the episode a quarter century later.[7] Immediately following the disaster, Powell shepherded a government report calling for big changes to the way that Treasury securities were sold to fix the vulnerabilities that had allowed the problem to develop. Quoting one of his counterparts on that project, *The New York Times* reported that Powell had achieved "far more consensus" than had been thought possible while heading the committee of Treasury, S.E.C., and Federal Reserve officials.[8]

Following his early stint in government, one that had left him respected in Washington, Powell had worked in banking briefly before moving in 1997 to Washington-based private equity giant The Carlyle Group. While his experience in government had begun to build up Powell's reputation, his time in private equity would complicate it. Thanks to its proximity to the seat of government power and intricate web of relationships in D.C., Carlyle was the subject of frequent criticism about the revolving door between Washington and finance.[9] Powell spent about eight years there, closing or helping to close deals worth hundreds of millions of dollars.[10] His time at Carlyle, and the debt-laden companies he left in his wake, would provide grist for his critics for decades.[11]

After he left Carlyle, Powell continued to dabble in private equity before making his way into the Washington think tank world and then to the Fed. Once he had been confirmed to the central bank, he chaired a range of committees and kept a low profile as he brought himself up to speed on a complicated array of topics. Monetary policy was anything but simple in the lackluster economic era that followed the 2008 financial crisis. Before he began to deliver speeches or appear in public, Powell spent long months studying, asking Fed economists for briefings, and researching the issues of the day so thoroughly that he built a reputation among the staff for intellectual modesty and extreme meticulousness. Powell might not have been a trained PhD economist, but he was bent on becoming an economic expert.

The job was an interesting one, and over the years Powell earned the esteem of Janet Yellen, then the chair, and his other colleagues for his willingness to take on assignments that ranged from large and consequential to small and mundane. He weighed in thoughtfully on policy decisions. He helped to monitor reserve bank affairs. He pitched in on minor building and budget issues at the Fed's Washington headquarters. Powell found life as a Fed governor frantically busy, but he was the type of person who thrived on activity. He still managed to spend time with his wife and teenage children at their home in Chevy Chase, Maryland, where he and his family were active community members,* and to ride his beloved road bike to and from work and around the paved paths that crisscross the Washington metro area. He also golfed and read for fun (spy novels by John le Carré were a favorite).[12]

Then Donald Trump surprised much of the nation in late 2016 by winning the election to be its forty-fifth president. As the Fed Board's sole Republican, Powell—though he didn't know it at that point— had been abruptly catapulted into the role of heir apparent to the most powerful job in the economic world.

Janet Yellen was in charge at the Fed when Trump took office, having become the first woman to lead the institution in its century-long history in 2014. Yellen was a storied labor economist who came across as professorial and polite. But beneath her friendly Brooklyn accent and dimpled smile she possessed a quiet force. Yellen had inherited rock-bottom interest rates meant to spur growth by encouraging spending. She spent her early tenure working to keep them low, leaning against a faction of the policy-setting Federal Open Market Committee that wanted to raise rates to cool the economy. Five years after the recession that spanned 2007 to 2009 had ended, the labor market was still clawing its way back from a deep abyss and inflation remained short of the Fed's goal for slow but steady price increases. Despite that, some policy makers surveyed the landscape and saw signs that the economic rebound might overheat. Once inflation took off, their logic went, it could become hard to control.

"The Committee can no longer justify its continued zero-rate policy," Jim Bullard, president of the St. Louis Fed, said at the central bank's December 2014 meeting, at a time when unemployment stood at 5.6 percent, well above the 4.4 percent level it had dipped to

---

* So active, in fact, that Elissa Powell's involvement in community governance afforded the financial press a moment of hilarity in 2019. News surfaced that a noisy dog park was dividing the elite Chevy Chase Village, and Elissa, chair of the local board, had to mediate the often overtly snobby fight between people who wanted a spot for their pups to play and those who wanted quiet restored. "At the center of it all is Elissa Leonard, chair of the village board and wife to Jerome H. Powell, who is also a chair," *The Washington Post*'s Jessica Contrera wrote.

during the prior economic expansion.[13] "These data are far too hot to rationalize what was really an unprecedented emergency policy in reaction to a very severe crisis."[14]

Yellen was conscious of the serious human consequences of weakening the job market rebound prematurely by acting to slow the economy. Job applicants would compete for fewer open positions and might fail to find work, permanently weakening their résumés, making it harder for them to land positions down the road, and leaving their families with lower incomes and more limited resources. She agreed that the Fed ought to lift interest rates before inflation picked up toward the central bank's target. "I think we have to base our decisions on where we think inflation and real activity are heading and not where they are," she told her colleagues not long after Bullard voiced his desire to get moving. Still, she first wanted to see signs that labor market conditions were genuinely heating up.

"There is more scope for improvement in the labor market before inflation pressures emerge," she said at the Fed's September 2015 gathering.[15] Once the Yellen Fed did lift the federal funds rate in December 2015, it followed a glacially slow path relative to history, moving rates once in 2016 and three times in 2017.

Yellen was far from the fieriest advocate for patience on the Fed's policy-setting committee. As chair, though, she was both the most powerful voice and the most accountable for the ultimate decision. Her gradualist approach earned her frequent criticism from conservatives on Capitol Hill, who favored higher rates. Yet time proved her patience right. The economy continued to grow, unemployment dropped to unanticipated lows, and inflation was nowhere to be found. For all the real-time warnings that the Fed was moving too slowly and too late, postmortems would eventually criticize the 2015 Fed for raising rates too *early*. Yellen and her colleagues had been so focused on preventing inflation from heating up that they had started to weigh down the job market to hold price pressures back sooner than was necessary, economists would argue in the years that followed.

That was a fairly minor quibble. The economy was chugging along at a respectable pace and Yellen's track record was widely regarded as positive by late 2017, as the end of her first term approached. Despite that, Trump decided to replace her, bucking a long-standing practice in which willing Fed chairs were reappointed even by presidents of the opposite party in a show of respect for the central bank's independence from partisan politics. When Trump had met Yellen for a job interview, a short woman with an elvish face and a white bob haircut sat across the desk from him. She did not, *The Washington Post* would later report, look the way the president thought a Fed chair should. Powell, a man with flawless gray suits and an extra eight or nine inches, evidently fit the mold better.

Whether Yellen's appearance really weighed heavily on the president's mind is hard to know. It is more clearly the case that Trump liked Yellen but felt from the outset that it would be better to have his own person in the job. At the same time, Trump liked low interest rates: He was a property developer, after all, and real estate was one of the biggest beneficiaries of cheap money. It was hard to find someone with conservative credentials who could match Yellen's stance on monetary policy. Powell more or less fit that bill. While he was not an unwavering fan of extensive help for the economy—during his early years as a Fed governor, he had internally questioned the Fed's policy of buying huge quantities of bonds out of concern that it might fuel financial instability—he was mostly aligned with the chair by 2017. In him, Trump and his team saw a way to retain Yellen's basic approach to policy without keeping Yellen.

Plus, Treasury Secretary Steven Mnuchin had interviewed all the candidates for the job, and while there were other Republican contenders, he liked Powell. Mnuchin had been collaborating with the Fed governor closely and found him to be genial and easy to work with. It was a common perception. Powell was a social chameleon who possessed a disarming ability to make whomever he was speaking with feel that he both liked them personally and empathized with their point of view. He never interrupted when others were speaking, he responded to disingenuous or poorly worded questions with courtesy, and he memorized small details about people that he would later unearth at opportune moments in conversation. Powell often let meetings run long, as though his interlocutor were the most important person he would speak with that day. *The New York Times* would eventually run a guest column, written by one of his former Fed economists, titling him "Washington's best-liked man."

Mnuchin's recommendation, Powell's business background and charisma, and the president's desire to leave his mark on the Fed carried the day. On Halloween 2017, as Washington prepared for trick-or-treat night, the president called Powell to inform him that he would get the job.[16] Powell was sworn into his new position at the very top of the American economy in February 2018.

Nearly two years later, the role had taken him to the school gym in postindustrial Connecticut just before Thanksgiving.

Powell had launched a two-pronged initiative as chair. Part one was a review of the Fed's whole approach to setting monetary policy. He was a big-picture guy, and the picture he inherited when he took charge of the Fed worried him and economists whom he respected. Growth had slowed compared to decades past, partly because the population was aging. As that happened, demand for money had declined. Less demand for cash meant that interest rates—which, at their most basic, are how much people will pay to use money today versus tomorrow—had also naturally declined. As a result, the rate setting at which Fed policy would begin to seriously weigh on the economy had dropped steadily lower. The change was sapping the central bank of its power to offset recessions and steady the business cycle by cutting borrowing costs. During the 2007–2009 recession, Ben Bernanke's Fed had slashed interest rates all the way to zero, then had bought unprecedented sums of government bonds to try to provide more help to the economy by lowering longer-term interest rates and by pushing money out of safe bonds and into riskier and more active uses. As of 2018, the jury was still out on how effective those so-called quantitative easing (or QE) programs had been. Economic progress had mostly been plodding, with surprising consequences.

Fed policy makers had spent the 1970s and 1980s trying to wrestle inflation lower, but as growth came up short, prices had begun to climb extremely slowly, languishing below the Fed's target for 2 percent annual gains. Tepid price increases may sound like a good thing, but with inflation low, rates could climb even less before they began to weigh on growth.* That further diminished how much room policy makers had to jump-start the economy in tough times. Weak inflation also increased the risk that prices would decline in a bad downturn, touching off what could be a destabilizing bout of deflation.† Plus, if businesses could not lift prices, they might also struggle to lift wages, sapping a once-dynamic labor market of its vim. A little bit of inflation could be like grease on the gears of the economy. Too little was like rust.

Powell thought it would be prudent to figure out how policy should work in the new low-growth, low-rate, low-inflation era. It seemed likely that policy tools like bond buying would be needed again, and the new chair thought that those programs should be vetted and discussed ahead of time. It also made sense to revisit whether officials were thinking about "full employment" correctly in a changing world. Other economies, including Canada, had held formal reviews for their policy-setting frameworks. It struck Powell as the right moment to follow suit.

Alongside the framework review, the Fed was holding a series of community outreach events. The logic was simple. Reworking the Fed's economic approach with input from the public would look a lot better than handing down a dictatorial new plan from on high, having consulted only bankers and economic policy insiders. The East Hartford gathering was the latest in the series, which the central bank had dubbed Fed Listens, lest the world miss the point.

Top Fed officials were trekking to charter schools near Philadelphia, food banks in Dallas, and panels in Chicago to hear from "ordinary" people: workers without much formal education beyond their high school diplomas, senior citizens, minority groups, and community

---

* The federal funds rate is what economists call a "nominal" rate, meaning it includes whatever price level change is happening in the economy. If prices were climbing by 2 percent, theoretically that meant that the Fed had an extra 2 percent of room to raise rates before it started to constrain the economy.
† The logic here is that declining prices might prompt people to hold off on purchases as they waited for things they wanted to buy—cars, televisions, you name it—to become cheaper. Without consumer spending, which makes up 70 percent of the economy, growth would likely struggle to recover, miring America in a downward spiral.

development organizations. Fed officials, in turn, tried to explain in basic terms what they were up to and how their policies were playing out in the real world. The point was to make it clear to lawmakers, to the press, and ultimately to the American public that the modern Fed was not the central bank of decades past.

That old Fed had been obscure. Alan Greenspan, the chairman who presided over the prosperous 1990s and early 2000s, had once declared that his role had made him an expert at "mumbling with great incoherence." Monetary policy's inscrutability had been a sort of merit badge. America was happy with the economy in those days, and content to leave the Fed to tend to Wall Street. Greenspan, a fixture in Washington high society who dated and eventually married a television journalist and who had, in his youth, palled around with the libertarian icon Ayn Rand, was received as a sort of monetary oracle. Investigative journalist Bob Woodward dubbed him the "maestro." One of his myriad biographies was titled *The Man Who Knew.*[*]

Greenspan's cult of personality owed in part to the era he oversaw. He had been dealt a winning economic hand by history, presiding at a time of globalization hypercharged by a relatively young working-age population and big advances in computer technology, one in which laissez-faire economics and animal spirits were celebrated as engines of prosperity. Thirty years later, Powell had taken the other side of that shuffle. He had inherited an American economy facing graying demographics and a global backdrop made more tenuous by a destabilizing surge in nationalism, rampant inequality, and obvious financial vulnerabilities. Instead of celebrating the triumphs of modern capitalism, Americans were questioning its foundations, from free trade to the unfettered pursuit of profits.

Powell could have tried to become a modern Greenspan, attending D.C. society events and operating from behind a curtain. He might even have succeeded, because he certainly had the credentials. He was the richest Fed chairman in more than half a century, with a fortune of as much as $55 million at the time of his nomination (it's hard to

---

[*] Greenspan had inherited a secretive Fed from Paul Volcker, and he embraced obscurity during his early time as Fed chair, but the central bank did become more transparent later on in his tenure. We will get into the whole story later.

nail down with precision, since government financial disclosures use ranges). He had spent his adult life around a crowd that made that level of wealth feel quotidian. Warren Buffett remained a friendly contact. He had won bipartisan admiration in a hyperpartisan era. Inside-D.C. types still casually recounted conversations with "Jay" or "Janet," referring to Powell and Yellen, just as they had once name-dropped "Alan." The role of Fed chair had lost some of its mystery but none of its cachet.

But Greenspan's high-flying approach to the job wasn't Powell's personal style. He had once told a business school student that his career advice was to work hard and keep his head down, because competent people self-sabotaged all the time.* He was studiously low-key. Nor was aloofness right for the historical moment. The elite university graduates and unelected officials who strolled the Fed's marble halls were destined to attract skepticism as the nation experienced a populist resurgence that spanned both parties, one that had first landed a new brand of outspoken Tea Party Republicans in Congress, which later put Trump in the White House, and which would eventually help to empower a spate of young and progressive Democrats in Congress. America's central bank was not positioned to win any popularity contests as citizens questioned the value of institutions and fretted that the economic deck was stacked against the poor and working class.

The 2008 financial crisis had intensified that reality. It had generated shock waves that ricocheted through society for years, influencing both the way that people saw the Fed and the way that the Fed saw its role so profoundly that the effect was hard to exaggerate.

That was partly because of how the crisis had played out. Commercial and investment banks had spent the early 2000s making risky bets in the housing market and in housing-related securities, lending to subprime borrowers and rolling those bad loans into complicated and rickety financial securities that were sliced, diced, and shuffled around the banking and insurance system. The Fed had relatively few tools to neatly address the growing vulnerabilities, some of which fell under the purview of other regulators, and it had been

---

* Nick Timiraos reported this anecdote in *The Wall Street Journal* in 2017. The student was Sean Gillespie, who went on to work in software.

slow to use those it did have. It did not want to choke off business needlessly and it did not recognize the extent of the problem until too late.

It had been quick, however, to save the system as the mortgage debt piles began to crumble, working with the elected government to roll out rescue programs for the bank Bear Stearns and the insurer American International Group. Under Ben Bernanke's leadership, the Fed had dusted off its emergency lending powers to backstop an array of markets, and it enacted three massive bond-buying programs between 2008 and 2014. The policies propped up asset prices and kept the wheels of credit creation turning in an attempt first to soothe markets and later to prevent economic stagnation.

Many researchers credited the Fed's robust response for staving off a far worse disaster and preventing a rerun of the 1930s Great Depression. But the interventions had also saved irresponsible bankers. Before long, the Fed's policies had helped to send stock prices soaring, even as unemployment remained high and homeowners continued to face life-upending foreclosures. As the deep downturn gave way to a halting recovery, people blamed the central bank for distorting markets and worsening inequality. The libertarian lawmaker Ron Paul had in 2009 published a book titled *End the Fed*, the Occupy Wall Street protest movement that started in New York City in 2011 had explicitly criticized the central bank, and Texas governor Rick Perry had in 2012 suggested that the Fed's policies were "treasonous." Gallup survey data showed that public opinions of the Fed plummeted throughout the 2000s and only slowly began to haltingly recover years after the recession.[17]

The consequences of the Great Recession were real and painful. Opioid addiction tore through America, a public health tragedy that would come to be seen as partly economic, as a lack of opportunity bred hopelessness. Economists documented a surge in "deaths of despair," as people overdosed, died by suicide, or drank themselves to death.* Once-vibrant manufacturing hubs that had fallen on hard times before the downturn had decayed almost into ghost towns in

---

* This research was primarily carried out by Anne Case and Angus Deaton, who eventually turned it into a book titled *Deaths of Despair and the Future of Capitalism.*

its wake. A sense that something had been lost had taken hold across big parts of the country.

Powell had witnessed cynicism festering throughout the decade that followed the downturn. It was easy to understand why much of the country was skeptical about the economic order and the Fed's place in it. Powell expected people to question the Fed's policies as the nation's growth continued at a historically weak rate, and he and his colleagues had decided to answer that public concern with transparency.

Powell found himself in a strange position. Here was a man who had been privileged from birth, who had cut his teeth in corporate law and high finance, and who had amassed and enjoyed fabulous wealth. Yet he was positioning himself as a sort of champion of the proletariat at the Fed because it was what the moment called for. Powell was unfailingly practical.

Fortunately, the one gift history had bestowed upon the chair gave him a chance to offer the public a glimmer of hope. The postcrisis rebound had been sluggish, but that gradual healing included a long stretch of steady job gains, ones that proceeded month after month and pulled would-be workers back into paid employment. The unemployment rate had dropped to a half-century low in 2019 without stoking unsustainable wage growth or higher prices, to economists' widespread surprise. The improvement came at least partly because of the Yellen Fed's patient approach, which Powell had basically continued.[*]

The era of low inflation had enabled the Fed's gradualism. A set of goods and services that had cost $20 in 1970 had more than doubled in price to $41 by 1980, requiring an aggressive Fed response, but inflation had slowed so much by the twenty-first century that a $20 bundle of goods in 2010 cost just $24 by 2020.[18] Consumers and businesses alike had come to expect a steady creep upward in prices, not the kind of rocketing changes that would influence their decisions about what to buy and when. Perhaps partly because families and businesses had adjusted their behavior, accepting slower wage increases and raising prices less vigorously, low unemployment no longer came alongside high inflation the way it had in the 1970s. Pur-

---

* With some caveats. We'll discuss this at greater length in Chapter 6.

suing very low joblessness did not obviously come at a risk of sending prices sharply up.

Where the Fed of decades past had focused on the unpopular task of controlling inflation, the Powell Fed could declare loudly and often that its policies were helping the little guy by driving the jobless rates lower without worrying too much that $1 today would buy far less a year from now. That was a pleasant message for Powell to spread during his many meetings on Capitol Hill and at central bank outreach events.

Evangelizing the good labor market news was part of the goal in East Hartford, where Powell had been shuttled onto a packed tour bus alongside community group members, Boston Fed staffers, and reporters. The excursion took him to see cracked parking lots outside abandoned movie theaters and whisked him past the shell of an abandoned Pizza Hut. Signs of decay waited around every bend. Still, so did signs that employers had begun stretching into the forgotten community to find productive workers. Cars crowded the local food market lot, and some of them were new. In the elementary school gym, after the tour, the chairman had met an eighteen-year-old named Jasmine Ayala who had recently landed a $29-per-hour manufacturing job.* The driven young woman, who was putting herself through college by working late shifts, had convinced her managers at Pratt & Whitney to let her miss work that day for a chance to meet the Fed chair.

"Keep going to school," he had instructed her jovially during their brief conversation, sounding like the dad of three that he is.

He had also chatted with young students, leaning toward them as photographers snapped their pictures. The stories, and the images, would run in publications around the country and online. If Greenspan had mumbled strategically, Powell mingled strategically.

"There is still plenty of room for building on these gains," Powell would declare that same night in a dimly lit hotel conference hall in nearby Providence, Rhode Island, as an assembly of business leaders gathered before him, sipping after-dinner coffee as he spoke.

The optimistic speech had earned him a standing ovation, not a

---

* Chris Rugaber, a journalist at the Associated Press, first reported on Ayala's attendance at the event.

frequent occurrence after orations about monetary policy. The cheerful message had been just interesting enough, coming from the leader of the American economy, that it would be repeated in newspaper headlines across the country the following day.

Powell could not know on that brisk November evening that within months, the job gains of the last decade would be nothing but a memory. The businesspeople before him, contentedly nibbling their desserts, would find themselves fighting to keep their companies alive. Within two years, the era of quiescent inflation would stage a sudden reversal. And as the world changed abruptly, the very idea that the Fed, a collection of economists with finance-specific tools, could listen to and serve a constituency beyond Midtown Manhattan and Wall Street would face trial by virus.

Chapter 2

THE MONTH MARKETS MELTED

Economics is a highly sophisticated field of thought that is superb at explaining to policy makers precisely why the choices they made in the past were wrong. About the future, not so much.

—*Ben Bernanke, then Fed chair, 2013 Princeton University commencement speech*

THE GLOBAL FINANCIAL ORDER nearly crumbled in mid-March 2020. The disaster revealed itself quietly, when a financial analyst at TD Securities in Midtown Manhattan stepped into a meeting with a worried trader, one of the people in charge of buying and selling bonds for the bank. It had already been a disorienting month for the poor analyst. He had been out of the office the prior week with a terrible flu, one that he had picked up while in the Atlanta airport. Still congested and bleary-eyed, he had returned to work to find himself a pariah. A novel coronavirus that seemed to have originated in China had begun to tear through New York City, and while most offices remained open, people were on edge. One of his older colleagues made a point of rapidly backing away anytime the analyst entered a room.

Adding to the strangeness, his desk had been moved away from his boss's and placed onto a half-empty trading floor in a different part of the office building. There, he worked alongside twenty colleagues from different teams. He thought of it as the "Noah's Ark" approach to virus defense: If some people in the office fell ill with the mysterious sickness, there was no way that an entire team would be put out of commission. Still, sitting far from his team was a major inconvenience at a time of plummeting stock prices and wild gyrations in bond markets, where both governments and corporations go to raise money.

The meeting with the trader took the analyst's slow-building sense of foreboding and gave it a focal point. The guy wasn't freaking out, exactly. People like him moved tens of millions of dollars in milliseconds and were generally unflappable. But something weird was happening in the government debt market, he explained. It had become hard to sell some old Treasury bonds, not the ones most recently issued by the government, but securities that still had months or years left before they would expire and pay out invested cash to bondholders.

Bond traders monitored a stream of security sale data on their computers throughout the day, so they knew what was available and at what price it was selling. As a rule, only huge transactions could "move the market," because so many people are buying and selling United States Treasury bonds at any given moment that any new deals were just a drop in the ocean. The Treasury market, as people liked to say, was the deepest and most liquid in the world. But it was as if the ability to trade on a dime without sending out ripples, that famed liquidity, had evaporated overnight. Suddenly, the trader reported, even the tiniest deals were causing prices to bounce. It was clear that hardly anybody else was buying or selling. And the reason that the market had dried up was becoming obvious. Sellers who wanted to off-load the securities were asking far more for them than what would-be buyers were willing to pay. Offers to buy, called bids in bond parlance, were nonsensically low.

What the trader was really saying hit the analyst like a bucket of ice water. *Nobody wanted to purchase U.S. Treasuries.*

It is hard to describe how insane that was. The market for U.S. debt had, up until that moment, been regarded as risk-free, meaning that holding a Treasury security was basically as safe as holding cash. It paid out interest because you were tying up your money for a given amount of time, not because there was a chance that you might never see it again. If ever you needed to sell a Treasury, a buyer would stand ready to take it off your hands at a predictable price.

If it was becoming hard to offload Treasuries when you needed to do so, that safety was no longer certain. Worry and confusion reigned on Wall Street that week as other bond-watchers came to the same conclusion. The Treasury market was breaking down as investors panicked about the new coronavirus and scrambled for cash, as foreign holders ditched the bonds, and as popular debt trades turned unprofitable, causing hedge funds and other investors who had been holding Treasuries to try to dump them.

If Treasury debt would not trade, the strategist wondered, what would?

The answer, it turned out, was hardly anything. The Treasury breakdown was both a symptom of and fuel to a larger drama playing out across markets. Investors seemed to be attempting to sell off entire portfolios, and they were struggling to do so. Commercial paper, the short-term debt companies use to fund themselves, was hard to renew. Investment-grade company bonds were difficult to trade, junk bonds all but impossible. Money market mutual funds, where companies and investors park their cash to make tiny returns, were seeing massive outflows. Financial publications reported that several hedge funds, including Capula and Bridgewater,[1] were sustaining heavy losses. Word had reached some employees at the New York Fed that several funds might be on the brink of collapse. Another rumor was swirling that major investment vehicles were about to try to liquidate large portfolios of mortgage-tied debt. If they did, that would flood the market with securities it could not handle. The fabric of modern capitalism was coming apart at the seams. The fallout, if it continued and deepened, might make the financial crisis in 2008, which had thrown millions out of work and plunged the world into years of upheaval, look like a mere prelude.

Carnage in markets may seem a step removed from the real economy, but this was 2020. Wall Street was intertwined with everyday life. Already, the pain in stock markets had wiped out huge portions of American households' savings: Net worth would ultimately sink by 5.5 percent in the first three months of 2020, falling across wealth and income groups.[2] If something went drastically wrong in the Treasury market, the broader system of debt that stood behind mortgages, car loans, and corporate payrolls could quickly unravel. The problems would not stop there. Investors around the globe might question the sanctity of America's IOUs. And while they would probably conclude that the debt was safe, because the U.S. government can raise taxes to pay back its obligations, the simple reality that a bout of stress could halt trading in Treasury markets would doubtless make owning those bonds less attractive. Debt might end up becoming more expensive without that truly risk-free backbone, and the market less efficient at getting money to people who wanted to use it. The safety and liquidity of the Treasury market had enabled an era of global financialization; its breakdown could upend it.

The Federal Reserve averted such a world-changing crisis.

The central bank was already stepping up by the time the TD analyst took his meeting. Lorie Logan, a Federal Reserve Bank of New York official, had spent the tumultuous early weeks of March gathering information from contacts on trading floors alongside her team. Logan had worked at the New York Fed since 1999[3] and had been a key official by the 2008 global financial crisis, coming back from maternity leave to help design and execute the Fed's sweeping rescue as banks and financial institutions teetered on the brink of collapse. By 2020, she led the Federal Reserve System's entire trading account, which it used to buy and sell debt, transactions that were key to monetary policy and sometimes to fostering smooth market functioning.* It was a relatively new job for her, and one that made her the central bank's closest direct conduit to markets. She was the official whom insiders sometimes called "the chief technician of monetary policy."[4]

Logan was fitting into the job well. She did not cut an imposing figure: Her voice was youthful, her manner of talking friendly and direct, and she favored simple, dark outfits. She lacked an economics or finance doctorate at an institution where academics

* A nerdy point on market operations and rate setting: Prior to the 2008 financial crisis, asset purchases were used to set the Fed's main policy interest rate by either pumping more central bank cash into the system or draining it out. In the wake of the downturn, as the Fed's bond buying kept the system awash in central bank cash all of the time, such purchases could no longer work as well to guide interest rates. Instead, the funds rate was set by paying banks a certain rate to park money at the Fed. The markets desk still bought securities as part of quantitative easing programs and other operations.

dominated, having studied political science at Davidson College and public administration at Columbia. Yet her understated demeanor concealed a sharp intellect, and her lack of ego allowed her to carry out her job with a level head. That was important. When things went wrong in markets and the economy, the Fed was the government's first line of defense. The first line of defense within the Fed was New York's markets desk and the portfolio Logan managed. Paul Volcker, the former Fed chair, referred to it as "the holy of holies" in his autobiography.[5]

As the pandemic shut down entire cities and sent markets into a tailspin, Logan's team in New York had tried out nearly every policy it could enact on its own authority and in consultation with the Board in Washington. It had offered massive infusions of overnight and short-term funding to the firms at the center of the financial system. At Powell's instruction, it had accelerated planned bond purchases. Nothing seemed to do enough. Spooked investors wanted cold, hard cash, and they were dumping assets too fast for the system to handle. The banks and broker-dealers that serve as go-betweens to the entire market were choked with a massive inventory of securities and deposits, and banking regulations enacted over the prior decade to protect against crisis seemed to have limited how much they were willing to hold.[6] The Fed's bond purchases were too small to absorb the avalanche of assets suddenly for sale.

There was an obvious solution. The Fed needed to become a backup buyer at a massive scale.

Stock indexes had closed in disarray on Friday, March 13. By then, Fed officials had made what would come to seem like an obvious call. They would meet over the weekend. That way, they could act to stem the crisis before Asian markets opened on Monday, which would be Sunday evening in Washington. It was a familiar playbook from the 2008 meltdown, when the Fed had regularly met before stocks began trading on Monday morning in Asia to make momentous decisions. (Ben Bernanke, chairman of the Fed during the crisis, had famously joked that he would title his memoir *Before Asia Opens*.) The whole situation carried a sense of sick déjà vu. The global financial crisis that swept the world starting in 2007 was supposed to be a once-in-a-century disaster, but conditions in key markets were at least as bad as they had been at its depths. And this time, they had deteriorated over days and hours rather than months and years.

Logan gave the first meaningful speech at the meeting, which started at 10:00 A.M. and was held remotely, on account of its suddenness and in recognition of the new threat posed by the virus. Her colleagues were arrayed before her on a screen as she began to speak. Three of the Fed's five Washington-based governors and top central bank staff had gathered in the boardroom at the central bank's headquarters on Constitution Avenue, leaving spaces in between them at the mahogany table in the spirit of maintaining proper social distance—still a new concept. Each of their twelve regional colleagues dialed in via teleconference, as did the Fed's vice-chair for bank supervision, Randal Quarles, who was at his family's home in Utah and joined from a regional Fed outpost.

Logan and her fellow New York Fed officials were huddled in their fortresslike offices on Manhattan's Maiden Lane, along with Vice-chair Richard Clarida, who had come in from his home in Connecticut that morning. The palazzo-style building was decked in wrought iron décor that conjured an almost medieval atmosphere on the sunniest of days. Given the backdrop, it was unapologetically dire.

On the webcast, Logan found herself pronouncing phrases that would have been unfathomable a few weeks earlier. Parts of the Treasury market had ceased to function, she explained. Business debt financing was nonexistent. None of the fixes she and her team could carry out on their own authority seemed to be helping sufficiently. Things were getting bad, and they would get worse unless the Fed stepped in. She told the policy makers gathered on the screen in front of her that if they authorized the buying of huge amounts of Treasuries and mortgage-backed debt—dusting off and scaling up a policy that had been used before to soothe troubled markets—her desk could make those purchases aggressively at first.

It was a suggestion, one that Fed chair Jerome Powell promptly echoed as an outright proposal. And the idea was that policy needed to go big. The central bank's top officials had drawn up the plan ahead of the meeting, and it sounded like a doctor's orders to a desperately ill patient. They were laying out what the voting members of the Federal Open Market Committee needed to do to keep the financial world from crashing.

The Fed's presidents and governors, who totaled seventeen in March 2020, were an argumentative bunch. True to form, there was debate that day over how much they should lower interest rates. Most of the committee wanted to cut a full percentage point, taking short-term borrowing costs straight to zero to keep borrowing as cheap as possible as the virus rattled commerce, but a few officials favored a smaller reduction, hoping to save ammunition for later. Nobody, however, questioned that they needed to do whatever they could to fix the government bond market.

So it was, on a Sunday in March, that the central bank voted to begin rescuing Wall Street and the economy for the second time in a dozen years.

The root cause of the crisis in 2020 was a global pandemic, not irresponsible risk-taking by banks and investors. Likewise, the solution was no repeat of the bank-specific bailouts of 2008. This time around, the Fed would buy government-backed bonds—huge sums of them—until the market traded more normally. It was a pumped-up version of a bond-buying program that had first been enacted more than a decade earlier.[7] Of course, some investors would undeniably benefit, including hedge funds that had amassed huge Treasury holdings as part of a trade that was usually safe but that had turned disastrous in the face of the March 2020 volatility. Big Fed market actions almost always benefited someone who had taken a gamble. But the goal was not to rescue some of the world's wealthiest investors: It was to save the entire system. It wasn't just one fund, one player, that would collapse if the Treasury market staggered. If the backbone of finance went down, it was going to take the Main Street economy with it.

"When stresses arise in the Treasury market, they can reverberate through the entire financial system and the economy," Chair Powell explained that Sunday, once the announcement had been made, at an impromptu remote press conference. Reporters had dialed in to the hastily organized gathering on the chilly, overcast afternoon, their connections stilted, the atmosphere haphazard. "We thought we had to do more, and we knew what we had to do."

The Fed's move that weekend would not stop the bleeding immediately. The S&P 500 stock index would fall 12 percent on March 16, its worst performance since a meltdown in 1987 so infamous that it was commonly known as Black Monday. Oil prices would slide to $30 a barrel, a four-year low. The following week would also remain messy in Treasury markets—analysts would call March 17, for instance, "disastrous." The coronavirus had killed almost six thousand people and sickened about two hundred thousand heading into the third week of March,[8] tiny numbers compared to the devastation it would eventually inflict. But the economy was beginning to shut down and America was opening its eyes to the inevitable pain to come. People were panicking.

March 15, 2020, would mark an early foray into a broader rescue, one that would be unveiled day by day over the course of the following two months. The massive bond market intervention, combined with a steady drip of new credit-providing programs, would ultimately calm investors, averting a system-wide collapse. It would also force the Fed to push into areas where it had never ventured.

Because of the critical role the dollar played in the global economy and markets, the pandemic meltdown would put the Fed's role as an economic leader to the world on full display. It would be inescapably clear that America's economic and financial future, and to a more limited extent the international system's, hinged on decisions made by technocrats sitting in a stately building on Washington's Constitution Avenue—or, thanks to the pandemic, at their houses up and down the Eastern Seaboard—and at a dozen Fed branches sprinkled across the country.

The 2020 rescue would differ from the Fed's actions during the 2008 financial crisis in an important way. The Fed would try to extend its help far beyond Wall Street this time around. The bank-specific solutions a decade earlier had drummed up widespread resentment for the Fed, inspiring congressional challenges to its independence and making former chair Ben Bernanke's name a dirty word in libertarian and some liberal circles alike. As the world faced months of lockdown, Fed officials wanted to make sure they supported the flow of credit not just to financial players but to any business that might be at risk of cutting jobs if it couldn't borrow.

The question was whether the Fed had the firepower to make a broader policy package effective and whether the broader government would step up with an adequate economic rescue effort of its own. At the time of that Sunday morning meeting, Minneapolis Fed president Neel Kashkari had his concerns.

Kashkari, the forty-six-year-old son of Indian immigrants, was a veteran of the last crisis and bore its scars more visibly than any other sitting Fed official. He'd been an idealistic thirtysomething when markets had crashed the last time around, newly installed at the Treasury Department by what he had initially believed to be a happy accident. He had been working at Goldman Sachs when CEO Hank Paulson was named Treasury secretary. Bored with the private sector and eager for something new, a young Kashkari had cold-called Paulson and asked to follow him to Washington. It had, unbelievably, worked.

When the subprime mortgage market blew up the following year, plunging the nation into the financial crisis, Kashkari found himself helping to craft the government bailout of Wall Street banks and massive automakers. He was one of the original architects of the Troubled Assets Relief Program, or TARP, the $700 billion plan meant to stabilize the financial system by buying and guaranteeing problem-laden securities.* Nothing about the nation's response to the mortgage meltdown went to plan—it was too limited, often too late, and too political. TARP itself was a public relations land mine, and as the program's administrator (or, as he was unaffectionately known, the "TARP czar"), Kashkari was torn apart in congressional hearings for its failings. He gained twenty pounds as he spent months eating Cool Ranch Doritos for dinner at his Treasury desk. He slept in the office. Washington, and frankly much of America, seemed to hate him for his efforts.

After the crisis, Kashkari moved to a cabin in the middle of a Sierra Nevada pine forest in northeast California to detox. He chopped wood and relived everything that had gone wrong.[9] When he returned to civilization, he joined the asset manager Pacific Investment Management Company in 2009. It wasn't a good fit, and he quit in 2013. He

---

* TARP was later reduced in value to $475 billion. It would also ultimately be used to inject capital directly into banks and financial institutions, given the complexity of buying troubled assets.

attempted a colorful run at California's governorship, trying for the job as a Republican with a social justice bent. At one point he spent several days living on the streets on a shoestring budget, shooting a campaign video meant to highlight the plight of the state's homeless population. The unconventional effort—some might call it a stunt— was not enough to clinch a victory, but the run for office spoke to Kashkari's insatiable ambition. Kashkari was a still-young man who had started his career as a rocket scientist before trying his hand at Wall Street and Washington, and he remained hungry for the next interesting thing.*

But his adventures in the wilderness and in state politics weren't enough to get 2008 off his mind. When the Minneapolis Fed's board selected him as president in 2016, Kashkari remained haunted by his time as "TARP czar." He kicked off his tenure by running a series of research conferences examining whether the issue of so-called Too Big to Fail banks had truly been dealt with, annoying many within the Fed by relitigating something that the entire system had been working on for years. The conclusion of the analyses and conferences, perhaps unsurprisingly, was that the changes had not gone far enough. As a central banker, Kashkari struck a pro-worker posture, arguing that the job market had more room to heal even a decade after the start of the 2008 crisis. When the Fed lifted interest rates, he argued in internal meetings and public town halls that it should keep them lower for longer, pointing to weak wage gains and nonexistent inflation as arguments for continued patience.

Now, as Wall Street again came under stress and the economy headed for an all-but-certain recession, Kashkari watched with alarm. The defining—and in many ways the worst—era of his life seemed like it could at least partly repeat itself.

In Minnesota, he was far removed from the action this time around. He had traded nights in his sad government office for evenings at home, surrounded by his wife, Christine, their baby daughter, and their fuzzy Newfoundland dogs. He had begun to do the family's grocery shopping and had introduced Christine to cheese-

---

* Kashkari worked as an aerospace engineer after graduating from the University of Illinois at Urbana–Champaign.

burger macaroni Hamburger Helper (which she kind of liked) and Manwich (a ground meat and tomato sauce combination that she hated). It was a more pleasant environment, but the situation was still unsettling. Powell and his board colleagues kept the regional presidents in the loop, calling regularly to let them know what was happening, and Kashkari spent his days talking to local business leaders and his research staff to get a read on the economy.

What he heard worried him. Workers were being sent home. Capital spending plans were being scrapped. Wages were being suspended or cut. The descent, if it was not blunted by a massive policy response—the kind that had failed to fully materialize following the housing meltdown—could have serious, dangerous consequences. Kashkari knew that the Fed would find itself short on tools to coax growth back from the abyss. Most of its policies worked via interest rates, which were already extraordinarily low. When it came to emergency lending policies, which the central bank could deploy in times of crisis to keep key markets functioning, Kashkari had no official say. The Board of Governors in Washington handled those tools. But he hoped—and thought—his colleagues would do everything in their power to soothe conditions.

If Kashkari had learned one thing in 2008, it was that caution and crises did not mix. He decided it was time to begin peddling a message, directed at Congress as much as the Fed: Go big.

When *60 Minutes,* the CBS news show, was looking for a Fed official to speak about the nascent meltdown just a few days after the March 15 Sunday afternoon rate cut, the producers turned to Kashkari, whose 2008 experience made him a recognizable voice on the issue. He was just one of the Fed's seventeen sitting officials, and as a regional president he did not hold a constant vote on monetary policy or exceptional sway over the central bank's decisions, but he could offer his battle-weathered perspective. The interview recorded on March 19 to air on March 22. In a sign of the anxious times, CBS's Scott Pelley surprised Kashkari by giving voice to a question worrying central bankers everywhere on that uncertain Thursday, as Wall Street investors dashed for cash and newspapers reported that some banks in Manhattan had run short of high-denomination bills amid rapid withdrawals.[10]

"To the person who is about to grab their car keys and go to the ATM and take out three thousand dollars, you say what?"

Kashkari thought about what message America might hear in his response. If he said "Don't" with alarm, they might take it as a sign that running to pull their money from their banks was their best option. He had learned that the best thing an official could do at such a moment was to reassure.

"You don't need to. Your ATM is safe. Your banks are safe. There's enough cash in the financial system," he replied. In what would become one of the more iconic lines of the 2020 meltdown, he added: "And there's an infinite amount of cash at the Federal Reserve."

The rest of his message during the appearance was directed to America's policy makers.

After 2008, "it took more than ten years to put America fully back to work, relative to where they were before the crisis," Kashkari told Pelley. "Ten years. And so that's what we have to try to avoid, having these mass layoffs. We can't have another ten-year recovery."

Yet "we can't" would not automatically equal "we won't." Aggressive, and often uncomfortable, choices would be required to get American workers and businesses through a calamitous period without lasting damage. The Fed could play a role in that by keeping markets functional and by lowering rates to help the recovery when it came. In the near term, though, making borrowing cheaper might not do much to help an economy that state and local officials were rapidly locking down in an effort to stop the spread of the coronavirus.

For all its reorientation toward Main Street in recent years, it was not obvious what the Fed could do to support the millions of American businesses that were about to see their fortunes take a dramatic turn for the worse. Still, it seemed clear that central bankers were going to have to try whatever they could to help.

"We were always too slow and too timid in responding to the crisis," Kashkari told *60 Minutes,* referencing the prior meltdown.[11] "Today, whether it's healthcare policy makers, fiscal policy makers, which means Congress, or the Federal Reserve, we should all be erring on the side of overreacting to try to avoid the worst economic outcomes."

The Fed would do just that in the months ahead. In the spring of 2020 and over the two years that followed, as the global pandemic first imperiled society's most important financial markets and then—together with massive government spending—touched off an unexpected chain of events that revived long-dormant inflation, America's central bank would more fully embrace its role as the most powerful economic institution the modern world had ever known.

It was a status that had been more than a century in the making.

Chapter 3

ONE NATION, UNDER BANKS

History doesn't repeat itself, but it often rhymes.

—*attributed to Mark Twain, regularly quoted by Jay Powell*

AROUND HIS FORTIETH BIRTHDAY, Marriner S. Eccles began to suspect that his late father's economic thinking suffered from some fundamental flaws. He wasn't the first person to develop a delayed sense of filial skepticism, nor would he be the last. But in his case, the realization came around 1932, just in time to shape the course of American economic history.

Eccles had been born in Logan, Utah, in 1890 to the second wife of a Mormon business magnate. His father had immigrated from Scotland and started from the very bottom of the economic ladder. The ancestral Eccleses had scraped by as producers of homemade wooden kitchen utensils, as Marriner would put it in his eventual autobiography, "one thread away from nakedness and one crust from starvation."[1] After converting to Mormonism, the family had set out on a journey to America in 1863, moving to what Eccles (and other Latter-day Saints at the time) called the "Promised Land in Utah." For them, the dream delivered. David Eccles, Marriner's father, worked obsessively to gain a foothold in his new country. He followed the famed trail to Oregon as a young man, then returned to Utah to work in logging and other enterprises, and eventually became an entrepreneur, amassing a budding business empire that stretched from railroads to banks. He built a fortune while carrying on a thrifty personal existence and avoiding debt of any kind. By the time Marriner was born, the oldest of David's nine children by his second wife,* his family was fantastically rich.

Despite the Eccleses' wealth, Marriner began working summers at age eight, because his parents believed idleness was bad for a boy. He left school at eighteen and worked for his father before embarking upon a two-year, two-month mission trip to Scotland, during which he made few converts but, "nevertheless," had "an interesting and instructive time."[2]

Afterward, Eccles, a young man with sideswept dark hair, piercing eyes, and a drive to make his parents proud, returned to Utah and the family businesses. He was overseeing a hydroelectric power plant project in a canyon ten miles southeast of Logan when, in early December 1912, he received shocking news: His father had died of a heart attack.[3] The elder Eccles left behind an estate worth $7 million (more than $200 million today), twenty-one children, and a web of lumber operations, sugar factories, coal mines, and construction and banking interests. Marriner, just twenty-two, was left running a minority share of the sprawling enterprise, while his older brothers by his father's first wife took other parts.

The family eventually quarreled over control, and Marriner prevailed in taking stewardship of several businesses (a fact he later less-than-modestly credited to his superior acumen and careful maneuvering). He spent nearly two decades building upon the businesses with great success. He lived his life frugally, in a way that would have made his father and the religion he belonged to proud, and he valued the other creed David Eccles had held dear: laissez-faire capitalism.

"The magic words of his career had been 'thrift' and 'hard work,'" Eccles recalled in his memoir. "They multiplied benefits in his day. I thought they could always do that."[4]

Then came the 1930s. The Depression was a turning point for Eccles and, partly through him, for America and the world.

Understanding the Fed's origin story requires rewinding the clock to a point several millennia before Marriner Eccles walked the streets

* The family was polygamist.

of Logan and Ogden, one well before the phrase "Great Depression" entered the human lexicon. The story of central banking starts around the dawn of money.

"What is money?" is both a simple and an incredibly complicated question. It is the $5 bill in your wallet or the one-euro coin in your pocket. But it's also, fundamentally, imaginary. Societies have used one thing of symbolic value—cowrie shell, embossed metal—to trade for other things of tangible value—food, shelter—as far back as well-documented history stretches. Grain-backed money systems prevailed in ancient Mesopotamia, while shells were once accepted as currency across Oceania, Asia, and the Americas. Lydians, in western Turkey, were using gold coins twenty-five hundred years ago.[5] Money has varied in form over time, but a single underlying reality has tied the diverse systems together. Value lies less in its physical substance than in what its users understand it to signify as a medium of exchange, store of value, and unit of account. Money is an idea that we buy into, and common belief makes it work.

Over the centuries and across human civilizations, people have used some combination of cash and debt—a promise to hand over cash or something else of value at some future date—to pay for goods and services. Credit systems stretch back to at least 3500 B.C., when Sumerian temple administrators had developed a system that allowed people to purchase products in advance and pay in grain at harvesttime without ever exchanging physical cash, anthropologists have documented.[6]

That system of debt, credit, and currency has often been supported by what we now call a "fractional" banking system. Historians have argued that such systems were present in ancient Rome,[7] common in Europe by the 1400s,[8] and had grown pervasive in many parts of the world by the 1700s. The way they worked was simple enough. Households and companies who owned whatever was accepted as money—often gold—did not want to keep it all under the mattress, for security reasons and because it was heavy to lug around. They would leave it with goldsmiths, and eventually banks, in exchange for paper slips that evidenced their deposit. Often, they did not even need to take out the gold to make transactions; they could just exchange the paper claim, backed by the gold, as a means of payment.

But as the monetary system developed, bankers found that they needn't keep enough gold in storage to back all the claims in circulation. It was vanishingly unlikely that everyone would redeem their notes at the same time. They started to lend out the gold itself or to write additional paper notes against it, so that their outstanding claims exceeded the gold on reserve in their vaults.[9] Money in the overall economy was multiplied, and more commerce could be undertaken. A deposit pile that was worth ten bills could generate more—maybe fifteen, maybe twenty, maybe thirty—depending on the risk tolerance of the banker and, in some cases, its agreements with its depositors.

Unfortunately, fractional reserve arrangements had a destabilizing flaw. Fractional lenders without insurance were susceptible to runs. If people became nervous that a bank could not cover its obligations, they would rush to grab their deposits before there was nothing left. If the bank was unable to meet the redemptions, it would be broken. As financial systems grew larger and more interconnected, broken banks could damage entire economies. As financial markets developed and became more complex, dash-for-cash runs in the face of trouble would remain a constant feature and threat.

Bank runs were far from the only problem that dogged the financial system by the late 1700s, when America won its independence from England.[10] The foreign currencies and precious metals that the North American banking system had revolved around in colonial times were often available in finite quantities and served as a rigid superstructure for the nation's fledgling commercial system.[11] The supply of money could struggle to expand to keep pace with rising demand for cash during wars, harvests, or economic boom times. When authorities printed cash without some sort of anchor, though, they could overdo it—reducing the worth of the currency, causing prices to inflate, and leaving people with cash savings able to buy fewer goods and services. That happened dramatically as the nascent American government scrambled to fund the Revolutionary War. The infant country emerged victorious but with a disorganized and devalued currency.[12]

Alexander Hamilton had devised a solution, proposed to Congress in a 1790 report and passed into existence in 1791. It was a central bank that would print cash that could be used to pay taxes, which would serve as a safe place to store public funds, and which could serve as the government's agent in carrying out transactions.[13] The idea drew on the model set forth by the Bank of England, which had been created in 1694 to assist government war finance but enjoyed a partial monopoly on issuing banknotes by the mid-1700s.[14]

America's first attempt at central banking opened for business in Philadelphia, the nation's capital at the time, that December. It issued banknotes, ultimately backed by precious metals, which were widely used and provided some stability to American commerce. In addition to its banking services for private citizens, the bank made loans to the government and managed the Treasury's interest payments to foreign investors. While it did not officially determine how much money was flowing through the economy—the supply of silver primarily dictated that—the bank could alter money and credit around the edges by tweaking its lending policies.[15] Lawmakers remained wary of concentrating financial power with federal authorities, though, and the bank's existence was brief. Congress voted against extending its charter in 1811, defeating it by one vote in each chamber.

When inflation came knocking after the War of 1812 and the government found itself deeply indebted but with no central authority to help manage its financial affairs, people questioned the decision to let the First Bank of the United States die.[16] At the urging of prominent financiers and businessmen, the Second Bank of the United States was formed. It opened in Philadelphia in 1817, right around the corner from its predecessor, had a twenty-year charter, and operated as both a commercial bank and an agent of the government.[17]

Nicholas Biddle, the son of a prominent Philadelphia merchant family, served as its head starting in 1823 and became the driving force behind its power. A prodigy who graduated from Princeton University at fifteen, Biddle had a reputation as a Renaissance man as an adult. He served as secretary to an American emissary in London before establishing himself as a lawyer and financial expert, then wrote a history of Lewis and Clark's famous expedition from the explorers' notes.[18] He brought his domineering personality and tenacity to the Second Bank, which under his watch regulated commercial banks, rescued them in times of financial panic, and even began crudely setting interest rates.

Yet the bank's growing authority drew the ire of President Andrew Jackson, who was Biddle's near-perfect foil. Born in a South Carolina backwater and educated sporadically before making his reputation as a lawyer in Tennessee and as a war hero, Jackson was skeptical of finance by nature and experience. He had lost a great deal of money after investing with a land speculator who went bust, and he trusted neither credit nor paper cash. If Biddle was the foremost advocate of organizing banking and finance, Jackson was a champion of decentralization.[19]

Biddle did his institution no favors when it came to winning Jackson's support. He pushed for the government to renew the bank's charter earlier than was strictly necessary, wagering that Jackson would be voted out of office if he neglected to extend it. Jackson took the other side of that bet, vetoing the renewal in 1832 and making the bank a central issue in that year's presidential election. "The bank," Jackson told Martin Van Buren, his vice president and soon-to-be successor, "is trying to kill me, but I will kill it!"[20] When Jackson beat Henry Clay and retained office, he interpreted his victory as a mandate to end the nation's second try at central banking.[21] In 1833, he ordered that government deposits be moved to state banks, stripping Biddle's institution of its power. The gutted bank's charter formally expired in 1836.

America's early attempts at establishing a monetary authority had met with occasional successes, but they carried too much of a taste of authoritarianism for a country that had so recently fought to throw off the yoke of monarchy. They were seen as servants to New York's finance industry rather than as public entities that would serve farmers and producers scattered across the country. The experiments laid bare a tension that would come to define monetary policy in America. It was clearly more efficient to consolidate control over money, but it felt profoundly undemocratic to concentrate such power in a few pairs of unelected hands. Doing so seemed destined to tip the scales in the favor of elite interests.

Still, instability dogged the decentralized system that took shape in the 1800s. Banking rules varied from state to state, and a chaotic array of paper notes was issued by the so-called state banks. The bills were theoretically supported by gold and silver, but often the backing proved insufficient in practice. The system was prone to runs.[22]

An example of that weakness reared its head shortly after Jackson killed the Second Bank. Reserves, the cash banks kept in their vaults to meet demand, spread inefficiently around the country, piling up in places where they were less needed. Meanwhile, America's state banks began to take on risk by vigorously extending loans.[23] That combination—increased risk-taking and the lack of easy access to money in a pinch—paved the way for a sweeping financial crisis in 1837 that ultimately plunged the economy into a depression, one in which widespread bank failures dovetailed with crop failures to leave American laborers starving.[24] Historians since have blamed Jackson's policies for the disaster, but politically, it was his successor, Van Buren, who paid. He had taken the White House just weeks before the panic commenced, and it ranked high among the factors that made him a one-term president.[25] Congress attempted to establish a third central bank in 1841, but it was vetoed by America's tenth president, the states' rights aficionado John Tyler.[26]

America's monetary system was ripe for improvement by the latter half of the 1800s, and the onset of the Civil War in 1861 set changes into motion. Looking to fund the expensive conflict, President Lincoln's government borrowed heavily and issued paper notes not immediately backed by gold—so-called greenbacks—between 1862 and 1865.[27] Because the government could not guarantee their convertibility to existing gold reserves, the notes were at least closer to being a fiat currency, one that depended on the faith and credit of the government instead of deriving its value from precious metal. Their existence made America's money supply less rigid.

Driven by necessity, standardization also began to sweep America's money supply during the Civil War. Legislation passed starting in 1863 created the basis for a national banking system, one in which banks could apply for federal charters and in turn were required to keep government bonds on deposit at the newly created Office of the Comptroller of the Currency.[28] The setup was a good money-raising device for the government, creating a natural source of demand for its debt. It was also a decent deal for banks, who earned interest on the deposited bonds. The legislation paved the way for a more uniform currency because the new national banks were allowed to issue so-called national bank notes against their collateral on deposit. The notes came to replace diverse state bank offerings after the government slapped a tariff on state bank money to discourage its use.

America exited the Civil War with a more flexible and tidier monetary system, but some conservatives—often lenders who wanted to clamp down on wartime inflation, which was eating away at the value of their outstanding loans—quickly began agitating for the end of the greenback and a full return to the gold standard. Reversion would provide a sounder basis for the economy, they insisted, an argument that gained purchase following a financial panic in 1873. *The New York Times* on December 9, 1874, reprinted a passage from *The Utica Herald* that pointed out that business had ebbed and demand for cash was low, making the moment ripe for a switch back to metal-backed money, sometimes called specie. The economy's "revival can just as well begin upon a specie basis as upon the rotten, fickle basis of cheap money which brought about the very panic from which the country has been endeavoring in vain to recover," the *Herald* had argued.[29] (The crisis had been triggered by a stock market crash in Europe, which had caused overseas investors to dump U.S. railroad bonds. Without a way to finance themselves, railroads went bankrupt, ruining a major Philadelphia bank that had heavily invested in them and touching off a broader run on the banking system.)[30]

Farmers across the Midwest were unconvinced that the expanded money supply had the destabilizing effect coastal bankers claimed. Many thought more flexible dollar access would help them to avoid bouts of ruinously high interest rates, and they favored keeping greenbacks ample. A letter to the *Times* editor, published amid the national debate, argued for the continuation of greenback currency on the basis that "the people" would have their interests served by such a system, "except usurers and money lenders." To punctuate his or her motivation and worldview, the writer signed the piece "Labor Reformer."[31]

Conservatives triumphed in 1875. That year, Congress decided to remove greenbacks in circulation until the currency was worth its former exchange rate with gold—causing the monetary supply to constrict in fits and starts until parity was achieved in 1879.[32] The decision came as America industrialized, railroads proliferated, and productivity boomed, and it exacerbated an intense deflation that had begun to take hold after 1867. Agriculture prices plummeted and the loans farmers had taken out became crushing as they struggled to bring in enough cash from crop sales to pay them back.[33]

The pain forged an early version of American populism. Monetary reform was a major issue for a movement that began in Lampasas County, Texas, in the 1870s, and which would come to be called the Farmers' Alliance.* It was also the central cause of the so-called Greenback Party, a team effort between organized workers and farmers that rose to challenge the industrialists of the day. The Greenback Party was eventually subsumed into the People's Party, which in turn merged with Democrats. As the movements evolved, their initial support for fiat greenback currency switched to an allegiance to a bimetal system that incorporated silver-backed money—a plan made famous by the politician William Jennings Bryan's famous "Cross of Gold" speech.[34] A common thread through the efforts, though, was a belief that more money pumping through the economic system, and even a little inflation, was good for the laboring farm and industrial classes.

Easy money had become the preferred policy of the American working class, a precedent that would have important echoes in the twenty-first century.

While it often strikes modern audiences as arcane, the nation's monetary system was a topic of popular discussion and discontent heading into the twentieth century. Because the money supply did not expand easily to meet seasonal fluctuations in demand for cash, it regularly posed a problem at harvesttime. Every fall, farmers had to pay their workers before they sold their crops, causing a short-term spike in borrowing. Clearinghouses could help to funnel cash out of big banking centers and into rural areas where it was needed, but the system did not always work quickly or efficiently.[35] Often, dollars became concentrated in places where they were less necessary, causing a rush for cash in places with high demand for money but an insufficient supply, which set off cascading bank runs. Financial panics struck the rickety system not only in 1873 but also in 1884, 1890, and 1893.[36]

The underdeveloped banking and currency system also held back the United States' money market, preventing it from expanding to a point where it would rival England's. In financial journalist Walter

* You can find a discussion of this movement throughout William Greider's *Secrets of the Temple: How the Federal Reserve Runs the Country.*

Bagehot's seminal 1873 book, *Lombard Street: A Description of the Money Market,* the author recounts that London banks held 120 million pounds of deposits around the time of publication; New York's, just 40 million.[37] Bagehot explained in detail why that mattered: If a merchant were to use 50,000 pounds of his own money to earn 5,000 pounds over a year, he would make a 10 percent return. But if the same merchant could use 10,000 of his own pounds and borrow 40,000 at a 5 percent rate to earn that same 5,000, he would finish with 3,000 after paying interest—a 30 percent return. He could charge less, trade more, and earn bigger profits by leveraging his capital, helping to expand not only his own economic pie but also that of the nation to which he belonged. To unleash that prosperity machine, a country needed a stable banking system that could make large amounts of capital available at relatively low interest rates.

It was America's combination of financial inefficiency and regular meltdowns that helped to spur another attempt at central banking.

The catalyst came in 1906, when a massive earthquake tore San Francisco asunder, killing three thousand people, leaving sections of the city in ruins, and touching off instability in global money markets as foreign insurers scrambled for cash so that they could pay claims on California policies. Gold lurched toward the damaged city, leaving banks in New York with few reserves and preventing them from extending new loans.[38] Global monetary policies worsened the predicament. Gold tended to flow toward wherever it could earn the highest return, so the Bank of England's decision that autumn to raise interest rates induced investors to move savings toward London, further depleting U.S. banks' capital holdings. At the same time, the Bank of England instructed British lenders to cut off short-term credit to American companies, worried that the younger nation's economy was overheating.

Money suddenly became hard to access in America, slowing the borrowing and spending that had been fueling growth in the economy and a boom on Wall Street.[39] The twin blows left U.S. capitalism teetering on an unstable foundation when the critical turning point arrived the following year, during what we now know as the Panic of 1907.

The drama started in earnest that October. Mining businessman and investor F. Augustus Heinze, his brother Otto, and their business associate Charles Morse tried to corner the stock of Heinze's company, United Copper. The plan was to buy up so many of the outstanding shares of United Copper that it forced investors who were selling the stock short—effectively betting against the company—to buy the securities at a high price to settle their trades. It may have been a clever plot, but it was not clever enough: The collaborators miscalculated how much stock they needed to win control. When other investors realized that the so-called short squeeze* had failed, the stock price plummeted. The losses were so spectacular that nervous investors began to pull their money from any banking institution tied to the financiers.

The New York Clearing House was able to stem the initial runs by taking over management of the imperiled banks and lending to them. But a series of implicated trust companies—which, as nonbanks, were not part of the Clearing House system—were ineligible for that sort of help. As their antsy depositors came calling, they had to find salvation elsewhere.

They turned to John Pierpont Morgan, the towering founder of the firm that would go on to become JP Morgan Chase. Mustachioed with a crop of white hair and a bulbous nose, Morgan was treated as a moral leader and elder statesman on Wall Street. He had organized a private bank bailout for the United States Treasury in 1895, and as the fresh crisis reared its head, he helped to orchestrate rescues for various Wall Street companies. The bailouts were at times theatrical. During one particularly dicey moment in the meltdown, Morgan locked Wall Street's dominant bankers into his private library for a fraught planning session that lasted into the wee hours of the morning. Beneath Flemish masterworks, against a backdrop of crimson damask wallpaper, they came up with a plan to save their hard-hit counterparts for the sake of the broader financial system.[40]

But even with the bank-led rescue programs, businesses closed, people lost jobs, and the economy suffered as financing conditions limped back. And while other financiers including John D. Rocke-

---

* This term may be familiar to readers. A similar maneuver would be used by Robinhood traders 114 years later to counter institutional investors who were shorting the company GameStop.

feller played major roles in 1907, Morgan's position at the very center of the rescue was not lost on America's politicians and policy thinkers. A single, mortal man had been the main thing standing between the banking system and deeper disaster.[*]

The panic and its aftermath spurred calls for change—ones that demanded the attention of Senator Nelson Aldrich, the powerful Republican chair of the Senate Committee on Finance.

At sixty-six, Aldrich had been a longtime supporter of the national banknote system that had emerged after the Civil War. But it was inescapable that some monetary reform legislation was politically necessary following 1907, and he decided to make the project his long career's capstone. In 1908, he led a delegation to Europe to study central banking on the Continent and in England, where central banks had been a reality for centuries. The Swedish Riksbank had been created to serve the crown in 1668,[41] and the Bank of England had been established a few decades later. While the Bank of England remained private, it had by the early twentieth century grown into an issuer of currency, the government's banker, and an implicit lender of last resort—meaning an entity that would keep cash flowing to commercial banks during times of panic, making sure that short-term runs did not kill off fundamentally healthy institutions. Bagehot, the nineteenth-century financial journalist, is most famous for explaining that function: The central bank needed to lend to whoever needed it in a crisis to prevent the situation from spiraling out of control. "The object is to stay alarm," Bagehot wrote. "If it is known that the Bank of England is freely advancing on what in ordinary times is reckoned a good security—on what is then commonly pledged and easily convertible—the alarm of the solvent merchants and bankers will be stayed. But if securities, really good and usually convertible, are refused by the Bank, the alarm will not abate, the other loans made will fail in obtaining their end, and the panic will become worse and worse."[42]

It demonstrated that a central bank could do what J. P. Morgan had done in America: keep banks from collapsing amid panic by

---

[*] One of the bankers present, Thomas Lamont, would recall in a book he later penned that Morgan's role that evening was that of a "modern Medici"—referring to the family that, through financial power, dominated Renaissance Florence.

making it clear that they could access whatever capital they needed in order to satisfy withdrawals and keep credit flowing.

The Aldrich expedition found a lot to envy in the systematic European approach, which shored up confidence in the currency system and allowed banks to operate with far less capital on hand. The senator himself, long dubious of the merits of a central bank, was converted somewhere between London, Berlin, and Paris.[43] After decades without one, America was on its way toward a more centralized system of money.

European ideals fresh in mind, Senator Aldrich in 1910 organized a secret meeting at the exclusive Jekyll Island Club off the coast of Georgia to turn the group's research into an actual plan. The attendees—Paul Warburg and Frank Vanderlip, leading bankers; a senior Treasury official named Henry Davison; A. Piatt Andrew, a Harvard economics professor; Aldrich's personal secretary, Arthur Shelton; and Aldrich himself—were sworn to secrecy and left New York under the pretense of going duck hunting, traveling south on Aldrich's private railcar. Because they referred to one another only by their first names to keep their real identities secret even from the staff, they have been known in the decades since as the "First Name Club."*

The clandestine behavior had a cold logic. Aldrich was asking finance-industry insiders to figure out how to resolve the country's monetary problems, in which they had a vested interest.[44] The optics were terrible, and he worried that they could kill his budding plan's chances. It foreshadowed a problem that would forever haunt the central bank that was to come. On one hand, the matter in question was complicated and bankers were nearly unique in truly knowing their way around the issues. On the other, allowing bankers or those who sympathized with them to design policy would beget a system that benefited finance, perhaps to the detriment of the broader public.

Once installed at the main house of the Jekyll Island Club, in

---

* Benjamin Strong, vice president of the Bankers Trust Company and J. P. Morgan's close associate, worked with the group and was also part of the "club," though historians have debated whether he attended the undercover Jekyll Island meeting.

a space that J. P. Morgan himself had ensured was devoid of other guests,[45] the six men hashed out a blueprint for what would become the Federal Reserve. They envisioned a fifteen-branch central bank that would have power over money printing and bank regulation and that could support troubled banks in crises.[46] Each branch would be governed by boards elected by member banks in their district; bigger banks would have more votes and thus more representation. The branches would hold reserves, issue currency, support the short-term business debt market, clear checks, and keep money moving around the country. What the bankers designed was not an arm of government so much as a private, government-sponsored organizing body, one that could halt panics and make sure that reserves—so often stuck in far-flung places and frozen entirely amid panics—would be centralized.

Plan in hand, the Jekyll Island group returned home, where its members reached out to financiers in New York, commercial groups, and western bankers to nudge them into positions on a hypothetical central bank that were consistent with their still-secret design.[47] Full details of the Jekyll Island meeting would not come out until the 1930s, but it was relatively widespread knowledge that something was afoot. Interest groups began to push their points: The founder of the investment bank Goldman Sachs lobbied for institutions like his to be able to work with the new central bank, which was then envisioned as a cooperative of commercial banks (which take on deposits) that would leave out investment banks (which help corporations with financing and deal in securities).[48]

But the Jekyll Island blueprint hit a roadblock. By the time the workshopped outline was formally announced in mid-January 1912, Aldrich's political popularity was waning, victim to his continued support for an unpopular tariff. To compound the injury, his Republican Party was soon to lose control of the Senate.

Thanks to the shift in power, turning the rough draft into a law fell largely to Carter Glass, a Virginia Democrat and former newspaperman who became chairman of the House Committee on Banking and Currency in 1913.[49] Glass sponsored and championed the Federal Reserve Act alongside the newly elected president, Woodrow Wilson, who was a political scholar and had been head of Princeton University.[50]

From the outset, the freshly empowered Democrats loudly criticized the Aldrich plan. Glass would go on to refer to the proposal as "a central bank, for banks, and by banks" in his eventual memoir, in which he also complained that Aldrich's research effort had forced the American taxpayer to foot the bill for a library on banking and currency that cost the Treasury more than one hundred thousand dollars, "along with other very considerable expenditures."[51] But even as the Democrats denounced the very idea of a privately controlled central bank and complained about Republican largesse, they borrowed heavily from Aldrich's draft. The Jekyll Island idea offered a carefully thought-out structure. It was also, some historians have pointed out, relatively decentralized and thus in line with Glass's broader political philosophy. The Virginian had a long history of maneuvering to keep government power dispersed—doing so was key to protecting white supremacy in the South.[52]

Even so, admitting that the eventual Federal Reserve Act mirrored the Republican outline in important ways was unthinkable. It was a plan created by bankers that envisioned a system effectively run by them, and public opinion was fast turning against the leaders of American finance.

By the time Woodrow Wilson had taken office in 1913, Congress and voters had begun to see the banking industry as an oligopoly, an industry where power is concentrated in too few hands and customers suffer for it. Congressional lawmakers had been publicly investigating the so-called Money Trust, a spectacle that captured the press's attention and peaked with a headline-grabbing interrogation of Morgan himself at a hearing in 1912 (a reputational besmirchment the senior banker found so incredibly painful that his family blamed it for his death mere weeks later).[53]

As Glass and Wilson worked on a plan to reform the currency against that finance-skeptical backdrop, the president insisted that the new central bank must be under public control. He did not want regional reserve branches to operate on their own, answering mainly to private interests. "Which of you gentlemen thinks the railroads should select members of the Interstate Commerce Commission?" Wilson gibed at a meeting with Glass and bankers in the Oval Office, arguing that it made no more sense to allow the banks to regulate America's financial infrastructure.[54] The final version of the Federal

Reserve Act carved out a middle ground, mixing Aldrich's bank-controlled and decentralized setup with the publicly controlled body that Wilson favored. The president signed the bill Glass had shepherded into existence just before Christmas of that year, on December 23.

The structure created in 1913 was a prototype of the Fed as it exists today. The act created a new national currency—Federal Reserve notes—and required banks that belonged to the system to hold reserve balances with their local Federal Reserve branches.[55] Those regional Fed Reserve banks would range in number between eight and twelve (the law left that detail to be imminently decided) and would be owned by stockholding commercial banks. The financial fiefdoms would be coordinated by a public supervising authority in Washington, the Federal Reserve Board, whose members would include five presidential appointees working alongside the comptroller of the currency and the Treasury secretary.[56*] The goal of the system was to smooth over seasonal disruptions in money flow both by centralizing reserves and by allowing the Fed banks to support short-term loans backed by agreements between suppliers and producers, called "real bills,"[57] to make sure that sufficient money was available at times when it was in high demand.

The newly created Federal Reserve System was not especially powerful at its inception, nor did it have a spelled-out responsibility for either price stability or encouraging employment, which would go on to become its most well-known missions.[58] It was supposed to protect the system against painful panics and keep credit flowing by lending to member banks against good collateral when they needed cash to avoid a crunch. It was also intended to elevate the prominence of the little-used United States dollar in global trade.[59] Its ambitions more or less stopped there. Issuance of currency had to be tied to gold and to actual economic activity, which implicitly guarded against inflation by limiting the supply of money. Supporting speculative stock or bond investing was out of the question.[60] Glass, right up through his memoir, saw the Fed not as a central

* As an aside, the act specified that Board members would make $12,000 annually, about $345,000 in today's dollars. Governors today actually make around $200,000. Their wages haven't kept up with inflation.

bank like those in Europe, but as a means of currency reform and organization.[61]

The details of the legislation had been hotly and popularly debated, to the point that a *New York Times* editorial published on Christmas Day in 1913 complained that the public was getting too little credit for shaping the Fed's design. "It has seemed to us that the enactment of this measure in the form in which it received the President's assent is one of the most striking proofs in recent history of the efficiency of representative institutions," the paper griped, annoyed, in jest or in earnest, that Glass and Wilson were hogging the glory. The writers, supporters of the reform, said that the press, private bankers, and chambers of commerce had pressed improvements "with force, with patience, with iteration, and with success."[62] The *Times* writers weren't the only ones outraged at not getting credit. Many people would claim authorship of the ideas that became the Fed in the decades to come, publishing warring histories of its institutional parentage. Glass would write an entire book on the founding out of spite, after a Yale historian attributed the central bank's creation to a man whom he viewed as a more tangential character. Glass's account was full of choice words for the historian and the book in question, including: "Nothing comparable to it adorns the annals of legislative contrivance." The takeaway from the often-petty debate over the Fed's origin story is that America's central bank was a complex compromise, built on the ideas and interests of varied people and groups. The Fed was an exercise in the possible, not the ideal, from its very founding.

The interested parties may have been many, but they were not diverse. It was a system set up to service banks and serve those with access to them, which at the time of its founding largely meant America's white, male, and monied citizens.

As the Fed plan passed into law, nationally chartered banks, which were required to join the system, rushed to do so—the *Times* reported that the National Reserve Bank of Washington had telegrammed President Wilson asking to join eleven minutes before he had signed the actual legislation.[63] Public attention turned to the unresolved question: Which cities would get a reserve bank?

—

It is an inevitable reality of Washington that where there are spoils there will be lobbying, and cities began to compete for the honor and perceived economic advantage of hosting a regional Fed bank before the ink was dry on the legislation creating them.

The law had charged Treasury Secretary William McAdoo, the secretary of agriculture, and the comptroller of the currency—a trio of Democrats—with designating the eight to twelve lucky winners. Early speculation suggested that they would pick New York, Chicago, Boston, St. Louis, and Pittsburgh, but from the start it was clear that more than a dozen cities would want their own Fed outpost. In all, thirty-seven tried for a regional branch.[64] The twelve that prevailed, identified in April 1914, were all politically important banking centers, and the locations have never been amended in the century-plus since, even as America's population and commercial centers have shifted. The quirky result is that Missouri is home to two Fed branches, one in Kansas City and one in St. Louis. San Francisco, meanwhile, oversees all seven states west of the Rocky Mountains, plus Hawaii and Alaska. (The other reserve bank locations were, and still are, New York, Boston, Philadelphia, Cleveland, Richmond, Atlanta, Minneapolis, and Dallas.)

The winning cities seemed to accomplish three goals: dispersing money and credit beyond the bank-heavy Northeast, satisfying bankers and the business community, and, at the margin, rewarding progressive allies. Missouri's windfall is a case in point. St. Louis was a historically important reserve city and practically destined to get a bank, but it wasn't obvious how to keep money flowing farther west. While places like Omaha and Denver were under consideration, the search committee's polling showed that bankers preferred Kansas City, which was a buzzing commercial hub and had a booming nightlife scene.[65] It probably didn't hurt that both the Democratic House speaker, Champ Clark, and the agriculture secretary in charge of picking locales had ties to Missouri.[66] Richmond, both Democratic and Southern, won out over Baltimore. The latter sat in Maryland, which was less reliably left leaning and which had more ties to the North. Poor Pittsburgh, nestled between Philadelphia and Cleveland, was snubbed in the interest of regional balance and, as some critics at the time alleged, over its comparative lack of political connection.[67]

McAdoo and his colleagues had designed their map thoughtfully, but that did not prevent outcry over the results. Blowback over the fact that New Orleans, Omaha, Denver, and Baltimore had been deprived reserve banks was so immediate and so severe that the selection committee released a defense of its decision, chiding bankers for making such a fuss and arguing that hosting a reserve bank bestowed no great financial advantage.

"Every city which has the foundations for prosperity and progress will continue to grow and expand, whether it has such a reserve bank or not, and well-informed bankers, especially, are aware of this," the committee harrumphed in its April 10, 1914, statement.[68]

Controversial as they were, the results stuck, and the Fed set about organizing itself. The Treasury secretary often dominated the Fed Board in its early days, serving as the ex officio head and housing the institution at the Treasury Department building in Washington. The leaders of the Fed itself were tasked with setting up shop.[69] For the central bank's first official chairman—just called "governor" in those days—Wilson turned to Charles Sumner Hamlin. An effective political operator behind the scenes, Hamlin was a little-remarked-upon lawyer and former Treasury official who, if it is any sign of his prominence, merited fewer column inches in *The New York Times* obituary pages in 1938 than the son of a once-prominent rear admiral.[70] The institution that took shape under both him and his successor, William P. G. Harding, was heavily involved in financing the war raging through Europe, which it did by marketing war bonds and by lending to member banks at low interest rates if the banks then used the proceeds to purchase government securities.[71] When, in 1920, the Fed did begin to exercise some of its own control and discretion, it raised rates to lure gold back from abroad in a bid to secure the dollar's backing, precipitating a deep recession and deflation.[72]

Yet the Fed's limited role as an organizing body that narrowly served the elected government's objectives and defended the gold standard would not last. As the 1920s roared on, Benjamin Strong, Jr., emerged as the most powerful central banker in America and began to change the fabric of the institution he dominated.

Strong had been a young star of Wall Street during the 1907 meltdown and had personally helped Morgan to analyze the financial health of failing trusts. He had gone on to become a member of the

First Name Club, helping to draw up Aldrich's rough outline for the Fed. And in 1914, he became the first head of the New York Fed. He had some reservations about taking the job, which paid just $30,000 (his 8,000-square-foot Manhattan apartment rented for $15,000 per year).[73] Even so, when he ultimately accepted the Fed post, he took it on with vigor. Under his guidance, New York, the very city the anti–Wall Street advocates had hoped to disempower with the Fed's decentralized structure, became the nucleus of the new system.[*]

Strong, whose secretary later recalled him as a man with "eyes that could see right through you,"[74] was a natural leader. He came up with a system to loosely coordinate asset buying across regional banks, ultimately forming the Open Market Investment Committee, of which he was chair.[75] Buying government bonds had not initially been an important function of the regional banks: The Fed had been expected to foster the creation of only a very short-term market for borrowed money in the United States. But the reserve banks had tiptoed into longer-term government securities during World War I because the Treasury needed a buyer for its debt, and they had later realized they could use the purchases to earn a return for their own accounts.[76] It turned out that the buying also came with an economic bonus for the broader economy. When the regional banks bought securities, that increased reserves—central bank cash—on the balance sheets of the banks from whom they made the purchases. The banks then lent against those reserves, so that when the Fed bought more bonds and short-term notes, more loans flowed to consumers, and the economy tended to grow more rapidly.[77]

"There were no substantial historical precedents for this new venture in central banking," W. Randolph Burgess, who worked as a statistician at the New York Fed at the time, would later write. "For the first time in history, a bank of issue could direct its policy decisions to the whole economic picture."

Under Strong's watch, the Fed began to engage in macroeconomic

---

[*] In fact, many parts of the original goals were overturned in these years. "The Federal Reserve developed much more activist procedures than envisaged by the authors of the Federal Reserve Act or practiced in earlier years, and policy actions became more centralized," Allan Meltzer, the central bank historian, wrote in his chapter on the 1923–1929 period.

management. It guided the cost of borrowing in a way that aimed to keep the business cycle steady while supporting the international gold standard.

As the Fed found its footing during those early years, becoming more of a powerful, private interest–controlled, New York–centric institution than Wilson and Glass had envisioned, it drew occasional criticisms. A former comptroller of the currency printed a scathing review in *The New York Times* blasting the Fed for spending $25,646,409 on a "palatial" New York building that its author swore would "make Solomon's temple of old seem quite cheap in comparison."[78] In fact, the New York Fed faced such scrutiny over its budget that it began calling its fifty-person team of statisticians the "reports department."[79] Statisticians sounded fancy.

Nevertheless, the Fed was on the whole seen as a success. It had initially been chartered for twenty years and was made permanent in the 1927 McFadden Act, escaping the fate that had befallen the First and Second Banks of the United States.[80] "The best tribute to the efficiency of the Federal Reserve System is that no panic has developed since its inception," Marriner Eccles, then one of the institution's fans, would tell the Rotary Club of Ogden in 1928.[81]

The Federal Reserve may have gained some early supporters, but troubles were brewing for the nation's third shot at centralizing its money system. Wall Street speculation was running rampant by 1928, helped by the Fed's policies, when Strong died at just fifty-five. His passing created a leadership vacuum at precisely the wrong moment. Officials, concerned that their own credit policies were propping up the booming stock market, tightened policy to restrict the flow of money starting that year even though the economy was not especially strong. In early 1929, the Federal Reserve Board issued guidelines meant to prohibit banks that made stock market loans from borrowing at their regional Feds.[82]

To what extent the Fed's decisions—first easy money, and then an abrupt reversal of that patience—set the stage for the Great Depression has long been a topic of historical debate. What is widely accepted is that the Fed did far too little to suppress the crisis once it had begun.

The stock market crashed, regional bank panics took hold, and the financial system had all but collapsed by the end of 1933.[83] Instead of helping the economy through the disaster, the Fed focused on maintaining the gold standard.[84] The government was required to back 40 cents of each dollar with gold, which did not typically constrain the Fed's ability to maneuver, because the central bank generally had more gold on deposit than it needed. Global interest rate differentials could change that, though, luring gold stores from American vaults. Higher rates elsewhere could prompt (or force) the central bank to carry out policy in a way that would lift interest rates domestically, in hopes of pulling gold back from overseas. That is exactly what played out at the onset of the Depression.* Fed officials kept policy tight, choking off lending and spending, initially to keep gold from flowing to France.[85]

Moralistic arguments also influenced policy. A few regional central bankers felt that a crisis would prune out weak institutions and reckless gamblers—and as the Fed found itself locked in a disagreement over what role it should play in blunting the crisis, it failed to help troubled banks. As the financial system teetered and the economy contracted, money became scarce, pushing up its value, and prices fell. Deflation crushed debtors as the sums they owed became more expensive relative to what they could earn with their businesses or labor. Franklin Delano Roosevelt rolled out a number of policies to stop the unraveling, including a move to break the link between the dollar and gold, a banking holiday, and the start of federal deposit insurance. They helped. Even so, a long period of mass bankruptcy and widespread privation that would send unemployment to about 25 percent had taken hold. It would end fully only with the mobilization for World War II.

Before that, change would come to the Fed, much of it the handiwork of Marriner Eccles.

---

* Ben Bernanke, the former Fed chair, documented in a co-authored 1991 paper that across a sample of twenty-four major countries during the interwar period, "there was a strong link between adherence to the gold standard and the severity of both deflation and depression."

—

Eccles—by then in his thirties, still pale and slim, still unfailingly fiery—had entered the late 1920s at the pinnacle of the business world.

He had secured his place at the head of the sort of dynasty that had become possible in that capitalistic century, one built on wealth and enterprise instead of the pedigrees of past eras. He believed that the Fed had succeeded at stabilizing the financial system and, as was fashionably accepted among the economic thinkers of his era, that business cycles were a bygone phenomenon. It was a new age of roaring prosperity.

Then came the stock market crash of 1929, which left children starving to death and villages of families living in cardboard shacks.[86] Eccles, watching businesses fail by the dozen and staring down hard decisions about layoffs and belt-tightening himself, found doubt creeping into his mind.

One of the banks Eccles owned in Ogden, Utah, narrowly avoided a crushing run in 1931, in an episode that helped to set the rest of his story into motion. The debacle started in earnest one weekend in August, when Eccles got word that a nearby—and highly respected— bank was in terrible shape because of the ongoing national deflation and economic malaise. It would fail to open its doors that Monday. The news seemed likely to set off a local panic as investors rushed to pull their money, which boded ill for Eccles's business empire. Ogden was the very heart of his First Security Corporation* banking network, so he knew that if disaster were to hit there, it would likely ripple through his other banks.

It was critical to kill the meltdown before it even started. He called together his officers that Sunday. First, he told them, they were to call all of their business contacts who held accounts at the failing bank and assure them that Eccles's institution stood prepared to do business with them. That should shore up commercial confidence, he thought, and keep deposits flowing into his banks at a time when withdrawals were sure to come.

The second part of the plan focused on nervous clients. Eccles

* FSC would, eventually, become part of Wells Fargo.

would put out a statement, via telegram, to outside accounts that Monday morning, explaining that First Security had known about the coming bank failure, had gotten ready, and stood "fully prepared to meet any and all demands."

Then came the critical act of theater. Eccles issued clear instructions to his employees about how they were to act on that pivotal Monday: "Go about your business as though nothing unusual was happening. Smile, be pleasant, talk about the weather, show no signs of panic. The main burden is going to fall on you boys in the savings department. Instead of the three windows we normally use, we are going to use all four of them today. They must be manned at all times because if any teller's or clerk's window in this bank closes for even a short time, that will stir up more panic. We'll have sandwiches brought in; no one can go out to lunch."

People were going to come in by the droves to pull out cash, he said. The tellers were going to pay them, every last one. But they were going to do it very, very, very slowly. The goal was to avoid depleting the bank's funds, which were too small to satisfy all customers.

As Eccles had anticipated, the run came. The lines snaked out the bank's doors as tellers handed out money at a snail's pace, counting out the bills with flair. Eccles could see the taut lines creasing faces as his customers waited, and he could sense the nervous buzz in their voices. When the bank's cash delivery came from the regional Fed branch, Eccles pulled the Fed officer who came with it up to the bank's counter.

"Just a minute!" he said, waiting for a hush to fall over the lobby. He launched into a short speech about why the sense of dread pervading the room was needless.

"There is no justification for the excitement or the apparent panicky attitude on the part of some depositors. As all of you have seen, we have just had brought up from Salt Lake City a large amount of currency that will take care of all your requirements. There is plenty more where that came from."

He neglected to mention that the Fed's cash was neither owned by nor accessible to his bank. Minor details. He pointed out the Fed employee to his customers, and even asked him to say a few words.

The showmanship, and a promise that the bank would stay open late that day so that every person who wanted money had time to withdraw it, reassured the masses. People stayed in line, but the tone shifted.

Eccles opened his doors early the next morning. Instead of paying out cash slowly, he told the tellers to do it unusually quickly. No lines were to form. None did. Customers that day were greeted by a mostly empty bank staffed with employees calmly going about their business. No signs of abnormality were allowed to manifest, even though the bank paid out far more than it had on Monday.

"On Tuesday customers came into the doorway of the bank, looked furtively around the lobby, and, seeing that things were peaceful and serene, walked away," Eccles would later recount, adding smugly: "And that was the end of that run."

The episode is a textbook example of what banking panics are all about: confidence. By reassuring depositors, just as J. P. Morgan had once done by supporting chaos-stricken lenders, Eccles was able to keep his financial institution operating and functional. And while the dramatics of the episode are hard to corroborate, Eccles's feats during the Depression earned him national attention.

Eccles was one of the wealthiest men in the West and by the 1930s had amassed an immense but indeterminate fortune across a range of businesses from banking to beet sugar. He was left standing after the darkest days of the Depression crushed much of his class. Because of that reputation, politicians in Washington sought Eccles's expert opinion on the disaster that had befallen the American economy.

When they did, they found someone who held a fundamentally different view on the matter than one might have expected from a leading capitalist—and, in fact, a very different perspective than he himself had espoused even a few years earlier. The Depression had set off the kind of soul-searching for Eccles that his missionary work had never inspired. After much stress and many hours of worry, he had concluded that the core tenets of his father's economics didn't work in his day and age. When he as a business owner buckled down, stopped spending, stopped lending, and operated prudently in the face of stress, it was just making things worse for everyone, creating a downward spiral in which less money was changing hands and less economic activity was happening. It was a situation that no self-interested private company could heal. Eccles had come around to believing in what economics textbooks now teach as "the paradox of thrift."

"It took a general economic collapse to show that 'thrift' as it was practiced—quite correctly—in a former epoch, could, in the present one, be a source of great danger to the nation as a whole when practiced in excess," Eccles would recall. He had convinced himself that only one force could save the economy from such danger, and that was the government.

When Eccles went to Capitol Hill to testify on the ongoing crisis, one of several businessmen to do so, he did not mince words. He advocated for his newfound beliefs, which closely resembled what would become known as Keynesian doctrine after the now-famous economist John Maynard Keynes himself set the principles out in writing several years later.[87] "Is it necessary to conserve Government credit to the point of providing a starvation existence for millions of our people in a land of superabundance?" Eccles asked during his congressional testimony in 1933.[88]

Eccles laid out a five-point spending program proposal during that testimony, one that would help to inform and set out a basis for Franklin D. Roosevelt's New Deal. His advocacy for a forceful federal response—at a time when almost everyone else, including Roosevelt himself, had called for a balanced budget—earned him the president's ear. He won a brief appointment to the Treasury Department.

Yet Roosevelt had a different job in mind for the Utahn. Eccles was stunned when, one blistering August day in Washington, the Treasury secretary floated an idea to him in whispered tones during a White House conference. The president was thinking of making Eccles the head of the Federal Reserve. "For once in my life I was mum," Eccles recalled later. It wasn't the good kind of stunned silence. Eccles might have said nice things about the Fed's role in stabilizing the system before the Depression, but the episode had greatly diminished the central bank's reputation. More to the point for Eccles, the D.C.-based Board had very little power compared to the regional banks. To drive that reality home, the post he was being offered had become available because Eugene Black, the incumbent, had resigned so that he could go lead the Atlanta Fed. Legislation passed in 1933 had given the Board the authority to approve monetary policy plans,[89] but it had no power to initiate them. The regional reserve bank's top officials would agree on a purchase plan and then submit it to the Board for sign-off in a system that was somewhere between clunky and dysfunctional. Eccles saw the diffuse power as a way for the New York financial interests, through the New York Fed, to exert outsize influence on national economic policy.

He was not enthused.

"Private interests, acting through the Reserve banks, had made the System an effective instrument by which private interests alone could be served," Eccles recalled telling the president when, a month later, Roosevelt personally asked him to take the job. He would do it only if he could fundamentally reform the Fed.

The president told Eccles to come up with a plan.

And so it was that, a few years after helping to inspire the most ambitious series of public works projects America had ever seen— a triumph of fiscal policy, the government's taxing and spending tools—Eccles helped to rewrite the rules of central banking in America.

The Banking Act of 1935, which Eccles helped to shape, is sometimes referred to as the Fed's "second founding."[90] The reform took power away from the private reserve banks and concentrated it at the presidentially appointed Board in Washington, now officially called the Board of Governors of the Federal Reserve System. Regional heads, once called governors, were nominally demoted to presidents. The leader of the Board was newly titled "chairman." All seven governors would hold votes on the rate-setting Federal Open Market Committee. Carter Glass, by then an aging senator, maneuvered to reserve five voting seats for his beloved reserve banks, which would include a constant vote for New York, but the public appointees now held the majority.[91]

America's experiments in central banking had long been a balancing act between centralized control in the hands of the government and dispersed control in the hands of bankers, and the 1935 reform heavily tilted the scale toward the public.

At the same time, the reform began to establish the central bank's independence from more political bodies. Meetings were moved from the Treasury Department to a new building on Constitution Avenue in Washington, D.C., which runs parallel to the stretch of grass and monuments called the National Mall. The comptroller and Treasury secretary lost their seats at the Fed's decision-making table.

In 1936, having secured and separated the Fed's power core in Washington, Eccles became the first person to claim the title "Fed chair." Troubles continued to plague the nation—analysts have since estimated that the unemployment rate might have been as high as 17 percent. Given the brutal context, the changes happening in the economic policy sphere drew notice.

"Many people believe Marriner S. Eccles is the only thing standing between the United States and disaster," *Time* magazine wrote in a cover story that year.[92]

Chapter 4

THE FED'S SECOND ACT

At the time of its creation, proponents and opponents
recognized a principal issue: Would the Federal Reserve
be controlled by bankers operating in their interest or by
politicians operating in theirs?

—*Allan H. Meltzer,* A History of the Federal Reserve,
Volume 2, Book 1, 1951–1969

I N 1951, LONG AFTER *Time* had declared him America's best hope
to avert cataclysm, Marriner Eccles had come to believe that he
might truly have a key role to play in saving the nation. The circumstances were nearly the opposite of the ones that had prevailed
fifteen years earlier.

Eccles had guided the economy through the painful post-
Depression years and had helped the financial system to weather
World War II, which had fully pulled growth out of its long malaise.
Even so, he had entered the 1950s as a storied public servant with a
smarting ego.

In late January 1948 President Harry Truman had surprised
Eccles—and the rest of Washington—by declining to reappoint him
as chair in what appeared to be a snap decision, the motivation of
which would remain an enduring mystery in economic policy circles.
The deposed Eccles chose to stay on at the Fed, enabled by the fact
that the chair holds one of the Board's seven governor seats. Those
positions carry much longer tenures than the leadership roles. Eccles

would go on to capture his feeling about his decision to stick around by quoting an old Scottish ballad in his memoir:

"A little I'm hurt, but yet not slain;
I'll but lie down and bleed awhile,
And then I'll rise and fight again."

The Truman White House didn't realize what it was in for.

The next step in Eccles's career would kick off a pivotal era in Fed history. In the half century stretching from 1950 to 2000, the Fed would become far more independent of the White House, more focused on fighting inflation, and increasingly dominated by economists and economic theory instead of men of industry with more ad hoc belief systems. Those decades would also see the central bank become vastly more powerful.

The seeds of the change had been planted while Eccles was still chair. It was a debate over inflation—which was, at its heart, a struggle over what role the Fed would play in the postwar order—that would cement his legacy.

Midway through the twentieth century, both postwar peace agreements and the destruction in Europe had locked America into place at the head of the global geopolitical pack. The nation's economy was growing robustly, fueled by booming fertility, an ascendant middle class, the entry of women into the labor market, and the migration of Black Americans into industrial cities in the North. From Detroit to Pittsburgh, factories were pumping out the new essentials of American life: cars and radios, steel and washing machines.

The Fed was enabling the surge by nurturing borrowing and spending, but it was doing so quietly and outside the public's eye. Money supply was not the center of debate it had been at the dawn of the twentieth century. When the Fed was considered at all by the general public, it was seen as a technocratic entity.[1]

The Fed had spent much of the post-Depression period focused on helping to keep rates low so that the government could finance World War II, but by the late 1940s, Eccles and his colleagues had

begun itching to use the Fed's monetary powers to contain a burst
of high inflation. The Fed's authority to guide economic conditions independently of the elected government remained ill-defined,
though, and the prospect of higher rates proved unpopular with the
administration.

The Truman White House paid lip service to controlling price
increases. But its actions spoke more loudly than its words. The
administration rolled out policy changes that would fuel inflation—
lifting wage and price caps and ending a tax on excess profits. When
it came to Fed policy, the Truman Treasury suffered from a "chronic
bias for cheap money in all seasons," Eccles would later write.[2] The
administration did not want the Fed to make it more expensive for
the government to borrow money by lifting interest rates, a position
that it maintained after cutting Eccles from the top spot and installing his successor, Thomas McCabe.* President Truman and Treasury
Secretary John Snyder wanted the Fed to continue a wartime practice
of holding the rate on government bonds at low levels, often called
pegging.

As Fed chair during the war, Eccles had willingly kept a lid on
rates by buying government securities.[†] He had believed that it was
the Fed's job to cooperate with fiscal authorities in times of crisis,
even though the approach left it with limited ability to control
prices. He did not think the setup should be a permanent state of
affairs, however. Eccles thought economy-stoking monetary and
government spending policies should be reserved for moments of
dire need.

By the start of the 1950s, he and his colleagues at the Fed had
firmly come to believe that economic policy should turn more restrictive during times of relative prosperity, like the one the country was
entering. The Depression was a distant memory and the economy

* Eccles initially thought he had lost his job because he had been too aggressive
in overseeing a bank, Transamerica, and it had lobbied to have him sacked. He
later wondered if it was his monetary policy stance. The real reason never became
clear, though his *New York Times* obituary blamed his differences with the White
House over inflation.
† Such purchases are not direct. When the Fed buys bonds, it purchases them from
specially designated banks. Those banks get "reserves"—deposits at the central
bank—in exchange.

was growing strongly. As the Korean War started and intensified, the Fed found itself facing the prospect of having to buy a fresh wave of government debt, continuing what is now commonly known as monetary financing, even as prices climbed.

The Fed, by Eccles's account and based on records from the time, offered lawmakers and the White House an array of options that would have given a measure of control over inflation to the central bank in a gradual way to avoid risking a painful disruption. Such friendly overtures did not move the White House or Secretary Snyder, who was fast emerging as Eccles's nemesis. Truman and Snyder were "populists who believed that banks, not the market forces of supply and demand, set interest rates," according to an account written by one of the Fed staff economists present for much of the episode.[3] Prices continued to climb as the government dallied. It was a worrisome development during an era in which out-of-control inflation was seen as a fomenter of unrest, given the interwar experience of Germany and Italy. "By wiping out the middle classes" inflation had "paved the way for fascism and communism on the continent of Europe," Senator Paul Douglas, Democrat of Illinois and an economist, said on the Senate floor in 1951.[4]

The situation came to a head in January of that year. Treasury Secretary Snyder announced in public at a luncheon on the eighteenth that the government's long-term rate would be kept at 2.5 percent—and he implied that the Fed had agreed to that plan.[5] It had done no such thing. McCabe, the newly installed Fed chair, could not see how he could publicly contradict the announcement without resigning. As a result, it was Eccles—freed, ironically, by his demotion—who answered lawmakers' questions about Snyder's announcement. He openly contradicted it.[6]

On January 31, Truman upped the ante by summoning the entire Federal Open Market Committee to the White House to pressure it to set policy as he demanded, the first and last time that such a dressing-down has ever happened. After the gathering, Truman and his Treasury Department announced to the press that the central bankers had agreed to maintain the Treasury financing arrangement.[7] The president even sent Fed chair McCabe a letter, swiftly released to the press, in which Truman asked McCabe to "convey to all the members of your group my warm appreciation of their cooperative attitude."[8] The trouble was that, again, the Fed had agreed to no such cooperation. The Truman White House was bluffing, trying to bully the central bank into compliance.

Livid, Eccles decided that it was time for him to take matters into his own hands more dramatically. It wasn't the disaster *Time* had foreseen him fighting, but it was a calamity, nonetheless. He summoned the Board's secretary and asked for a review copy of the committee's internal account of the meeting. He then called a favorite reporter to the hotel where he was living and arranged for him to publish an account of it in *The New York Times* while also distributing it to *The Washington Post* and the Washington *Evening Star.*[9] The nation's most prominent newspapers carried stories calling out the administration's lie.

Eccles's Fed colleagues were surprised that he had released the document, but they either kept quiet about his decision or supported it, he would later recall. The Fed had come to accept fighting price instability as a key part of its job, and the White House was tying its hands.

"If we fail in this task, history may well record that we were responsible in great measure for helping to bring about the destruction of the very system our defense effort is designed to protect," Eccles told his colleagues at an emergency meeting the next day. He then referenced a set of duties that had just years earlier been set out in the Employment Act of 1946. The law dictated that the federal government should not only promote maximum employment, but should also protect purchasing power.[10] "If Congress objects to our actions, it can change the law; but until it does that, we have a clear responsibility to check inflation."

Sensing defeat, William McChesney Martin, Jr., a Treasury assistant secretary who would soon lead the central bank, negotiated a compromise with several members of the Fed Board in which it would withdraw its help from the government bond market only gradually. On March 4, 1951, the two entities released what is now known as the Treasury-Fed Accord, announcing that the Fed would stop supporting government bond issuance. The document set forth the foundation for monetary policy independence, freeing the Fed from political domination.

—

Another momentous change had taken place over the course of Eccles's tenure: America and the world had shifted away from the gold standard and toward a new currency system.

The United States had used gold as at least a partial basis for its currency for practically its entire history, with occasional suspensions, and had formally adopted the gold standard in 1900. The standard had been kept in place through the passage of the 1913 Federal Reserve Act, with the requirement that the central bank maintain gold holdings equivalent to 40 percent of the currency it issued.[11] Yet that ratio had become difficult to maintain amid the Depression and in the tumultuous decades that followed. During the financial carnage of 1933, gold had flowed out of vaults as panicked consumers fled to its relative safety and as foreign holders moved their money out of the crisis-stricken United States. The Roosevelt administration had first ended creditors' right to demand repayment in gold and then taken a series of actions that nationalized the gold stock.[12] Legislation in 1933 and 1934 gave the president the power to set the price of gold: It had been at $20.67 per ounce in 1933, then was raised to $35 per ounce in early 1934, helping to devalue the dollar and fight back against Depression-era deflation.

Other nations had also suspended their gold standards during the 1930s, and in 1944 delegates from forty-four countries met in Bretton Woods, New Hampshire, to hash out a new plan for global monetary governance that would foster cooperation and growth following World War II. Eccles, still Fed chair at the time, attended on America's behalf, John Maynard Keynes on Britain's. Despite sharing similar philosophies about the government's role in stemming crises, they hated each other. "It's no wonder the man is Mormon. No single woman could stand him," Keynes is said to have remarked. (It is worth noting that Eccles, though he professed himself to be a less-than-fabulous husband, was not a polygamist, and the Mormon church had banned the practice.)[13]

What emerged from Bretton Woods was a system in which currencies were convertible into dollars, and dollars convertible to gold, at a set price, so that the United States had to adjust the global supply of dollars to maintain the desired value.[14] The plan required maintenance of the dollar's link to gold at $35 per ounce, which at times curtailed the Fed's ability to maneuver after the system became fully operational.[15]

When Eccles resigned in 1951, he had played a central role in consolidating the Fed's power in Washington, in establishing monetary independence from the White House and Treasury, and in witnessing the establishment of a new money standard that formally placed the dollar at the core of the entire global financial system.

Maintaining Bretton Woods gold convertibility was hardly the Fed's only concern in setting monetary policy in mid-century America. Congress had declared in 1946 that it was the government's responsibility to "use all practicable means" to promote "maximum employment, production and purchasing power." That law, the one Eccles had referenced during his battle with the White House, had given the Fed, as an independent agency of the executive branch, an early version of its two-part mandate. William McChesney Martin moved from Treasury to chair the Fed in 1951, and his central bank spent the 1950s interpreting the law as a directive to balance the goals of fostering low unemployment and moderate price increases.

Martin himself believed the Fed should occupy a limited position in society. The Fed stopped buying longer-term bonds during his tenure in an effort to play less of a role in markets. It moved to a policy that emphasized purchasing short-term debt only, one that would essentially hold until 2008.[16]

Martin's colleagues, however, did not always share his humble view of the Fed's position in society. The painful memory of the Great Depression's rampant unemployment lingered, and Martin's fellow policy makers prioritized creating the strongest job market possible. They began to try to "buy" additional employment, allowing inflation to move slightly higher without decisively counteracting it by adjusting monetary policy.[17] Their nudging, historians have since concluded, eventually overshot.

Output had been growing nicely leading into the mid-1960s, inflation was low, and the unemployment rate was falling. Economics as a profession, once held in similar esteem to accounting or insurance, had gained an aura of importance. Economists had "descended in force from their ivory towers" and now sat "confidently at the elbow of almost every important leader in Government and business," *Time* declared in 1965.[18] As the technicians took power, officials began to believe that they could guide the economy with a more surgical precision. "The choice was seen as a social judgment," Allan Meltzer, a Carnegie Mellon University economist and Fed historian, wrote in his 2009 book. "At the cost of a small additional tax on cash balances, society could employ more people, especially people with low marginal productivity and little education and skill."

The economist and historian Michael Bordo has summed up the Keynesian doctrine that dominated that era even more concisely: "The welfare costs of inflation were perceived as lower than the costs of unemployment."[19]

Chair Martin wanted to raise interest rates as unemployment slipped below 4.5 percent, but his colleagues resisted. When he did cajole the policy-setting committee into a discount rate increase in December 1965, with the jobless rate near 4 percent, three of the seven governors dissented, calling the decision "premature" in the absence of more actual inflation.[20]*

Price increases began to move higher the following year, rising above a 2 percent pace substantially and steadily for the first time in nearly a decade. Convinced that achieving full employment meant driving the jobless rate down to 4 percent, and focused on reaching that mark, Martin's colleagues continued to resist interest rate increases. The central bank in that era was still intellectually disorganized: Officials didn't make official economic forecasts, didn't ascribe to similar views on what pushed prices up across the entire economy, and did not have any clear and agreed-upon framework for how to weigh trade-offs. In the cacophony that resulted, they let prices pick up for years on end without forcefully resisting the trend.[21] The slow

---

* As a technical aside, the discount rate is the interest rate the Fed charges commercial banks for short-term loans, whereas the federal funds rate is the rate banks charge one another. The discount rate was a major tool for communicating policy prior to the mid-1970s, and the Board still sets it, but it has become less important with time. The funds rate is today the target policy rate, the one used to guide economy-wide credit costs.

response to rapidly rising prices that started under Martin's watch was the first, and more minor, error. The second, pressing mistake came after 1970, when Martin was replaced at the Fed's helm by Arthur Burns.

President Richard Nixon pressured Burns to accommodate the economy headed into the 1972 election, the president's tape recordings would later make clear. During one colorful private telephone conversation, Nixon encouraged Burns to lead his colleagues at the central bank along toward lower rates. "Just kick 'em in the rump a little," the president advised.[22] Despite the backdrop of quick inflation, Burns kept borrowing cheap enough that lending and spending chugged along without major inhibition. The stage was set for disaster. Easy monetary policy, many economists now believe, helped to send prices into the stratosphere, especially after years of government spending on the Vietnam War and new social programs aimed at poverty alleviation that had helped to create an imbalance between supply and demand.

Nixon tried to solve the problem with his own policy tools. As inflation took off, and in a bid to shore up domestic manufacturing, the president on August 15, 1971, announced economic reforms meant to contain rapid price increases and bolster the domestic job market. The country would suspend the practice of tying the dollar's value to gold in any way, would institute wage and price freezes, and would slap a charge on imports.

The so-called Nixon shock was the dying gasp of a gold-tied global monetary system, setting the stage for an era in which currencies fluctuated with national policies and market forces. Cutting the gold anchor, however necessary, set the stage for a drop in the dollar's value in global currency markets. The price freeze Nixon instituted paved the way for further trouble. Instead of stopping inflation, it merely delayed it.[23] An oil embargo in 1973 coincided with the end of controls to send prices much higher, and they remained elevated through a second oil crisis in 1979. By the early 1980s, prices were climbing at a double-digit pace.

Short-term inflation was not the Fed's fault, the conventional wisdom now holds, but it was central bank inaction that allowed fast price gains to become a regular feature of the American economic landscape. As the Fed failed to act decisively to choke off rapid inflation, workers began to expect higher costs and demand higher wages each year. Businesses steadily charged more to cover those climbing wage bills. There was no end in sight to the destabilizing situation, which was eroding savings piles and making it hard for companies and households to plan. What would become known as the Great Inflation is the defining moment in late twentieth-century monetary history, a mistake that has haunted central bankers' nightmares—and informed their policy decisions—ever since.

Paul Volcker became chair of the Fed in 1979 as inflation ratcheted up above 10 percent. A towering economist from Teaneck, New Jersey, Volcker led a campaign that pushed interest rates to nearly 20 percent in a bid to control price increases. Builders famously mailed him two-by-fours because his policies were making mortgages so expensive, and crippling the homebuilding industry so much, that they could no longer use the wood to build houses. Car dealers sent the Fed keys from automobiles they could not sell.

As Volcker's Fed instituted its inflation-fighting policy, the United States entered a punishing downturn and unemployment skyrocketed to a peak of 10.8 percent, a height it wouldn't touch again until 2020. People everywhere paid amid the adjustment, but they also stopped spending money. Supply caught up and prices came down.

As it implemented the restrictive policy, Volcker's Fed briefly practiced what he would later call practical monetarism. Rather than officially targeting interest rates, he focused on reserves in the banking system. Milton Friedman and Anna Schwartz had argued in a book published in 1963 that money supply was a major driver of economic outcomes in the United States. While Friedman's ideas did not catch hold at first—Keynesianism still ruled the day—they gained attention as the orthodoxy failed to address inflation, the concern of the moment. "It always seemed to me that there is a kind of common-sense view that inflation is too much money chasing too few goods. You could oversimplify it and say that inflation is just a monetary phenomenon," Volcker would later explain in a published interview. "So I think we could explain what we had to do to stop inflation better that way than simply by saying that we've got to raise interest rates."[24]

Less charitably, pushing rates up to the crushing levels they reached would have been difficult to explain to the public and to lawmakers. By focusing on how much money was pumping through the system and saying that the "market" was setting interest rates, Volcker could dodge some of that blame while still doing what he had deemed necessary to wrangle inflation.

Volcker had plenty of reason to worry about the optics. From the mid-1970s, even before the Fed began to stage a particularly forceful response, lawmakers hated that the Fed was depressing business and sending joblessness higher in pursuit of stable prices. They passed the legislation to prove it. Congress in 1975 adopted a resolution that instructed the Fed specifically to aim for "goals of maximum employment, stable prices, and moderate long-term interest rates." It put what is now known as the Fed's dual mandate into law in 1977.[25] Senator Hubert Humphrey, a Democrat from Minnesota and formerly Lyndon Johnson's vice president, pushed even further in the Full Employment and Balanced Growth Act. Humphrey died in 1978, but the act passed into law not long after, laying out a set of lofty goals: Adult unemployment should not exceed 3 percent, inflation should be brought below 3 percent and eventually less, and the employment goal should dominate if there were ever a question of priorities.[26]

Volcker fell short of that ambitious (and probably unrealistic) mark as he pushed interest rates relentlessly higher, slowing demand and throwing people out of jobs in pursuit of stable prices. Unemployment averaged 9.7 percent in 1982, higher than its average during the worst year of the Great Recession. Critics argued that the Fed's assault on price pressures amounted to picking sides in a class war as America's laboring masses lost jobs and high rates helped the owners of capital to reap profits. By choosing to stabilize inflation, critics argued that the Fed was choosing to protect the status quo— people who had money or were owed it found that it kept its value— even if those just getting started economically could not borrow to build houses or start businesses. "In the name of stability, the past was defended, and the future was denied," the journalist William Greider would go on to write in his 1987 book *Secrets of the Temple*.

Volcker was blasted at congressional hearings, which were newly held twice yearly per a requirement in the Humphrey–Hawkins legislation. He helped to cost Jimmy Carter his reelection.* At one Capitol Hill appearance in 1983, a senator remarked that his colleagues had blamed Volcker for just about everything except for "herpes and giving away the Panama Canal," then quipped, "but we're not through with the hearing yet."[27] It didn't aid Volcker's cause that he was more of an autocrat than a consensus broker and that his Fed operated in an intentional obscurity. Lawmakers often saw his power and privateness as an unattractive combination. Frank Annunzio, an Illinois Democrat, once told the Fed chair that he "would make a very excellent prisoner of war" because he "wouldn't tell the enemy a thing."[28]

Both popular opinion and the economic consensus shifted dramatically in Volcker's favor in the years and decades following his reign, as inflation moderated, growth stabilized, and the damage his decisions had inflicted on lives and livelihoods faded. He put the economy through a painful period that, many researchers now believe, laid the groundwork for decades of healthy growth. During the late 1980s and 1990s, an era often called the Great Moderation, unemployment trended steadily lower, productivity took off, and the debate over whether the Fed was setting its priorities incorrectly largely disappeared. Slower inflation was seen as a victory by economists and politicians alike. Volcker went from contemporary villain to historical hero.

In fact, the resolution of the 1970s and 1980s price burst secured the Fed's position at the top of the nation's economic order. During Eccles's time, monetary policy had been treated as a secondary power, one that helped to stimulate or restrain growth around the edges while often playing backup to Congress's fiscal spending and taxing powers. That reputation had remained intact during William McChesney Martin's and Arthur Burns's tenures, which saw the Fed working alongside the White House and Congress and exercising autonomy but in a limited way—or, at times, arguably not at all. Volcker's assault on inflation catapulted the Fed's monetary powers to the very forefront of economic management and made it clear that

---

* Volcker reflected on the political repercussions in his memoir. "Years later, on a fishing trip with Carter, I asked him if he thought the Federal Reserve monetary policy had cost him the 1980s election," he wrote. "A wry smile spread over his face as he said, 'I think there were a few other factors as well.'"

the central bank could choose the economy's near-term path all on its own. The government began to treat inflation and macroeconomic guidance as largely the Fed's job, not a joint project of elected officials and central bank technocrats.

The shift was practical. The Nixon efforts had shown that the central bank was, at least in that instance, better equipped to contain inflation than the elected government. It was also politically expedient. Politicians did have tools that could help to achieve and sustain higher employment levels, but the Fed could make a convenient scapegoat if it fell short.

The central bank remained well shy of omnipotence. Congress still controlled taxes, social benefits, and education, all of which shaped who earned money in the first place and whether they could hold on to it in the longer run. Most economists believed that the Fed's policies could smooth over fluctuations in the business cycle but could not fundamentally alter how much growth the economy was capable of achieving. Even so, it had become clear that the Fed's authority to determine how much it paid to have and lend money—and whether that money retained its value over time or was inflated away—could shape the course of economic history.

Plus, the Fed's power extended beyond America's shores in an increasingly critical way: Monetary policy helped to determine the value of the dollar, which remained dominant in global commerce. While the Treasury, as America's finance ministry, was officially in charge of exchange rate policy in the new era of floating currency values, in practice Fed policy rates could draw investors toward or push them away from the dollar. "It is the central bank, in its conduct of monetary policy, that inevitably exerts an influence, sometimes a dominant influence, on exchange rates," Volcker would write.[29] Through interconnected currency markets, the Fed had become more than just a powerful domestic economic agenda-setter. It had become central banker to the world.

Such was the legacy, and the mighty influence, that Alan Greenspan inherited when he became chair of the Fed in 1987, a job he would hold until 2006. Greenspan, a New Yorker who had made his reputation in economic consulting, presided over a golden era for the

Fed. After two reputationally bruising decades, the central bank had gained an air of mystique.

Free market economics had come back into vogue during Ronald Reagan's presidency in America and Margaret Thatcher's time as prime minister in the United Kingdom, and Greenspan's Fed embraced the philosophy. Gone was the gospel of practiced Keynesianism, with its focus on labor. In was a desire to allow markets to decide what was fair. As in Eccles's frontier youth, many subscribed to the idea that unleashing businesses and wealth to pursue profits with minimal interference would lead to maximum prosperity. The tilt unquestionably helped the rich, but the poor were also benefiting from a strong labor market in the 1990s as trends including globalization, young demographics, and climbing productivity combined to create a strong economy. The class tensions that have often resulted in Fed criticisms throughout its history were, while present, relatively quiet. The Fed chair felt comfortable enough in his place in Washington that he even weighed in on congressional debates, at one point supporting the George H. W. Bush administration's tax cuts.[30] Through it all, Greenspan was celebrated as a sort of high priest; his oversight of his temple was rarely questioned by anyone with serious power.

Greenspan focused carefully on controlling inflation, but he did not pursue that goal blindly. He was a skilled analyst who spent much of his time collecting alternative data points that informed his decisions rather than relying solely on models. During the late 1990s, for instance, he resisted the idea of preemptive interest rate hikes because he suspected that a burst in productivity from new technologies, like computers and software, might allow for lower unemployment without a corresponding increase in inflation.[31] He was right. The shock that eventually brought that expansion to its knees was not runaway price gains but a stock market bubble centered on internet and technology companies.

Even as Greenspan's careful judgment shored up his status, and interest in the central bank's decisions abounded on Wall Street, the Fed continued to operate in the shadows. The Fed had in the 1980s shifted away from Volcker's practice of targeting a rate of growth in the nation's money supply and back to focusing on interest rates—specifically, the federal funds rate, which commercial banks charge one another to borrow reserves overnight.[32] But that transition went unannounced, and the Fed remained silent about when it actually made policy rate adjustments.[33] Wall Street typically figured out whether there had been a rate change by watching market movements as the New York Fed's markets desk bought and sold securities.

Early in Greenspan's tenure, secrecy was an aim itself: The Fed believed that being too clear about its plans would lock in market expectations and limit its room to maneuver. By the late 1990s, it was driven by decades of tradition, a desire to retain space for scholarly debate, and a low estimation of the public's ability to understand what the Fed was up to. Even as America's central bank became more professional, more dogmatic about pursuing its goals based on some unifying theory, and more influential than perhaps any global monetary authority that had come before, it had not become much more accountable—under Volcker, it had become even more of an enigma. There was little internal appetite to change the undemocratic state of affairs.

Greenspan himself explained in 2001 that the "undeniable, though regrettable, fact is that the most effective policymaking is done outside of the immediate glare of the press."[34]

Chapter 5

THE TEMPLE IS UNDER
NEW MANAGEMENT

The issue which must be resolved, indeed has to be, is
the balance between accountability, which is essential in a
democratic society, and effectiveness of monetary policy.
Anyone who thinks they have the unquestioned answer
to that balance has not dealt with this subject in any very
great detail.

—*Alan Greenspan, in congressional testimony, October 1993*

W E SHOULD NOT PRETEND the Federal Reserve, of all institutions in government, is infallible," Henry Gonzalez, a Texas
Democrat and chairman of the House Banking Committee,
declared at a hearing on October 13, 1993.[1] The seventy-seven-year-
old representative leaned forward in his high-backed chair, peering
down at the bespectacled Fed chairman hunched over the witness
table below him.[2]

Alan Greenspan, sporting a comb-over and a digital watch, wore
an expression that registered something between boredom and polite
exasperation as he waited to respond, resting his mouth on his hand
and arching his eyebrows slightly. While he was generally treated as
a sort of conqueror in Washington, cracks in that status did occasionally surface, and often at Gonzalez's hands. The representative's
tone was almost friendly as he took the Fed to task, but his message was anything but. Gonzalez had introduced several proposals
to make the Fed more accountable. He wanted to audit monetary

policy operations and expenditures. He had suggested that the Fed begin videotaping its meetings and releasing the tapes to the public at a lag.* Finally, he wanted the Fed to hire more diversely, taking issue with the fact that its top ranks were so heavily dominated by white men.

"I want to take the 'bankers and their friends' sign off the door to this exclusive club and open it up to all competent Americans," he told Greenspan on that autumn day.[3]

The Fed chair opposed the criticisms, and Mr. Gonzalez's ideas for addressing them, intensely. When it was his turn to speak, he warned that "if accountability is achieved by putting the conduct of monetary policy under the close influence of politicians subject to short-term election cycle pressures," poor economic management would result. Inflation would be the likely outcome. It was a logic that had become the golden principle in central banking: Volcker's war on inflation had proven that, sometimes, macroeconomic management required extremely difficult short-term decisions, ones that no rational politician would make. And while Greenspan agreed that diversity was critical, the Fed was making progress, he insisted. (That was overstated. Decades later, the central bank would remain a heavily white and male institution.)[4]

In the early 1990s, though, Greenspan had reason to hope that there was little danger of externally imposed reform. Congress remained the Fed's boss, but the central bank enjoyed support from the Clinton White House and from other lawmakers in the House and Senate. It was capable of resisting calls for change, a reality Gonzalez himself recognized.

"This is not radical reform, and there is no cause for the Federal Reserve to proceed as if barbarians are at the gate and it is the end of Western civilization," Gonzalez said at the hearing. He quoted another lawmaker, who had said that "if you talk about fixing the door jamb at the Fed, they accuse you of being a building demolition crew."

The Fed's insulation from congressional tinkering was not abso-

---

* "Could even be accessible to cable, and even with musical background," Gonzalez ad-libbed at the hearing.

lute, though, and the central bank was destined for some measure of modernization. Fed transcripts—word-by-word accounts of the behind-closed-door meetings where it set interest rates—had become an object of Gonzalez's attention. Back in 1975, the head of the banking committee was Fed critic Wright Patman, another Texas Democrat. He had asked Fed chair Arthur Burns for a detailed account of the Fed's proceedings, but Burns provided only an edited rundown of the meeting.[5] Somewhat surprisingly, given the pall cast over anything that even roughly resembled government secrecy in the wake of the Watergate political scandal, the issue faded. But in 1993, Democrats were again calling for detailed accounts of Fed deliberations, inspired in part by a high-profile series of what seemed to be leaks.[6] The Fed had a practice of publishing its decisions six weeks after they were made, but *The Wall Street Journal* was accurately reporting them within days.[7] The situation gave sophisticated market-watchers who subscribed to the paper an advantage over the public in understanding what the central bank was doing.

The push for better transparency gained a new life. Yet when lawmakers asked Greenspan whether the Fed kept detailed meeting transcripts or recordings, the chair obfuscated. He explained that while the events were taped, those tapes were turned into general notes and then taped over.

"There is no permanent electronic record, that is correct. We obviously have rough notes," he said at a hearing on October 19, 1993.[8]

The trouble was that transcripts of the Federal Open Market Committee meetings existed, and that reality quickly became public knowledge. In an analysis publication released a little more than a week after that Greenspan statement, Christopher Whalen wrote that "Gonzalez and his veteran staff hear increasingly from insider sources that, contrary to the party line from the Fed's bureaucratic mandarins in Washington, a nearly complete set of verbatim written transcripts does exist of the FOMC's secret deliberations."[9] It would later emerge that Greenspan and his fellow policy makers had held a special conference call in preparation for the October 19 hearing four days earlier, on October 15, specifically to discuss what to do about the transcripts.* In introducing the topic of the call, the chairman noted that "fairly recently [we became aware that] we have raw, unedited transcripts" going back to 1976. He himself had known about the documents for a year and other governors had known longer, though several reserve bank presidents—to their dismay—had been entirely unaware of them.[10]

Greenspan had his reasons for wanting to keep those meeting records private. When it came to the older rough transcripts, he feared that they might include inaccuracies, having been taken down by secretaries and not experts. He fretted that former committee members, now dead, would have no chance to correct the record. When it came to the new ones, he worried about the precedent of releasing them. Freewheeling debate would stop when subjected to the glare of public attention. Fed meetings might become an exercise in reading from prepared testimonies rather than an intellectual exchange.

The reality that Greenspan had been less than forthcoming with Congress about the existence of historical transcripts—less charitably, downright misleading—propelled the issue onto newspaper front pages. Gonzalez pushed for a release of the full set of historical notes. Knowing that Congress could push for the older transcripts, and concerned that the Justice Department's newly aggressive reading of government freedom of information laws meant that it would not back the Fed up if officials tried to maintain the veil of secrecy, the central bank agreed to release old meeting accounts on a five-year lag.

The Fed also began to publish details related to its policy decisions to eliminate the advantage sophisticated investors had over the public in understanding policy changes. Starting in February 1994, Greenspan's Fed began to announce changes to the federal funds rate, something that was initially set up to be a one-off. The Fed was about to increase interest rates for the first time in years, and it seemed valuable to explain what was happening.[11] "Chairman Greenspan decided

---

* On that call, Greenspan acknowledged that he was getting nervous about congressional action. "I was uncomfortable because I sensed a certain very peculiar view, and not only amongst those who have historically been concerned about the Federal Reserve as an elite, secretive temple of monetary manipulation but also from a number of people who have generally been very supportive of the Federal Reserve or were somewhat uncertain."

to announce this action immediately so as to avoid any misunderstanding of the Committee's purposes, given the fact that this is the first firming of reserve market conditions by the Committee since early 1989," the first statement noted. The practice stuck,[12] and by May, the full committee was releasing rate decisions. In 1999, the Fed started publishing statements after each of its meetings, regardless of whether it had changed interest rates.*

The Fed was lurching reluctantly into the public eye. Transparency, officials increasingly acknowledged, was necessary to effective and fair policy communication and to protection from political attack. One regional Fed president in 1994 suggested at a policy meeting that explaining policy decisions offered a "public relations benefit." Yet it came with side effects. It took away some of the Fed's mystery and, in reducing policy makers to the status of mere mortals, opened their actions to still more scrutiny. *The Wall Street Journal* compared the Fed's newfound candor to the scene in *The Wizard of Oz* in which the wizard is revealed to be nothing but a man behind a curtain "frantically yanking on the levers."[13] Despite that, the shift toward greater openness marched inexorably forward—and the pace accelerated sharply after Ben Bernanke took charge as the head of the central bank.

Greenspan stepped down in 2006, and his successor was a quiet but convicted Princeton University economics professor and Great Depression scholar. Bernanke had long felt that Greenspan was unnecessarily obscure when it came to monetary policy goals, and that the Fed would benefit from being clearer about its intentions. He had spent years quietly pushing for greater openness, both when he was a Fed governor between 2002 and 2005 and from outside the building as a leading economist and thinker on monetary policy. When he took over as chair, he had the chance to make his ambitions reality. But more pressing issues confronted him. He started his term just in time for an overextended housing market to face a price

---

* It's worth noting that one concern about creating a precedent of announcing changes to the Fed funds rate was that it would take away power from discount rate changes, which were at that time announced, disempowering the regional bank boards—made up heavily of bankers—who voted on those policies. That concern was founded. Discount rate changes became a nonevent.

correction. What could have been just one symptom in a run-of-the-mill cyclical economic downturn instead set fire to Wall Street's inner workings.

The problems started in the real world. Bank and nonbank lenders had spent years cheerfully extending unrealistic mortgages, requiring little or no money down and offering loans to borrowers with limited incomes who could not reasonably hope to pay them back. Borrowers, sensing their chance to participate in a version of the American dream—a big home, maybe one that would house a dog or a kid—took on more than they could handle, convinced that housing was an investment and that prices only ever rose. As homeowners began to miss payments and house prices slipped from astronomical levels, that risky behavior began to bite. Lenders took a closer look at their iffy mortgage portfolios and promptly stopped extending so much credit. With few homebuyers, prices slumped, and the popular practice of using houses as piggy banks to finance consumption stopped working. Economic activity slowed. Homeowners lost jobs, and the big loans they could never really afford went into forbearance and eventually default.

A catastrophic chain reaction rippled through the financial system. Banks and other financial institutions had spent years bundling up bad mortgages so that their individual risks would cancel each other out, slicing those bundles into shares, and sometimes selling them off as relatively safe investments—while often holding them on their own balance sheets. Rates were low, and people were eager to buy something that looked solid but offered a high return, as the mortgage-backed debt bundles did. When those securities proved highly risky and plummeted in value, banks and insurance companies lost massive sums, so much so that key institutions tiptoed on the brink of failure. The financial crisis would topple the investment bank Lehman Brothers, echo around the world, and turn the fledgling economic downturn into the worst recession America had faced since the 1930s.

Wall Street took the public blame for the debacle, but some of the fault lay in Washington, including at the Fed. Greenspan had championed a light-touch approach to financial oversight, and along with his fellow regulators tended to take the view that the free hand of the market would allocate resources far more efficiently than some stodgy bureaucrats in Washington might. Banks, the logic went, would want to protect their stock owners and would limit their risk-taking with that in mind. But in the years leading up to 2008, financial institutions gave out home loans like candy, paying little to no attention to borrower earning prospects or indebtedness, and failed to examine the risks hiding within mortgage securities.

The Fed suspected something was going wrong even as it was happening. At the Fed's monetary policy meeting in June 2005, San Francisco Fed vice president John Williams, board staffer Andreas Lehnert, and their colleagues gave an extensive presentation on whether the housing market was overheating.[14] Strikingly, the working assumption in the presentation was that housing might be 20 percent overvalued, meaning that bringing prices back in line would shave $3.6 trillion off American wealth—a drop equivalent to 30 percent of the nation's annual economic output. "Of course, if house prices continue to soar—and in the San Francisco Bay Area, at least, they show no signs of slowing—the magnitude of the housing overvaluation problem will rise as well," Williams noted.

The Fed could have curbed the excesses somewhat. At that 2005 meeting, the committee debated whether it made sense to set monetary policy with an eye on containing the bubble, something Australia was doing with some success at the time. It concluded that the costs would probably outweigh the benefits. Whether raising rates more to cool things down would've helped remains an open question, though many analysts think that the Fed should have.

What is less debatable is that the central bank also had regulatory tools that could have curbed some of the bad behavior, and it didn't use them. It could prevent deceptive mortgage lending under a 1994 law, for instance, but took little action to implement and use those regulations until 2008. At that point, it was far too late.[15] The Fed could have also instructed its army of bank supervisors to take a more thorough look at what the firms they oversaw were getting up to, but bank oversight was imperfectly coordinated and gave significant discretion to the Fed's regional branches. For many of them, flexing supervisory muscles was not a priority. During the committee's 2005 discussion, Tim Geithner, then the president of the Federal Reserve Bank of New York, asked if the Fed had a history of successfully using bank supervision to deflate housing bubbles (a question that may have been tongue in cheek; it didn't). Several of his colleagues responded by teasing him. Susan Bies, a Fed governor who was particularly focused on financial stability, responded earnestly and at length by describing what the Fed was doing to limit the headiest bank practices as fancy securitization became a regular feature of the mortgage market and lending standards dipped drastically. Shortly before she concluded her analysis, she acknowledged, "We haven't done a sterling job."

"Shall we break for coffee?" Greenspan responded to her monologue, transcripts of the gathering show.

The slow-motion financial implosion that the country experienced starting in 2007 looked, in many ways, like a return to 1929. As mortgage borrowers failed to keep up with unrealistic loans and the edifice of debt crumbled, though, Ben Bernanke's central bank did what the 1930s Fed had failed to do. It stepped in to save a flailing system.

Bernanke was quiet and occasionally gruff, with a shiny balding head and signature beard. He dressed a little bit sloppily, the sort of person who was much more concerned with what was happening within the confines of his head than with the fact that his $10-for-four beige socks from the Gap were not quite the thing in Washington's rarefied circles. Originally from Dillon, South Carolina, he had left the small town where his family owned a drugstore for a spot at Harvard. He went on to earn an economics doctorate at the Massachusetts Institute of Technology and became a tenured professor at Princeton before moving to Washington in 2002 to join the Fed as a governor. That role was followed by a top economics job in George W. Bush's White House, which ultimately appointed him Fed chair.

Bernanke's background in economic theory paradoxically made him perhaps uniquely qualified to helm the central bank at a time when the real world seemed to be coming apart. As a Great Depression scholar, he knew what had gone wrong the last time the Fed had stared down such a sweeping implosion. He used his knowledge of the Fed's history and powers to stretch the institution into new frontiers and, in doing so, helped to prevent a rerun.

After the 1930s, the Fed had gained broader powers to act as a "lender of last resort" in times of crisis, authorities that by 2007 allowed it to provide backup funding to a wide variety of financial market counterparties. Bernanke and his lawyers made unprecedented use of those emergency lending powers to keep markets functioning—rolling out commercial paper,* money market, and even credit card and auto loan backstops. It also used them to enable rescues for the investment bank Bear Stearns and the insurance giant American International Group. By contrast, the government allowed Lehman Brothers to fail, citing its own legal limitations—although some lawyers and academics have argued in the time since that it was politics and caution, not strict rules, that drove the decision.

The emergency programs came in addition to monetary policy moves aimed at cushioning the entire economy. The Fed slashed rates effectively to zero. In late 2008, as the housing and mortgage markets deteriorated and investors dumped mortgage-backed debt, the Fed stepped in to buy $600 billion of mortgage-backed securities and other government-backed housing debt. It was a move Bernanke approved unilaterally at first, relying on a Fed rule that allowed the chair to react to financial developments in between meetings. Some members of the Federal Open Market Committee were irritated that he had taken such a major action on his own, worried about the precedent that it could set. The committee ultimately approved the purchases before they began.

While bond buying was initially used to keep markets functioning, it would progress to become a clear monetary policy—one aimed at speeding up the economy. Buying massive quantities of government-backed debt helped to push down longer-term interest rates, stoking asset prices and encouraging borrowing and growth.[16]

If the Great Inflation era had secured the Fed's place as the central global economic policymaking body, Bernanke's experimentation in 2008 and after made it the world's financial market backstop. The Fed's rescue programs, rolled out month after month, prevented entire markets from crashing, helped to arrest the labor market's free fall, and may have prevented America and its trading partners from experiencing another Great Depression. They built on playbooks

---

* Commercial paper is short-term debt banks and other businesses use to fund operations.

that other central banks had written: The Bank of England's financial rescues in the mid-1800s set an example that central banks had followed since,[17] and the Bank of Japan had been carrying out massive asset purchases since 2001.[18] But because the United States had the deepest capital markets in the world—and because the Fed, as the steward of those markets and the powerful currency backing them, held such massive sway—the wide-ranging rescue sent a critical message to investors. If a market, asset class, or financial institution was important to the soundness of the overall system, the U.S. government would swoop in to fix things.

That implicit backstop, called moral hazard, became an angry buzzword on Capitol Hill after 2008 and 2009. Some lawmakers, economists, and interest groups were livid that Wall Street had received a huge helping hand, and others were mad that the government had interfered in the working of the market. Indictments of crisis policies won clicks on the internet and scored political points, but they often failed to address what should have happened instead. Without some sort of intervention, more financial institutions would almost certainly have failed, and the costs would have reverberated to harm businesses and households. Lehman's collapse stood as a cautionary case in point. Panic reigned after the investment bank crumbled, and credit provision ground to a halt. The disaster worsened the recession, which stretched from 2007 to 2009 and briefly pushed unemployment as high as 10 percent. The lingering labor market damage took years to heal, instilling a sense of uncertainty that would fundamentally shape an entire generation's approach to economic life.

Central banking in the early twenty-first century was, as had been the case during Volcker's reign in the 1980s, an exercise in picking least-worst options. Bernanke's choice was to prevent the economy from collapsing, and to deal with the consequences later.

Bernanke tried to communicate what was happening as broadly as possible during the crisis, hoping to both reassure Americans and secure public support for the Fed's many-front rescue mission. He appeared on CBS's *60 Minutes* in 2009 and in 2010. In April 2011, he held the first-ever Fed post-meeting press conference. An excited media corps noted that he wore a gray suit, sat behind a mahogany desk, and said basically nothing new.[19] Still, it was a watershed moment. A central bank that had long cloaked itself in secrecy was making it clear that the public should and could expect it to explain itself.* The crisis, and the Fed's leader, had fast-tracked what had been a slow and grinding push toward greater openness.

The Fed had also introduced a new practice, starting in 2008, in which it released anonymized economic forecasts from Fed presidents and governors each quarter.[20] The forecasts helped the public to better understand what officials were thinking as they set policy, and how they were weighting the trade-off between their two goals. For instance, the Summary of Economic Projections made it obvious that the Fed had no intention of letting inflation run much higher, even if that helped to return employment to its long-run potential level faster. Starting in 2012, the Fed also released a so-called dot plot, in which light blue dots are arrayed along an axis of interest rate estimates to show where individual, unnamed officials see borrowing costs headed over the coming two years and in the longer run. (Wall Street became so fixated on the so-called dots that Chair Jerome Powell would at one point compare the release to a painting by famed pointillist Georges Seurat. By focusing on the individual dots, he warned, people could miss the big picture. He projected a slide featuring *A Sunday Afternoon on the Island of La Grande Jatte* over his shoulder during a speech to bring the point home, looking momentarily more like a high school art history teacher than a Fed chair.)[21]

Bernanke and his colleagues had taken another step in 2012 that seemed incremental at the time, but which was both internally controversial and enormously consequential: The Federal Open Market Committee formally committed to trying to hit 2 percent inflation as a target. Doing so helped to underline to investors that the Fed was

---

* Bernanke's press conferences—and those held by his successor, Janet Yellen— occurred once every three months. Shortly after Jerome Powell took over the Fed chair job from Yellen in early 2018, he moved the gatherings from one per quarter to one after each of the central bank's nine annual meetings.

not trying to quash inflation absolutely but rather trying to maintain it at a relatively low level. It also annoyed practically everyone who noticed the move. On the left, Fed-watchers fretted that the central bank would focus on driving inflation down to the total exclusion of its full-employment goal. On the right, it ignited renewed hatred among a group of critics who felt that the Fed ought to aim for no inflation at all.

"Central bankers who are willing to tolerate a little more inflation usually wind up getting a whole lot more than they expected," Republican Paul Ryan chided Bernanke in 2012, quoting Paul Volcker.[22]

America's journey to a 2 percent inflation target is a story packed with strong personalities, and it's one that came with big consequences. It was under way in earnest while Greenspan was still the chair. He and Janet Yellen, then a member of the Fed's Board of Governors, sparred collegially over the Fed's price stability goal at the central bank's July 1996 meeting, for instance. While Congress had instructed the central bank to stabilize prices, it had become clear that nobody really knew what that meant in practice.

"Mr. Chairman, will you define 'price stability' for me?" Yellen had asked.[23]

"Price stability is that state in which expected changes in the general price level do not effectively alter business or household decisions," Greenspan replied.

"Could you please put a number on that?" Yellen parried, drawing laughter from her colleagues.

"I would say the number is zero, if inflation is properly measured," Greenspan answered.

"Improperly measured, I believe that heading toward 2 percent inflation would be a good idea, and that we should do so in a slow fashion, looking at what happens along the way," Yellen rejoined. She had earlier elaborated on why she thought some inflation might be desirable: Keeping prices locked in place would lead to "permanently less employment and higher unemployment," and she saw the Fed's job as striking the right trade-off, weighing steady prices against a strong labor market.

"I do not read the Federal Reserve Act as unambiguously telling us that we should choose price stability and forgo maximum employment," she had said.[*]

Officials did target an inflation rate in their private deliberations in the following years—generally 1.5 percent.[24] But as the twenty-first century started, years of weak price gains began to spur concerns that the economy was getting too close to a destabilizing deflation. The FOMC took a major step by publicly signaling in 2003 that a fall in inflation would be "unwelcome," the first time in many decades that it had suggested out loud that slower price gains could be anything but good.[25]

Even as the committee came to embrace the idea that some inflation was desirable, Greenspan was dead set against putting a number on what level of price gains was, in fact, welcome. Bernanke privately urged Greenspan to make the target explicit, convinced that doing so would help to guide public expectations. By the time he took over, he knew he wanted to adopt a formal target, and the committee discussed doing so in detail in 2009. By that point, consensus had formed around targeting 2 percent inflation using an index produced by the Commerce Department. The goal mirrored the official inflation target other central banks around the world had spent decades steadily adopting, starting with New Zealand in 1989. While the unfolding financial crisis made an inflation declaration temporarily unattractive, after 2009 it is clear from committee transcripts and economic projections that officials were targeting something like a 2 percent rate of change. In 2012, policy makers made it happen on paper. The new approach meant that if inflation either sagged or soared, it would be obvious just how badly the Fed was missing its goal.

Still, Bernanke believed communicating the target more clearly could help the Fed to achieve its targets more effectively. His push toward transparency in general was also politically smart at a moment when the Fed remained an object of popular ire, beset by an animos-

---

[*] Yellen went on to become a celebrated proponent of low rates and full employment, but she meant it in the 1990s when she said she looked at the target as a balancing game. She and a fellow Board member went to Greenspan's office later in 1996 and tried, unsuccessfully, to convince him to raise interest rates to head off inflation. He reportedly listened carefully, then ignored the advice.

ity that had brimmed to the point of overflowing five years after the start of the financial crisis.

Following the 2008 meltdown, Wall Street executives had walked away from a disaster of their own making with big bonuses and few visible repercussions, even as ordinary Americans lost jobs by the millions. The contention that the Fed had acted to protect the broader public rang hollow from Fox News to the Far Left. Even the Fed's policies to coax the economy back to health seemed to be aimed at helping big financial players at the expense of the little guy. Its policy of bond buying, for instance, lowered the payback on many types of debt and pushed investors into riskier assets, like stocks—sending the S&P 500 soaring and visibly helping the already-wealthy owners of capital. Only about half of Americans held any meaningful amount of wealth in stock, either directly or through retirement portfolios. Even among those who did hold stocks, the very wealthy owned the lion's share.[26] The Fed's purchases probably also benefited the working classes, but in far less salient ways: Bond buying may have averted a massive market meltdown that could have deepened and worsened the recession, and super-low rates probably prompted a stronger economic rebound. Economists themselves could not agree on the size of those benefits.

By 2011, activists who pitted themselves against the "1 percent" criticized the central bank's role in saving fat-cat bank executives. It had not helped the Fed's image that Bernanke himself sounded unsympathetic or dismissive of criticism at times. He said at a news conference that year that the Occupy Wall Street movement's criticisms were based on a misconception of what the Fed had done, and while "a very simplistic interpretation" of the bank bailouts was that the Fed wanted to preserve banker salaries, "that is obviously not the case."[27] Nor did it help that the Fed's programs to rescue American International Group and Bear Stearns had involved after-the-fact reporting, with transactions released to the public only much later, and closed-door decision-making.

Lawmakers made political hay out of bashing the Fed. Some of that might have been purely opportunistic. The Fed is a punching bag that cannot hit back, because it avoids getting drawn into the political fray. Bernanke had also talked to some members of Congress in jargon that they could not understand, and several remained salty about his tone even years later. People in power didn't like the Fed, and at least some especially didn't like Bernanke's version of it.

The idea that the Fed needed to be "audited" went from crackpot suggestion to rallying cry, with Representative Ron Paul and his son, Senator Rand Paul of Kentucky, repeatedly introducing bills that would review central bank monetary policy decisions. Bernie Sanders, the Vermont Independent, championed the movement on the political left. The Fed's financial statements were already audited, but the movement to subject its monetary policy decisions and other internal deliberations to review captured the deep ill will. In a rare moment of bipartisan cooperation, one version of the bill passed the House in 2014 with votes from both parties—333 lawmakers voted for it, 106 of them Democrats. It was doomed from the start, since there was no signal that President Obama would sign such legislation, but the momentum said something about the prevailing attitude.[28]

When Bernanke stepped down in early 2014, he was celebrated as a hero in some quarters, but his public fêting came with caveats. "History will credit the Fed chairman with preventing a second Depression," Bloomberg's opinion writers declared.[29] "There is no doubt Mr. Bernanke has been one of the most consequential Fed Chairmen in history, but his legacy is still far from clear and is at best more mixed than the effusive praise suggests," *The Wall Street Journal*'s opinion pages cautioned in January 2014, days before he stepped down.[30] CNBC would later run an article titled "Bernanke's Legacy: A Fed That Did Too Much?"[31]

Bernanke's Fed had explored its vast powers and experimented with clearer communication for the sake of better policy outcomes and improved public understanding. It was a legacy of activism. His successor, Janet Yellen, would usher in what seemed on the surface like an era of continuity—while laying the groundwork for an even bigger experiment.

Janet Yellen was already a top labor economist with decades of public policy experience by the time Barack Obama nominated her to lead the Fed. Born in Bay Ridge, Brooklyn, to an elementary school teacher and a family doctor, she had been a childhood overachiever. She did a Q and A with herself for the student paper during her senior year at her public high school because it was a tradition for the publication's editor in chief to interview the valedictorian, and she was both. ("Mineralogy has always been a major interest," Janet told Janet.) When she wasn't collecting rocks, she was studying probability, matrix algebra, and finite dimensional vector spaces and enjoying off-Broadway theater.[32] She attended Brown University's Pembroke College for her undergraduate degree, and it was there that she fell in love with the practical public policy implications in economics. She went on to a doctorate at Yale, then worked at Harvard before taking a role at the Federal Reserve Board in Washington. At a Fed lunch in 1977, she met her future husband, the economist George Akerlof. They bonded over their shared devotion to Keynesian economics— the idea that the government has an active role to play in resolving market breakdowns—and married less than a year later. They would go on to collaborate extensively, especially while they both worked at the University of California, Berkeley. While Akerlof was an academic who would go on to win a Nobel Prize for his work on market imperfections, Yellen would gravitate toward more policy-focused roles, first serving as a governor at the Fed Board, then at Clinton's Council of Economic Advisers, then as president of the Federal Reserve Bank of San Francisco. She became vice-chair of the Fed in the wake of the financial crisis and, in 2014, the central bank's first-ever female chair.

Yellen knew when she took on the leadership role that it would be her job to return policy to more "normal" settings after years of cheap money. She brought her lifelong focus on employment to the task. Yellen urged her fellow officials to look at a variety of job market indicators—not just the headline unemployment rate—as they tried to figure out whether the labor market had fully healed from the shock of the Great Recession. With an eye on how gradually wages were increasing even as the jobless rate fell, Yellen and her colleagues tiptoed toward lifting rates. The Fed made just one quarter-point increase in 2015, one in 2016, and three in 2017, allowing the expansion to chug along and laying the groundwork for a strong labor market that would drive the unemployment rate to its lowest level in half a century.

Yellen's time as chair marked a pendulum swing away from the inflation-containing focus of the Volcker era and much of the Greenspan era and toward a more balanced approach in which job market strength weighed heavily in policy discussions. Fed officials increasingly sounded like their labor-focused predecessors in the 1950s and '60s, though they did not treat the pursuit of full employment with the same single-minded fervor.

"Unemployment rates for young African American and Hispanic men without a college degree remain especially high, and one important benefit from further improvement in the labor market would be increased job opportunities for these men and other groups that currently still experience high unemployment," Yellen said at a particularly revelatory speech in Philadelphia in 2016.[33] Still, the Fed chair didn't return to the Keynesian ideal of the 1960s, which saw the central bank as an important player in the push to improve opportunities for marginalized workers. She hinted at but did not fully embrace running the economy hot—allowing for higher inflation in a bid to pull more sidelined workers into the economy.

"To be sure, many of the factors that contribute to the labor market outcomes of minority groups are not amenable to monetary policy, and measures beyond the scope of monetary policy should be considered to alleviate the economic challenges that these and other Americans face," she caveated that day in Philadelphia.

Even so, the Fed's cautious patience during the Yellen years laid the groundwork for the longest economic expansion on record, one in which unemployment dipped to its lowest in half a century. The share of people working or looking for work recovered steadily, despite widespread predictions that it never would. Marginalized groups of people—those with limited education or long gaps in their work history, people with felony records—benefited the most, finally getting a shot at decent work. The period showed what the Fed could and could not achieve. On one hand, its long period of low rates helped the economy to expand gradually and for a long time. On the other, interest rates had fallen around the globe as households and businesses displayed relatively limited demand for money, and even rock-bottom borrowing costs were not enough to drastically speed up business conditions. As the economy spent year after year of expansion at more of a brisk walk than an all-out sprint, companies found it hard to raise prices without losing customers. Inflation hovered at low levels, and investors began to see the Fed's by then well-established 2 percent goal as a ceiling that they would never breach.

The Fed had been ambitious, but it had not been able to stave off the stagnation sweeping many advanced economies. By raising interest rates even slowly, many economists would argue by 2019, it locked in low inflation. It had tamped down household demand, and it had signaled to markets that it would always take the cautious route. What came to be seen as the mistake of the Yellen years—excessive caution—would echo through monetary policy decision-making in fateful ways in the years to come.

Yellen had her reasons for tiptoeing. For one thing, monetary policy truly was not a panacea—it could not improve childhood education, equalize health outcomes, right an unbalanced criminal justice system, or solve the myriad other problems holding people back in American society. Plus, most economists at the time, Yellen included, believed that lower unemployment would eventually spur price increases. Keeping price pressures under control with preemptive policy action could allow for years of healthy expansion rather than a repeat of the Volcker experience in which the committee had to crush the economy to slow price increases.

While there was no sign that it influenced policy, Yellen was regularly taken to task by lawmakers during her Capitol Hill testimonies, typically for keeping interest rates too low. Key Republicans clamored for more hikes, faster, and continued to blast the Fed for its crisis-era policies. With Republicans in control of the House and Senate starting in 2015 and animosity toward the central bank still alive and well among Democrats, the possibility of a successful movement to "audit the Fed" was an ever-present threat.[34]

Subjecting the Fed to greater oversight "would be an important step towards making the Federal Reserve a more democratic institution that is responsive to the needs of ordinary Americans rather than the billionaires on Wall Street," Senator Sanders wrote in a 2016 news release.[35]

The Fed remained resolute in fighting such a measure. "Audit the Fed is a bill that would politicize monetary policy, would bring short-term political pressures to bear on the Fed," Yellen said of the proposal. "Beyond a shadow of a doubt, independent central banks perform better."[36]

—

Even as Fed officials tried to protect their freedom to set economic policy without political interference in the wake of the 2008 melt-down, they were willing to examine and try to fix what had gone wrong with regulation. It was obvious that everyone—Congress, financial regulators, and central bankers themselves—had failed to curb reckless risk-taking in the years leading up to the crisis. Law-makers' answer to that was the Dodd–Frank Wall Street Reform and Consumer Protection Act, a sweeping overhaul of financial regula-tion that created the new Consumer Financial Protection Bureau and a Financial Stability Oversight Council, a consortium of regula-tors headed by the Treasury Department that was meant to identify emerging financial risks. The Fed had gained new powers to regu-late systemically important financial institutions, the "too big to fail" giants that had brought the system to its knees and required gov-ernment bailouts. While it's a lesser-known fact, the Fed itself made important changes behind the scenes, tearing discretion over bank supervision away from its regional branches and consolidating it in Washington. Bank overseers were newly rotated around institutions, instead of embedded for longer stretches. It was an attempt to pre-vent Fed supervisors from becoming excessively cozy with the banks they oversaw.

Still, stark limitations plagued the new regulatory regime. Banks had been made safer—for small ones, the new regulations were onerous—while hedge funds and nonbank lenders remained outside the central bank's purview, with oversight split among other regula-tors who did not have similarly clear mandates for protecting system-wide financial stability. Nonbank regulation remained flawed. In one of the clearest examples of that, Securities and Exchange Commis-sion money market fund reforms did not go far enough to prevent mass withdrawals at the first sign of major trouble thanks largely to a major industry lobbying push. In fact, onlookers warned as the regu-lations were passing that they probably made the funds even more dangerous.[37]

And by the time Powell succeeded Yellen in 2018, the newly built and incomplete regulatory infrastructure—meant to erect a safety barrier around Wall Street so that its future blowups wouldn't hit innocent bystanders—was poised for a quiet dismantling at the hands of President Donald J. Trump's appointees.

The chipping away had started at other regulators, and in particular the Treasury that Secretary Steven Mnuchin newly presided over. In 2018 and 2019, though, a deregulatory bent had also begun to take hold within the central bank itself. The tiny, expertly precise series of changes were spearheaded by Randal K. Quarles, a modern-day relative by marriage of Marriner Eccles who had served as Powell's assistant at Treasury in the 1990s and who remained his good friend.* Quarles had been confirmed as the Fed's first-ever official vice-chair for supervision in October 2017.

The changes taking place across the government in the early Trump era weren't "exposing the soft underbelly" of the banking system, as Quarles liked to say. Some were lucrative for individual firms, but most stopped short of the more meaningful rollbacks the industry was clamoring for. Nevertheless, the tweaks almost uniformly cut in one direction, and that was toward lighter oversight. It amounted to a statement: The post-2008 reforms had gone far enough to insulate the system from disaster, and in some cases too far.

"The key question will be ensuring that, as we continue to refine the system over time, we do so while maintaining the robust resilience of the system to shocks," Quarles, who always spoke with a genteel enunciation, told lawmakers at his nomination hearing.[38]

His contention that it was resilient in the first place was destined for a once-in-a-century test.

---

* We'll meet Quarles in greater depth in the next chapter.

Chapter 6

A POLARIZED FED

To say a central banker is ideological is to say that a
central banker is human.

—*Peter Conti-Brown,* The Power and
Independence of the Federal Reserve

A MERCHANT FROM A BUSTLING seafood market in Wuhan,
China, lay in a hospital bed suffering through an unidentified
virus vaguely resembling bronchitis in mid-December 2019. She
was one of several workers from the Hua'nan market in emergency
wards across the city, and she showed symptoms that some three
dozen other patients would exhibit in the coming days.[1]

Half a world away in Washington, just a handful of wrap-up
meetings—briefings with staff and a lunch with the White House's
National Economic Council director, Larry Kudlow—stood between
Fed chair Jerome Powell and winter vacation. It was about a month
after Powell's trip to East Hartford and Providence, and he was looking forward to the upcoming break. While there had been definite
bright spots, his first twenty-two months as Fed chair had often been
a wild and challenging ride.

Powell's tenure had started off smoothly enough. After Powell had
taken office the prior year, President Donald Trump had ignored the
Fed for a few months. But by mid-2018, as the Fed raised interest
rates slowly but steadily to guard against the possibility of higher
inflation, Trump had broken the decades-old norm in which sitting
presidents avoid critiquing central bank policy out of deference to

Fed independence. Once he was commenting, it was not long before he began to do so melodramatically.

The president had started small, saying in July 2018 that he was "not thrilled" with Fed policy. The venom intensified quickly, and by October he told Fox News that the central bank was "going loco" as it raised rates. In November, he told *The Washington Post* that he knew the central bank was erring in its approach, declaring, "I have a gut and my gut tells me more sometimes than anybody else's brain can ever tell me."[2]

Things had especially escalated in December 2018. The Federal Open Market Committee had closed out Powell's first year as chair with a fourth and final rate increase. The move came even as inflation hovered below the central bank's goal and as Trump waged trade wars that had put markets on edge. The committee thought the outlook for the economy was still decent despite the uncertainties, and many officials wanted to get policy back to what they considered to be a "neutral" policy setting, one where the Fed's interest rate was neither helping nor hurting the economy. Stocks declined a little bit after the Fed announced its rate increase and released a set of economic projections showing that officials expected to make two more moves in 2019.

Then problems had started in earnest during Powell's post-meeting news conference. Asked about the central bank's balance sheet, Powell suggested that the Fed would continue to shrink its bond holdings— its other policy to remove monetary help—according to a preset plan, taking a little bit of pep out of markets each month. The comment suggested to investors that the Fed was paying insufficient attention to what they saw as a worrying backdrop. Stock indexes plummeted.

"I don't think it is like an airplane that can really fly on autopilot, and we can all feel comfortable," DoubleLine Capital's deputy chief investment officer told CNBC that afternoon, calling the comment "scary."[3]

The president, who often measured his administration's success in stock charts, was livid. Rumors swiftly crossed the newswires that Trump was furious with Powell and was contemplating trying to fire him. Journalists scrambled to figure out whether ousting the Fed chair would even be legal, ultimately landing on the conclusion that the answer was almost certainly no. Still, the issue was put to rest only after Mick Mulvaney, the acting White House chief of staff, appeared on ABC's *This Week* two days before Christmas and said that Trump had "put out a tweet last night specifically saying that he now realizes he does not have the ability" to fire Powell. Mulvaney was mistaken: The tweet in question had come from the Treasury secretary, Steven Mnuchin. Nevertheless, the moment seemed to clarify both that removing Powell had been a live discussion and that it had hit a wall.[4]

Even if Powell's job was secure, the economic situation and investor confidence in the Fed had both ended that year in bad shape. The chair had spent his 2018 family Christmas gathering in South Florida scribbling on a notepad, trying to find the perfect words to convince onlookers that the Fed wouldn't imperil the expansion. He was scheduled to speak on a panel alongside former Fed chairs Janet Yellen and Ben Bernanke at an annual conference for academic economists just over a week later. It would give him a chance to clear the air, but he needed to nail the tone.[5]

Neil Irwin, a veteran Fed journalist and the moderator, opened the conference by noting that markets had been volatile and asking Powell for his economic outlook.

"Thanks very much, Neil," the famously unscripted and chatty Fed chair said, lifting from his lap a sheaf of white papers with purple tabs hanging from the side. He proceeded to read from it directly, describing the latest economic data and how they informed his thinking and declaring that "there is no preset path for policy." The Fed was "always prepared to shift the stance of policy, and to shift it significantly, if necessary." Once he finished delivering his short and reassuring speech, he took off his black-framed glasses, audibly took a deep breath, and rolled up his notes.

Markets rose in relief almost instantly. Powell was paying attention to them and to the economy, they had determined, and he was not going to blindly pull back policy support until it caused a recession.

Crisis had been averted with that early 2019 speech, but the challenges that year had remained formidable. Trump was still carrying out a trade war with China, even though many of his fellow Republicans opposed the idea, and stock prices shuddered with every new tariff announcement. As the S&P 500 sank, Trump grew more incensed with the Fed, blaming monetary policy rather than his own actions for unsettling investors and imperiling growth. He began tweeting about the central bank daily, lobbing a series of creative insults at Powell personally.

At one point, the president likened Powell to "a golfer who can't putt, has no touch." (Powell was, in fact, an avid golfer, and in private conversation, his friends and acquaintances vouched that he could certainly putt.) At another juncture, he called Powell and his colleagues a collection of "boneheads." In a tweet posted while Powell was delivering his most important speech of the year that August, Trump asked whether Chinese president Xi Jinping or Powell was the bigger "enemy."

Nearly every president in history would have preferred to have low interest rates, which encourage lending and spending and bolster growth. No leader in United States history had declared that desire so flamboyantly.

Powell and his colleagues at the Fed ignored the president in public with a military discipline, though officials internally chafed at the running commentary. (When Trump published the "enemy" tweet and Fed communications lead Michelle Smith emailed it to Richard Clarida, the vice-chair, he had replied with an "Ugh, ugh.")[6]

The other problems confronting the Fed that year were less ignorable than presidential blustering. The stock market's gyrations were a symptom of a pullback taking hold across the broader economy. Manufacturing was slowing sharply and business confidence, which had been buoyant after Trump cut corporate taxes, had begun to decline. In February, the economy added just 24,000 jobs, not the 150,000-plus that had become the norm. The slowdown was due in large part to the upheaval happening in global trade, but it also tied back at least a little to the cumulative effect of the Fed's interest rate increases over the prior four years. A recession seemed possible.

The 2019 economy had called for a pivot, one that Powell had needed to spearhead.

Powell had typically been collaborative, not dictatorial, as a leader. When he was appointed as chair, people had regularly questioned whether he would be able to function well in the high-power role as a lawyer with a background in private equity—not a PhD economist. The Fed's staff economists, once downplayed by William McChesney Martin, but later embraced and carefully consulted by Ben Bernanke and Janet Yellen alike, had come to heavily influence monetary policymaking by the time Powell took over the institution.

Powell had largely made his lack of a doctorate a nonissue. He had always made a point of seeking out and then earnestly listening to the staff economic experts, befriending them and winning their respect in the process of mastering the content. On the committee, he had shored up his power by being a levelheaded leader. He did not dominate discussions or flex his power by trying to push through policies, at least in those early years of his tenure.

But conditions were changing so rapidly as Trump tried to remake global capitalism, threatening an otherwise stable expansion, that a prompt response seemed necessary. Trained economists were hesitant to declare the trade war a major threat before they could see the damage spelled out in data. Powell, lacking their devotion to models, was nimbler. He hinted during a June speech in Chicago that the central bank might cut interest rates, and he worked the phones to make sure that his colleagues would vote for the change. Officials slashed borrowing costs first in July, then again in September and October.

The trio of mid–business cycle adjustments were a risky move. It was a major reorientation after four years of gradual rate hikes, especially for a slow-moving and contemplative institution. Business television pundits and Wall Street financiers promptly speculated that the Fed had bowed to Trump's pressure campaign, questioning whether cracks were emerging in its prized independence from political interference. That autonomy, won during Marriner Eccles's time as governor in the 1950s and reinforced during Paul Volcker's chairmanship in the 1980s, was treated as nearly sacred by 2019.

Powell realized early on that the politics of the moment would color the public's perception of the reorientation. But it would be worse to delay warranted rate cuts. Independence from politics meant doing what policy makers viewed as the right thing, no matter what the White House was saying. After the Fed announced its first quarter-percentage-point rate decrease in July 2019, CNN's Donna Borak used her news conference question to ask Powell to address the speculation that he had been influenced by the president.

"We never take into account political considerations," he said. "We also don't conduct monetary policy in order to prove our independence. We conduct monetary policy in order to move as close as possible to our statutory goals, and that's what we're always going to do."

"At the end, we'll—you know, we'll live with the results," he said.

The result was a continued attack. Trump remained unsatisfied and kept up his criticism, framing it in terms of global competition. The United States still had higher borrowing costs than Europe, where the economy was growing much more slowly and the European Central Bank had set its policy rate below zero in a bid to discourage saving.

"What the Market wanted to hear from Jay Powell and the Federal Reserve was that this was the beginning of a lengthy and aggressive rate-cutting cycle which would keep pace with China, the European Union and other countries around the world," Trump had tweeted just after the first rate cut announcement. "As usual, Powell let us down."[*]

The presidential onslaught continued throughout the year, but by the end of 2019, the chair was proud of the course he and his colleagues charted, no matter what kind of feedback it was earning from the White House. They had communicated responsiveness to deteriorating economic conditions with their trio of rate cuts. They had also emphasized their independence from the presidential administration by making it clear that they would stop reducing borrowing costs following the three adjustments, even as the president called for more action, and faster. Powell had capped an active year with a satisfied message at his December press conference. Policy makers were in no hurry to change rates in either direction. They had done enough. Trade tensions seemed to be waning, the job market was at its strongest in half a century, and the outlook for 2020 seemed bright.

"Of course, if developments emerge that cause a material reassessment of our outlook, we would respond accordingly," Powell had said, as he always did.

In the wake of the meeting, as he started the chilly Washington morning with his usual predawn scan of the major newspapers—the *Financial Times, The Washington Post, The Wall Street Journal,* and *The New York Times*—Powell had a happy holiday season stretching out before him.

---

[*] Monetary policy from the ECB applies to the euro area, also called the eurozone, which is a subset of the European Union rather than the whole thing.

He and his wife would be celebrating more than Christmas and New Year's in Florida that holiday season. Sam, the oldest of their three children, would be married in Palm Beach on January 4, an optimistic start to what promised to be a better year.

Some eight thousand miles away, though, a microscopic threat had firmly taken hold by that middle week of December 2019. Within months, it would upend the bright economic outlook Powell and his colleagues had so painstakingly secured.

Powell planned to use the relative calm that 2020 promised to finish his major project at the central bank: the Fed's review of its monetary policy. The institution he had inherited was facing down a slow-burn threat that was stealthily reshaping the global economy, but which had crept up so gradually that its magnitude had only recently become accepted as obvious. Interest rates had dropped.

That statement often baffled people. The Fed had the power to set interest rates, after all. But central bankers didn't have the luxury of setting policy in a vacuum: What interest rate would speed up the economy or slow it down depended on other economic trends and changed over time.

The magic number under which rates sped up the economy, and over which they slowed it down, was often referred to as the "neutral" or "natural" rate. If growth was running below what the economy was capable of based on labor force and productivity trends, keeping rates below neutral could help to heat it up and fend off deflation. If it was above its potential, higher rates could cool it down and fend off inflation. While the concept sounded academic and amorphous, it actually made sense as a simple description of what had happened in practice in the wake of the 2008 meltdown: Central bankers around the world had discovered that they could not lift rates very much at all without tanking economic growth.

Unfortunately, it was very difficult to guess in real time how much rates could increase before they would begin crimping the economy. Economists tried to estimate the neutral rate with models, and those suggested that it might be steadily falling. By early 2020, the most popular model suggested that it was around 2.5 percent, assuming prices were climbing at about 2 percent a year. Rates had been able to rise to 5.5 percent without choking off growth as recently as 2000.

The drift lower in neutral rates had happened across advanced economies. Big forces seemed to be driving the decline, including demographics and inequality. As the population in many nations aged, it pushed up demand for retirement savings. Likewise, rich people tended to save more of each dollar they earned. More saving lowered demand for cash, which in turn lowered interest rates.

As the natural rate sank, it was robbing central banks of ammunition to cut the cost of borrowing during downturns. Because central banks could not do much to stoke spending and heat up business conditions, countries could get stuck in yearslong recessions in which lackluster consumer demand and poor labor market conditions fed on one another. By 2020, that trap seemed very real: The scenario had played out in Japan starting in the 1990s, then in Europe following 2008. Even the United States was experiencing unimpressive growth by historical standards, though its rebound from the 2008 downturn had been stronger and its economy could still handle slightly higher interest rates than other advanced economies.

In fact, economists within the Fed thought rates might be stuck at rock bottom around a third of the time in the United States, risking chronically slower recoveries from recessions.[7] By Powell's tenure, that grim conclusion was repeated often, a scene-setting statement for a bleak economic future.

By the time Powell was chair, the predicament seemed to be worsening. Wage gains had slowed after years of weak demand in which workers were plentiful and competing for a limited supply of jobs. Companies felt that they did not have the power to charge more, in part because their poorly paid and cash-strapped consumers would simply stop buying if they did. Interest rates incorporated price increases, so tepid inflation made for even less room to cut them in times of trouble. The combination of weak price increases and declining interest rates threatened to create a snowball effect in which economic stagnation became worse with time.

The Fed had witnessed a sobering preview of what running short on ammunition could mean in the wake of the 2007–2009 downturn. Central bankers had been unable to cut rates low enough to keep up with the pace of contraction during that financial crisis, having slashed them to near zero for the first time in U.S. history in late 2008. Congress could have swooped in to do what the Fed could not, jump-starting the economy with big spending programs, but fears about government indebtedness and partisan strife prevented that from happening. The central bank was the only game in town.*

Fed officials had tried other policies to goose demand, rolling out their three rounds of large-scale buying of Treasury bonds and mortgage-backed securities to push money into riskier assets and provide a jolt to the economy.† Unfortunately, it was hard to judge how effective those policies were at stoking growth because it was impossible to know how the economy would have fared in their absence. Because they encouraged financial gambling by design and pushed up asset prices, it was also clear that they came with less-than-ideal side effects, including the possibility of bubbles and higher wealth inequality.‡ Policy makers struggled to gauge whether the benefits of the approach, called quantitative easing, or QE, justified the costs.

"I think we are actually at a point of encouraging risk-taking, and that should give us pause," Powell himself had said during a Federal Open Market Committee meeting in 2012, not long after he had joined as governor. "Investors really do understand now that we will be there to prevent serious losses. It is not that it is easy for them to make money but that they have every incentive to take more risk, and they are doing so."

He added, "Our models will always tell us that we are helping the economy, and I will probably always feel that those benefits are overestimated."[8]

The best argument for quantitative easing often seemed to be that

---

* Paul Volcker originally applied the phrase to the Fed. It was further popularized when Mohamed El-Erian, the Pacific Investment Management Company adviser, wrote a *New York Times* bestseller about the Fed in 2016 called *The Only Game in Town.*

† These programs were enacted under Ben Bernanke and are the same ones discussed in the previous chapter.

‡ We'll go over the Fed's impact on and interactions with income inequality (the differences in how much people earn each year) and wealth inequality (differences in their net worth) at much greater length in Chapter 11. It is also worth noting that, in 2015 remarks, Powell observed that his fears about QE had not materialized and the programs did have benefits.

it was better than doing nothing. Keeping money coursing through markets may have helped risky asset owners and came with a chance of inflating bubbles, but it also kept financing cheap for companies and encouraged them to keep hiring, and it meant mortgages continued flowing to potential buyers. Providing the boost seemed superior to just allowing everyone to languish. Congressional stimulus spending would have been better, some economists at the time argued and many later agreed. But lawmakers were struggling to reach standard agreements to keep the government funded, let alone pass meaningful legislation.

Even the unconventional monetary policy was not potent enough to stimulate the economy back to full health quickly. More than a decade after the recession ended in 2009, the unemployment rate was still coming down and people were slowly returning to the job market. The years would-be workers had spent on the sidelines came at an enormous human cost, leaving families poorer and costing individuals the fulfillment a job can bring. Price gains and inflation slid lower as demand came up short. The "Japanification" that economists had come to fear—the idea that growth could become mired at disappointing levels for years, as it had in the Asian nation—seemed to be on the verge of playing out in the United States.

When he took the helm of the Fed in 2018, Powell became the first chair to preside over the institution at a time when the threat of tepid growth and inflation across advanced economies was widely accepted as reality. When Yellen was in charge, people were only beginning to appreciate the extent of the issue. Larry Summers, the prominent Harvard economist and former Clinton administration Treasury secretary, had first dusted off the old concept of "secular stagnation" during a 2013 speech at the International Monetary Fund. The phrase had been coined in 1938 to describe a market-based economy doomed to little or no growth. Summers suggested, not exactly full-throatedly, that the idea might explain what was happening in Japan and "may not be without relevance to America's experience today."[9]

Mainstream economists generally nodded along with the analysis, though some differed on the details. Yet even as the thesis began to take hold, it took time to follow the line of thinking to its logical conclusion: Growth and interest rates were probably not going to snap back to historically normal levels anytime soon.

John Williams, then the president of the Federal Reserve Bank of San Francisco, argued that interest rates were unlikely to move higher anytime soon in a 2017 paper co-authored with Board economist Thomas Laubach and Kathryn Holston, a prodigy of a research assistant.[10] Other Fed officials were slower to adopt the outlook. Fed policy makers released long-run estimates of interest rates each quarter, and while they had nudged lower over the years, it took until mid-2019 for them to roughly match Williams's humdrum interest rate projection.

Given how much the economic world had changed, Powell and his colleagues believed that central bankers needed a plan. If officials could keep inflation from slipping below 2 percent on a permanent basis, they might be able to prevent the downward spiral that was playing out in Japan and Europe from taking hold. They also believed it was worth talking out what backup policy responses the Fed would use to make up for their limited room to cut rates.

Perhaps most salient for the typical American, it seemed clear that against a backdrop of low rates and low inflation, the trade-off between unemployment and price increases—the one that the Fed was famously believed to have pushed too far in the 1960s and '70s, feeding the Great Inflation—had broken down. Very low joblessness was no longer spurring faster price increases, and the Fed needed to reconsider how it was balancing those goals. Doing so could help to avoid a repeat of the 2015–2018 rate-increases cycle, when officials had raised interest rates slowly but substantially because the job market looked strong, only to realize later that at least some of that tightening might have been unnecessary. The Fed's formal review was meant to make sure that the future approach to policy was well suited to a new era.

Of course, policy impotence was not the only problem the age of near-zero rates posed. Low rates on safe investments, like government bonds, presented a dilemma for anyone who had been counting a certain level of payback into their financial planning—like soon-to-be or recent retirees. Investors had become more aggressive with their cash management, putting their savings at risk as they tried to earn a little bit of interest. Corporate borrowing had also exploded, because piling on debt was cheap to do. The era was a devil's playground for financial vulnerability.

Critics occasionally blamed the Fed's rate setting for these vulnerabilities, often ignoring that interest rates are partially a function of real-world conditions and are not purely a policy choice. Such arguments rarely grappled with the reality that rates were very low around much of the world, or that the economy had faltered when the Fed raised rates even moderately.

Still, the potential for financial danger made it ironic that, just as Powell's Fed busied itself with a review focused on how to deal with a future of rock-bottom borrowing costs, it and the broader government were also embarking on a quest to "tailor" and "right-size" regulation—buzzwords that critics worried would ultimately mean "weaken."

Randal Quarles had started as the Fed's first-ever official vice-chair for bank supervision on October 13, 2017, making him the person most central to the central bank's regulatory tinkering. Quarles's job was new, created by lawmakers as they grappled with what had gone wrong in the mortgage market following the 2008 crash. Besides setting up the Financial Stability Oversight Council to identify threats facing the entire system following the crisis, the 848-page Dodd–Frank legislation that had passed in 2010 had given the bank supervisors at the twelve Fed reserve banks a more official boss.

"We can't legislate morality, and goodness knows we can't legislate wisdom," Chris Dodd, one of the law's sponsors, said upon its adoption. "All we can do is establish a comprehensive framework and a clear path forward. And that is what we have done. The regulators still have to interpret and enforce the law."[11]

Like the chair and vice-chair, the vice-chair for supervision served a four-year term, meaning that every new presidential administration would have an opportunity to replace them. But in sharp contrast with the Fed's monetary policy leadership roles, it was clear from the outset that the Fed's top supervisory official would be more political. Financial regulation was inherently somewhat partisan. Democrats would want to rein in banks to protect the little guy and squeeze financiers. Republicans would want to free them of their shackles so that they could pursue profits and fuel growth. Rules would change somewhat with political cycles.

Fed governor Daniel Tarullo had never been formally nominated to the vice-chair for supervision job, but he had carried out many of the seat's responsibilities on an unofficial basis during the Obama years. Throughout his tenure, the government slowly ratcheted up oversight of the large banks and the Fed shook up its supervisory practices across regional banks, concentrating more power in Washington. Banks became more cautious and spent more money on complying with rules that they often complained were excessive or poorly designed. Many policy makers in Washington were proud of the fixes made during the postcrisis era; others fretted that they had gone too far and were keeping small businesses and families locked out of credit markets while forcing tiny banks to consolidate to compete. When a Republican was elected to the White House, it was obvious that regulation would face changes. The Trump administration had chosen Quarles as its man for the job at the Fed.

Straight-backed and square-jawed, a crisp pocket square often tucked into the pocket of his expensive suit, Quarles was a well-known figure in Washington. He had spent time at Treasury during George H. W. Bush's administration, working on financial regulation in response to a wave of savings and loan industry failures, and had then been a senior official at the Treasury during George W. Bush's administration. Much of his career had been dedicated to the law firm Davis Polk & Wardwell, where he focused on the financial industry, and he had worked as a partner at the private equity firm The Carlyle Group. He just missed Powell there, starting in 2006 as Powell was leaving.

Quarles was not born a creature of Washington, however. He had grown up as the son of a ranching family in Colorado and Utah before attending Columbia University and later Yale Law School, and he always retained a love of the American West. After taking one trip out to the Hamptons as a young lawyer and spending long hours stuck in Long Island traffic, he eschewed the Manhattan high life scene for quick weekend trips back to Salt Lake throughout his twenties and thirties. It was there that he met Hope Eccles, Marriner's grandniece, while searching for a condo near an exclusive Utah ski resort where she ran a luxury hotel. His real estate agent—the mother of a friend from college—had set them up.

Randy, Hope, and their three children had relocated to Washington when Quarles took a job at Treasury during the George W. Bush years, and then remained there while he worked at Carlyle. But his heart was always in the West, and the family eventually moved back to Utah, where Quarles set up a boutique asset management firm, which in part invested the family money.* By the time he got the Fed job, the kids were established and the family decided to stay put, so Quarles spent his weeks commuting on late-night flights. This time around, he took up part-time residence in Washington's swank Willard Hotel. It was somewhat ironic that one of the most lobbied men in modern Washington lived in the very place where the word "lobby" was, according to D.C. lore, perhaps coined and at any rate popularized. Ulysses S. Grant frequented the bar at the Willard when he was president, and interest group representatives used to cluster near the hotel entrance to vie for his attention. President Grant, the story goes, called them the "damn lobbyists."

From the start, Quarles was an unusually colorful character for a Fed official. He was rich and clever and had no qualms about airing that. He talked about his passion for piloting in his central banking speeches and punctuated his writing with phrases like "kaleidoscopic gallimaufry." (The latter is a real word, for the curious and the uninitiated, meaning "a confused jumble.") He was also vocally proud of his western roots, and of his place in one of the region's most storied families. He had been known to affectionately refer to his long-deceased connection as "Uncle Marriner."

In fact, familial pride in Uncle Marriner had given rise to a particularly weird drama, one that reads more like an episode of *Gossip Girl* than a chapter in central banking history.

The palaver started around 2008, when a group of Utahns tried to donate a six-foot-tall bronze statue of the Eccles family monetary maven to the Fed's main building. Metal Marriner did not meet with the enthusiastic reception his sponsors had expected, perhaps because he was not a work of especially pronounced beauty.† The task of taking possession of the bronze casting fell to Fed governor Kevin Warsh, a politically connected lawyer by training who had, much like Quarles, married into a fabulously wealthy and prominent family. His wife was an heiress to the Estée Lauder makeup fortune.

---

* The firm's name was The Cynosure Group for the ship that brought Marriner Eccles's father, David, across the Atlantic from Scotland.
† This was the estimation of several people who were loosely involved in, or familiar with, the episode.

As the months dragged by, Warsh and his colleagues worked on accepting the statue, but it was a slow process. The Fed fretted over fire codes and tax laws, had calls with representatives from the Eccles family, and worked ploddingly on the details of the transfer. The statue was eventually accepted, and a ceremony was held in 2014, but that was well after Warsh had departed the central bank.[12] Even then, it was placed in an out-of-the-way spot instead of in the striking central atrium where at least some of its sponsors had envisioned it standing.

When Warsh's name came up for Fed chair, Bloomberg's Rob Schmidt first reported the tale in a story titled "Warsh vs. Quarles Feud Has Been Renewed by Trump Fed Search."[13] *Politico* followed up with "Fed Fight Gets Even Weirder."[14] Quarles and Warsh had reportedly clashed while working in George W. Bush's administration, and the idea that a statue had worsened the bad blood between them was too delicious for Washington to ignore. Whether Quarles actually blamed Warsh for the incident (people would later insist that he did not) was irrelevant. The story became D.C. folklore overnight, elevating both men to topic du jour on the local cocktail party circuit.

Some within the Trump administration took the Bloomberg story as a sign that Quarles, already installed at the Fed, and Warsh, a contender for the chairmanship, would work badly together. Warsh's track record of supporting higher interest rates had already hurt his chances at the Fed job, and the saga was another nail in the coffin of his bid to lead the central bank.

Powell, already under more serious consideration, got the nod instead. Years later, at a White House event, a regretful Trump would see Warsh in the audience and ask: "Why weren't you more forceful, Kevin? You're a forceful person. I could've used you a little bit here," apparently assuming that he would have had more luck in convincing Warsh to bow to his campaign for lower interest rates than he'd had with Powell.[15]

Quarles's family ties to the Fed made for good stories, but they did not seem to dramatically influence the ideology he brought to the institution. Eccles had urged public spending in lean times, worried that wealth concentrated in the hands of too few people would harm the economy, and had in general embraced his role as a "class traitor," to use his words. His grandnephew by marriage did not harbor similar sentiments.

The men did share some similarities. Quarles was a member of the Church of Jesus Christ of Latter-day Saints like Eccles and exhibited a similar meticulousness. He also shared Eccles's flair for rhetorical drama. (Quarles had been a volunteer church membership clerk in college, and the job had once prompted him to send a letter to his church elders complaining about the reams of misaddressed mail coming in to the Manhattan chapter, which he was required to redirect. "I should be at a Broadway play tonight with a beautiful girl on my arm, the shriek of the city in my ears, and the double beat of summer love in my heart. . . . And what am I doing? I am stuffing envelopes. I am stapling," a young Quarles griped.)

But where Eccles had become a Keynesian before the word even existed, Quarles remained a steadfast devotee of free market capitalism, albeit a version that came with guardrails. He wanted to create a transparent system in which companies could understand regulations and pursue profits within clear-cut guidelines. He laid out his philosophy especially clearly in a 2010 law article, in which he argued that "governments can limit both moral hazard and uncertainty by refraining from intervention when possible and, when action of some sort is inherent in the government's mandate (as in issuing debt or executing monetary policy), by developing and sticking to clear, predictable rules for action, thus putting boundaries on what decisions can result from a weighing of the pros and cons."[16] Basically, he did not want bureaucrats to get in capitalists' way.

That light-touch posture could lead to bad calls. Quarles was arguing for regulation that was exactly strict enough, without being too strict, in a world where those perfect lines were nearly impossible to draw. When he was at Treasury in 2005, Quarles had argued that if regulators weren't playing catch-up with markets, it would be a sign that they were stifling innovation. "Markets are always ahead of the regulators, and frankly that's how it should be. It's analogous to the advice that my father provided me that if you don't miss at least two or three planes a year, you're spending too much time in airports," Quarles said, even as he called for better integration of global regulation instead of a race to the bottom in financial oversight.[17] Yet the downfalls of letting financial innovation get ahead of the government's ability to police it had soon become evident as American mortgage markets began to show cracks. In 2006, Quarles acknowledged that officials were looking into requiring greater transparency in nontraditional mortgages and that he and other officials at the Treasury were "doing everything in our power to make our financial system even more resilient in the future,"[18] but he also seemed to play down risks building in the housing market. He said that he "would not expect to see a substantial drop in housing prices as long as income is rising and interest rates remain moderate." A year later, home prices had fallen precipitously from their run-up, and risk-taking in mortgage-tied markets with excessively light regulation caused banks and large financial institutions to implode.

Still, when Quarles was appointed to the Fed, many pro-regulation onlookers quietly admitted—though rarely or never with their names attached—that they had feared Trump would pick someone far more disruptive. Quarles was not the type of person who would burn up the rule book. Still, he was an expert in how regulations worked, how they interacted, how they could be gamed, and who could suffer or benefit from small alterations. He was perfectly suited to make tiny changes that would offer significant results.

"His motto seems to be: Whatever the big banks want, give it to them," Elizabeth Warren, the Massachusetts Democrat who had made it her personal mission to police the financial industry, warned after Quarles's 2017 confirmation.[19]

"We look forward to working with Vice Chair Quarles in crafting a regulatory program that fosters economic growth and allows banks of all sizes to better serve their customers and communities without compromising safety and soundness," Rob Nichols, president of the lobby group the American Bankers Association, declared hopefully in his own post-confirmation statement.[20]

Quarles had fulfilled some but not all expectations in his early years on the job, moving slowly but deliberately to recalibrate regulation. He had undertaken three big projects at the Fed: tailoring the way regulations were applied to reflect legislation that had recently passed Congress, streamlining much-maligned annual bank stress tests to make them more predictable, and reducing the amount of discretion supervisors had over the banks they oversaw. More than any of his concrete actions, though, his very presence seemed to have a soothing effect on the largest banks. They began to draw down their holdings of capital—assets that could be used to maintain financial health in bad times—soon after the new vice-chair walked in the door.[21] The shift in tone mattered.

Powell was close with Quarles, whom he had personally recommended for the vice-chair for supervision role. Quarles never voted against or publicly undermined the Fed's monetary policy decisions, though he had previously made it clear that he was in favor of higher rates and a more predictable approach to setting policy than the Powell Fed had pursued.[22] Powell, for his part, consistently voted in support of Quarles's changes to bank oversight. Powell pushed the powerful central bank to be as accountable to the public as was possible within its existing structure, and he seemed to view the vice-chair for supervision as a tie to democratic legitimacy for bank-related work.

Even so, Quarles was not going about his regulatory business unchecked. Nearly every major regulatory change he implemented between 2018 and 2020 had earned a no vote from his colleague Lael Brainard.

Brainard was by then the last Democrat left on the Fed Board. She had joined the central bank in 2014, following a stint as the undersecretary for international affairs at the Obama Treasury Department and a long career in Washington's global policy circles. The fifty-eight-year-old macroeconomist was an established D.C. insider, easily recognizable in a conference crowd by her sheet of long white blond hair and her habit of wearing chunky silver jewelry.

Brainard's professional life had flowed naturally from an internationalist childhood. Born in Hamburg, Germany, to a Foreign Service officer and a teacher, she had been raised in Cold War Poland and Germany before its reunification following the fall of the Berlin Wall. Her upbringing heavily informed her worldview. "I was fascinated by how two countries so close in geography and resources could diverge so sharply simply by being separated by the Iron Curtain," she had told graduates at a commencement ceremony in 2014.[23] "Germany built a vibrant market democracy oriented to the West while Poland suffocated under a heavy state apparatus oriented to the Soviet Union. Life in Poland was grim and individual initiative stifled."

The family moved back to the United States when she was a teenager, and she attended the prestigious George School in Pennsylvania, graduating in 1979 and going on to study at Wesleyan University. After Wesleyan, she did a stint at McKinsey as a consultant, where she worked with "U.S. car manufacturers struggling to maintain share against Asian competitors and U.S. financial institution clients competing in increasingly complex global markets," she would later tell senators.[24]

Consulting did not provide her with the fulfillment she sought. Brainard left McKinsey to pursue an economics doctorate at Harvard University. She had chosen the field because she knew she wanted to work on policy, but she also craved an intellectually disciplined route to answering the world's big problems. From MIT, Brainard spent what she would later call an "eventful year" at the White House Council of Economic Advisers following the fall of the Berlin Wall, working on Poland's democratic transition plan. She then returned to academia, earning a reputation as a rising star in the economics world while teaching at the Massachusetts Institute of Technology in the 1990s.

But Washington retained a hold on Brainard, and she started as a White House Fellow in the Clinton administration. Her leave from MIT—meant to be temporary—quickly turned indefinite. She stayed on as deputy assistant to the president, working to shape China's entry into the World Trade Organization, among other global issues. She ultimately became the president's Sherpa, or personal representative, at global diplomatic meetings, establishing a reputation as a fierce and strategic negotiator. She won many fans during those years, who called her driven and intelligent. She also developed some big enemies, who labeled her ambitious and said that she had "sharp elbows."

Brainard was known around D.C. as half of one of her generation's mightier power couples. She had in 1998 married Kurt Campbell, a defense expert who held prominent positions in the Clinton and Obama administrations and who would go on to found the Center for a New American Security think tank.[25] The pair had met in the atrium of Harvard's Kennedy School while she was a graduate student and he was a young associate professor, and they wed on their vintage Civil War farm in Rappahannock County, Virginia.

By the 2010s, Brainard and Campbell lived in a six-bedroom house in Chevy Chase[26] with their three daughters, who attended Sidwell Friends School (they were slightly younger than President Obama's daughters and the Powell children, who were also alums).[27] Campbell had in 2013 co-founded the Asia Group,[28] a strategic advisory firm that helped big U.S. companies with expansion across the Pacific and provided consulting services to investors. The couple occasionally made the who's who lists popular among inside-Washington media publications, despite Brainard's intense sense of personal privacy and reticence when it came to talking about herself in all but the most controlled public settings. But D.C.-famous and famous-famous were different things. In 2012, *Foreign Policy* listed her in an article about "The Most Powerful Women You've Never Heard Of."[29]

Brainard had spent her post-Clinton years at the Brookings Institution think tank before becoming a counselor to the Treasury Department in 2009, at the start of the Obama administration, and then an undersecretary. She held that all-consuming job even as her kids were growing up. People who knew her recounted stories of walking into important meetings to find her youngest at the table with a coloring book. Brainard sometimes took work calls while driving to soccer practice.

News broke in 2013 that she was planning to leave the Treasury, and in 2014 she was confirmed as one of Obama's nominated Fed governors.

"In the Obama administration, Ms. Brainard has won a reputation as a tireless diplomat and firm negotiator," Annie Lowery had written in *The New York Times* when the news that she was leaving Treasury came out. "She has pressed Europe to mount a much more decisive and larger response to its long-simmering debt crisis" and "she has also urged Beijing to hasten its reforms to the Chinese economy, reorienting away from investment and toward domestic consumption, and making it easier for foreign companies to compete with Chinese businesses."[30]

The Fed seemed like a new challenge for an expert in global economics—but it took Brainard time to find her place at the institution, which had a different metabolism and pace of decision-making than the crisis-era Treasury she had just left. Brainard occasionally riled her colleagues, some of whom felt she was not collaborative enough. She also drew major criticism from the press when she donated the personal maximum to Hillary Clinton's campaign in the 2016 election. "At a time when Federal Reserve officials are making the case that monetary policy needs to be non-partisan and independent, a sitting governor has given money to Hillary Clinton," Bloomberg's Craig Torres wrote in the story that uncovered the news.[31] Many in Washington doubted that she would stay at the Fed, suggesting the job was a résumé-builder and just one chapter in her broader ascent. Brainard was often mentioned as a possible pick for Treasury secretary should Clinton win, and was nearly as often quietly judged for being so ambitious.*

Then Trump triumphed instead. Lael Brainard's fate shifted suddenly and sharply: She found herself in the unlikely role of lone liberal sitting at the Fed Board. Unexpected as it was, Brainard used her position to become a one-woman obstacle to the Fed's push toward lighter regulation.

The role was an awkward one. She began to cast a volley of dissents at an institution where polite consensus generally dominated. She released statements alongside her votes, laying out in detail why the changes Quarles was making to regulatory policy might prove dangerous. As her opposition campaign hardened, it also began to prove effective. She had no hope of actually stopping the rulemaking, but journalists made a practice of starting with her dissent, rather than the press release, whenever the Fed posted a piece of regulatory news. She was placing changes that might have otherwise passed in obscurity under a spotlight and laying out a map in case future officials wanted to reverse them.

Brainard also took strong stances on monetary policy, which she laid out in careful speeches. She favored ambitious unconventional

---

* Fed officials who were seen as being openly ambitious were often faulted for it on Wall Street, among academics, and even by colleagues. Brainard and Kashkari both faced snide commentary along these lines. Oddly, it never really came up regarding Powell, who had positioned himself at a Washington think tank on his way to a cool government job and who had publicly said that, earlier in his life, it had been his dream to be Treasury secretary one day.

While both men and women sometimes took heat for ambition, Brainard also faced overt sexism. For instance, the number of people (particularly men) who have mentioned her blue eyes and long hair or commented on her fashion choices to this reporter, often in conversations about her ideas or career, far exceeds the number of people who have offered unsolicited commentary on Powell's or Quarles's appearance.

policies when times were bad—making big promises to keep rates low for a long time, for instance. While she had voted for the Fed's rate increases in 2018, she was generally considered a "dove," meaning she favored low rates. She made a point of being a Fed governor who paid close attention to labor concerns, engaging with worker organizations and focusing on the job market in her speeches.

Brainard's positions on financial regulation and focus on labor were politically astute for someone who hoped for an even bigger job in a future Democratic administration. But she also seemed to genuinely believe in what she was doing. She often worked to further her causes far from the eyes of reporters. She attended community development events unadvertised. She had made hiring and promoting a varied set of researchers a personal mission, and research assistants would often report that she was the governor who regularly showed up at diversity-focused internal events.

The Fed's future role in markets and society also preoccupied Brainard, which partly reflected the committees she had been assigned to at the Board and partly reflected her own interests. She held regular market intelligence calls with Wall Street analysts to understand the financial stability landscape, and she tended to catch on to trends quickly. She began speaking about blockchain technologies in 2016, before central bankers were widely focused on them, and before long became focused on the Fed's potential role in developing and policing digital currency technologies.[32] She was the governor who most believed that the central bank had responsibility for understanding and talking about climate change's economic and financial risks, a topic many of her colleagues kept at a careful distance, given its political divisiveness.*

Owing in large part to her thoroughness and competence, Brainard maintained the respect of her colleagues, even though she was out of step with them ideologically—in Powell's case, slightly, and in Quarles's, very. She was often prepared to the point of absurdity. Staffers told stories about times they had been sent to brief her only to realize that she knew as much about the topic at hand as they did.

Her influence at the Fed was no secret, and big investors parsed

---

* This book will deal with digital currency and climate change at length in Chapter 14.

her every word. At times, she had even been seen as a sort of contrarian bellwether for committee decisions. In one comical (depending on your vantage point) instance in 2016, markets reacted sharply because the Chicago Council on Global Affairs announced that she had a speech coming up the following week, just before the Fed entered its typical pre-meeting quiet period. Investors interpreted the impromptu scheduling to mean that she was poised to argue against a coming rate hike, and stocks jerked lower, newly anticipating an increase.[33] The speech had been scheduled weeks earlier and the timing was simple bad luck.

Both Brainard and Quarles possessed a quality that tended to be useful in policymaking: They were able to work effectively across partisan lines. Despite their many differences, the pair limited their public beefs to questions of policy. In fact, inside the building they had struck up a sort of oddball friendship, one based on mutual respect in the face of near-total disagreement. On one particularly acrimonious morning in their shared policy lives, as Brainard dissented on a set of rules that would tailor regulations for big banks—saying that they would "go beyond what is required by law and weaken the safeguards at the core of the system before they have been tested through a full cycle"—she sat relaxed at Quarles's right throughout the open hearing on the decision, at one point laughing at a joke he had cracked. A slight, ironic smile tugged at her lips as she cast her definitive no vote.[34]

Both Quarles and Brainard had Powell's trust and confidence, and he consulted with them on matters of importance, Quarles because of his title, role, and deep banking knowledge and Brainard because of her economic, international, and financial stability expertise. Still, the fact that the two had prominent voices in policy discussions made for a polarized Fed. To one side sat a near-libertarian lawyer who felt that a central bank should have stark limitations in a democratic and capitalistic society, and to the other a Democrat-aligned economist who thought the Fed had a responsibility to use policy more expansively to safeguard finance and support the economy.* Powell existed in the space between.

---

* Both Quarles and Brainard were moderate compared to many of the conservative Republicans and progressive Democrats in Washington during this period. They were nevertheless quite far from each other, ideologically.

—

Brainard and Quarles were far from the only policy makers working alongside Powell to drive the Fed through its moment of twenty-first-century change. The Fed's decentralization and preference for consensus meant that all of its officials—its Washington-based governors and its twelve regional presidents—could at times matter critically for policy. Given how unwieldy the committee could be, the central bank had long had a nerve center when it came to shaping monetary policy. That was the so-called "troika" made up of the Fed's chair, vice-chair, and the New York Fed president.

The group of three had historically set the Fed's tone, pre-discussing key decisions and helping to shepherd the large Federal Open Market Committee toward consensus. Powell had carefully built his own central trio. White House administrations typically consulted the Fed chair when appointing other governors, and Trump's early Fed nominees fit that pattern, giving Powell a say in who would become his vice-chair.

News broke in early 2018 that the Trump administration was considering filling that role with John Williams, then the head of the Federal Reserve Bank of San Francisco.[35] Anyone familiar with both Trump's and Williams's personalities could have predicted that the presidential interview would go badly. Williams was a famed economic theorist who, alongside his colleague and friend Thomas Laubach, came up with the most commonly used estimate for the Fed's not-hot-not-cold neutral interest rate. Outside of work, he loved video games (*Dark Souls*), science fiction and magical realism (Haruki Murakami, David Mitchell), and modern art. His father had been a policy adviser to California governors from both parties, and his ideology-spanning example exerted an enormous influence on how Williams thought about himself and his career.

President Trump had demonstrated in his other agency picks that he didn't have an issue with quirky people, but it also seemed like he was looking for powerful bankers straight from central casting who were members of his own party. Williams came off as anything but: He was jovial, chatty, independent-minded, and hardly a devout Republican. His hair was perpetually disheveled, and he'd been known to enthusiastically forgo a tie. The interview flopped.

The vice-chair job went instead to Richard Clarida, the clean-cut Columbia professor and Pimco adviser whom Obama had almost nominated instead of Powell.

Powell had hit it off with Clarida when he interviewed him, and he supported Trump's decision to nominate him. The Fed chair had called Clarida up to congratulate him the day of his confirmation, asking when the new vice-chair could get started—and floating the idea of the monetary policy framework review that he wanted to launch. Powell wanted the economist to lead what would become the cornerstone project of his term, adding intellectual heft and academic gravitas. Clarida was unsure at first, especially about the public element, but he said yes. Rethinking the future of monetary policy clearly ranked right at the top of Powell's list of priorities.

While he was pleased to have Clarida on board, Powell still admired Williams, who had done some of the most groundbreaking research of his generation. Fortunately, there was another key job open: The New York Fed needed a president.

Powell also had significant say over who got the New York position. While six of the nine directors on regional Fed boards select regional bank presidents, the Board had a veto vote, allowing it to guide the result. Beyond that, Powell was well connected to the process through Glenn Hutchins, a financier who sat on the New York Fed's board and who was leading the search for the new president.* Williams made a good impression on the other search committee members because he had managed a huge organization in the San Francisco Fed, and he seemed thoroughly prepared for the executive and academic sides of the job. That, combined with the fact that Powell had signaled via Hutchins that he liked Williams, sealed the deal.

The selection met with immediate backlash. The New York Fed

---

* Hutchins had spent years developing a network across the Fed's system, setting up the Hutchins Center on Fiscal and Monetary Policy at the Brookings Institution in Washington. Ben Bernanke, Janet Yellen, and Don Kohn all worked there after they left the Fed—their hallway was jokingly called the "FOMC, or Former Open Market Committee." Friends roundly said Hutchins's interest in monetary policy and involvement at the Fed was born of his intellectual fascination with the topic. In any case, it put him in a good position to be a conduit to the Fed Board as the New York Fed's directors thought about who to put atop the most powerful regional central bank.

had gone to extreme lengths to advertise that its president search would be far-reaching and consider diverse candidates. Arguably the only thing optically worse in 2018 than picking a white man for a top job in a field that was still dominated by them was doing it after you had supposedly looked at everyone else. (News outlets had widely reported that the directors had considered several women, including Brainard, for the position.)

Despite his management experience, Williams cared little about markets compared to a typical New York Fed pick, treating them as an almost quotidian reality underlying the more interesting macroeconomic questions of the day. He had made a yearslong habit of bragging about not spending his days glued to a Bloomberg, the ubiquitous data machine of finance. He seemed to view economics as a higher pursuit that should exist on a plane above the day-to-day drama of stock and bond movements, often a well-received sentiment among academics and PhD economists. It was less welcome to bankers and traders. Placing him into a role that Wall Street had long viewed as their key conduit to—and advocate at—the Fed offended many in the industry.*

Since the days of Benjamin Strong, the powerful first head of the New York Fed, big banks and market participants had viewed the institution as their own personal branch. While Eccles had done his best to make Washington the center of Fed power, the Board under subsequent chairs, including Greenspan, treated the New York Fed as the bastion of the system's financial expertise. For its part, the New York Fed had been happy to take on the role of finance leader. The bank had always viewed itself as the "first among equals," both because it held a constant vote on monetary policy—unlike the other eleven reserve banks, whose presidents voted only on a rotating basis—and because it carried out all Fed trading activity and linked the central bank to Wall Street. The New York Fed president was the highest-paid official in the Fed system, earning $497,000 in 2019.

---

* Williams's free-spirited attitude had fit nicely in San Francisco, where the staff wore sneakers to the office, but at times clashed in New York, where people wore ties and dress shoes. He also butted heads with his new senior staff, a reality that would eventually lead to ousters and resignations.

Powell, whose salary was set by Congress, made about $200,000.[36] Placing a lifelong Fed economist at the helm seemed sure to more closely integrate the branch into the system, potentially diminishing what made it special and separate.[37]

New York problems aside, Powell's troika operated smoothly when it came to advice and idea formation. Williams had decades of central banking experience and clear ideas about the economy's future. Clarida was an intellectual, academic type with an unbeatable memory for names and personalities, and he was often used to float what officials sometimes called "trial balloons," ideas that the Fed was testing out but which it didn't want to turn into official policy until it had prepared the public and felt out its reaction. Wall Street knew about Clarida's communication role and gave his words extra weight.

The trio also got along well personally. Powell and Clarida, who both played the guitar, had even teamed up to play the Barenaked Ladies' version of "God Rest Ye Merry Gentlemen" at the Fed's 2018 holiday party. The next year, they performed an encore, adding on a rendition of "What the World Needs Now Is Love."

Still, the troika was not all-important in Powell's Fed. Powell was the type of leader who set out a large goal and then delegated major tasks. He wanted to spend his tenure as chair making sure the Fed was ready to confront the challenges of the twenty-first century, but he wanted that effort to involve the entire central bank.

The outreach portion of Powell's signature policy framework review was perhaps the clearest display of both the collaborative way in which the Fed worked in those days and what it hoped to achieve as it approached its big overhaul in 2019 and 2020. Powell, Fed chief of staff Michelle Smith, and Clarida had fine-tuned the idea to run the series of community events across the central bank's national system alongside the academic review of the Fed's framework, hoping for public feedback and buy-in.* Once they brought a broader commit-

---

* The original idea may have come from Fed staffers, but the timeline is a little bit unclear.

tee of Fed officials and staff members into the loop, it was Brainard who branded the push.

At one of the early internal discussions on the outreach plan, Fed officials and economists had grappled with the framing. How should they make it clear that the Fed was holding educational events that would both explain monetary policy to community groups and take their views into account? What was the point they were trying to convey? How could they avoid sounding cheesy or inauthentic? It was not the case that they were going to draw up a new framework for setting America's monetary policy on some Rotary Club's recommendations, and that would be obvious from the get-go, so they needed to avoid overpromising. The people around the table chattered back and forth, bandying about a fourteen-word title for the initiative.

Brainard, silent for most of the meeting, suddenly drummed her fingers on the table before her. Heads turned in her direction.

"Fed Listens," she stated, simply but definitively, sitting back in her chair.

"That's it," Clarida replied.

With a two-word phrase, she seemed to capture the Powell Fed's deepest aspiration. The central bank wanted to be transparent not because it made policy more effective—the Bernanke innovation— but because it wanted the public to feel heard.

"Surveys show that all over the world people are losing faith in large institutions, so we're paddling against the current in trying to sustain public faith in the Fed," Powell would at one point explain to a town hall of teachers.[38]

Beyond that, there was plenty of evidence that the Fed needed to improve its listening skills for reasons beyond reputation. The 2008 crisis and its policy aftermath were increasingly seen as a tragedy in two parts. Economists hadn't paid enough attention to what was happening outside their models to see excesses building in the housing market, and afterward many hadn't listened to displaced laborers closely enough to realize how many wanted to return to the job market. If they had, they might have set policy differently, leaving rates lower for even longer.*

---

* There were policy makers, in both instances, raising these issues. Famously, Janet Yellen was internally warning about the housing bubble from her then seat at

The Fed's leadership and the bulk of its staff had attended the very best universities and enjoyed excellent professional connections. Many of them had spent large portions of their adult lives in New York or Washington, often in the bubble of high society. Powell, Brainard, and Quarles might have represented a range of political views, but they were all plainly wealthy. Most high-ranking Fed officials were at least well-off. Many had never—or at least had not recently—experienced the daily economic challenges that faced the median American and practically every family in the bottom half of the income distribution, from wondering whether they would be able to help their kids pay for college to losing sleep over a doctor's bill. Given how much their economic experiences diverged from the typical American's, listening was essential.

The Powell Fed didn't know what was coming next as it entered 2020. But officials did know that when trouble struck the economy again, they didn't want to miss critical details.

---

the Federal Reserve Bank of San Francisco; in the 2015–2018 rate-increase cycle, presidents including Mary Daly and Neel Kashkari voiced skepticism about how tight the labor market was. They were not, however, voicing the dominant understanding in those moments.

MARCH MADNESS

Fear is the most contagious disease you can imagine.

—*Warren Buffett, speech in 2020*

AWN BROKE IN WASHINGTON on February 28, 2020, to find President Trump gearing up for a Friday night campaign rally in South Carolina. He would brag about the United States' low coronavirus infection rate while telling an arena packed elbow to elbow with supporters that liberals were turning the illness into a new political "hoax."[1]

Fed chair Powell woke at his home on a tree-lined street in Chevy Chase, Maryland, in a very different frame of mind.

The year had gotten off to an auspicious enough start: His son's wedding had been beautiful, unemployment was entering the new decade at a half-century low of 3.5 percent, and the trade war that had roiled markets and kept central bankers awake at night in 2019 seemed to be calming. Reports of a novel coronavirus in China had begun to dominate headlines, but when Powell had arrived in Riyadh, Saudi Arabia, the week earlier for a Group of Twenty meeting of global economic officials, Powell had believed that the outbreak might be contained in Asia. The United States might feel spillover effects as China locked down its economy to contain the spread, cutting off a crucial customer base for global goods and services and disrupting supply lines, but the economic problem was likely to remain mostly regional.*

Events promptly changed his thinking. Powell had spent the weekend watching headlines report a rising infection tally in South Korea and an outbreak in Iran. As he attended meetings at the King Abdulaziz International Conference Center and at a palm tree–ringed Ritz Carlton on Saturday, February 22, dozens of new cases were reported in northern Italy.[2] The tone of conversations about the virus began to shift with the European case count, becoming more worried with each passing outbreak announcement. Geography was not going to be a barrier, one that would construct defenses around the United States' borders and keep contagion at bay. By the time Powell boarded a plane back to America—he flew commercial, as Fed chairs typically do, and dressed casually for the flight in the lightweight wool Allbirds sneakers then popular among millennials and cool dads[3]—it had become clear that the virus would span the world.

From Riyadh, the Fed chair had contacted his colleagues and asked them to research the government's emergency powers. How would America respond to a global pandemic, and how would the Fed fit into that response?

By the time he landed in Washington's Dulles Airport after his fourteen-hour flight on Monday, February 24, his preparations had ceased to seem like overcautious contingency planning. He turned on his phone to a raft of missed emails and messages. Stock indexes were plummeting. The concern Powell had begun to feel was also infecting society's collective psyche.

Conditions deteriorated from there. Clarida, the Fed's vice-chair, was slated to deliver a speech at the National Association for Business Economics on Tuesday, February 25. Because the Fed often used his speeches to signal ideas it was testing out but not yet ready to turn

---

* For context, the events related on the pages ahead came chronologically before—in fact, in the lead-up to—the more drastic Fed response detailed in Chapter 2. They explain how Fed officials thought about the coronavirus at its advent, and how that view evolved into the response that materialized in mid-March 2020 (the subject of Chapter 2).

into policy, the appearance offered the central bank a chance to mark out its position on how big a threat the virus posed.

But what if they sounded too alarmed? When Powell and Clarida discussed the speech text, they decided that it was important to strike the right balance. The best economic forecasters in the business were still only penciling in a minor hit to growth from the spreading infection, not any kind of full-blown crisis. If they came out sounding too concerned, markets would think they knew something about the coronavirus that the public didn't—which wasn't true. While Powell had become more anxious about the U.S. implications of the virus, Clarida still thought the major fallout would be concentrated in Asia, and that the consequences for America would mostly emanate from a slowdown there.

Clarida had been surprised by a question on the pandemic during an appearance on Bloomberg Television in late January and had called the virus a "wild card." He settled on language that would stick to that wary, but not panicked, vibe. The virus could pose a threat to the global economy, but as of late February, it was too soon to tell how big that threat would be.

By Wednesday, February 26, the CDC had confirmed a coronavirus case in California that hadn't originated in China—suggesting that the illness was spreading in American communities.[4] Italian case counts continued to skyrocket. The coronavirus was quickly gaining enough momentum to shutter entire sectors of the global economy, and the world was waking up to that reality. At the Fed's main building in Washington, officials were beginning to become much more concerned.

Powell met with Clarida and top staffers—including Thomas Laubach, director of monetary affairs; Andreas Lehnert, financial stability director; chief of staff Michelle Smith; and a small crowd of other economists and officials—in an hour-long planning meeting. That the session was happening at all was a testament to how worried the central bank's leaders were rapidly becoming.

The situation was serious, Powell told his colleagues. They needed to think it through.

They ran through an analysis of what could happen with the virus and what it would mean. What were the economics of a pandemic in 2020?

"There could be a very large social distancing impact on demand," Stacey Tevlin, the Fed Board's head of research and statistics, told her colleagues. The phrase "social distance" was still a new one. It sounded alien, almost funny.

"How bad are we talking, Rich?" Powell asked his second-in-command, searching for a worst-case scenario.

"Probability distributions have means, right tails, left tails," Clarida hemmed, referencing the common statistical bell curve: The right tail includes low-probability good outcomes, the left low-probability bad ones, and the middle is made up of more likely, less exciting scenarios.

The fact that he was offering a Stats 101 lesson instead of answering did not bode well.

"The global financial crisis?" Powell asked, referencing the 2007–2009 meltdown.

"No," Clarida answered, looking at his colleague through the thick black frames of his glasses. He spoke, as always, with the practiced calm of a college professor.

"No, the worst-case scenario means it basically looks like the Great Depression."

The comment hung in the air for a moment, and then Clarida explained his forecast. If entire cities had to shut down overnight, as was happening in Italy, it would not ripple through the financial sector and slowly come to hurt the real economy, as the financial crisis had. People would lose their livelihoods immediately. Families would stop paying mortgages, and shops would stop paying rent. No part of the economy or of markets would be spared from disruption. Businesses were highly indebted, so that abrupt kink in cash flow could destabilize a mountain of bonds and mortgage investments.

The question was how to respond. The central bankers didn't discuss the policy playbook at that meeting, but officials knew from the start that their tools to combat what was coming might prove limited.

The Fed's first line of defense, as always, would be interest rates. The federal funds rate stood at 1.5 to 1.75 percent, giving the Fed room for either six normal-sized interest rate cuts, since moves usually come in quarter-point increments, or the shock and awe of a few supersized cuts. But it wasn't obvious that trying to encourage borrowing to bolster demand was the right solution to the problem at hand.

The scenario that confronted officials in late February 2020 was not one in which consumers stopped buying houses, cars, and couches because they were worried about the economic outlook, but one in which they were kept away from stores and restaurants altogether out of fear of a deadly virus. Plus, as worried banks and financial firms took a more cautious approach to lending amid the uncertainty, it wasn't clear that cheap borrowing costs would be passed along. Who was going to underwrite a business loan for a new restaurant when the entire economy was staring down a shutdown of indeterminate length?

By Friday, February 28, the day of Trump's South Carolina speech, the Dow Jones Industrial Average stock index was headed for its worst five-day streak since the 2008 financial crisis. It had plunged 1,200 points the prior day, for the worst single session in its history.[5] The White House was taking a halting approach to a coronavirus response. It had set up a task force and enacted a travel ban from China at the end of January, and it had requested $2.5 billion in supplemental funding for vaccine development and other virus responses on February 24.[6*] Trump had predicted during a news conference on February 27 that the nation's coronavirus total, then estimated at around fifteen people, "within a couple of days is going to be down close to zero."

"That's a pretty good job we've done," he said, congratulating himself.[7]

Senator Mitch McConnell of Kentucky, the Republican majority leader, had acknowledged on the Senate floor on February 27 that there seemed to be little question that the virus would cause "some degree of disruption" in America. He then launched into an attack on Democratic minority leader Chuck Schumer, of New York, for "moving the goalposts" on how much money was needed for the initial response. Schumer had also taken to the floor, blasting Trump

---

* To put this in context, that is less than one two-thousandth of what would ultimately be allocated for the coronavirus response.

for cutting money from infectious disease research and public health programs and for downplaying the situation, accusing him of "towering and dangerous incompetence."[8]

In a further demonstration of the partisan wrangling that had kicked off, Elizabeth Warren, the progressive Democrat from Massachusetts, had introduced a bill suggesting that money meant to fund Trump's border wall with Mexico be redirected toward the Department of Health and Human Services for virus response efforts.[9]

The virus had infected more than eighty thousand people globally and killed three thousand by late that week. The front page of *The New York Times* that Friday morning relayed that investors had begun to fear an imminent economic recession, and that "the outbreak could crush consumer demand, as people limit travel or stay home even without a government order to do so."[10]

Something would need to be done to blunt the economic and financial fallout that Covid-19 seemed destined to create. As political bickering kicked off, it also appeared more and more likely that the Fed—unelected and agile—would be the part of government that was willing and able to respond swiftly, whether or not its tools were suited to the cause.

The mounting economic danger weighed on Powell's mind as he completed his morning routine that Friday, February 28, scrolling through Twitter and scanning the major news stories. He and Clarida had begun discussing whether some sort of action might be necessary. Changing policy promptly might be seen as reactive, but better to be early and overreact than to be late and fail to shore up the economy against a once-in-a-lifetime shock. The risk loomed ahead ominously as Powell climbed into his chauffeured car, black and nondescript, to head to his weekly breakfast with Treasury Secretary Steven Mnuchin.

Powell and the Treasury secretary met in the private room at the Fed's stately Eccles Building. Completed in 1937 and flanked in Georgian marble,[11] the Fed's headquarters sat about a mile from the White House and just a bit farther from the Treasury Department—the metaphorical opposite of Powell's position. The Fed chair rarely spoke to the president after the long months of attack he had endured, but he maintained a good working relationship with Mnuchin. The pair shared backgrounds in private equity and a no-nonsense approach to the policy world.

Otherwise, they were about as superficially dissimilar as two privileged white men could be. Powell was older, having just turned sixty-seven, and classic in his wealth. In 1971, he had graduated from Georgetown Preparatory, a boys-only Jesuit campus, a class ahead of Robert F. Kennedy, Jr., and a dozen years before future Supreme Court justice Brett Kavanaugh. The Powell family had belonged to the prestigious Chevy Chase Club when Jerome, whom everyone called "Jay," was growing up. After his education at Princeton and Georgetown and his entry into law and investment banking, he had joined the tony members-only New York Athletic Club in his thirties (lest non-Manhattanites wonder whether this is just a gym, the membership page boldly states in orange capital letters that the institution "opens the way to an exclusive world." It is basically a social club for the 1 percent).[12] By his tenure as Fed chair, he was thoroughly connected in Washington's most elite circles. Still, friends said Powell was the type of person who had money without living for it. The fact that he had chosen to cap his career with public service roles probably spoke to that.*

Mnuchin was a decade Powell's junior, richer—his net worth was estimated to be as high as $200 million, four times Powell's—and flashier. He drove a red Porsche with custom plaid interior in college, according to *The New York Times*,[13] and worked at Goldman Sachs before founding a hedge fund, Dune Capital, which he named for a spot—presumably a pile of sand—near his house in the Hamptons. He had helped to bankroll films, including *The Lego Movie* and *Avatar*, and married his third wife, Scottish movie star Louise Linton, in a 2017 ceremony officiated by the vice president.[14] The pair had drawn public ire that year when Linton tagged the various high-end designers she was wearing in an Instagram post about a Treasury trip (spe-

---

* "Probably" because it is not clear, as of this writing, what Powell will do once he is no longer Fed chair. His predecessors have made millions giving speeches and consulting with Wall Street firms, and Powell during his renomination declined to sign an ethics promise Elizabeth Warren had suggested that would ban him from working in or for financial services for four years after leaving government.

cifically, #rolandmouret, #hermesscarf, #tomford, and #valentino), then got in a fight in the comments with an Oregon woman who implied that the couple's travel was a poor use of government dollars.

"Aw!!! Did you think this was a personal trip?! Adorable!" Linton had replied, before trotting out choice phrases that included: "I'm pretty sure we paid more taxes toward our day 'trip' than you did."[15*]

Mnuchin himself generally cut a less dramatic figure. Still, he was an anomaly in Washington circles and was typically described as either a policy lightweight or a sycophant to the president by Wall Street executives and analysts. Despite that, Powell found him to be competent and the pair worked together effectively. Their weekly meetings, held over breakfast or lunch, were productive.

A sober atmosphere prevailed as Powell arrived to this one, though. As he tucked into his usual yogurt and fruit—the Treasury secretary had blueberries, egg whites, and coffee—the pair talked over the potential depth of the fallout from the fast-spreading virus. Bond markets were gyrating as stocks continued to plummet. Nothing was at a breaking point yet, but that could change quickly.

Powell pondered the problems facing the world and his central bank while walking back to his office after breakfast, his shoes clacking softly on cold floors as he made his way through the high-ceilinged halls of the Eccles Building. It was time to send a clear signal.

Investors believed that the Fed was watching the pandemic unfold with, if not the same indifference that the administration was exhibiting, something bordering it. James Bullard, the president of the Federal Reserve Bank of St. Louis, had been labeling worries about the virus premature. He had told CNBC just a week earlier that there was "a high probability that the coronavirus will blow over." Clarida's speech earlier in the week had been intentionally vague, but the press had homed in on his statement that it was "too soon to tell" what the virus's fallout would be, rather than his veiled warning that it might prove grim.

* As a gossipy addition to this contrast, both Powell's and Mnuchin's wives have made films. Elissa Leonard's *Sally Pacholok* traces an emergency room nurse's crusade to have B-12 deficiency properly diagnosed. Louise Linton's *Me You Madness* features Linton herself as a fashion- and sex-obsessed hedge fund manager who moonlights as a cannibalistic serial killer.

It would be wise to signal that the central bank was aware of the risks and prepared to respond to them, Powell had decided. He would release a statement.

Powell spent hours checking in with many of the twelve regional Fed presidents, asking what they were hearing from business leaders in their districts. Calls with foreign counterparts—the Bank of England, the European Central Bank—were woven into his schedule. At noon, he, Clarida, and Williams, the Fed's leadership trio, talked through the unfolding situation and response. Throughout the day, the Fed chair kept CNBC playing on the television and one eye on his Bloomberg screen. The data terminal was delivering nothing but bad news.

At 2:30 P.M. on February 28, as markets bled, Powell released his statement: Coronavirus posed an evolving risk, and the Fed was "closely monitoring" developments. It would "act as appropriate" to support the economy.

It was a highly unusual, and entirely intentional, effort to let America know that the Fed was preparing to respond, possibly with a rate cut before its planned March 18 meeting. Stocks breathed a temporary sigh of relief. Powell went back to working the phones within minutes of the release.

By the following Monday, Powell was ready to set a plan to cushion the economy into action. Mnuchin had scheduled a Group of Seven call for the morning of Tuesday, March 3, and Powell had decided that if the Fed was going to cut rates, it would make sense to do it near that meeting.

Over about twenty back-to-back calls that Monday, he talked with national and global leaders, including outgoing Bank of England governor Mark Carney and Christine Lagarde at the European Central Bank. There was little scope for a coordinated global response, because central bank policy interest rates were hovering at historically low levels across the world. The United States was in the best position to kick off the monetary response to the unfolding crisis.

Powell had lined up a consensus among his own colleagues and, by late that afternoon, everything was on track for the Fed to cut interest rates in their first emergency move since 2008. Given the weight of the decision, the conversations had been surprisingly painless. After watching markets bleed and quarantines clamp down across Europe, even usually feisty Fed officials were comfortable with moving rates early to get ahead of whatever disaster might soon arrive on America's shores. The Fed held a formal video conference to discuss the change starting at 7:30 P.M. From Boston to San Francisco, presidents and their staff economists dialed in from remote offices. Because the committee's normal boardroom wasn't equipped with the technology needed for the teleconference, Powell gathered with the other governors in the Fed's special library, a small room lined with bookshelves. There hadn't been time to arrange a dinner and there were no good food outposts near the Fed—even the closest Starbucks was a walk—so most attendees in Washington hadn't really eaten. At least one official had settled for scarfing down a yogurt and a Diet Coke from the Fed's convenience shop shortly before the meeting started. The minor privation only contributed to the growing sense of strangeness and alarm.

Lorie Logan, the markets desk head from the New York Fed, gave the prognosis from a conference room in the Manhattan building. Markets were on edge. After Powell's Friday statement, some investors were expecting a coordinated rate cut across global central banks, she reported, reminiscent of one that international policy makers had made in tandem during the depths of the financial crisis.

Officials agreed that they needed to move early to stave off economic damage after the Group of Seven meeting the following morning. A few differed on details—some favored acting immediately—but the group opted to wait until Tuesday so that communications could be arranged, and so that the chair and Fed staff would have time to prepare for an emergency news conference. Powell held off on his vote so that the committee could wait until the next morning to release the announcement.

As stock markets opened in free fall on March 3, Powell cast his vote, making the decision to slash borrowing costs official. The Fed announced the move in a 10:00 A.M. statement.[16] The half-point reduction lowered the central bank's key rate to a range of 1 percent to 1.25 percent and placed the Fed firmly at the front of the country's economic response to the virus.

The market reaction to the shock-and-awe move ranked between disappointing and concerning. Stocks bounced momentarily before resuming their decline, which many analysts attributed to the fact that investors had been looking for an action that had been coordinated with other global central banks—or that, no matter how powerful the Fed was, it was no match for a once-in-a-century pandemic.

Lowering interest rates would make it slightly cheaper for companies and consumers to borrow, and it might reassure markets that the Fed was paying attention, helping to keep them calm. But it was hardly a cure-all. Though it was the policy option available to Powell and his colleagues at that moment, it wouldn't reopen closed factories, it wouldn't bring Chinese tourists to the United States, and it wouldn't fix the shortfall as U.S. factories missed out on parts from China.

As analysts and reporters raced to explain the Fed's move and Wall Street's indifference, Powell headed to his hastily scheduled press conference, held in the chilly basement of a nondescript office building on Washington's I Street. Approaching the lectern, he straightened his thin lavender tie and prepared to answer tough questions. Some Fed-watchers would accuse him of using the virus outbreak as an excuse to bow to Trump. Even before that morning's cut, analysts had penned notes warning that the Fed would waste precious policy space with an emergency move. Central banks, they pointed out, could not solve everything.

As was often the case with Powell, it became clear which criticisms were weighing on his mind shortly after he began to speak.

"A rate cut will not reduce the rate of infection. It won't fix a broken supply chain. We get that," the Fed chair acknowledged. "We don't think we have all the answers."

In possession of answers or not, the Fed needed to come up with more of a solution than a single rate cut, a reality that became inescapable in the following days. People were beginning to panic as colleges canceled classes and cities issued notices telling businesses to close their doors. The world had experienced nothing like the pandemic in a century. On March 10, a week after the Fed's move, Seattle closed public schools, making it the first major city in the United States to do so.[17] Anthony Fauci, director of the National Institute of Allergy and Infectious Diseases, told members of Congress that the coronavirus was ten times as deadly as seasonal flu. News broke the following day that March Madness, the college basketball tournament, would be played without fans.

It was not clear that elected politicians were going to respond quickly to the unfolding crisis. Despite Mexico's near-zero case count, President Trump seized the moment to push for his long-sought wall on the nation's southern border, tweeting, "We need the Wall more than ever!"[18] He also took the new opportunity to critique Powell, posting that "our pathetic, slow moving Federal Reserve, headed by Jay Powell" should have cut interest rates by more.

As fear began to grip society, tumult on Wall Street was magnifying the tension. Monday, March 9, had seen stock futures—which traders use to bet on the market before it opens at 9:30 A.M.—plunge so swiftly that they triggered what is called a "circuit breaker," in which exchanges halt trading for fifteen minutes to avert a downward spiral of panic selling.[*] Rapid declines continued from there.[19] Markets breathed a short-lived sigh of relief as the Trump administration floated the possibility of a government stimulus package on March 10, but swiftly worsened again. On March 11, as the World Health Organization officially declared the coronavirus a global pandemic,[20] the Dow dove 10 percent in its worst percentage drop since 1987.[21]

"Stocks plummeted once again on Thursday after President Donald Trump and the Federal Reserve both failed to quell concerns over the economic slowdown stemming from the coronavirus," CNBC declared. It was evident where investors were looking for relief. The stock market mirrored what was happening in financial markets more broadly.

Before getting into a more detailed account of the carnage—the episode in this book's introduction—it is worth going over how the different markets that had begun to break down worked in normal times.

When someone buys a stock, they are buying an ownership stake in a company, often referred to as equity. Stocks offer high paybacks—

---

[*] This happened partly because Russian and Saudi Arabian authorities failed to agree on oil production cuts the night before, sending prices lower, worsening the outlook for energy companies and rocking already-worried stock investors.

"returns," in financial lingo—because they are risky. Stockholders own part of the company they have invested in, so they are on the hook for its success or failure, and they are the last to be paid back if the company fails. Popular stock indexes like the S&P 500, Nasdaq, and the Dow Jones Industrial Average track a bundle of individual stocks, and they are the most closely followed real-time financial data because they reflect assets that are held widely, trade quickly, and are easy to understand. When you turn on CNBC or Bloomberg Television at any given moment, you're likely to see trackers of the indexes flash across the bottom of the screen in bright red and green, quoted in point and percentage terms.

Individual company stock prices fluctuate as investors become more or less confident about the business's future, but they can also move because they are caught up in broader market sentiment. For instance, if investors are worried about the economy, they may ditch the stocks of even healthy companies so that they can shift their money into safer places. Because indexes lump together many firms, their movements tend to reflect the business environment. That's what the plummeting stock market gauges in the first and second week of March were saying: The outlook had taken a sudden, precipitous turn for the worse.

Stocks are just part of the financial story on any given day. Debt markets, where companies and governments borrow money to pay for their operations or investments, are an even more critical part of the world's financial infrastructure—totaling $105.9 trillion in 2020, compared to $95 trillion socked in global stock markets.[22] Companies, federal governments, and municipalities use so-called primary debt markets to sell bonds, which are basically IOUs that promise repayment at a future date, generally with regular payments in the interim. The people who buy the bonds can hold them to maturity, profiting from those interest payments, or can trade them on a "secondary market," where the bond's price and yield—the amount a holder earns for hanging on to the security over time—fluctuate as time passes and economic conditions change.

A bond's price moves in the opposite direction of its yield. Let's say you bought a bond from your favorite doughnut company for $100, and it promised to pay 2 percent annual coupons over three years. That bond is always going to pay back the same amount: $2 three times, and $100 at the end of the contract. But things can change over the course of those years. Maybe interest rates across the economy shoot higher, so that the $6 you're earning for tying up your money is suddenly lackluster. Maybe the doughnut company finds itself in financial distress amid a croissant craze, it looks like the business might go bankrupt, and the risk that it will not pay back the $100 in full and on time increases. Such changes will cause the bond's price to fall on the secondary market. As the bond's price falls, let's say to $95, the yield rises. Someone who buys the bond is still going to get $106 over the course of the bond's life. But instead of being a $6 return on a $100 investment, that is now an $11 return on their $95 investment.

It is trickier to read bond market movements as a signal of whether the economy is experiencing good or bad news because many drivers cause bond prices to fluctuate. For instance, worried stockholders tend to shift their cash into safe bonds during times of trouble because bondholders get paid back before stock owners if a company goes into bankruptcy. Scared investors especially flock into U.S. government debt, called Treasuries. American government debt is seen as very safe, and is generally easy to buy and sell.

While the term "bond" is generally used to refer to long-term debt, companies—especially banks—also borrow money for short periods of time in debt markets by issuing what is called commercial paper. Short-term borrowing makes up what is commonly called the money market, along with other types of debt that mature within a year, including short-term Treasury debt, called bills. Money market mutual funds, which ordinary investors use to stash cash and earn a slightly higher return, invest heavily in commercial paper and government bills.

Debt markets are traded in heavily by big market players like hedge funds and exchange-traded funds, and are interconnected with stock, currency, and commodity markets by a series of short-term borrowing and lending arrangements. Together, they make an intricate financial spiderweb that exists on the edges of traditional banking.[23] The March 2020 crisis touched every part of that universe.

Through March 9, markets were selling off, but conditions were orderly. It was clear that investors wanted to drop holdings that were likely to be affected by the health crisis, like stocks and risky corporate bonds, in search of safer investments. Prices on longer-term Treasury bonds climbed and yields dipped as people scrambled to put money somewhere safe. Everything looked more or less like one would expect, given the huge economic shock the pandemic seemed sure to bring. When the New York Fed ramped up temporary cash infusions for major players in short-term markets that day, analysts labeled the move prudent but precautionary.[24]

Fed officials in Washington spent that Monday—about a week out from their surprise rate cut—talking about whether they might need to make another move at their upcoming meeting on March 18. They were far from fixed on that plan. In fact, they had begun to think about how they could tweak the language in their post-meeting statement to leave their options open without cutting immediately.

Then, over a short forty-eight hours, markets began to fall apart.

The change started on March 11, when the announcement that the world was officially experiencing a pandemic helped to send the stock market into free fall. After that day, what had looked like an orderly withdrawal from money market funds began to look more like the modern version of a run on the bank. Investors asked for their investments back en masse, and funds had to shuffle to free up cash.[25] In the process, they stopped buying commercial paper. Worried companies, seeing that they would lose a crucial source of funding as the short-term debt market froze, rushed to draw on their lines of credit with banks.

Banks too began to run into a problem: Their balance sheets were getting bigger as customers drew down loans and kept cash on deposit and as securities began to rapidly change hands. The biggest banks were required to maintain easy-to-tap capital—essentially equity from shareholders that could cover possible losses—in proportion to their exposures thanks to one of the key regulations that had been beefed up after the 2008 crisis. The regulation in question did not distinguish between risky and non-risky holdings: Banks would need to have the same capital whether they were holding a dicey loan or a Treasury loan. As banks and their affiliated dealers swelled their balance sheets and tiptoed close to the constraint, it could discourage them from carrying out low-risk, low-reward activities—like temporarily holding government debt.[26] Banks did not want to breach those limits, because maintaining more capital would cost them. They stopped serving as market go-betweens willing to buy and sell bonds. Their hesitance was compounded by financial reality. The bonds increasingly looked like they might be hard to off-load, and nobody wanted to wind up stuck with them.

As people tried to sell investments of all varieties and few buyers stepped up to meet that rush of supply, things started to get messy.

Foreign companies had issued a huge amount of debt denominated in dollars in the preceding years, and suddenly they found themselves struggling to renew it—an issue exacerbated by the turmoil in short-term money markets, where many of the firms turned to raise dollars. Both companies abroad and foreign central banks had begun to sell Treasury securities to make sure they would have dollars to pay the bills and, in the case of the central banks, to keep their own currencies stable. As that happened, normal price relationships in Treasury markets began to jump out of whack.

Market problems quickly went from serious to catastrophic. Hedge funds were maintaining a popular trade that went bad amid gyrations in the government bond market, and they alone would dump $90 billion in Treasuries in March, by one estimate, as foreign holders sold $300 billion.[27] As so many investors rushed to sell, trading in the U.S. government debt that formed the backbone of all other markets started to deteriorate.

The Fed was desperate to restore normalcy. Allowing the Treasury market to remain broken would risk permanently damaging its reputation for safety—something that would weaken the very foundation of global finance. Powell, Clarida, Williams, Logan, and a handful of other Fed staff officials had spent those early weeks in March deciding how to respond to a crisis that was metastasizing before their very eyes. On March 12, the New York Fed announced that it would accelerate a series of already-planned government debt purchases, ones that they had been performing just to maintain market smoothness. They would also buy longer-dated bonds, not just shorter-term bills, taking the other side of transactions as investors across the market tried to sell government debt that nobody wanted to buy.[28] Despite the intervention, markets continued to perform badly. On Friday, March 13, the New York Fed announced that it would buy half of its monthly bond purchase allotment in a single day in what was a quick-fire, powerful change, at least on paper.[29] It fixed nothing. The central bank clearly needed to meet over the weekend.

On March 15—the Sunday detailed at the start of this book—the Fed took dramatic action. Central bankers slashed interest rates from 1 percent, where they'd been since March 3, to zero. They rolled out a massive bond-buying program and improved the conditions offered on swap lines, which allowed foreign central banks to more easily access dollar funding, which they could then funnel to banks and businesses in their jurisdictions that needed dollars to make good on debts or carry out everyday transactions. The package meant business: The Fed was trying to say that it would do whatever it took to restore markets to normality.

"We're going to go in strong starting tomorrow," Powell said during his post-meeting press conference, as he was describing the planned bond purchases. "We're really going to use our tools to do what we need to do here, which is restore these important markets to normal function."

Powell and his colleagues knew that the March 15 package, as sweeping as it was, would not be enough. The Fed was moving more quickly than it ever had in any crisis across its more than century-long history, but there were real questions about whether it was moving fast enough. Markets were not built on the assumption that a worldwide shock could cause global commerce to grind to a halt in a matter of days.

That was exactly what was happening. States across the country were imposing lockdowns and curfews, leaving an army of waitresses, bartenders, and other service workers without jobs or any obvious way to make ends meet.[30] Broadway had shut down on March 12. As central bank officials were announcing that they would slash rates to zero, New York City's government was rolling out news of its own: It would impose a shutdown on tens of thousands of bars and restaurants, along with the local public school system, to contain the spreading pandemic.[31]

Many investors were hoping the Fed would come up with a no-holds-barred response that would rescue the corners of markets that still looked perilous. The central bank had done a lot on that frantic Sunday, but it hadn't put forward any specific programs to help commercial paper issuers and investors or to stop the bleeding at money market funds. Low rates would do little to fix the meltdown under way, and with the Treasury market functioning badly, it wasn't clear that super-cheap borrowing costs would even make it to consumers. The turmoil was enough to gum up the flow of new credit as banks waited to see what would happen next. The Fed desperately needed to unclog the financial pipes.

"If the Fed waits too long," Bank of America strategists had written in a note about money market funds the Friday before, "the risk of a large-scale run could increase."[32]

After Fed officials had wrapped up their March 15 meeting, the boardroom where policy makers usually sat elbow to elbow eerily empty, Powell pulled Andreas Lehnert to the side. Lehnert, who had led the Board's fifty-person financial stability division since 2016, had been looking into what tools the Fed had to rescue markets. While the central bank had used its emergency lending authorities extensively during the financial meltdown that had swept the globe twelve years earlier, postcrisis reforms had changed the so-called lender of last resort powers, and markets themselves had evolved. Lehnert and his team had been working with their colleagues in New York and at the Boston Fed to sketch out rough outlines of how they could reestablish the programs that had supported key money markets in and after 2008, given the new constraints.

It was time, Powell said, to get them ready.

Lehnert left the meeting room, walked through the Fed's echoing hallways to a temporary office he was using amid renovations—a musty, cramped space with glaring lights—and got to work. The Fed had the rough contours of a plan, but enacting it quickly was going to be no easy task. The cerebral economist, who had a quick and quirky sense of humor and read books on disasters for fun, knew he was in for a string of long nights.

He was in his office plugging away, messaging colleagues and liaising with lawyers, when the next morning dawned, strange and terrifying. Even after the Fed's massive Sunday announcement, stock futures plunged before trading began, hitting the "limit down" trigger meant to stop irrational selling. When the actual market opened, it plummeted 8 percent immediately and tripped another "circuit breaker" intended to stop the downward spiral.[33]

An array of corporations seemed likely to face a credit downgrade and investors were pulling money from funds that track junk bonds, the lowest-rated company debt. Investment trusts holding real estate bonds were tap-dancing on the brink of a meltdown, and though the Fed was buying some mortgage-backed debt, that was no cure-all.[34] The market for state and local bonds had ground to a complete standstill. New municipal bond issuances were being put on hold, raising questions about how public entities would raise the money they needed to pay the costs associated with the unfolding public health crisis.[35] Even as the Fed pledged to buy massive quantities of Treasury bonds, the market for government debt remained clogged. It was like the financial crisis that had rocked the global system in 2008 all over again, but it extended to markets that had remained safe in the depths of that global panic. So many were melting down in tandem that even seasoned investors did not know exactly what was happening. It wasn't clear where disaster was going to rear its head next.

Chair Powell sent out emails before and around 7:00 A.M. that Monday making it clear that it was time to start the next phase of the rescue. America's central bank had a lot of work to do to keep the world's financial system from tearing apart.

Randy Quarles, the Fed's vice-chair for supervision, had always been the type to work long hours. Friends who had traveled internationally with him when he was at Treasury joked that while everyone else brought magazines on overnight flights or slept, Quarles would pull a serious volume out of his bag and plug away throughout the trip.

The early weeks of March 2020 were putting even his habits to the test.

He had spent the end of February on the phone or in meetings with the increasingly panicked elites of global finance. He had traveled to San Francisco late on the afternoon of Thursday, February 27, to meet with bank supervisors and had added on a Friday meeting with David Marcus, the Facebook executive spearheading the tech giant's attempted digital currency product, which was running into regulatory hurdles.* But instead of focusing on the future of currency on February 28, Quarles had found himself taking calls from worried colleagues and contacts from an office inside the San Francisco Fed. By the following week, his life had become a never-ending series of conversations centered on the unfolding crisis.

He dialed in to the Fed's March 2 meeting from San Francisco, then traveled back to Washington on a late-night flight the next day. He caught a few hours of sleep in his suite at the Willard Hotel before heading back to his office at the Fed's board to get on a 7:00 A.M. conference call with Fed staff. He joined back-to-back calls and meetings on the hour or half hour that entire day—including one with Daniel Tarullo, his unofficial predecessor and sometimes critic. On March 10, he checked in with large foreign banks as the Fed tried to make sure that they would remain safe at a time of extreme stress, speaking with Barclays' CEO, Credit Suisse's managing director, Deutsche Bank USA's managing director, and a gamut of Treasury and global financial stability officials. The pace of work was frantic; so, increasingly, was the tone on Wall Street.

Quarles caught his typical late-night flight from Washington's Dulles Airport back to Salt Lake City that Thursday, leaving unfinished papers on his desk in Washington. By Sunday, March 15, things had devolved so sharply that he realized a nonstop lineup of crisis calls would prevent him from flying back across the country that night. By the middle of the week, it was clear that a one- or two-day delay would stretch into something far longer—the Fed's headquarters was shutting down amid lockdowns meant to contain the virus, without an obvious return date. After years of commuting, Quarles was about to shift to work-from-home from the mountain West, where he would be logging on each day from his library-like home office, an opulent room lined with backlit bookshelves and a sleek fireplace. He

---

* Randall Guynn, a Davis Polk lawyer, had previously pled Libra's case to Quarles in D.C., *The Washington Post* had reported in 2019. Guynn was Quarles's former colleague and close personal friend, and the vice-chair met with him and other Davis Polk lawyers far more often than with other banking lawyers, his calendars showed, and far more than his predecessor ever had. It was an unusually clear case of coziness between a regulator and the representatives of the regulated.

had spent his career hoping to spend more time in Utah, but a global pandemic was not the catalyst he had envisioned.

In late February, Quarles had been slow to believe that the coronavirus would be the big deal Powell was convinced it was destined to become. But by the time the central bank began its rescue operation and the world shifted to work-from-home mode, he had snapped into action as the Fed's eyes and ears at the big banks.

Quarles found himself facing down a potentially huge job. The global crisis a decade earlier had made clear that if a meltdown tanked big, interconnected financial institutions, it would make credit hard to access for families and businesses, deepening and lengthening the economic disaster as spending dried up and firms were forced to tighten their belts and fire their employees. The first critical thing was to make sure that the banks sitting at the center of the system were prepared for whatever might lay ahead.

As the Fed had prepared to roll out its massive policy package that Sunday, Quarles had scheduled a call with Randall Guynn at Davis Polk and Rodgin Cohen at Sullivan & Cromwell, two of the nation's leading bank lawyers. The top legal minds were also the most efficient way to quickly take the banks' pulse.

The always-punctual Fed vice-chair left the pair waiting for an hour and a half as he and his fellow Fed governor Michelle Bowman discussed the Fed's Sunday policy package, which both had misgivings about. He thought they should vote for it in a show of unanimity if nothing else.* With no assistants around in his new setup, he had no way to flag to the lawyers that he would be late. He was mortified.

When he dialed in, deeply apologetic, the pair reaffirmed what he had expected. Postcrisis regulatory reforms had left the biggest banks with what they hoped would be manageable exposures and far more capital to cover losses than they had held in 2008, but nobody really knew how things would play out at a moment of such grave uncertainty. The banks themselves were worried about the remainder of the system. If the market for corporate bonds remained effectively

---

* Bowman, a Trump appointee who was focused on community banks, did ultimately vote for the rate cut; Loretta Mester, the Federal Reserve Bank of Cleveland president, was the sole dissenter. Quarles himself deferred to Powell when it came to monetary policy, airing any disagreements he had privately.

closed, and if trading in Treasuries continued to break down, it would echo through all of finance.

While Quarles thought that banks had enough capital to weather even a very severe storm—and he had consistently favored less regulation and fewer restrictions for banks—he was also realistic about the politics of the moment. In 2007 and 2008, banks had continued paying out dividends to shareholders and buying back their own stock to push up share prices even as their prospects took a dramatic turn for the worse amid the unfolding mortgage meltdown. The actions had been intended to project strength. Instead, handing out capital as the world burned had left the firms weaker as they teetered on the brink of bankruptcy, making the crisis even worse than it needed to be.

The Fed did not want to witness a pandemic-era rerun, and Quarles expected that if banks did not take some action early on, they would be forced to cut both buybacks and dividends down the road. Buybacks made up about 70 percent of capital payouts and were comparatively easy to suspend. Dividends made up the smaller chunk but were given so much psychological importance that cutting them might spook investors and send bank stock prices plummeting— cutting into executive stock-based pay packages and, ironically, leaving the banks with less capital, since stock valuation was a big part of the equation.

Quarles had begun pressuring banks to suspend their share buybacks around March 10. His push started with JP Morgan Chase, but his efforts to communicate with it were complicated by the fact that CEO Jamie Dimon had been hospitalized following an aortic tear. Dimon's dangerous heart rupture had happened in the wee hours of March 5, when the chief executive officer had awoken at 4:00 A.M. worrying about the doom about to befall the economy thanks to the unfolding pandemic. After calling his colleagues in London and Mumbai, he had settled in to read some newspapers and promptly felt a ripping in his chest. He was out of commission for that critical week.

Fortunately, the executives Quarles was talking with at other banks were receptive to his message. It would be better for them to announce that they were suspending share buybacks than to wait for regulators to force them to cut off everything. James Gorman, the Morgan Stanley chief executive, had begun to talk to his fellow bank heads about a voluntary suspension, coaxing the grudging into an agreement.

The optics would be better if big banks made and announced a suspension themselves than if the Fed mandated one. If it seemed like the government had forced banks to stop some payouts, investors would suspect they were not healthy. On the morning of March 15, the nation's largest banks announced that they were choosing—of their own volition—to cut off share buybacks. Bank of America, Bank of New York Mellon, Citigroup, Goldman Sachs, JP Morgan Chase, Morgan Stanley, State Street Corporation, and Wells Fargo would all begin conserving capital.*

"The decision is consistent with actions by the Federal Reserve, the administration, and the Congress," the Financial Services Forum, the consortium of the largest banks' chief executives, wrote in an announcement explaining the decision.[36]

"We have the capabilities and balance sheet to support the financial system and all of our constituencies," JP Morgan said in a press release. "We stand ready to support our government in any way we can."[37]

As the announcement rolled out, Quarles was already on to the next goal. He wanted to convince banks to tap the pressure valve the Fed offered them during times of trouble. The discount window had been around since the Fed's very inception, and it allowed deposit-taking banks to take what were effectively short-term loans from the Fed. While it could be a valuable source of funding in times of trouble, stigma had dogged it for years. Banks were concerned that touching it would signal that they were in trouble and tank their stock prices.

The Fed knew that some banks—not the big ones at the center of the financial system, but ones that were big enough to matter—could probably use the funding in those uncertain days of the early pandemic but wouldn't take it unless prodded. Policy makers had sweetened the discount window's terms on March 15, hoping to lessen their hesitation.

That alone probably would not be enough, Quarles knew. He and

---

* The decision came together just in time: Gorman, who had orchestrated it, would be diagnosed with a symptomatic case of coronavirus early that week.

his colleagues had helped the biggest banks to coalesce around a plan to essentially hold hands and jump, tapping the window in hopes that slightly smaller firms would follow suit. Gorman's Morgan Stanley went first on March 16. It was then quickly followed by seven of its peers, including Goldman Sachs and JP Morgan.[38]

The banks insisted that they had plenty of funding access, but "it is important to lead by demonstrating the value of the Federal Reserve's discount window facility," read a Financial Services Forum release following the action.[39] Investors should not take the move as a sign of weakness, in short, but other banks should take it as a sign that the discount window was open for business.

The delicate dance Quarles, his colleagues at the Fed, and banks were performing midway through March, as the world around them melted down, showed how much the 2008 disaster and the bank failures it spawned remained burned into the psyche of regulators and institutions alike. The onset of the pandemic had eerie similarities, and nobody wanted another banking crisis. Nor did regulators want a situation in which banks went into hibernation mode, battening down the hatches and refusing to lend or make markets until the outlook cleared. The banks, for their part, wanted to redeem themselves and show just how much they had matured in the dozen years since they had helped to crash the global economy.

As the hours crawled by in an endless stream of negative headlines and declining stock quotes, though, the unfolding cash crunch also demonstrated how 2020 was different. A dozen years earlier, weakness had surfaced in the guts of the financial system and poured outward, ricocheting through the global economy. This time around, the shock had come from outside, and major cracks had yet to surface in the banking system.

Even so, a meltdown appeared to be strengthening its grip on markets, as investors struggled to dump even seemingly valuable assets. Banks might have looked well prepared, but the same could not be said for money market mutual funds, corporate bond funds, real estate investment trusts, and investment vehicles of many types. The same regulations that had left the banks themselves able to weather the pandemic shock had pushed financial activities into more lightly regulated nonbank companies.

Bank of America, JP Morgan, and their counterparts were not be-all, end-all players in the modern financial system. Ensuring their safety and soundness was just a first step.

Powell spent that Monday, March 16, scrambling to figure out a fix to the wider-ranging problems. He had shifted to working from home in Maryland for the first time that day. He joined phone calls with staff and Treasury Secretary Steven Mnuchin as Pippa, the family terrier, ran in and out of his office, excited to have Dad around. Susie, his youngest daughter, had been forced to come home from her senior year at Princeton, so the house was fuller than usual.

Always an early riser, Powell had begun his morning by emailing his colleagues to get the ball rolling on a rescue package for still-flailing markets. His schedule was packed with calls with staff and global central bankers, interspersed with unscheduled consultations with his close lieutenants and other government officials. His conversations were punctuated by the bad news flashing across his television screen: The Dow Jones Industrial Average sank so much at the 9:30 A.M. market opening that trading was again halted. Panic reigned not just in stocks but across Wall Street.

As ordinary Americans hoarded toilet paper and nonperishables, companies were trying to hoard cash, but some were struggling to maintain even their normal borrowing levels. Royal Caribbean Cruises had been hit hard as the virus canceled vacations and as images of disease-stricken boats held at sea deterred new bookings. Its short-term funding costs had skyrocketed from a roughly 2 percent interest rate to more than 4 percent over the course of that mid-March weekend. The utility company Exelon had seen its financing costs rise by a similar degree, people familiar with the matter said.[40] The Fed's moves had done next to nothing to restore order to the commercial paper market, which remained at a standstill in part because the money market funds that typically bought short-term securities were barely functioning. If companies could not fund themselves by renewing their debt, which looked increasingly likely, the consequences would cascade through the real economy. Businesses and banks would come up short on cash to pay the bills and keep the lights on. Powell knew that the solution to the market's problems had to lie in the emergency lending powers he had asked Andreas Lehnert and his team to investigate—often called 13(3) after the section of the Federal Reserve Act that enables them.

Crisis-fighting was part of the Fed's founding rationale, but the early Fed had lacked sufficiently expansive powers to stave off big problems. After its 1913 founding, the Fed could loan commercial member banks short-term money against only gold or real bills,* allowing it to support one very specific corner of financial markets. Emphasizing the limited scope of those powers, the Virginian lawmaker and Fed architect Carter Glass had told the Senate in January 1922 that the reserve banks "do not loan, cannot loan, a dollar to any individual in the United States nor to any concern or corporation in the United States, but only to stockholding banks,"[41] calling the regional reserve outlets "banks of banks."

Throughout the 1910s and 1920s, the government created separate enterprises to support specific kinds of credit—be it rural credit or war finance—when it thought they were necessary.[42] Then came the Great Depression. As banks failed widely and finance came to a screeching halt, President Herbert Hoover asked Congress to widen the types of securities that the Fed could lend against, hoping to create a more useful security net for the whole of the system.

Glass had told him, almost literally, that such a change would happen over his dead body. "Congress will never consent to it while I am alive and my health is excellent," *The Baltimore Sun* reportedly quoted the eternally saucy senator.[43] Before long, the near collapse of the gold standard changed Glass's mind. As business dried up, real bills were in short supply, so the Fed was suddenly scrambling for gold to back notes and meet the public's demand for money. It became clear that the country would suspend convertibility as its gold supply failed to keep up with the country's needs. Glass tried to forestall that.

A first Glass–Steagall Act, passed in February 1932, gave the Fed the ability to issue notes against government securities. It also gave Fed banks a temporary authority to loan to member banks against "satisfactory" collateral, at high interest rates, when the borrowing bank had used up its typically eligible assets. "The decline of the real bills doctrine brought by the Glass–Steagall Act of 1932 opened the

---

* As a reminder, these are agreements between suppliers and producers backed by physical goods and soon to be settled.

door for further legislation that expanded the Fed's powers," Parinitha Sastry would write in a carefully researched history of the Fed's authority.[44]

Charles Sumner Hamlin, the Fed governor, saw the open door and walked right through it. At Hamlin's private urging, Glass proposed an amendment to section 13 of the Federal Reserve Act that July. The new measure allowed the Fed, "in unusual and exigent circumstances," to lend against eligible securities so long as that collateral was "secured to the satisfaction of the Federal Reserve Bank" and the borrower was "unable to secure adequate credit accommodations from other banking institutions." After some minor changes, the proposal passed into law, expanding the types of companies the Fed could keep cash flowing to in times of trouble.

The Fed was a pure banker's bank no more, at least in theory. Yet what the new wording meant was immediately controversial, especially at the Fed Board itself. Officials chose to take a narrow reading of what kind of assets they were allowed to lend against and who they were allowed to lend to, at least at first, and the Fed barely flexed its 13(3) muscles in those early years. Only 123 loans were made with the authority between 1932 and 1936 (among them, reportedly, were loans to a winery secured by barrels of brandy and rum, and loans to another company secured by a marble shipment).[45]

The Fed's power to save flailing companies and investors outside the banking system faded from view in the decades that followed. The authority was occasionally built upon and broadened, but those changes mostly flew under the radar. In 1966, the Board revisited the narrow interpretation it had set out in the 1930s, extending its powers to cover nonmember banks in times of trouble.[46] A critical congressional change to 13(3) in 1987, following the stock market crash that year, broadened the rule's criteria so that it could be used to lend against a wider variety of collateral. The change was meant to enable the Fed to provide loans to securities firms in need.[47]

The cumulative effect of seventy-five years of tinkering came to bear in 2008. As banks and insurance companies found themselves in peril at the height of the financial crisis and as money markets seized up, Bernanke's Fed used its emergency lending powers on a massive scale. Unlike the 1932 Fed, and given more explicit legal latitude by the changes that had happened in the interim, the modern

Fed took an expansive reading of what the 13(3) powers allowed it to do in "unusual and exigent" circumstances. Bernanke and the central bank's creative lawyers rolled out program after program to back up various markets teetering on the brink of disaster. The authority was also used as the legal basis for the big bank bailouts. By November 2008, the programs had made about $700 billion in loans.[48]

Bernanke's Fed had created an emergency loan program template that could be pulled off the shelf and reused for various markets. It had a standard basic structure. The Fed would make a loan to a "special-purpose vehicle," a legal entity set up purely to carry out the program and keep its activities organized. The vehicle could then purchase securities or offer loans to investors in exchange for specific collateral—bundles of car loans, municipal debt, or small business loans. The interest rates and strings attached on most of the market-wide programs were set so that they would be used as a last-ditch option, not as a replacement for private credit. The idea was to convince investors in critical markets that if things got bad enough, the central bank would be there to buy temporarily troubled securities. That knowledge would prevent investors from dumping the holdings in a rush to limit losses. The programs could act as a stabilizing force.

It was a more sophisticated version of what Marriner Eccles had done when he turned the attention of his panicked bank lobby to the Federal Reserve's money delivery in an effort to break his bank run in the 1930s: The mere act of making it clear that cash would remain accessible—and of saying "there's plenty more where that came from"—had a calming effect. During 2008, Bernanke's Fed rolled out sixteen separate facilities, including ones aimed at supporting individual institutions like Bear Stearns or Citigroup as they went through mergers or tried to survive particularly turbulent periods.[49]

Yet the scope of those bailouts irked Congress. Riding a wave of popular anger at the bank rescues, lawmakers had mandated in post-crisis reforms that future emergency Fed programs should be available to a broad-based set of borrowers (lawyers in 2020 said that would likely be interpreted to mean at least five eligible users). Lawmakers also made it clear that the Treasury secretary would need to approve any decision to use 13(3), along with program terms.

Bernanke had shown off how mighty the Fed's lending programs could be. Congress, recognizing that power, had wanted the Fed's technocrats to have buy-in from the government's politically account-able actors. In 2020, that would mean that Powell needed Mnuchin's signature for any market rescue.

Powell and Mnuchin had begun to speak about resurrecting some of the Bernanke Fed's market rescue programs shortly after Riyadh, and Mnuchin was receptive. By that painful week in mid-March, he had agreed to back up the programs with Treasury money, which would make them easier to get off the ground quickly and at scale.

Powell had asked Lael Brainard to oversee design of the programs alongside the Fed's lawyers, led by Mark E. Van Der Weide, and Andreas Lehnert. Brainard had been at the nexus of markets, econom-ics, and politics long enough to be the right person for the delicate job. Plus, Lehnert and the rest of the financial stability staff reported to her because she chaired the Board's financial stability committee. By the middle of March, Powell had also asked Brainard to join the decision-making troika, a testament to the key position she was play-ing in a turbulent time.

Like Powell, Brainard had since late February been worried about the pandemic turning into an American economic disaster. She had spent the early days of the pandemic's global spread in Amsterdam for a global financial stability meeting, one attended by Singaporeans who were already facing an initial wave of the virus. As she walked through the bustle and rush of the Frankfurt airport on the way home, watching travelers from all over the world whisk off to other corners of the globe, it had hit her clearly: This thing is going to spread. When she got back to the Fed Board, she had popped her head into colleagues' offices. *This,* she told them, *is going to be bad.*

Unfortunately, recognizing the scale of the disaster and getting on top of it were different things. Brainard, Lehnert, the Fed's lawyers, and other staff members had been scrambling to draw up the legal paperwork and agreements with the Treasury that they needed to restart market rescue programs in 2008 and set up new ones that seemed likely to be needed, but the crisis was moving faster than they could. Even though Fed staff members in Washington, New York, and Boston were working around the clock, it took time to adjust the old designs so that they would work in 2020 and comply with the law. Meanwhile, the market for short-term company debt was disastrous, and it seemed possible that money market mutual funds would face runs before the Fed could unveil a rescue. Officials were racing against chaos, but by mid-March, they were losing.

"The only surprising thing is that it took them this long to do it," an economist at an asset manager told *The New York Times* on Tuesday, March 17, after the Fed and Treasury announced that they would restart the Commercial Paper Funding Facility, or CPFF. He was expressing a widely shared sentiment.[50]

Investors were relieved to see the 10:45 A.M. press release, and happy to know that the 2008 throwback would rescue the choked market. The commercial paper market was used by big businesses like Pfizer, Royal Dominion, and DuPont for short-term financing, so restarting it was essential to keeping companies current on payroll and paying their utility bills. The Fed would go on that day to offer a second program, one that could get short-term funding to banks at the core of the financial system, another welcome development. Stock indexes in the United States rallied and closed higher that day partly because it was becoming clear that the central bank would come to the rescue with more than just rate cuts.

But the moves also left Wall Street wondering: What took so long, when will there be more, and do they recognize how bad this is?

"It's on the mend," a TD Securities analyst said. "But it's not healed yet."

Unfinished business abounded, and it was becoming clearer with each passing day that the Fed was going to need to push its powers well past the 2008 playbook. Treasury markets were still disastrous. Investors continued to worry about the corporate bond market, which at $10 trillion dwarfed the $1 trillion commercial paper market.

Lehnert's financial stability division at the Fed had been set up in 2010 as a sort of disaster planning and response team, and this was clearly showtime.* He and his colleagues had begun to map out

---

* "We have spent many years thinking about events that were unlikely, improbable, and, frankly, weird," Lehnert would go on to tell Bloomberg. One of those out-of-the-box catastrophes? A global pandemic.

which markets the jobs in America's economy depended upon. Keeping corporate debt, municipal debt, and midsize business borrowing functional would be key to keeping America employed, they determined. Lehnert began to refer to the strategy internally as "covering the waterfront."

Central bankers were, again, learning from the recent past. In 2008, the Fed had saved the banks and the key money markets while hoping that Congress would step in to help other types of businesses and households, which the central bank's powers were less well suited to assist. A debt-wary and divided legislature failed to deliver, passing spending programs that were too small for the job at hand and leaving much of the rescue to the central bank. Families lost their homes, workers lost jobs, and companies closed shop as slow demand made business untenable. An anemic recovery followed.

Much like that earlier episode, when Congress and the White House had passed relief packages that were too small to deal with the problem at hand amid partisan bickering and deficit worries, it was not clear in mid-March how effective the elected government's response would be. By that week, as America's death toll from the virus exceeded one hundred for the first time, the Trump administration was at least coalescing around the idea that the virus was a major problem: "I felt it was a pandemic long before it was called a pandemic," the president had said from a White House lectern on Tuesday, March 17.

Trump had signed an $8.3 billion relief bill on March 6 that kicked off vaccine research and gave states money for a health response, among other measures, but no one mistook that for a sufficient response.[51] The administration had been suggesting a payroll tax holiday to deal with the remainder of the problem, but lawmakers had shown little enthusiasm for a form of relief that would do nothing to help the legions of newly unemployed.

The administration announced that Tuesday that it was proposing $1 trillion in relief spending, including sending $250 billion in checks to millions of Americans. The idea echoed something former Obama administration economic official Jason Furman had suggested in the opinion pages of The Wall Street Journal a little more than a week earlier and a proposal that Utah Republican Mitt Romney was making, so the policy seemed likely to garner some bipartisan support.[52] Still, it was not clear how much of the administration's package would realistically pass into law. In fact, it wasn't even obvious what the broader package would look like. Mnuchin, whom Trump had chosen to quarterback the effort, was not yet disclosing particulars.

"The Treasury secretary declined to share details of his proposal, including a dollar figure for the direct payments to Americans," *The New York Times* reported.

"It is a big number," he had told reporters on Capitol Hill.[53]

At the Fed, officials did not want to repeat the mistake of saving Wall Street as the rest of America was left hanging, hoping that enough help would come from the rest of the government.

"My goal, our goal, is to bring this to Main Street," Patrick Harker, president of the Federal Reserve Bank of Philadelphia, said that Tuesday.[54]

The ambition was nice. The question was how to make it reality.

Chapter 8

A CORPORATE HOUSE OF CARDS

Mike Tyson actually said it so much more colorfully
when he noted that everyone has a plan until they get
punched in the mouth.

—*Jerome Powell, 2016 FOMC transcripts*

W HEN PEPSICO, EXXONMOBIL, VERIZON, and a handful
of other major investment-grade companies issued bonds on
March 17, 2020, Wall Street practically cheered.[1]
The terms, by any reasonable metric that had existed before the
pandemic took hold, were terrible. Oil giant Exxon had paid the
same amount to borrow $8.5 billion that it had the prior August,[2]
even though interest rates for safe government debt had dipped
sharply since, which should have made for cheaper corporate borrowing costs.[3] Much of what was happening was desperation fund-
raising: Short-term markets were a disaster, so firms were trying to
ensure they had cash on hand to keep up with their obligations by
borrowing longer-term, which is usually more expensive.

But after tense days in which the corporate bond market had been
essentially shut, it was a headline-grabbing miracle that a handful of
America's largest companies had managed to issue at all. "The opportunities to bring new offerings have been few and often far between,"
Bloomberg reported. The coronavirus pandemic had made investors
take a warier look at the massive debt pile sitting on corporate balance
sheets. Even for the companies with the highest ratings and the lowest chance of default, spreads—the premium corporations were pay-

ing to borrow relative to rates on government bonds—had roughly doubled since the start of March. The riskier high-yield bond market hadn't been open to companies looking to raise cash since March 4, as their spreads rocketed to the highest level in nine years.

The momentary relief in parts of the corporate debt market had been enabled by the Fed's Sunday afternoon rate cut and bond-buying announcement, paired with its Monday afternoon pledge to shore up commercial paper. The volley of quick action had stoked investor hopes that more help was on the way. Even amid the reprieve, it was only the healthiest and most well-established companies managing to sell bonds. The outlook for credit markets globally remained perilous.

Private debt markets—an important corner of finance where companies could raise cash without meaningful involvement from banks—had ground to a standstill. By Wednesday morning, U.S. state and local government bond markets were suffering badly, as mutual funds that held the debt were forced to sell their holdings to meet an ongoing wave of redemptions from their own investors. News headlines were calling it the "worst muni rout since 1984."[4] Some $13 billion in scheduled state and local bond offerings had been put on hold or canceled as the market stopped working, by Bloomberg's estimate. Credit rating agencies were steadily slashing their evaluation of companies' prospects, cutting Occidental Petroleum Corporation from investment-grade to junk status two days after slashing Lufthansa into speculative territory.[5] Moody's Investors Service analysts were warning that more downgrades were coming.[6] Indexes that tracked risky debt were posting massive outflows.

From where Fed and Treasury officials sat, it was clear that a financial crisis remained possible. On Wall Street, analysts had begun to whisper that one had already arrived.

Camped out at kitchen tables and hastily assembled home offices, Fed staff members and officials were collecting information on the ongoing collapse cascading across financial markets. Financial stability director Andreas Lehnert and his team had finished the "cover the waterfront" table showing which parts of the economy were likely to cost the most jobs and had begun to circulate it.[7] Small businesses, state and local governments, and big companies might fire people by the tens of thousands if the financial arrangements underpinning them—the web of long-term bonds and short-term borrowing that enables the modern economy—suddenly tanked. Fed governor Lael Brainard, who was working from the attic office of her crowded house in Chevy Chase (all three of her daughters and her niece were home for the lockdown), consulted it so often that the map of America's layoff risks would remain burned in her brain for years to come.

The threat that a mountain of debt could go bad was shifting from hypothetical to highly possible. As demonstrated by the media's sudden and intense interest in which companies could issue bonds and which could not, corporate debt had emerged as a towering financial vulnerability. Other big investment categories, from real estate debt to money market funds, looked hazardous.

Brainard, Lehnert, and their colleagues knew how shaky the financial structures that underpinned American economic life might prove to be if the crisis dragged on. An unexpected shock had set the unraveling into action, but the weaknesses in the system that made the stakes so high in 2020 had been building in plain sight for years.

Jerome Powell had in 2016, when he was a Fed governor, described America's financial system as having an "unwieldy regulatory apparatus and vibrant shadow banking sector."[*] It was that unfortunate combination that was suddenly coming to bear.

"Shadow banks" were lenders and financial companies that were typically much less regulated than official banks. They had been a feature of the American system for generations, from the trust companies of the 1907 panic to the big life insurers and investment companies that spiraled in the 2008 crisis. But as markets had grown more important and more complex, shadow banks had exploded in size. Post-2008 regulation had expanded them further by squeezing some dangerous behaviors out of the banking system and into the murkier world of nonbanks,[8] and the global oversight body called

---

[*] In fact, he had suggested in July 2016, as the Fed was winding down its 2008 emergency lending programs—the original versions of the facilities the Fed was now rolling out—that it could be smart to keep them as part of the tool kit, "unplugged and in dry storage." He suggested that the Fed's role as a lender of last resort in troubled times would probably need to "continue to evolve ever further from the traditional bank-based model."

the Financial Stability Board estimated that the world's nonbanks accounted for about 49.5 percent of the financial system in 2019, up from 42 percent in 2008. By the start of 2020, shadow banks included the mutual funds where companies and ordinary people store their money, the hedge funds that invest for pensions and school endowments, and real estate investment trusts that underpin the nation's hotels and office spaces, to name a few—and they were gambling in ways that U.S. and global financial supervisors had flagged as risky.

Unfortunately, nobody in government had managed to do much to stop it.

The Securities and Exchange Commission, which oversees hedge funds and mutual funds, had been reluctant during the post-2008 years to take on a systemic risk-regulating role, a hesitance outside experts attributed to bandwidth, institutional culture, and legal limitations.[9] The Fed did have a stability mandate, but it was a narrow one. If something was not going to imperil the large banks it oversaw, like Goldman Sachs and Morgan Stanley, it was hard for the Fed to argue that it had any authority to stop the activity. It could and did point out problems with hedge funds or mutual funds, but it did not have tools well tailored to rectify them.

Even the Financial Stability Oversight Council, created specifically to fill in the cracks, did "not generally have clear authority to address broader risks that are not specific to a particular financial entity," a Government Accountability Office report would later find.[10] The council had dialed back some of the sway it did have under Mnuchin's watch. The Trump administration Treasury had stopped the policy of designating shadow banks as systemically important, which would have subjected them to stronger oversight, opting to designate activities as risky instead. The council had continued to release assessments of risks to the system, but those were the hopes-and-prayers version of oversight. They typically pointed to problems in gentle language without setting out much of a road map toward solving them.

It was not shocking that Congress had failed to give its patchwork of financial agencies more clear-cut authority to regulate more effectively, or that the regulators had failed to more wholeheartedly employ what powers they did have. Financial regulation could be complex and hard to communicate to voters: Beating up on big banks might win elections, but criticizing securitized debt vehicles lacked the same charm. Meanwhile, the people profiting from lax oversight were often deep-pocketed donors who financed Democratic and Republican campaigns alike (at times simultaneously, in a signal that the goal was currying favor rather than installing one ideology into power).[11]

Financial regulators themselves often came from the industry and in some cases planned to return to it once their time in government was over. In 2020, Powell, Clarida, Mnuchin, and Quarles all had private equity or asset management backgrounds, and it seemed likely that some or all of them would return to working in finance once their government service terms ended.* The loudest critics of the revolving door argued that it meant that officials who kept loopholes intact could benefit down the road. Even if one looked at it more charitably, the setup meant that the people in charge of writing the rules had at some point benefited from the system as it existed, and often had friends and former colleagues seated among Wall Street's top brass.

Washington also had practical reasons for failing to tightly police the nonbank financial system: Regulation could stifle innovation and access to credit. The many and varied firms operating on Wall Street enabled deep and broad markets, which in turn allowed the United States government to borrow cheaply, provided the cold hard cash that helped to turn an entrepreneur's dreams into reality, and attracted investment from around the globe to U.S. companies. But those advantages—the fact that so many people could get rich, and that growth could be served so well—could make it tempting to set simple, permissive rules in the face of growing risks, as had been the case in the housing market in the run-up to the 2008 bust.

Whatever motivated it, regulatory inaction leading up to 2020 had again left the financial system with flawed defenses just as the low-rate era was encouraging investors to take ever more dangerous bets.

---

* Quarles would return to asset management after his time in government; Clarida would consult with investment managers before going back to Pimco; Mnuchin would run investment funds; Powell, while still in government at the time of this book's writing, had declined to sign an ethics agreement that would have prevented him from working with financial services companies for four years following his service.

The long years of rock-bottom policy rates and bond buying that the Fed had used to bring the economy back to life following the Great Recession had pushed investors into riskier assets in search of higher returns.

Fed officials knew that was happening, and some, like Eric Rosengren at the Federal Reserve Bank of Boston, had wanted to raise interest rates to prevent it. Most, though, did not think that using Fed rate policy to curb financial excess was worth the cost. Higher rates might slow a building bubble, but they would do so inefficiently by harming the overall economy. Powell had, during a 2016 Fed discussion on the topic, said that he had long accepted the "conventional wisdom" that monetary policy generally shouldn't be used to "lean against the wind" of financial instability—although he counseled against ruling it out altogether. It might make sense in unusual cases.

"I'm thinking of a situation in which a broad range of asset prices are moving up well beyond what fundamentals would justify; where the other tools we have don't seem to be addressing the problem or have failed to do so; and where low interest rates are pushing up asset prices and driving credit to excessive levels," he had said.

The excesses bubbling up in some corners of finance in the years leading up to 2020 seemed narrower than the broad, system-wide problems he had described, but they were still serious. Money market reform had not gone far enough to insulate funds from the kind of runs that had imperiled them in 2008, and other vulnerabilities dotted the shadow banking universe.

Obvious, unchecked risk-taking had surfaced at hedge funds in the late 2010s, for instance. Financial regulators knew that funds had been making trades that took advantage of a common Treasury pricing quirk and allowed them to make tiny profits.[12*] To turn those

---

* This is obviously a simplified description of this trading strategy. The nerdy version: Treasury basis trades were a commonly used strategy that took advantage of a difference between cash and futures prices on government debt securities. That difference was called the basis. If the basis was bigger than the cost of buying the Treasury and financing the purchase with short-term debt (repo), the trade was profitable. But if things went wrong in the repo market, if traders suddenly and surprisingly had to come up with money to meet margin calls on the futures contracts, or if the ability to quickly trade Treasuries dried up, they could run into major short-term problems.

little payoffs into big ones, they scaled the trade up to incredible sizes using cheap borrowed money. The trades could go sour if ordinary relationships between asset prices broke down, though, forcing the funds to rapidly "unwind" them by dumping the Treasury securities.

The fact had been regularly flagged in oversight reports, and for a time a task force was looking into what could be done. "Forced sales by hedge funds could cause a sharp change in asset prices, leading to further selling, substantial losses or funding problems for other firms with similar holdings," a Treasury official had at one point warned the group. "This could significantly disrupt trading or funding in key markets."[13] The task force had suffered a silent death by inaction, though, and the risk was allowed to continue unresolved. It came to bear in March 2020.

Lehnert, Clarida, and staff members at the Fed were hearing by the middle of the month that the so-called basis trade was going wrong, to disastrous effect, as were members of the media: Bloomberg ran a story on March 17 titled "How a Little-Known Trade Upended the U.S. Treasury Market."[14] The piece argued that the way money was reshuffling as the hedge fund trade went bad had also sucked cash out of commercial paper markets and was touching off strain in other parts of the financial system. It seemed like the well-known risk might have turned out to be a sweeping vulnerability, one that was intensifying the need for massive Fed intervention.

"Seemed like" was the operative term. Data on hedge funds was so sparse that it wasn't clear then—and it would be hard to establish even much later—whether the funds were a key source of the broader tumult in markets or a minor side effect. The episode underlined just how much the rise of shadow banking had obscured regulator understanding of the financial system, its weak spots and its risks.

The embattled corporate bond market stood out as another source of evident fragility in early 2020, and it presented a trickier problem. The Fed could counterbalance a wave of hedge fund bond selling simply by stepping in as a major buyer of Treasury debt, taking the other side as positions were unwound. The bond market that companies used to raise money would need a more creative emergency fix, because the Fed could not buy corporate bonds in the straightforward way in which it bought Treasury bonds. Its ordinary powers only allowed it to purchase government-backed debt.

Weaknesses in the business bond market had been building over the five years leading up to the pandemic as corporate borrowing took fire. Companies had issued roughly twice as much debt in the year through the first quarter of 2020 as had been normal a decade earlier.[15] The financing had also gotten much riskier. About half of investment-grade company debt was just one notch above junk debt status, a rating called BBB, up from a third back in 2009. That pile of BBB debt in the United States totaled more than $3 trillion as of 2019.[16]

As a result, many of America's companies were on the brink of having their bond ratings slashed into junk territory—a designation signaling a higher risk of default—by rating agencies if something went awry. If that happened, it would force many mutual and pension funds to sell the debt, because their investment rules banned low-rated bonds from their portfolios. With fewer buyers, the cost of funding corporate operations would skyrocket overnight. Companies would find themselves unable to pay the bills as they were forced to pare back on borrowed money. They might resort to mass layoffs and other cost-cutting measures that would hit workers and customers. The disaster would move from Wall Street to Main Street, and it would do so rapidly.

The ominously titled "BBB cliff" was far from the only weakness in the financial system stemming from overindebted businesses. Leveraged loans, which banks and other financial institutions extend to already-indebted companies, had also ballooned and totaled about $1.2 trillion, roughly twice pre-2008 crisis levels.[17] That giant pile of already-precarious debt might turn unstable as state and local lockdowns spread and business dried up, leaving companies little room to make good on interest payments and with few options to renew their debt. To put those numbers into context, Americans had $1.3 trillion in outstanding subprime mortgages headed into the 2008 crisis,[18] and when those debts went bad, it had helped to knock the financial system to its knees.

If a silver lining existed, it was where the riskiest corporate loans were not. Banks appeared to be far less exposed to leveraged borrowers than they had been to exotic debt bundles during the housing crisis. Unfortunately, nobody had perfect insight into just where the leveraged loans were. In a 2019 report, the Financial Stability Board had been able to directly identify the holders of eight in ten leveraged loans. "Little is known, in particular, about the direct exposures of certain non-bank investors to these markets," the FSB had acknowledged.[19]

As recently as their January meeting, Fed officials had worried that "financial imbalances—including overvaluation and excessive indebtedness—could amplify an adverse shock to the economy."[20] In 2019, Powell himself had warned that "a highly leveraged business sector could amplify any economic downturn as companies are forced to lay off workers and cut back on investments."[21] He was an expert on the topic: He had helped to pile debt onto companies during his work in the private sector and had himself questioned whether the Fed's bond purchases risked sowing the seeds of instability during his early days as a Fed governor.

The Fed and its fellow regulators had little power to stop unwise corporate borrowing. Businesses are free to load up on debt as they see fit. The Fed had briefly tried to use supervision to prevent banks from making some of the riskiest loans, but that practice had drawn lawmaker ire and backlash, earning the Fed a wrist slap for overstepping its mandate.[22] Plus, it wasn't clear how much difference supervision would have made, given that most of the rise in riskier borrowing had been enabled by nonbank lenders, and was thus outside of the Fed's oversight.[23]

It was not guaranteed that the corporate debt markets would be to 2020 what the mortgage market had been to 2008, but the potential for system-wide problems clearly existed. If debt-laden corporations were forced into bankruptcy, it would be the people who worked at their factories or hotel brands who paid with their livelihoods, not the private equity giants or clever chief financial officers who had structured their finances in the first place. Bond funds invested in the debt were already facing outflows, which risked triggering fire sales and further destabilizing markets. Plus, if bond markets remained shut down, it wouldn't just be dangerously indebted companies that paid: Even healthy firms were struggling to issue debt.

In a sign of just how large the risks loomed, the central bank's two most recent former chairs jointly penned a column on Wednesday, March 18, warning about the risk and suggesting a solution.

Ben Bernanke and Janet Yellen's opinion piece in the *Financial Times* suggested that the Fed ought to ask Congress for the authority to buy corporate bonds. That they were giving such public advice was surprising—they usually did not—and the contents were even more shocking. Central bankers are typically allergic to asking Congress to change the Fed's powers, afraid it will open the door to unwanted meddling. A possible corporate bond collapse was enough to change the calculus.

"If critical economic relationships are disrupted by months of low activity, the economy may take a very long time to recover," the former economic officials had warned. They had suggested that the "Fed could ask Congress for the authority to buy limited amounts of investment-grade corporate debt. Most central banks already have this power, and the European Central Bank and the Bank of England regularly use it." The goal, they said, would be to restart choked corporate bond markets, which were under "significant stress."[24]

"The Fed can help mitigate the economic effects of the outbreak, particularly by assuring that, once the virus's direct effects are controlled, the economy can rebound quickly," they wrote, setting out a rationale that would become a mantra for the central bank in the months to come.

The Fed would not need to ask Congress for new powers, and that is because the 2020 crisis differed from the prior crisis in two critical ways: The year 2008 had set out a proven road map for rescuing troubled markets, and Steven Mnuchin was Jerome Powell's counterpart at the Treasury Department.

During the 2008 implosion, Treasury Secretary Hank Paulson had been hesitant to back up some of Bernanke's emergency lending with the elected government's money.* The Fed had never made such extensive use of its emergency lending authorities, and it was unclear how they would work out. Paulson, it seemed, was worried they might deplete the funds he had available. The lack of Treasury help was a problem because the Fed's lawyers had determined that it could not legally expect to lose money on the programs: Gambling

---

* As a reminder, emergency lending programs are the ones carried out under the Fed Act section 13(3), the privileges created in response to the Great Depression and expanded in the decades since.

to lose amounted to "spending," and it only had "lending" powers. Without Treasury cash to insure against losses in the commercial paper program, for instance, the Fed had been forced to come up with a creative design that used private-sector money, collected by charging participants fees, as a backstop.

Mnuchin, by contrast, had already made it clear to Powell by the time of the Yellen and Bernanke piece that he was willing to support a broader set of market backstops than had been used in 2008. That meant that the Powell Fed would be able to aid a variety of markets— including that for corporate bonds.

There was a logic to Mnuchin's willingness to give a Fed corporate backstop Treasury's sign-off. Bernanke's experimentation during the earlier crisis had made it obvious that Fed emergency loan programs could be a useful tool, one that would allow the government to provide trillions of dollars of backup to financial markets while spending barely anything. Potentially, nothing.

It looked like monetary sorcery on paper, but the setup was simple. The Fed didn't need Congress to give it money to buy or borrow assets. Because the Fed could simply create cash in the form of reserves, it could do that with the push of a button, crediting a bank's balance sheet in exchange for the securities. The Fed simply required a layer of insurance. The money could be used to cover early rounds of losses if the assets the Fed had taken on turned out to be dented or worthless. But every dollar of insurance could support several dollars of lending, since it was unlikely that all the assets a program bought or supported would go bad at once. That meant that $1 of insurance could translate to $8 or maybe even $10 in firepower to support the economy.

Officials in 2020 saw a model in which Treasury, rather than the private sector, insured the programs as the way to go. It allowed the politically accountable government to demonstrate that it was behind the programs, which felt more democratic. And fortunately for the government, it was highly unlikely that the programs would end up losing much. They were designed to support healthy securities that were simply having short-term problems.[25]

The talking point was excellent. For every $100 billion Mnuchin agreed to dedicate to the insurance, Mnuchin would be able to promise $1 trillion in economic aid. History—from Bagehot's England to the 2008 crisis—offered plenty of evidence that being able to pledge a forceful response like that in critical moments could stop a meltdown in its tracks.

Yet a flaw in the plan surfaced as Fed officials began to think through how a broader set of market rescues might be structured. Mnuchin's war chest looked likely to be too limited for the turmoil at hand.

The Treasury had tapped an unused pot of money, the Exchange Stabilization Fund, to serve as the insurance layer on the commercial paper program that the Fed had unveiled March 16. The fund contained about $94 billion, and Treasury staff thought they could comfortably earmark perhaps $50 billion of that, since some of the money was technically supposed to remain available for exchange stabilization. Assuming the Fed required $1 insurance for every $10 in debt support—which was optimistically low—that worked out to about $500 billion in total firepower. That would not be enough to cope with the vast debt piles that looked like they might come tumbling down. If even a third of the "BBB cliff" was downgraded to junk status, funds might be forced to sell a sizable chunk of $1 trillion in bonds practically overnight, and that was only one of the markets plunging into disaster.

That was why Mnuchin was asking Congress for more money. A lot more.

Congress, by then, had its hands full. As it became inescapably clear that the government would need to provide relief to pandemic-shuttered businesses and sidelined workers, Capitol Hill was swinging into action.

Mnuchin, like Powell, had realized at the late February meetings in Riyadh that the infections sweeping China and the rest of Asia could present economic problems—but at that point he had publicly cautioned against jumping to any conclusions.

"Within the next few more weeks, we'll all have a better assessment as there's more data around the rate of the virus spreading," he told Reuters that Sunday night.[26]

He remained unsure, in the early days of March, that the coronavirus would turn into a full-fledged crisis. But by March 9, as the virus began to show signs of exponential growth in the United States, he was becoming convinced.[27] He had spoken with Democratic House Speaker Nancy Pelosi about the possibility of a crisis response the following afternoon, and he had called Senator McConnell and asked for his approval to begin coming up with a package.

"The secretary of the Treasury is going to have ball control for the administration," McConnell told reporters on March 10. Still, at that point, Mnuchin said it was too early to call the conversations "negotiations." Pelosi, *Politico* reported, called her chat with the Treasury secretary "pleasant"[28]—not the kind of term one would use on hardball dealmaking.

Genial chats had quickly progressed into actual, frantic planning as early March worries ceded to mid-March panic. The administration was approaching the House and Senate without a clear idea in hand, because no obvious legislative playbook existed for a global pandemic. Different congressional committees began to draft ideas that would be combined into one big program to save the country and economy from disaster, with Mnuchin serving as a sort of conductor, weaving the sections into a coordinated performance. On Monday, March 16, as the Fed was announcing its first emergency lending programs, Mnuchin was logging long hours hopping between huddles with McConnell, Pelosi, and Wall Street magnates including Goldman Sachs's David Solomon and Blackstone's Stephen Schwarzman. He called Powell's cell repeatedly, keeping him posted on the progress and staying apprised of what the Fed was doing and seeing.[29]

On Tuesday, March 17, Mnuchin made his way to Capitol Hill for the Senate's regular closed-door lunch. Dressed in a crisp white shirt and royal blue tie, lines of exhaustion under his eyes the only sign of the kind of week he was having behind the scenes, he unveiled the details of the $1 trillion proposal that he had been cobbling together and was now hoping to pass through Congress. Besides sending checks to households and offering families other sources of aid to help them to make it through state and local lockdowns, it would offer small businesses and cash-strapped airlines relief. It would also inject substantial funding into programs run by the Fed, supercharging the central bank's powers as an emergency backstop for markets.

What was noted nearly as prominently in major newspapers on March 17, 2020, though, was Mnuchin's solemn mood as he had announced the suite of ideas. He had warned senators that the unemployment rate might spike as high as 20 percent if the government did not step in forcefully to save markets and the economy.[30] That pronouncement was surprising, coming from an administration official who perennially played up optimistic economic talking points.

So, in a way, was the relief package. The Treasury secretary was asking Republicans, who had spent years scolding about the dangers of high deficits,* to get behind a huge government spending package that would help people and entities whom they had not traditionally championed—states and localities, for instance—without even pretending to pay for it. He was hoping to empower a Fed that Trump, his boss, had spent years publicly bashing. The package coming into existence was evidence that he, and members of both parties, were taking the task before them seriously as they prepared to fight the largest public challenge any of them had confronted.

"We are preparing bold steps to ensure that Main Street can access liquidity and credit during this extraordinary time," McConnell told a clutch of reporters after the lunch with Mnuchin, concern etched into his owlish visage.[31]

Still, getting a plan together was not going to be easy. In the disjointed scramble to devise a solution big enough to fit the problem, some parts of the economy seemed sure to fall through the cracks. Mark Warner, a Democrat from Virginia on the Senate Banking Committee, was becoming worried that midsize businesses were going to find themselves left out. It was clear by that Tuesday that the package would include relief for small businesses, and it seemed likely that it would also include some sort of backstop for corporations. But what would happen to firms too large for the grants the government would offer tiny companies, but too small to raise money in capital markets?

"I am proposing that we immediately set up a small and mid-sized business liquidity facility, jointly run by the Treasury Department and Federal Reserve, to provide companies affected by the virus with federally-guaranteed loans at low rates throughout the crisis," Warner said in a March 17 statement.[32] The language was ambitious:

---

* Republicans had grown the nation's deficits with tax cuts that had not paid for themselves, but they had at least tried to argue that they would be debt-neutral.

super-low interest rates, long terms, and very simple requirements, all meant to get the money out quickly and spread it widely. The loans also had a forgivable feature for companies that retained their employees. While the Fed could not lose money on its lending programs, the idea was that a sufficient backstop from the Treasury could ensure that the central bank would not have to pay out the cash itself. (It was ironic that, less than one hundred years after Carter Glass initially told Hoover to go to hell for suggesting that the Fed should lend to nonbanks, one of his home-state successors was proposing a plan that would push the Fed much farther—from lending to a range of counterparties to what was plainly spending.)

Fed staff were apoplectic. On a call with Hill negotiators, the central bank's top lawyer, Mark Van Der Weide, insisted that the proposal went beyond what the Fed would or should do. The Fed, its lawyers said, resisted "legislative prescription."

But the idea had garnered some attention on Capitol Hill, especially among members of the Senate Banking Committee. "There are a lot of members who want to give Treasury X dollars and then have the Fed use its 13(3) authority to set up lending facilities," one member of the committee's staff wrote in an email to Treasury officials and Fed lawyers that week, asking to set up a call to discuss what was possible. "Warner is talking to lots of members about his proposal."

As the government's plan to save the economy came into rough view during those early days of negotiation, it carried two distinct possibilities for America's central bank: The program would fail to become law in its sweeping, expensive form, leaving the Fed to pick up the pieces with its blunt economic tools. Or the ambitious legislation would pass, and it would ask the Fed's powers to work in ways they never had before.

Powell had been keeping his fingerprints off the partisan wrangling. But behind the scenes, he too insisted to senators that Congress needed to be careful not to stretch the Fed beyond its legal and historical limits, changing its very nature in the process. "The Fed can do lending, not spending," he told elected representatives in a refrain that would become one of his crisis-era taglines.

Powell spent most of his Tuesday afternoon on March 17 jumping between back-to-back calls addressing lawmakers' questions and concerns about the Fed's possible role in the rescue and exchanging information about what was happening in markets and the economy. Patrick Toomey was the first in line, shortly after lunchtime. The Pennsylvania Republican was concerned about what was happening in markets—were institutional failures likely? Mnuchin had, by that point, suggested that he would need about a $200 billion pot of money to back up the Fed facilities to support flailing markets. Toomey, a former trader himself, was hearing from market participants that $200 billion might be far too small. Powell, on the phone at his home desk, watching CNBC and Bloomberg anchors speak over tickers that were still flashing red, agreed that things in markets looked grim.

Then came Pelosi, the House Speaker. She had spent the entirety of the prior Friday—from 9:50 A.M. to 9:45 P.M., with brief interruptions—on the phone with Mnuchin hammering out a workable agreement. Pelosi and Powell had a good rapport. She wanted to know what he thought about the fiscal package coming together. How large should it be? How bad was this?

"Think big," he assured her. Interest rates were low, and the costs of servicing the debt would be small. Not doing enough would be the more serious mistake. Pelosi would turn the Fed chair's words into a motivational quote for the crisis era over the weeks and months ahead.

As Mnuchin, lawmakers, and Fed policy makers spent the week racing to stem the financial disaster, the pandemic itself was worsening. The United States and Canada had closed their borders to nonessential travel. States and cities around the nation had begun imposing restrictions meant to contain the virus. Bill Gates, the Microsoft founder and billionaire philanthropist, suggested that shutdowns could last for more than a month.

"If a country does a good job with testing and 'shut down' then within 6-10 weeks they should see very few cases and be able to open back up," he posted on the forum Reddit. It was dawning on America that a monthslong disruption unlike any it had ever experienced was the optimistic outlook.[33]

Trump, besides contradicting his statements from the preceding weeks by declaring that he had known the coronavirus was a pandemic for quite some time, had begun to tweet about how the "Chinese Virus" was a hidden enemy. The fight against it was a war, he said, promising that "WE WILL WIN!"[34]

Americans feared for both their jobs and their health. The sounds of sirens wailing were just beginning to haunt New York City apartments as the new coronavirus case count climbed from a little over fifty per day on March 15 to as many as eight hundred by March 17. New York was about to demonstrate for the nation what it meant to be on an exponential infection curve.

"Officials have grasped for comparisons to other catastrophes," Andy Newman wrote on the front page of *The New York Times* the following morning, in a story that wrapped around a photo of a verdant but eerily empty Central Park, a single jogger visible in the wide frame. New York mayor Bill de Blasio had tried to contextualize the disaster, Newman wrote.

"Mr. de Blasio said the economic fallout from the shutdown as a result of the virus could rival that of the Great Depression and the health impact that of the 1918 influenza epidemic that killed over 20,000 in the city."[35]

Financial markets echoed the ominous mood coursing through society. By the evening of March 18, they were still cascading through a painful meltdown. The Fed's massive bond purchases and rate cuts were doing little to reassure Wall Street. Rates on Treasury securities continued to climb, when they should have been falling as investors rushed toward safety. Money market funds were dumping short-term corporate and municipal debt frantically.

Fed vice-chair Clarida and Powell briefly discussed that evening whether they should roll out a yield curve control program, a drastic monetary policy tool in which a central bank promises to buy as much debt as is needed to keep key interest rates below a given level—essentially the "pegging" policy that had been used in Eccles's time, though not as explicitly coordinated with elected officials. The policy would have been an extreme resort, opening the possibility that the Fed would be left holding a large chunk of the entire debt market. They quickly rejected the idea, but that it was raised at all underlined the moment's desperation.

So did the action the Fed chose to take on that dire Tuesday. At thirty minutes to midnight, the central bank announced that it was rolling out a rescue program for money market mutual programs, which officials across the Fed system—and especially the Boston Fed—had been working frantically behind the scenes all week to design, struggling to forge a consensus across regulators and work through legal complexities. There had been real concern that the arrangement would not come together fast enough to prevent funds from beginning to collapse. Even though the programs were not fully ready to get started, it seemed prudent to get the broad-based details out. Delaying further would only increase the risk of disaster.

Wall Street's trading desks awoke to the news of the money market program on Thursday, March 19, though it didn't seem to change much. Markets continued to bleed. At 8:45 A.M., Maria Bartiromo, the longtime Fox Business host, turned to her guest that morning, Mnuchin, and posed the question on everyone's mind.[36]

"We appreciate all of your efforts," Bartiromo said to Mnuchin, who was dialed in by phone and pictured on an alarmingly red screen—red background, red chyron across the bottom blaring "Market Sell-Off," red market arrows pointing to the damage facing the Dow Jones and the S&P stock indexes. "It seems like you're putting everything including the kitchen sink on the table, and yet the markets are still selling off.

"There's real disappointment in your package, sir," she said.

Mnuchin pivoted, talking about the relief plan he was still drafting alongside leading senators. It would include $500 billion in direct checks to households under certain income thresholds, $300 billion in relief for small businesses, and $200 billion to support loans to hard-hit airlines and to back up new Fed facilities. The goal of that last bucket would be to supercharge Fed lending programs, averting financial disaster and keeping money flowing through markets and to corporate borrowers.

Bartiromo pushed Mnuchin on the timeline. Help three weeks from now would come too late. What could the Fed and Treasury do now?

"This is an unprecedented situation," he said. "This is not going to go on forever. We are going to beat this."

But it was not obvious, at that point, that his hope was justified.

Just as Mnuchin and his colleagues pushed for the massive package and pledged that help was on the way, opposition to the plan was crystallizing. The tension centered on the portion of the package related to the Fed and Treasury's rescue programs.

"Any taxpayer assistance that goes to giant corporations must come with real strings attached," Elizabeth Warren, the powerful Massachusetts Democrat, posted on Twitter late that Thursday, March 19.[37]

The full stakes of the pandemic meltdown were coming into view. As coronavirus lockdowns sent the economy crashing, the Fed was probably going to get a huge pot of money and a mandate to run a significant portion of the government's rescue. That support was going to bring with it intense scrutiny, as lawmakers insisted that the central bank try to funnel financial help far beyond the financial institutions it had been built to serve. The global crisis twelve years earlier had demonstrated the Fed's immense power as a first responder, but it had also illustrated the dangers of relying too heavily on the central bank's established tools.

"We can't have a repeat of 2008, where basically we shoved the money out the door to the big banks," Senator Warren declared on that frenzied March evening.

Chapter 9

THE DAY THE FED CHANGED

In wild periods of alarm, one failure makes many, and the best way to prevent the derivative failures is to arrest the primary failure which causes them.

—*Walter Bagehot,* Lombard Street

B Y THE END OF March 2020, a series of memes and short You-Tube videos had begun to make their way around the quirkier parts of the internet. One showed Jerome Powell, making a consternated face and cranking U.S. dollars out of a hand-turned printer from his press conference podium. Another showed a flat cartoon figure with gray hair next to a printer spewing dollars, below the Federal Reserve's official seal and above the phrase "haha money printer go brrrr."

As the month closed out, the saying had become ubiquitous in Twitter's finance-focused corners and had begun to seep out into the world beyond. Google search interest for "money printer" spiked and was most intense in Singapore, Canada, and Scandinavia, in a testament to how much the finance-focused world was watching American policy. On Etsy, the online marketplace for gifts and artwork frequented by America's twenty- and thirtysomethings, a seller who labeled themselves "Moneyprinterr" began to sell "brrrr" paraphernalia (among the kitsch: a stuffed printer holding a cigar and minting a dollar called the "money printer official plushie" and a "Jerome Powell, lord and savior" poster that pictured the Fed chair in red and blue robes, face framed by a golden halo).

It was not the first time a central banker had become a cultural touchpoint. Back in the 2008 crisis, Ben Bernanke had earned the label "Helicopter Ben" after he gave a speech mentioning a particularly novel type of monetary policy that involved a "helicopter drop" of money into the economy. It did not matter that the idea was theoretical and not what the Fed was actually doing. Cartoon artists across the nation had seized on the line, doodling the bearded and balding Bernanke chucking bags of cash out chopper doors.

Still, given the internet's primacy in everyday life as people languished at home with little to entertain them outside *Tiger King* and social media in spring 2020, the money printer series was the first time a Fed meme became quite so pervasive. At the heart of the "brrrr" phenomenon was the reality that by the time March turned into April, the Fed's actions were a major, even the primary, driver of markets.

That reputation had been cemented on March 23, 2020.

That day, a Monday, started menacingly. By 7:00 A.M. on America's East Coast, news had broken that German chancellor Angela Merkel was self-isolating after a virus exposure, Japan's Shinzo Abe had signaled that the Tokyo summer Olympics might be delayed, and U.S. stock futures had slumped so much that their trading had been suspended. After years of dysfunction, many worried that Congress would not agree to a relief package rapidly enough to preclude economic disaster, and Wall Street continued to nervously eye Washington.

Neel Kashkari had been on *60 Minutes* the prior night with his message that the Fed had "infinite cash" to help, but the handful of market programs it had rolled out at that point were cold comfort for a world staring down a lockdown of indeterminate length. For investors who continued to confront a breaking Treasury market, the world had gone topsy-turvy. Analysts wouldn't even begin to guess when stock and other asset prices might begin to recover.

"Markets and investors overall, right now, are predominantly focused on liquidity and the functioning of financial markets, before we can then move on," Sonja Laud, chief investment officer at the firm LGIM, said in an early-morning interview on Bloomberg Television.

"If we've reached those first two points, then let's start assessing when markets might bottom out," she continued, speaking to Francine Lacqua and Tom Keene. Keene, a bow-tied fixture on Wall Street's news scene, joined much of America in working remotely and sporting a stubble on that stressed morning.

Not much later, at 8:00 A.M., the headlines hit the newswires. The Fed was coming to the rescue, and in the process crossing nearly every barrier it had left standing after the 2008 crisis.

The announcement was sweeping. The Fed would revive a 2008 program that could help out the market for securitized loans, which bundle credit card balances, auto loans, and other types of debt and sell it off to investors in slices. It would also set up a series of totally novel emergency rescue plans. Officials promised two corporate bond programs, with the unwieldy titles Primary Market Corporate Credit Facility and Secondary Market Corporate Credit Facility. The first would buy company debt that had already been issued, and the latter would buy new bonds, to make sure that businesses could continue to raise money in the choked market. The goal was to keep corporate America supplied with borrowed cash so that the massive debt hanging over Wall Street's neck like a guillotine would not fall.

To help midsize businesses, the central bank also pledged to set up a Main Street loan program. Officials had been hoping Congress would come through with its own plan for the sector, but it had by then become clear that rescuing midsize companies would fall to the Fed. Central bankers had not come to a concrete enough agreement to release an outline of what Main Street would look like that Monday, so they simply announced that a rescue was coming.

In its release, the Fed also promised to buy as much government-backed debt as was needed to restore function to the disrupted Treasury and mortgage-backed bond markets. It wasn't the yield curve control Powell and Clarida had discussed, but the amped-up version of quantitative easing wasn't a million miles away, either. The media immediately took the Fed's series of market supports as the huge deal that they were.

"Fed Signals Unlimited QE, Adds Company Aid," the Bloomberg chyron read as economics reporter Mike McKee read the news live on air. "The Fed, throwing the kitchen sink and more, all the stuff under the stove and in the closet, at the markets," he bantered.

"Federal Reserve Chairman Jerome Powell's whatever-it-takes moment arrived Monday," a *Wall Street Journal* story declared.[1] "The Fed goes all-in," *The New York Times* agreed.[2]

As the headlines broke, stock futures began to bounce back from their worst week since 2008. Though equities would sink again that day, concerned about Congress's continued inaction, that Monday would mark a critical turning point in the fast-building financial crisis. Stocks would soar on Tuesday as they digested what the Fed's promises meant and as hope for congressional action grew. Across the bond and equity universe, March 23 was the date after which the pandemic financial shock began to reverse itself, setting up the most spectacular and sudden rally in U.S. market history.

The performance to shore up investor confidence had been carefully timed. Behind the scenes, Fed and Treasury officials had spent a harried weekend pulling together the programs, intent on unveiling the plans before Wall Street got off to another week of calamitous trading. Mnuchin had been simultaneously working with lawmakers to try to secure the massive pot of funding to back up the central bank's efforts, a sum that by that Sunday had swollen from $200 billion to more than $400 billion. There was still no guarantee that it would pass Congress, and the Fed programs announced on March 23 were mostly set up so that they could function at a small scale without it. Still, chances seemed to be on Mnuchin's side. Powell, from his desk in Chevy Chase, had been coordinating the political and practical planning, taking both scheduled calls from lawmakers and nonstop unscheduled ones from the Fed's staff.

The all-hands-on-deck effort, and the precedent-shattering package that it produced, were aimed squarely at staving off a financial crisis. That did not mean they would be costless. Powell and his colleagues knew, even as business news channels cheered on the forceful March 23 response that morning, that it would open his institution up to political criticism and possible mission creep. Accusations that the central bank was bailing out the corporate bond market seemed inevitable. Designing Main Street would be an exercise in deciding who would win and who would lose from the Fed's help, forcing the central bank to make awkward decisions that would anger many.

Main Street would also shift the Fed's modern role as an emergency lender in subtle but profound ways: The program could not function as a last-ditch backstop for a traded market the way the 2008 rescues had, because midsize businesses financed themselves with loans rather than by selling securities.[3] It seemed destined to make the Fed, at least in a small way, banker to the private sector.*

Even the basic mechanics of the new suite of programs were reputationally risky. Mnuchin and the Fed had chosen the financial crisis management arm of BlackRock, America's largest money manager, to run the corporate bond programs. That they had tapped the behemoth firm without obviously considering alternatives was guaranteed to draw criticism. The corporate bond program would inevitably end up helping BlackRock's own exchange-traded funds, which dominated the market, creating an appearance problem and a potential conflict of interest. But the company was experienced and Mnuchin had been consulting with Chief Executive Officer Laurence Fink for days. It seemed like the most expedient option at a moment that called for rapid action.

The Fed's bond buying could also end in backlash. The central bank had purchased hundreds of billions of dollars in Treasuries by the time of the March 23 announcement. After it, that pace of balance sheet buying would continue to skyrocket. Between March 1 and the end of April, the Fed's holdings would go from $2.5 trillion to about $4 trillion, growing by roughly the same amount as they had over the course of all three of the central bank's post-2008 quantitative easing programs. This time, instead of taking five years, the change would take two months, and it would leave the central bank holding about a quarter of all outstanding Treasury debt. It wasn't the same as in World War II, when the Fed and the government had coordinated to keep rates low and the market functioning. Even so, the massive scale of the purchases would clearly reverberate across government finance, making it easier for the Treasury to fund the

---

* This would not be a complete first for the Fed, given the lending it had done both under its emergency powers during the 1930s and, using other authorities, in the two decades that followed. It would be the first time the Fed so directly supported nonfinancial businesses in its modern era of pronounced political independence and economic power, though.

government's crisis response plan without pushing longer-term interest rates higher. Though the risk of setting off an inflationary spiral seemed distant to officials then—years of weak price gains had suggested that QE didn't do much to stoke those pressures—the Fed's independence was sure to come into question.

Those risks were worth taking to blunt the economic fallout from the crushing pandemic, Fed officials had decided. Powell spent the morning catching up with his staff, and then, for ten minutes starting at 11:43 A.M., talking with the president who had spent nearly two years deriding him. The profundity of the moment seemed to register on Pennsylvania Avenue (not historically home to Jerome Powell's fan club).

"He's really stepped up over the last week," Trump would say at a press conference later that afternoon. "I called him today and I said, 'Jerome, good job.'"[4]

As extensive as they were, the Fed's new plans did not fix everything. Markets broadly began to calm down, but some Treasury securities remained volatile. Powell spent that week trying to make sure everyone understood just how far the central bank was willing to go as it tried to keep the public health crisis from creating a lasting financial disaster. On Thursday, March 26, he made an exceedingly rare television appearance on the *Today* show. Powell appeared in the media more than his predecessors, but it was unusual for a central bank official to take an interview on a chatty program meant for such a broad audience.

Seated in a studio at the Fed's Eccles Building, with a decade's worth of formally bound Federal Reserve bulletins arrayed behind him, a small mic snapped onto his violet tie, he took questions from host Savannah Guthrie.

"Is there any limit to the amount of money that the Fed is willing to put into this economy to keep it afloat?" Guthrie asked.

"The only limit on that will be how much backstop we get from the Treasury Department," Powell replied, speaking calmly, steadily. "Essentially, the answer to your question is no—we can continue to make loans. And really the point of all that is to support the flow of credit in the economy to households and businesses."[5]

The Fed's power across a wide range of markets, Powell was acknowledging, was on the brink of becoming limitless.

Still, whether the Fed would have the insurance it needed to fully backstop markets and insulate the economy remained a live question.

Mnuchin had worked desperately to make the funding for the programs come through, but in those late days of negotiations the $500 billion pot for Treasury (it had gotten even bigger in the final hours) remained among the most contentious parts of the plan. The Treasury secretary had gone on CNBC hours after Powell and his colleagues had announced the spate of March 23 programs to argue that the actions were "very important" but that "we need Congress to approve additional funds today, so that we can move forward and support American workers in the American economy."[6]

A small flock of congressional staffers could be found huddled in the hallway outside Senator Chuck Schumer's office in the Senate's Hart Building in the days that followed, hammering out the final language with the Democrat minority leader's staff. Mnuchin himself shuttled between Senate Majority Leader Mitch McConnell's office and those of prominent Democrats as he tried to keep everyone on board. A micromanager to his core, he had at one point seated himself at a table with two staffers and reworked a key section of the bill line by line and comma by comma in a late-night drafting session.

Democrats, in a sign of the deep suspicion that existed between the parties even when they were cooperating, used the final series of agreements to excise loopholes from the language to make sure Mnuchin had to use the massive pot of funding to back up Fed emergency loan programs and could not use it to support friends of the administration. Democrats also made sure the legislation retained language urging the Fed to focus on a few of their priorities. Senator Warner's staffers saw the Fed's March 23 announcement of its Main Street lending program as a preemptive strike meant to keep Congress from telling the Fed what to do for midsize businesses, a point of some annoyance. Even so, the final draft of the bill included language stipulating that the Fed should investigate a small business loan program and some way to support state and local governments.

Neither provision was binding, but they helped to get the package over the finish line.

When the CARES Act passed the Senate on March 25, lawmakers voted for it 96 to 0, a level of agreement that was unheard of in modern legislative history on a package so expansive. McConnell had explained the rationale behind the broad support for the bill on the chamber's floor: "Our nation obviously is going through a crisis that is totally unprecedented in living memory."[7]

The Fed's ability to leverage the $454 billion ultimately earmarked for its programs calmed markets and gave the law its shock and awe, allowing the administration to advertise that their package would provide more than $6 trillion in help for the economy.[8] Sections of the legislation that had nothing to do with the Fed would provide essential help for America's businesses and workers during a challenging time. Companies with fewer than five hundred employees would have access to forgivable loans, workers who had lost their jobs would be able to tap an expanded unemployment insurance program, and people below a certain income threshold would receive $1,200 checks to tide them over.

The spending programs, which would be renewed and extended in the months to come, were a huge break from the 2008 crisis, when the government had curbed its ambitions over fear about the nation's swelling deficit. At $2.2 trillion, CARES dwarfed the $800 billion American Recovery and Reinvestment Act enacted in 2009. It also came at twice the price tag that Mnuchin and the White House had originally advertised, and hardly anyone had asked whether the nation could afford it.

Fighting the coronavirus, lawmakers seemed to have generally accepted, was a battle worth the resources.

Mnuchin, who would remain the Fed's key partner as it worked to cushion the fallout from the pandemic, had a lot riding on the new relief law. People involved in the negotiations—including those who disliked him immensely—were quick to acknowledge that without him the deal would never have come together at such a speed and size. The rescue was a chance to define his legacy.

Upon his arrival in Washington, Mnuchin had been painted

mostly as a money-hungry financier. He had spent years at Goldman Sachs and in the hedge fund business, but it was his job during the financial crisis that drew the most attention. Mnuchin had in 2008 helped to buy California-based IndyMac, a bank and mortgage servicer that the government had taken over and was looking to unload, then moved to a mansion in Bel Air to run it.[9] IndyMac had loaded up on mortgage-backed securities, mortgages, and commercial loans that seemed to have hit rock bottom and, as the Fed unrolled rescue packages, seemed likely to have at least some upside. Together with a handful of other wealthy investors—John Paulson, George Soros, Michael Dell, and Chris Flowers—Mnuchin cobbled it and other struggling portfolios into a bank called OneWest. Mnuchin was an expert in the sorts of securities IndyMac held, having headed up the mortgage department at Goldman.[10]

The move, as with many of Mnuchin's ventures, was a stunning success by any financial metric. The partners expanded the bank's capital base, rebranded it through partnerships with the Los Angeles Lakers and Angels, and expanded its consumer lending. Whether One-West was a winner from a societal standpoint proved more debatable. The bank foreclosed on mortgage holders who couldn't pay, something that was common in those days of widespread delinquency, but which OneWest did particularly aggressively. In 2015, Mnuchin and his partners sold OneWest to CIT Group Inc. for $3.4 billion,[11] but for all the financial gain, the intensity with which OneWest had cracked down on nonperforming loans earned Mnuchin and the bank a reputation in Southern California that reverberated all the way to Washington.

When Mnuchin appeared on Capitol Hill for his Treasury secretary confirmation hearing in January 2017, his eyes alert below a receding jet-black hairline, he had explaining to do.

The hearing was wild. Mnuchin's posse immediately underlined that he was not a typical creature of Washington: Louise Linton, then his fiancée, sat behind his right shoulder, her bangs perfectly side-swept, her lipstick slightly iridescent, diamond stud earrings glinting for the C-Span cameras. Aspirational movie starlets were not regulars at Senate Finance Committee hearings.[12] Foreshadowing the tone of the tenure that lay before him, Mnuchin used his opening statement to praise Donald Trump, recounting the first Trump rally he attended. The event in Indianapolis had been an "unforgettable experience" in which twenty thousand people had packed a stadium and cheered for the politician like he was a member of the Rolling Stones.

"I share the president-elect's goal of economically empowering every citizen," Mnuchin had said.

The Democratic politicians vetting Mnuchin for the job were not reassured. Over five hours of questioning, they took him to task for many apparent offenses: the fact that his hedge fund had registered to an offshore tax haven in the Cayman Islands (he said the move was something pensions and other investors demanded, not a personal tax dodge), that he had initially failed to disclose nearly $100 million in real estate holdings (he said the forms were complicated), and that it took too long for him to file his complete financial disclosures (seriously, seriously complicated). But the topic that came up time and again was Mnuchin's move to crack down on homeowners while at OneWest. He argued, consistently and in a polite tone, that he had done his best to keep borrowers in their homes but that his hands were tied by the government's own rules and by the harsh realities of the era.

It was clear that Mnuchin had come to the hearing knowing that he would take heat, ready with prepared answers. What wasn't clear over the course of those long and contentious hours was why—with his fortune and business career—Steven Mnuchin wanted to come to Washington in the first place. Treasury secretary is a top-flight government job that gives its holder social cachet and power to generate change. It is also characterized by relentless work and near-constant criticism. Mnuchin, interestingly, framed it as an extension of his life in finance.

"Throughout my career, my commitment was to my clients and shareholders," he had told senators during his confirmation. "Thirty years later, my commitment is now to the American people, for whom I will work tirelessly by helping to grow our economy and create jobs."

Whatever his motivations, once he got the job, Mnuchin hustled. He quickly proved that he was suited to flourish in Trump's Washington. He constantly praised a president who tolerated nothing less, professing loyalty no matter what edict or action came from the White House. Even when his views appeared to be at odds with

Trump's, he simply claimed that he was a nonexpert or kept silent on the topic in public. Other cabinet officials dropped like flies, victim to frequent firings that grabbed headlines and drove the news cycle, but Mnuchin retained the president's ear and, with some wobbles, his confidence.

As news headlines zeroed in on Trump's border wall and detained migrant children, Mnuchin downplayed or dodged questions about the burning political and moral issues of the day while ticking through a quiet but meaningful agenda of blander policy changes. He negotiated massive tax cuts, began to defang financial oversight, and brought his former OneWest colleagues into other top government and regulatory positions. He failed to hire a full staff for Treasury, but he nevertheless managed to work his way through a sort of libertarian wish list.

Now the coronavirus pandemic threatened the very growth he had pledged to unleash. Mnuchin had scrambled to come up with a package that would protect the administration's prized economy. Once the legislation passed, he was dead set on being seen as a good steward of the cash. Elizabeth Warren had made a habit of calling the pot of money for the Fed a "slush fund," miffing many at Treasury.

When Trump signed the CARES Act into law on March 27, McConnell and Mnuchin stood behind him at the Resolute desk in the White House's Oval Office as he announced the pandemic response legislation. The Treasury secretary, who always had the uncomfortable look during public appearances of someone who cannot quite figure out what to do with their arms, held his hands at his sides and blinked slightly as he focused directly on the camera, a faint smile on his face. It broke into an expression of unabashed happiness as the president introduced him.[13]

"Steve Mnuchin, you know how hard he's been working," Trump said.

"Mr. President, thank you very much for your leadership, and for the vice president's leadership," Mnuchin said, stepping forward slightly, his head bobbing a little. "You made it very clear to us last week that we should think big—that this was a war on the virus."

—

Powell's Fed was still kicking into full gear as CARES passed. It needed to design the newly pumped-up programs, and it needed to keep pulling other levers to make sure the fragile financial peace would last. If it hoped to keep domestic markets in good shape, it would have to live up to its reputation as central banker not just to America but to the world.

Foreign central banks were reporting a dire shortage of dollar funding in their economies, one that threatened to deepen global financial problems. During a Friday morning call held by the International Monetary and Financial Committee, a twenty-four-member group of central bankers and other economic policy makers that focused on the world's financial system, officials fretted about the pressures.

"A global health pandemic has turned into an economic and financial crisis," Kristalina Georgieva, managing director of the International Monetary Fund, and Lesetja Kganyago, chair of the financial committee, said in a joint statement released following the meeting.[14] The IMF would do what it could to release the tension: It pledged to use its $1 trillion in lending capacity to support countries that ran into trouble, it had unveiled debt relief options for the poorest nations, and it was improving credit options that could allow hard-hit countries to borrow. Still, something more needed to be done about the shortage in American cash.

By 2020, the dollar's role in global finance and development was complicated, often criticized, and nearly impossible to overstate. The dollar was used in about half of all international trade transactions, far outstripping America's 10 percent share in world trade.[15] In many nations, the difference was stark: Fully 60 percent of Turkey's imports were invoiced in dollars even though imports from the United States only made up 6 percent of its total, based on research by the economist Gita Gopinath.[16] Roughly two-thirds of foreign exchange reserves were held in America's currency, and a huge share of corporate bonds were dollar-denominated.[17] Mark Carney, then the outgoing leader of the Bank of England, had warned about the dollar's "domineering influence" in the global economy during a speech at the Fed's Jackson Hole meeting the prior year.[18]

The reality that companies around the world borrowed in dollars could create problems in times of crisis. If a palm oil firm in Malaysia, for instance, had a big load of dollar debt but suddenly could not swap the local ringgits it was earning from its customers into dollars to make interest payments, it might fall behind on the bills. Likewise, if the ringgit declined in value against the dollar suddenly and sharply, the firm might discover that its debts had gone from manageable to crushing overnight. A decline in the local currency might force the business to sell drastically more oil to make the same dollar interest payment.

Nations could guard their companies and economies against that kind of destabilizing situation. They could make sure that local banks were well stocked with dollar funding, and they could try to push up their own currency's value against the dollar. To do the latter, a nation's central bank could sell reserves including dollar-denominated debt—Treasuries—in exchange for their own currency, reducing the supply of local currency in circulation and increasing its worth.

By mid-March 2020, foreign governments were dumping their Treasury holdings with abandon—bad news for the Fed, which was still trying to keep the U.S. government bond market calm and functional. The Fed had at first relied on its 2008 crisis response playbook to fix the international side of things, sweetening agreements that allowed it to get dollars to foreign central banks, which could then funnel that cash out to banks and businesses. On March 19, it had expanded the arrangements to a broader set of foreign partners, bringing Australia, South Korea, Brazil, and Mexico into the set of countries that qualified for the easy dollar access.[19]

But the dollar continued to climb in value. Bank of America analysts had begun speculating that the United States was going to need to intervene in markets to weaken the currency, something nearly unheard of in the modern era.[20]

The idea that dollars might become scarce was at the core of the problem. If dollar funding wasn't easily getting to overseas companies and institutions, they were going to continue rushing for greenbacks wherever they could get them, forcing more foreign Treasury selling. To get conditions back to normal, the Fed needed to devise a way to shuttle dollars to governments with which it could not take the geopolitically cozy step of establishing a swap line.

Enter the nerdiest-sounding program in a crisis chock-full of them: a facility affectionately dubbed FIMA repo.

Formally called the "Temporary Foreign and International Monetary Authorities Repo Facility" and announced on March 31,[21] the program had a geeky elegance. It allowed roughly 170 central banks and foreign entities with accounts at the New York Fed potential access to a short-term dollar loan in exchange for safe collateral: Treasury bonds. FIMA repo could prevent foreign holders from dumping Treasuries into the market, and it could get dollar bills into hands that needed them. Best of all, it could do both through an existing New York Fed relationship. That made it boring instead of eyebrow-raising from a political standpoint.

Hardly anyone in the media got excited about the new program, which had been given a name destined to inspire indifference. "Fed's New Foreign Central Bank Repo Tool Seen Easing Market Strains," journalist Michael Derby's headline in *The Wall Street Journal* read—the closest thing the program got to clickbait. Most didn't even go so far as to speculate what the effect might be. "Fed Broadens Access to Dollars with Repo Agreement for Foreign Central Banks," the Reuters title read.

But FIMA worked. It is tough to pinpoint what it was that ultimately calmed the market, but together with the interventions already unveiled, the new program seemed to be the backup the world needed to see. By the second week of April, foreign investors began to buy Treasuries again and drew down the massive dollar-denominated cash piles they had been building up.[22] Powell's Fed was still scrambling, but it was finally beginning to pay off.

Neel Kashkari had spent the crazed weeks of late March watching his colleagues maneuver from his perch in Minneapolis. While presidents held no vote on the emergency lending programs, they were kept in the loop. He had been happy to see a large government spending package coming together and he felt relieved that the Fed was holding seemingly nothing back in its crisis response. He was also hopeful that the backlash to 2020 would be much less than what he and his colleagues had faced in 2008. Nobody would have expected everything to work perfectly when an interconnected world shut down unexpectedly. The public would not view the package as a bailout, he thought.

He was spending his early pandemic days talking with Minnesota politicians—Senator Amy Klobuchar and Representative Ilhan Omar, both Democrats—and chatting with businesspeople including Glenn Hutchins, the New York Fed director and financier, who was researching how the Troubled Asset Relief Program had been overseen back in the 2008 crisis. (Hutchins would go on to co-author a *Wall Street Journal* opinion piece suggesting that "since time is so limited, perhaps an oversight group could be selected from regional Federal Reserve Bank presidents and directors, whose qualifications and conflicts have already been vetted." He was essentially nominating himself and his colleagues.)[23]

Oversight was emerging as a very real concern. Even if financial institutions hadn't caused their own problems this time around, the March 23 decision to save new and never-rescued markets could raise uncomfortable questions.

It was obvious from the outset that the Fed was going to be incapable of satisfying all constituencies, no matter what it did. The language that Senator Mark Warner had fought to have included in the CARES Act said the Treasury secretary should "endeavor to seek" to set up a Fed lending program for midsize businesses and nonprofits, one that would require recipients to use the loans to maintain most of their payroll employees. No rational business owner was going to pile on debt to pay employees when they had no confidence about what the future held. Setting up a program based on such guidelines would be political showmanship. Not doing it would clearly invite criticism. It was a lose-lose situation.

The law itself required regular reporting and established a Congressional Oversight Commission to shepherd the rescue, a policing body that could help to deal with Democrats' concerns that the money would turn into a fund for Trump administration political favorites. The Fed was internally prepared to go even farther, to effectively show its work—besides disclosing term sheets to the programs immediately, the Board was already drawing up plans to report many of the transactions in near-real time.

The need for extreme transparency tied back to a well-established reality. Congress might have trusted the Fed more than the Treasury in 2020, but in general people were still skeptical of the central bank. Lawmakers expected it to cater to monied interests, as Warren's comments during the CARES debates had made clear.

Concerns about the Fed's Wall Street ties had dogged the first two central bank attempts, had caused the Jekyll Island group to pretend they were going duck hunting instead of coming up with an outline for monetary reform, had informed the design of the Fed when it was created in 1913, and had continued right up to the pandemic meltdown.

The Fed had given its skeptics plenty of fodder since the 2008 global financial crisis. Former central bank officials regularly made fat paychecks consulting for banks and asset managers as soon as they left the Fed's marble hallways: Ben Bernanke had begun consulting for Pimco shortly after stepping down from the chairmanship, and Janet Yellen had earned big speaking fees from financial institutions after leaving the Fed.* Former lower-level staffers sometimes admitted sheepishly that they had commanded salaries at banks and financial companies that their skills alone probably did not justify. Firms were willing to pay for inside-the-building expertise.

Officials could also benefit from Wall Street's successes while they were still at the central bank. Many held broad portfolios of financial assets that they actively managed heading into 2020. On March 23, as the central bank ramped up its efforts to save markets and the economy, the Board's ethics office sent the regional banks a note warning them not to trade as they were determining the fate of markets and the economy: "Please consider observing a trading blackout and avoid making unnecessary securities transactions for at least the next several months, or until the FOMC and Board policy actions return to their regularly scheduled timing," it read.[24†]

The idea that the Fed was going to be anything but extra-friendly to Wall Street when it was so closely intertwined with it struck many lawmakers as fanciful. That skepticism was sure to keep attention focused on how the programs were designed and who benefited from them.

But as the Fed and its friends coalesced around the idea that being up-front and clear about their actions could help them answer criticism, their attention to reputational risks came with its own potential

* It would later come to light that she had made nearly $7.3 million in speaking fees in 2019 and 2020.
† This foreshadowed a later scandal, which we will get to.

pitfalls. As Greenspan had intuited decades earlier, greater transparency sometimes translated into less room to maneuver. The Treasury and the Fed might not be generous enough to avert real economic damage if they were narrowly focused on keeping support away from bad actors, fearing backlash.

There was precedent. When Kashkari had helped to draw up and administer parts of the rescue during the 2008 crisis, officials had been so worried about avoiding the appearance of helping irresponsible people and companies that they had stopped short of what was necessary.

"We didn't end up helping many homeowners, and the housing downturn was more severe," Kashkari said repeatedly in those late days of March and early days of April. "We need to err on the side of being generous."[25]

In spring 2020, as the Fed rolled out its role-redefining rescue and Congress came to the nation's aid, Kashkari was personally witnessing how urgent it was to get the policy response right. His wife, Christine Ong Kashkari, had been working for a corporate travel management company that had laid off the majority of its workers—including Christine. April 1 had been her first day of unemployment. They were able to take the hit, financially, but Christine was the sort of person who loved to work. The possibility that her job, like those of millions around the country, might not come back hung ominously over their household. The news of the layoff, he told people at the time, had been "a shock."

Chapter 10

RACING ACROSS RED LINES

Had he not changed, any praise of his consistency would be praise of a valueless value. It would have been a consistency maintained at the price of a ruined economy.

—*Marriner Eccles, of Franklin Roosevelt, who abandoned a balanced budget doctrine in favor of the New Deal spending programs*

IT WAS APRIL 7 when Samantha Stephens decided she was desperate enough to turn to the internet for help.

Eight days earlier, she had found herself numbly emailing her commercial landlord in New York City's West Village to let him know that she would be missing rent that month. Her café, OatMeals, had been forced to close in mid-March. At first she had tried to hang on with takeout. But her shop, which abutted the New York University campus, suddenly had no customers coming through the door looking to buy build-your-own bowls with creative toppings or custom creations like "The Hot Date" (dried fruit, pecans, peanut butter, honey) and "Truffle RisOATto" (shaved Parmesan, truffle oil, cracked pepper). Without students rushing past on their way to class and office workers ordering in to impress clients with an unusual breakfast, there simply weren't enough orders to justify stocking perishable supplies.

"It was costing me more to open my doors than I could bring in," Stephens would recall. "I really wanted to stay open for the community, I love my regular customers, and they depend on their morning oatmeal."

OatMeals had been the realization of a longtime dream for Stephens, an impeccable dresser with a bright white smile. When she had come to New York City for college in 2000, she was a food lover in her element, living around some of the best restaurants on earth. Like many a college freshman before her, she put on an alarming amount of weight. To get fit and save money, she had turned to oatmeal—and she realized that besides being cheap and healthy, the grain was an underappreciated canvas. Everyone just sprinkled cinnamon and called it a day, but Stephens took a bowl of oats and made Cacio e Pepe, pumpkin pie, or any of a hundred other combinations. She thought she could build a business around her oat innovations, but she didn't jump into the restaurant scene immediately, instead taking a job as an executive assistant at an investment bank. The ambition lived on in her mind, and she enrolled in culinary classes at night. Eight years and hundreds of hours of careful planning later, she was ready to take the leap. She rented a 380-square-foot cubby in the trendy Village, not far from the famous basketball cages that border NYU, and set up shop.

The business had been tough from the start, because it was not easy to pay the rent on the profit earned from a $3 or $4 bowl of cereal. Slowly, though, she established a following in the area. She went on CNBC's *Shark Tank,* pitching the concept and seeking external partnerships. The deal she struck on the show had fallen through, but the exposure had helped her to secure a brand partnership with Quaker Oats, which helped to supplement the store's profits. By early 2020, she and her employees had been making about $45,000 in revenue per month, enough to cover her payroll and supply costs, to pay the shop's $6,300 in monthly rent, and to service its debt.

Now the money had abruptly stopped coming in the door, and those costs loomed large. Stephens had tried appealing to her insurance company, but it made it clear that it would not cover this kind of crisis. She had applied for a disaster relief loan the prior Saturday, but she wasn't confident that it had even been properly submitted: While she had taken a screenshot of the page after she filled it in, she had never received a confirmation email. She was spending all of her time camped out in her tiny New York City apartment, disoriented by her changed reality. No café to go to, no work to do. She passed the time googling to see how other restaurants were staying afloat. That is how she got the idea for the GoFundMe page.

She asked for $25,000 up front, which she planned to use for rent, utilities, and payroll. But she wasn't kidding herself on that day in early April. It was unlikely that internet crowdfunding was going to save her business, help her get her employees back on the clock, or keep her from personal financial disaster.

She decided to try for a Paycheck Protection Program loan. The new forgivable small business loan program had passed as part of Congress's coronavirus response package, and it was struggling to swing into motion.* Stephens applied through Chase, her bank, and the system registered her application on April 11. The final dollar of the so-called PPP was exhausted on April 16, and Stephens hadn't gotten any money.

"It's panic and worry, and it's fear," she would tell *The New York Times* later that week. "But over all, a bit of numbness right now, because this is all so weird."

March, the first month of the pandemic in the United States, had been filled with dread. Across America and the world, as companies laid off entire staffs and businesspeople like Stephens confronted the real possibility of failure, it was becoming clear that April was going to be a month of tough decisions. That extended to the Federal Reserve, where Powell, Brainard, and Quarles were realizing that they would have to do things that disquieted them—crossing lines American central bankers had long avoided breaching—as they tried to keep still-fragile markets and an at-risk economy afloat.

First, though, economic officials had to deal with a few technical challenges. As entrepreneurs like Stephens saw their dreams teetering that second week of April, the government's response was off to a rocky

---

* As a reminder, this is the program for very small businesses that did not work through the Fed. The central bank was running Main Street, a program for slightly larger businesses.

start. After a month of minute-by-minute dealmaking and sweeping public announcements, Mnuchin's Treasury had to get down to the difficult task of shuttling money out the door, and it was proving to be logistically thorny. The Paycheck Protection Program had launched at 8:30 A.M. on Friday, April 3, offering companies with fewer than five hundred employees loans that would be eligible for forgiveness if they used them to keep employees on payroll and pay their utility bills. From the first day, demand was torrid. The Small Business Administration, which was administering the program, was being asked to process in mere hours a volume of loans that it usually might do over the course of a busy year. For a fraught period the following Monday, its website had become so overwhelmed by the traffic that it crashed.[1]

The program worked through commercial banks, which were supposed to originate and service the loans in exchange for fees. There were clear benefits to channeling the program through the private sector: The government lacked the know-how and capacity to quickly underwrite a nation's worth of loans, and the banks already had relationships with customers. Yet problems of equity were already emerging, as rumors circulated that lenders were allowing big and important customers to jump the line, even as the tiny companies that the program was most intended to serve waited anxiously to be helped. Plus, based on the simple math of the matter, officials were concerned that some lenders might flatly decline to participate. Making government loans to customers would take up space on their balance sheets and would not necessarily pay enough to make that attractive. The problem wasn't hypothetical. Rebeca Romero Rainey, president of Independent Community Bankers of America, had sent a letter to the Treasury secretary that Saturday, urging him to come up with a solution to help banks free up the space to participate.

"This program should not be limited by the balance sheet capacity of participating lenders," she said.[2]

If a large group of banks opted out of the program or found themselves unable to roll it out at scale, it was going to create problems. Like Stephens, many of America's small businesses needed help immediately, so it would be crippling if the delivery channel caused the program to sputter. Two or three months down the road, once the kinks had been fully ironed out, would be two or three months too late for many small companies.

"The banks are doing a great job, they're just overwhelmed," Mnuchin kept saying.[3]

There was an obvious way to make sure lenders would see the small business program as a good bet, find themselves able to keep up with customer demand, and retain enough space to keep making other kinds of loans. The government could allow the banks to swap the loans for credit from the Fed. The lenders would still earn origination fees and make their customers happy, so participating in the program would be attractive. The loans were no real risk to the central bank or the taxpayer, since they were effectively grants— Congress had already earmarked the money to pay them off, and they were being treated as loans only to pressure employers who took them to stick to the rules.

Powell and Brainard enlisted Kashkari's Minneapolis Fed to manage such a program: Kashkari had Wall Street experience, and he got things done.[*] Powell and Mnuchin touched base at 7:00 A.M. on Monday, and at 2:00 P.M., the news hit the wires. "The Federal Reserve will establish a facility to provide term financing backed by PPP loans. Additional details will be announced this week." The announcement was terse, a mere thirty-seven words, but it got the point across.[4]

Promising a PPP solution for the banks was a useful step, and the facility would be widely used. It was not a final one. By Tuesday, a fresh problem had surfaced, and businesses like OatMeals were already feeling the brunt of it. Amid the deluge of demand, people were fretting that the $349 billion small business loan program was going to be too small to get to everyone who wanted or needed a loan. Mnuchin tried to counsel calm.

"The president has made clear that if we run out of money, he is going to go back to Congress," Mnuchin said on Fox Business

---

[*] The New York Fed and Boston Fed were running other programs, on account of their ties to finance and Boston Fed president Eric Rosengren's 2008 experience and general competence. Dallas Fed president Robert Kaplan, who also had long Wall Street experience, was consulting closely on design for several programs.

that morning. By Wednesday, in a testament to how fast the world was moving, he had asked Congress for $250 billion to revamp the program.

"We will not run out of money," the Treasury secretary said on CNBC, trying to soothe a concerned nation. "The money will be there."[5]

Logistical issues were far from the only lingering problem. State and local bond markets had ground to a standstill by early April, a freeze that came at the worst imaginable moment. Rates had shot so high that states and localities could no longer comfortably issue debt to raise money. That was terrible news when the governments were facing lower sales tax receipts, delayed income tax payments as the pandemic prompted the federal government to extend the filing deadline, and rocketing expenses as schools shifted to remote learning and the public health response ate into their savings. Rhode Island was a case in point. It estimated that it would miss out on $300 million in revenue in March and early April from the delayed taxes, while closed casinos cost it another $1 million per day. Meanwhile, on that Monday alone, it had spent $7 million on ventilators.[6]

Powell had known that the Fed would likely need to help municipal bond markets, and lawmakers had been clear in the CARES Act that they wanted the Fed to do so. The language was not binding, but it would be difficult for Powell and Mnuchin to explain why they had ignored the guideline.

Yet the market for state and local debt was an especially uncomfortable one for the central bank, and for Powell in particular. The Fed had studiously avoided getting involved in the municipal market over the years for good reason. Such bonds could fund everything from city parks and airports to schools, and they were far from standardized. They were paid back using different revenue streams and often according to different terms. Municipal bonds were not simply quoted on an exchange where they traded freely from minute to minute, so they would be hard to buy at scale.

They were also a political minefield. Rashida Tlaib, a freshman Democrat and a member of the squad of progressive Democrats then in the House, had long wanted the Fed to promise to jump into municipal debt come the next economic downturn. Powell had regularly batted back those suggestions, arguing that it would politicize his institution by forcing it to pick winners and losers. Did only cities with well-managed pensions deserve access? If everyone could tap it, was that just a bailout for poorly run states that had gotten themselves into financial trouble? Those concerns might have been momentarily alleviated by the dawn of the pandemic, but they had not disappeared entirely.

To complete the trifecta of problems, big money managers could end up as major beneficiaries if the Fed snapped up municipal debt. Money market mutual funds and exchange-traded funds were heavily invested, BlackRock called itself the world's largest municipal bond manager, and Nuveen and Pimco were major players in the market.

Despite the reasons for disquiet, the practical and political pressure to set up a municipal program was intense. On March 30, Senator Elizabeth Warren published a series of tweets saying that the $454 billion pot of congressional money allocated for Fed programs could and should be used to help municipal borrowers. "Secretary Mnuchin should meet every one of their needs before a single unnecessary cent goes to enrich CEOs," she wrote. "Let's discuss," Mnuchin wrote in an email to Powell and his deputy secretary, forwarding the thread.

News broke in late March that the Fed had hired Kent Hiteshew, who had been the first director of the Treasury Department's Office of State and Local Finance. Board officials had also been calling around to the twelve regional branches for insight into local conditions, and *The Wall Street Journal* had reported as early as March 27 that some sort of municipal bond plan was afoot.[7]

For Powell, that reality marked a complete about-face.

"We don't have authority, I don't believe, to lend to state and local governments," he had told Tlaib just nine months earlier, when she had pressed him on whether the Fed would set up a lending program for state and local governments come the next economic downturn. "I don't think we want that authority. I think that's something for Congress to do. I don't think we want to be picking winners and losers, we want to be helping the economy broadly."[8]

Tlaib, leaning into her microphone from her seat on the questioner's bench, had continued undaunted. Why had the commercial paper market gotten support in the 2008 crisis, while the municipal bond market, crucial to cities like Detroit, which she represented, got nothing?

"What's the difference for corporations? Why is there a different standard?" she asked.

"We devised programs to reopen the capital markets," he said of the 2008 response, adding that the point was to get money to a broad variety of borrowers across the economy.

"We could do something similar for state and local governments," Tlaib had pushed back, gesturing emphatically.

"You know, we can talk about this," Powell had dodged, the strain in his voice suggesting that he was slightly ruffled, a condition that was uncharacteristic for him.

In less than a year, the world had changed so wholly that his institution was going to race across that line. Crossing the barrier without any change to the law would prove something that careful Fed-watchers and, seemingly, Tlaib had known even in July 2019: Often when the Fed says that it cannot do something, what it really means is that it does not want to. Laws can be stretched. But Powell's reasons for wanting to ignore that flexibility remained real and present. Entering local debt markets would invite politicization.

So, inevitably, would the other red line the Fed was preparing to cross by early April. As Treasury and central bank officials monitored the corporate bond markets following the Fed's sweeping March 23 program announcements, an unfortunate truth was becoming clear. Backstopping investment-grade securities was not going to solve the many problems afflicting companies that sat right on the dividing line between investment and junk status. Big companies were facing ratings downgrades at a moment when the market for risky debt was barely functioning, and the Fed's new programs were ironically making junk bonds look even worse relative to their backstopped investment-grade counterparts. Credit ratings could become the difference between success and failure for companies that had been perfectly healthy before the pandemic.

Larry Fink, the BlackRock chief executive, had sent Powell and Mnuchin an email on March 30 spelling out which large companies sat on the dividing line between investment-grade and junk ratings and which ones had already fallen. Household names dotted the list of recent downgrades, with Ford Motor, Occidental Petroleum, and Kraft Heinz Company the largest among them.

Making matters worse, the growing divide between investment-grade and junk debt threatened to exacerbate problems for America's banks. Corporate executives who thought their debt might get downgraded—or who worried that new debt would prove impossible to issue—were rushing to shore up their cash supplies by drawing on their lines of credit with banks. While the banks had been perfectly capable of making good on the credit promises up to that point, the drawdowns left them with less capacity to carry out other kinds of lending and market-making.

There was an easy fix. The Fed could buy junk bonds.

It would deal with the problem, but very little else about that plan was attractive. In what may have been a testament to the sensitivity of the issue, Powell and Mnuchin discussed it mostly between themselves at first. No politician, no matter how much financial backing they received from Wall Street or big corporations, was likely to publicly cheer a decision to help companies that had chosen to take on big debt loads.

The way to help the junk market without helping specific companies seemed to be to buy lower-rated bonds via exchange-traded funds, or ETFs, which was akin to buying tiny slices of a huge range of debt. Unfortunately, that created another pitfall. The largest junk bond ETF was offered by BlackRock, the firm running the Fed's programs, and it had been hit by massive outflows. By backstopping the market, the Fed would be bolstering a product tied to the very company it was paying to carry out its rescue. The calculus was one that would make any policy maker squirm. A broad, fund-based junk bond purchase program was likely to be quick and efficient. It would probably work. It was guaranteed to look terrible.

It was the hardest decision in a crisis full of them, but the positives carried the day. Industry players were assuring Fed officials that things could get bad if they waited. Officials were keenly aware that corporations employing millions of people were built upon layers of risky bonds: Mnuchin and Powell themselves had helped to lay that foundation during their years in private equity. Now they needed to keep it from cracking.

Powell donned one of his preferred lavender ties and shrugged on a neatly tailored blue jacket on the morning of April 9, 2020. His hair, always shot with silver, had become increasingly dominated by it over his years as Fed chair.

As he climbed into his Tesla—he was able to drive himself into work on the rare occasions that he was compelled to go in amid lockdown[9]—he faced the day that the Fed would formally breach its long-maintained boundaries. The central bank planned to unveil the municipal loan program it had been developing, detail its plans to buy some junk bond funds and recently downgraded corporate bonds, and explain how much of the new CARES money Mnuchin had earmarked for each of the emergency backstop programs the Fed had announced. The Treasury was holding some of the money in reserve, but the firepower was substantial: The new emergency programs would have $2.3 trillion in total lending ability. At 8:30 A.M., at the same exact moment that the Labor Department announced that nearly seven million people had newly filed for unemployment in the prior week, the Fed put out its statement.[10]

"With $2.3 Trillion Injection, Fed's Plan Far Exceeds Its 2008 Rescue," *The New York Times* headline read. *Fortune* called the move "stunning."[11] CNBC labeled it an "even bigger bazooka." A mere ninety minutes later, after watching the initial reactions roll in, Powell joined a Brookings Institution webcast from the book-lined Fed studio he had begun to use for such events. He sounded hopeful, but certainly not lighthearted.

"These are programs we're developing at a high rate of speed—we don't have the luxury of taking our time the way we usually do. We're trying to get help quickly to the economy as it's needed," he said. "I worry that in hindsight, you will see that we could have done things differently."[12]

Then he did something that would have been completely uncharacteristic of him just months earlier. Powell had always studiously avoided telling lawmakers what to do, arguing that staying in his lane was an important way to protect Fed independence, and that sounding political might invite partisan backlash and interference. But that day, he recommended what Congress ought to prioritize going forward.

"In many cases, what people really need is direct fiscal support, rather than a loan—and what we can do is loans," he said, weighing in on the prospects of further support. "Not our job, but I would see that as more likely than not to be needed."

"This is what the great fiscal power of the United States is for—to protect these people, as best we can, from the hardships they are facing," Powell said. His words doubtless would have rung true in Sam Stephens's worry-filled Manhattan apartment.

They also pushed Powell over yet another of his personal lines.

Lael Brainard was having hard conversations of her own in those early days of April.

Her leading role in the Fed's emergency lending design process gave her an important voice in some of the most critical choices the central bank would make during the 2020 crisis—and also some of the most difficult. If the lending programs worked, they might keep businesses and municipalities healthy in the face of turmoil. If they failed, jobs would be lost and the economy would suffer.

Starting from March 31, Fed and Treasury officials had begun to discuss the nitty-gritty aspects of the various programs that had been announced on daily 5:00 p.m. calls. Planning had gotten off to a tense start. Brainard, Powell, Mnuchin, New York Fed president John Williams, and Fed and Treasury staff members—including the Fed's lawyers, led by Mark Van Der Weide, and financial stability staff led by Andreas Lehnert—were trying to come to agreements on how much risk the programs should take, who should qualify for help, and what the terms of the loans should be.

For an hour every evening, Brainard and Powell dialed in from their houses in Chevy Chase, while Mnuchin called in from his office (he lived in a $12.6 million mansion in D.C.'s Massachusetts Avenue Heights neighborhood,[13] but Treasury officials went in to work throughout the pandemic). The public image Mnuchin painted of those early meetings was one of studious cooperation.

"We're very focused on a Main Street lending program, for those businesses that are above the SBA program and below the corporate program," he told Fox's Lou Dobbs that first week of April.

Behind the scenes, though, things were quickly becoming stressed. The design choices were anything but simple, and wording the term sheets was a tense exercise. If programs like Main Street were designed too loosely, they could end up boosting sophisticated investors and highly indebted companies who figured out ways to exploit loopholes. That would invite accusations of favoritism and backdoor bailout. Mnuchin was extremely attuned to that risk, which made him cautious. Nor was he willing to lose a lot of money on the programs.

He saw the $454 billion Congress had approved to back up the lending as a sort of nuclearization of Fed policy. The pile of money was so big, so clearly all-overpowering if it were used, that its mere existence should deter turmoil in markets. There was no need to design the programs in a way that would put the appropriation at risk. It was whispered in policy circles that Mnuchin was trying to emulate Hank Paulson's 2008 emergency lending efforts, which had handed back basically every cent of the government's money. Early on, Mnuchin was open and frank about the fact that he did not plan to gamble with the cash.

"I think it's pretty clear if Congress wanted me to lose all of the money, that money would have been designed as subsidies and grants as opposed to credit support," he would tell a group of reporters in late April.[14]

Mnuchin's backstop philosophy basically checked out when it came to the corporate bond program, which had begun to soothe markets with its very existence. But Brainard and many of her colleagues thought that Treasury was being too stingy as the terms for both the municipal program and Main Street came together. The municipal terms should be at least as generous as the corporate bond program, Brainard felt, and Main Street simply wouldn't work to funnel cash to midsize businesses if officials were not willing to take the chance of losing some government money.

"We don't want to make the mistake of being timid," Brainard argued on the calls. Eric Rosengren, the Boston Fed president and the official that the Board had asked to run the Main Street program— thanks to both his personal competence and the strength of his team—backed her up. The Fed risked playing a bigger role in markets than it had wanted to by establishing the programs in the first place. If they were going to do it, Brainard and her colleagues wanted to make sure that the facilities worked.

To what extent it weighed on her mind is unclear, but being so enmeshed in crisis design came at an obvious risk to Brainard's reputation in Washington. She was not able to make decisions herself, because the process necessarily required compromising with Republican administration officials. Yet even seemingly minor design choices carried huge potential to spur backlash. (For instance, Trump's energy secretary would say on national television that an early adjustment to the Main Street program was meant to help oil and gas companies, a statement that drew immediate cries of dismay from Democrats.) The shadow of decisions made in the heat of the moment in 2020 could come back to haunt her policy future and her chances at higher office. As Kashkari had learned twelve years earlier, it is difficult to walk away from a critical role in crisis management with your name unblemished.

There was little chance that the public would remain innocent to the central position she was playing, because the news was already dribbling out. Lauren Hirsch, then a reporter at CNBC, would report later in April that Brainard was central to design work on the Main Street lending program.

"Her role in the program, which is being conducted under a Republican administration, is notable given her Democratic ties," Hirsch said. "Yet her involvement in the Main Street program may help soothe some partisan tensions as there is heightened scrutiny of loans being given to larger companies."[15]

Powell and Mnuchin were going to own the 2020 rescue. For better or for worse, so would Lael Brainard.

Quarles, too, found himself confronting a moment of discomfort as the pandemic response rolled out.

The Fed's vice-chair for supervision did not believe the government should gum up the gears of capitalism. He liked rules-based policies. He disliked discretionary decision-making that injected uncertainty for the people who made markets run. But in April 2020, the Fed was obviously going to need to make heavier use of its unelected power, and it was going to have to use it on the fly. Banks were about to start their annual stress testing cycle, and the scenario analysis the Fed had planned to run their balance sheets through suddenly looked almost laughably mild. The "severe stress" scenario had an unemployment rate far lower than the heights pandemic-spurred joblessness would likely touch.

Already, calls for the banks to restrict capital payouts had begun to escalate toward a fever pitch. The eight biggest banks had announced that they would stop buying back their own outstanding stock shares under behind-the-scenes pressure from Quarles, and that act of suasion had made him squirm. But the banks had still not halted dividends, and the Fed was regularly forced to defend why it had not intervened to make them.

"I think our banks are highly capitalized," Chair Powell had said on April 9. "I don't think that step is appropriate at this time."[16]

It was increasingly clear that the Fed was going to need to do something more to ensure that banks were safe enough to weather a long dry spell. Brainard was internally pushing back on the lack of action to cut off dividends, and she was in broad company. Former Fed officials had begun weighing in on the issue with uncharacteristic force. Janet Yellen, who did not often criticize the institution she had formerly led, had made it clear that she was in favor of suspending bank payouts.[17] Kashkari, in Minneapolis, was apoplectic: Given the experience in 2008, he could not believe that the Fed would even consider letting banks send money out the door at a time when the crisis might worsen.

"Large banks are eager to be part of the solution to the coronavirus crisis," he had penned in an opinion piece in the *Financial Times* on April 16. "The most patriotic thing they could do today would be to stop paying dividends and raise equity capital, to ensure that they can endure a deep economic downturn."[18]

Quarles remained adamant that he didn't want to constrain payouts excessively or randomly. Even so, he recognized the black eye that would come from doing nothing to shore up bank positions if they were to run into trouble down the road. The 2020 stress tests, he and his colleagues were deciding, were going to need a revamp.

Speaking on a webcast before the David Eccles School of Business—

ever a family man—Quarles on April 10 explained the Fed's plan for the first time. It would subject the banks to a series of scenario analyses in addition to their typical stress tests. The results would not be binding, so they would not require banks to raise more capital. It was hardly toothy, but it did introduce an element of unpredictability to bank oversight, something Quarles had made a career out of criticizing.*

"The right thing to do is for us to continue our stress tests but as part of them to analyze how banks' portfolios are responding to real, current events, not just to the hypothetical event that we announced earlier this year," Quarles said, speaking from his personal office, a fire crackling in his modern black marble hearth. Then the Fed could "use that analysis to inform determinations we make about the supervision and regulation of the financial sector."[19]

Details were still in the works, he implied. What he said next was more surprising, coming from Washington's most powerful champion of light-touch regulation. Quarles suggested that the Fed and the broader government were probably going to need to reassess nonbank regulations—the ones that govern savings vehicles like money market funds and hedge funds—in the wake of the March market turmoil.

"As the dust settles here," he said, it would be important to "think about whether we have the right macro-framework around that portion of the financial sector, because of the significant amount of intervention that was required at the outset of this event."[20]

The thing Randy Quarles disliked more than the government getting mixed up in the workings of capitalism was when capitalism demanded it. America's top economic officials were finding during those frantic days that a crisis is a time for pragmatism, even if in-the-moment decisions risked setting precedents that could come back to haunt you later. As Powell sometimes quoted: *There are no atheists*

---

* When they were run that June, the scenarios would suggest that some banks could find themselves in bad shape if the pandemic took a more dangerous turn. The Fed also temporarily capped dividends in that release, while stopping short of halting them entirely. A second set of stress tests in December would allow for payouts to resume.

in foxholes. Whatever your ideology might be, you reassessed in the trenches.

April 2020 was uneasy for the Fed, and tragic for the world. Coronavirus fatalities climbed steadily, uncertainty over the future remained intense, and America remained on edge, braced for things to get worse before they got better.

Chapter 11

CULTURE WARS AND CAPITAL

The United States . . . on the one hand this is a country
of egalitarian promise, a land of opportunity for millions
of immigrants of modest background; on the other hand,
it is a land of extremely brutal inequality, especially in
relation to race.

—*Thomas Piketty,* Capital in the Twenty-First Century

Y ES, EVERY LIFE LOST is one too many," the Pittsburgh, Pennsylvania, radio host Wendy Bell said into her Facebook Live camera on the first Sunday in April 2020, rocking back and forth
slightly, apparently gripped by the animating energy of outrage. She
appeared before a radio microphone, but her flawless bronzer and
constant gestures toward the camera made it clear that she was working for a visual medium.

"Yes, that's the talking point. That's what we're going to say. But
ultimately dollars and cents boil down to, 'Are you going to bankrupt
America and the future for less than 1 percent of our population?'
Many of whom are already ill or aged? I'm on a fence."

Bell's ambivalence about hundreds of thousands of potentially
preventable deaths drew outcry on social media but also spoke to a
dark tension running through society. As vaccines remained a distant hope and hospitals struggled under the weight of coronavirus
caseloads, America was tired of staying at home. Businesses had been
bludgeoned with lost revenues, and Trump and his administration
were increasingly intolerant of the lockdown as it erased their prized

economic progress and pushed unemployment to Great Depression levels. Across Bell's local Pittsburgh area, Governor Tom Wolf's name was becoming a dirty word, synonymous with government-enforced limitations meant to curb the virus. Shoppers at Giant Eagle, the regional grocery chain, audibly smarted at rules that required carts to flow in one direction. Staffers at a local Walmart could be heard complaining loudly about having to wear masks as face coverings rode below their noses.

By early May, as state and local governments slowly reopened with some restraints still in place, masks had evolved into a potent political symbol. A poll by the Associated Press and the NORC Center for Public Affairs Research found that while 76 percent of Democrats said they wore masks when they left home, 59 percent of Republicans did.[1] President Trump appeared at several public events without one, flouting his own government's guidance, and toward the end of May he shared a tweet mocking Democratic presidential candidate Joseph R. Biden, Jr., for wearing one.

"He's a fool," Biden said when asked about the incident on CNN. "This macho stuff."[2]

As it became clear that the pandemic was going to be difficult to control, and that the health crisis was likely to drag on until a vaccine became available and perhaps even after, federal and state and local government officials had begun to plan for ways to safely—or at least sort of safely—return to major parts of normal life even as the virus continued to burn slowly through communities. Midway through April, Trump's White House had released "Opening Up America Again" guidelines.[3] New York City was designing a phased reopening plan—restaurants might be able to place outdoor seating on closed streets, *Eater New York* reported hopefully in late April[4]— and Georgia had allowed indoor dining to resume on April 27. The moves couldn't come fast enough to satisfy many. When Michigan governor Gretchen Whitmer extended the state's stay-at-home order until May 15, hundreds of protesters descended on the state house, many without masks and some toting guns.[5] They called it an "American Patriot Rally," and Trump supporters dominated. Photos of the crowd were peppered with the cardinal red of "Make America Great Again" hats. Government skepticism and populism had taken on an anti-mask bent.

The coronavirus had intensified fissures that were running through American society, feeding divisiveness and unrest as that never-ending spring crawled toward the first pandemic summer. Some of the gaps were political. Democrats often emphasized the threat the virus posed, while Republicans often played it down. Others were economic: College-educated white-collar employees were working from home as their blue-collar counterparts lost jobs or labored on the front lines, exposed to the dangerous virus. But the spark that would ignite the societal fire that summer was racial.

By May, it was clear that Black, Hispanic, and Latino Americans were quietly bearing the heaviest brunt of the coronavirus pandemic when it came to public health and economic outcomes. Early in the pandemic, people from those demographics were hospitalized for coronavirus at nearly five times the rate of white people.[6] The unemployment rate for Black workers would spike to nearly 17 percent in May 2020—that for white workers had peaked the prior month at about 14 percent, and by then it was already coming down. Those disparities were just the latest expression of long-running inequities, and especially jarring ones in a nation that claimed equality of opportunity as its founding credo. America's minorities were more likely to have less education, work in low-income jobs, and live in places with limited healthcare, trends that had evolved from centuries of discrimination and disadvantage. In the years leading up to the pandemic, the nation had been grappling with the harsh reality that Black people were regularly killed at the hands of the police who were meant to protect them, with protests at times sweeping American cities.

The nine minutes that helped to turn the reaction to that centuries-long drumbeat of injustice into an even more momentous movement came on Tuesday, May 25, 2020. That was the day that Minneapolis police arrested George Floyd, a forty-six-year-old Black man who a convenience store clerk said had bought cigarettes with a counterfeit $20 bill. A white officer named Derek Chauvin kneeled on Floyd's neck until he died, a slow-motion killing that was captured on video and circulated across the internet.

Hundreds of protesters flooded Minneapolis's streets starting the next day, and by May 27 they were marching across major cities from Memphis to Los Angeles. Photos of people of all colors and creeds gathering in solidarity, holding posters emblazoned with the phrase

"I Can't Breathe"—George Floyd's last words—dominated social media, alongside images of boarded-up storefronts and broken glass.

The protests quickly became another partisan dividing line, with much of the left embracing them as some on the right painted them as disorderly riots. Chauvin was arrested and charged for Floyd's death on May 29, the same day that Trump posted on Twitter that the Minneapolis protesters were "thugs" and warned that "when the looting starts, the shooting starts."[7] The phrase, which had a racist history tracing back to the 1960s Civil Rights movement, was widely slammed for glorifying violence.[8]

The 2020 Black Lives Matter protests were an important moment for America. At the Federal Reserve, which had been slowly evolving to fit a changing nation, they marked a sort of tipping point. From his home office setup in Minneapolis, the very epicenter of the unfolding social action, Kashkari was watching the events play out with dismay. He had long been bothered by the fault lines dividing society in the twenty-first century, many of which were both economic and racial—so bothered, in fact, that he had years earlier launched an Opportunity & Inclusive Growth Institute to research the ways that the economy distributed its winnings. Much of its work mirrored research that was happening across the Fed's twelve-bank system, but Kashkari was especially active in communicating that it was happening, drawing news coverage and stoking conversation on social media.

In the tense early hours after George Floyd's murder, as Kashkari watched the city around him react with shock and sadness and shared in the protesters' outrage, he decided to talk about it on Twitter. On May 27, he posted a two-tweet series condemning police action.

"It was as if they were saying: this is what we've been trained to do. We are trained to use deadly force against black men. And if they die, it's their own fault for being in that situation," he wrote. "It indicates institutional racism that is actively taught and reinforced."[9]

Kashkari's statement would, in subsequent days and weeks, become the national consensus on the political left and often on the more moderate right. But at a time when people were still processing what had happened, it was a shocking assertion coming from a policy official at the usually staid Federal Reserve.

It was rare for a reserve bank president to take a declarative stance on a potentially controversial topic in a public setting. The central bank had spent the prior decades mostly steering clear of hot-button social issues, especially ones with even a whiff of partisanship. The usual carefulness was no accident: The Fed had at times faced intense backlash when it was perceived to have stepped out of its lane. When Janet Yellen had talked about exploding inequality in 2014—questioning "whether this trend is compatible with values rooted in our nation's history"—then congressman Mick Mulvaney lambasted her for being too political.

"You're sticking your nose in places that you have no business to be," Mr. Mulvaney said at a House hearing in 2015, talking over her and raising his voice to punctuate his theatrical outrage. One of his fellow Republicans accused her of political bias, saying the issue was a Democratic campaign point.[10]

Yellen had pushed back, her voice taut, and argued that it was an economic issue.

"I am not making political statements," she insisted. "I am discussing a significant problem that faces America."

The 2015 exchange elicited headlines and spurred discussion about the a-partisan Fed's appropriate place in debates about equity, which was clearly an economic issue, but also unavoidably a social and political one. Kashkari was going further than Yellen had in commenting on a partly social issue, and it was a mere five years later. While he had more freedom as a Fed president than she'd had as chair, the striking contrast also showed how much the central bank had shifted in the interim.

The Fed, as a major producer of research, had increasingly begun to see itself as an important voice on a range of issues. New and bigger datasets had enabled more detailed studies on race, equity, education, and opportunity. And it was becoming harder to avoid treading into political territory: As the anti-mask movement illustrated, practically every part of American life by 2020 had taken on some sort of partisan bent. Even so, George Floyd's death was a bright-line moment, one that took the Fed's growing openness and increasing role in a national conversation about fairness and crystallized them. The Fed had sometimes sided with the political left on divisive but clear-cut issues by 2020 (its officials took the virus seriously and advocated wearing a mask), but it had never weighed in full-throatedly on any button quite as hot as 2020 racial equity discussions and the Black Lives Matter protests would prove to be.

Kashkari's colleagues across the Fed system released their own statements of either condemnation for what had happened in Minneapolis or support for the Black community. Mary Daly in San Francisco wrote on Twitter that "hate thrives when people stay quiet. So, it's important for all of us to use this moment to speak up. We must say out loud that this is not okay." Raphael Bostic, the only Black person then among the Fed's top leadership, wrote a post about the economic and social imperative to combat systemic racism. The events were "yet another reminder that many of our fellow citizens endure the burden of unjust, exploitative, and abusive treatment by institutions in this country. Over the course of American history, the examples of such institutionalized racism are many," he wrote.[11]

Powell himself spoke about the killing and the protests that followed during his news conference on June 10, a moment that stood out to many within the Fed's cautious halls as bold for the institution. "I want to acknowledge the tragic events that have again put a spotlight on the pain of racial injustice in this country," he said. "I speak for my colleagues throughout the Federal Reserve System when I say that there is no place at the Federal Reserve for racism and there should be no place for it in our society."

Many of the Fed's officials were clearly trying to display moral leadership, but several also brought the topic back to the central bank's own job, anchoring their comments in terms of economics.

"Everyone deserves the opportunity to participate fully in our society and in our economy," Powell had said in his June statement. "These principles guide us in all we do."

Kashkari, as usual, was even blunter.

"Racism is an undercurrent of the status quo," he told *The New York Times*.[12] "You have huge chunks of our population who are not getting a good education, who do not have good job opportunities—it absolutely holds our economy back."

—

The new tone at the Fed in 2020 reflected practical reality: Politically charged though it might be, inequality had become such an enormous force shaping and defining America's economy that it was no longer something the nation's most important economic policy body could tiptoe around. And America's new Gilded Age of gaping wealth and income divides often broke along racial lines, a reality the data made inescapably clear.[13]

The typical Black worker earned 80 cents on the typical white worker's dollar each week, and Black unemployment was double white unemployment at the best of times.[14] Years of lower earnings and tenuous footholds in the job market could add up to lower wealth: In 2019, the median Black family had a net worth of roughly $36,000, compared to roughly $188,000 for the median white family.[15]

The building blocks of that divided economic reality began to stack up before Black children were even born. They were more likely to be the children of parents with fewer resources—which could translate to less one-on-one time and less individual attention in childcare. Black kids, on average, entered school (typically a worse one than the average white child was attending) at a disadvantage that only snowballed as they climbed through the grades.[16] College-bound Black students were more likely to end up at institutions with high tuition and low graduation rates, and far more likely to drop out than their white counterparts.[17] Then came the actual job application process, which research showed treated candidates who were racial minorities unfairly— "Black-sounding" names were much less likely to get a callback.[18]

Race was a painfully obvious dividing line in the American economy by that tumultuous summer of 2020, but it was not the only one. The gaping racial wealth divide was partly linked to a broader bifurcation. A huge and growing rift separated America's haves and have-nots more generally by the time the pandemic struck.

Income inequality had been climbing for decades,[19] and wealth inequality had exploded even more drastically. The median household in the top 10 percent of wealth holders in America had a net worth—assets, like stocks and houses, minus liabilities, like mortgages—of $2.6 million in 2019. A family at the middle of the distribution had one-twelfth that much, $224,000, and one in the bottom 25 percent had just $300. That meant the wealthy had $8,380 in wealth for every $1 the poor had, compared to just $718 to the poorer person's dollar as recently as 1995.

Those figures traced the milder kind of inequality, the kind you could see and sense in your grade school or at the local shopping mall. If one focused in on the top 1 percent, the disparity was mind-boggling. The poorer half of American families held just 1.8 percent of the nation's net worth—savings minus debt—in 2019. The top 1 percent held about 31 percent, based on the Fed's data, up from about 24 percent in 1989.[20]

The Fed played a complicated role in the way both income and wealth inequality had evolved. On one hand, simplistic arguments that blamed racial or even general wealth inequality largely on Fed policies—and particularly on quantitative easing—made little sense. The Fed's balance sheet had started to rapidly expand in 2008, whereas the share of the nation's wealth held by the nation's poorer half had been falling steadily since at least the early 1990s. While some Fed critics suggested that it was low rates, and not just bond buying, that caused wealth inequality, that also failed to square cleanly with the real-world data. The trend toward greater wealth inequality had continued with little disruption through economic cycles, including ones in which the Fed lifted interest rates substantially and for a sustained period.

While Fed policy seemed unlikely to be the main or only driver of wealth inequality, that was not to say that it played no role at all. Mass bond purchases in particular clearly did push up the value of risky assets by prodding savers to seek higher paybacks. That made returns on securities like stocks higher. Rich households tended to hold far more of their net worth in risky securities and investments, so that had the potential to privilege the wealthy.[21] The affluent were also better positioned to hire advisers and fund managers who could help them to invest in ways that took advantage of the low-rate era. And as investors searched for paybacks in a low-rate world, they reshaped the economy. For instance, Wall Street had helped to turn the housing market into an increasingly exclusive asset class: By 2020, private equity and other investment funds regularly purchased and rented or purchased and flipped homes, either themselves or through technology firms using algorithms to quickly price and acquire attractive properties. As house costs rocketed higher amid intense buyer competition that was in some markets exacerbated by institutional money, the towering price tags locked many would-be buyers out, forcing them to rent—and turning their monthly housing outlays into pure consumption, rather than an investment. Because housing had been a major avenue of wealth building for America's middle class, that had the potential to make the wealth divide between the middle and the top starker with time.[22]

Unfortunately, it was devilishly hard to figure out *how much* cheap money was increasing wealth inequality, because the economy was a big system and low rates influenced it in many ways. For instance, the Fed's policies made returns on safe investments lower, which also mattered for asset owners, particularly older people and retirees.

Plus, even if one accepted that the long-run trend toward lower rates tipped the scales toward the wealthy, it was difficult to figure out how much of that to blame on the Fed. Central banks did not set their borrowing costs in isolation: The trend toward lower rates spanned the globe, and seemed to be the long-running result of lower demand for capital, which owed partly to trends like aging demographics that monetary policy could do little to change.

To make matters even more complicated, monetary policy probably had a very different effect on income inequality—the divide between how much rich and poor people earn—because economy-stoking policy helped the job market and boosted laborers. The flip side of a booming stock market was that companies could access more capital to grow and hire. Based on decades of data, it was pretty clearly the case that low rates helped push down the unemployment rate and, if workers became scarce enough, speed up wage growth. Higher pay could allow people who relied on labor to save more, generating wealth of their own. That is why, from the time of the Greenback movement in the 1800s, low rates had often been a preferred policy of the working classes.

The biggest beneficiaries of long or strong economic expansions tended to be people who were disadvantaged in the job market. For instance, Black workers, people who hadn't gotten a college degree, and the formerly incarcerated had flowed into jobs during the long expansion that had ended at the start of the pandemic. In a strengthening economy with low rates, a rising tide could lift all boats, even if the very rich caught the crest of the wave.*

Keeping rates low late into the business cycle wasn't a simple decision or an unambiguous win for the laboring population and society's disadvantaged groups, though. Easy Fed policy could create a combustible economy. Cheap credit could make it easy for families to achieve higher standards of living by borrowing heavily, but that debt made them more vulnerable if they lost a job or took a pay cut and could not keep up with their big house payment or hefty car loan, as the world had discovered in 2008. And while low rates pushed up stock prices, they meant that it was hard for investors who were trying to earn interest on safer forms of saving, like certificates of deposit or government bonds, to eke out a decent return. That could prod retirees and other usually risk-averse savers to take gambles as they tried to earn more interest.

Low short-term interest rates also spurred betting on Wall Street, making it more profitable for big market players to invest on "margin," using borrowed money to multiply trades that made very little money individually, magnifying potential gains but also potential losses.

Cheap money, in short, could inflate bubbles. While it hadn't in generations, there was also the risk that it could help to fuel inflation by stoking demand and leaving too much money chasing too few goods, forcing the Fed to constrain an overheating economy.

When the burst from either an asset price or a consumer price bubble inevitably came, the very rich would see their wealth drop sharply on paper, but working families would pay with their jobs. The same people who were pulled in off the sidelines in a strong labor market were vulnerable to the first wave of firings in times of recession. The

---

* People occasionally argue that the Fed would not have dramatically restrained employment by lifting interest rates. However, the central bank's 2018 rate hiking cycle, and late 2018 signal that it would continue to raise interest rates into 2019, offer an obvious modern counterpoint to that contention. Employment growth slowed markedly in 2018 and into 2019, then began to rebound as the Fed made its emergency cuts. For more historical precedent, one can look to the Volcker era, when high rates clearly pushed joblessness higher.

dot-com market crash of 2000 and the housing market meltdown a few years later both started in excessive financial risk-taking and ended in lost work and diminished futures. In the aftermath of 2008, the stock market recovered long before the job market did, leaving laborers playing a losing game of catch-up. The Fed's 2020 rescue promised to perpetuate that cycle. Because the central bank's backstops limited how much value assets would lose in bad times, they allowed their prices—and thus the wealth of the rich—to soar to heights they could not have achieved without an implied government guarantee.

What were the Fed's options in a world where low rates could bolster the wealthy and create excesses, but where high ones could choke off strong labor markets? Some Fed critics argued that it should have raised rates by more in good times to guard against bubbles and lean against wealth inequality, but that was an oversimplification. Because rates were naturally low across advanced economies, the Fed had limited room to move them high enough to dent asset prices without tanking markets and restraining growth. Reducing the wealth of very rich asset owners by hurting employment, costing the poor and vulnerable their basic livelihoods, was a combination in which everyone lost.

The Fed could have tried to enact more stringent preemptive regulation to blunt the boom-and-bust financial cycle, lessening the need for big market rescues and allowing for longer and more stable expansions that benefited the working classes. But it lacked broad authority over the shadow banks that had been major sources of vulnerability in 2008 and 2020, and that seemed unlikely to change. In the heat of a meltdown, basically everyone agreed that it was critical to keep markets from crashing. Outside those urgent moments, there was rarely enough vigor and consensus to fully overhaul the status quo.

The approach to Fed policymaking that had emerged in 2008 and was being cemented in 2020 was one that seemed to have the potential to lower income inequality—assuming the Fed remained intently focused on achieving a strong labor market—while putting a floor under markets in a way that enabled profitable financial betting. It seemed a reasonable enough setup from within the central bank. The Fed's job was to lay the groundwork for prosperity, not to decide how it was distributed. If Congress wanted to fight gaping wealth inequality, it could use taxes and transfers to redistribute winnings with more precision than the Fed could ever hope to achieve. While trying to help disadvantaged groups was a noble cause, Fed officials insisted that they did not have good tools to try to even the playing field across different education or racial demographics.

Even if that made sense, the setup was primed to draw popular criticism. Book titles declared that the Fed was an "Engine of Inequality," and think pieces argued that the central bank's "fine intentions"[23] worsened wealth divides. It hardly helped that, for all their efforts to commune with Main Street America, the central bank's leadership team was made up of a group of people who stood to benefit in a society that boosted the rich, and who did not look much like the population they were meant to serve.

Monroe Gamble had been ecstatic when he first landed a job as a research assistant at the Federal Reserve Bank of San Francisco in 2018.

The twentysomething had grown up in Kansas City, Missouri, where he had been one of the few Black students in a heavily white school district. With his mother's encouragement, he had started college at Virginia Tech—but he couldn't find direction, he began to have health issues, and he dropped out. Years of searching for a pathway ensued, including a brief period in which he was homeless, surfing friends' couches and lugging around his few worldly possessions in yellow trash bags.

He remained an active reader through his ups and downs, and one day he happened upon a public library book on economics. The topic fascinated him. When he realized that a Black man had written the text, he thought, "I could do this." It took six years, several colleges, and five attempts at multivariate calculus, but he did it. Gamble graduated in 2017 with a degree in business, emphasis on economics, and a minor in mathematics from the University of Missouri.

He was enamored with the idea of working at the Fed and applied to position after position at regional Fed banks—only to get rejected. He attended an economics training program at Harvard University in hopes of beefing up his résumé to land one of the coveted spots. Getting the Ivy League name into his education history had paid off.

When Gamble arrived at the San Francisco branch, a graceful

modern building with a breezeway not far from the city's waterfront Embarcadero district, one filled with modern art and big thinkers, it didn't take him long to notice an uncomfortable reality. He was the only Black economist or economist-in-training at the regional Fed. Gamble did some digging, asking around and looking back at staff photos from years past. He quickly pieced together that he was the first Black research assistant the reserve bank had ever employed.

Diversity and racial equity may have become a topic of intense conversation at the Fed in 2020, but no matter how you cut it— by experience, by socioeconomic status, or by race—representation within the institution itself did not appear to have improved much since Greenspan's days. Of the Fed's twelve regional presidents and five governors in 2020, all were either economists or had worked in banking and finance. One was Black (Bostic of the Federal Reserve Bank of Atlanta), one was of Asian descent (Kashkari), and the rest were white.

Of the Fed system's 870 economists in 2020, a little bit more than 1 percent were Black.[24] Race was just one particularly measurable sign of diversity, and the Fed also scored badly on others. Anecdotally, many of the researchers who held the most important roles at the Fed came from affluent backgrounds. There was an innocent reason for this: To succeed in the field of economics, students had to more or less enter college knowing that it was what they wanted to do. Students who showed up to freshman or sophomore year with economics on the mind came from educated and upper-income families who had given them exposure to the field young.

There was also a less innocent reason. From the entry level up, Fed hiring processes had often screened candidates based on the schools they had attended, and the people coming from top-tier economic programs tended to be heavily white and well-off. During hiring for entry-level reserve bank jobs, candidates with backgrounds deemed imperfect—people with gap years or different pathways into college—were often taken out of the running early.

The Fed also heavily employed macroeconomists, and the field was known for a hard-charging culture that could be unwelcoming for people who did not instantly fit in. Online forums like the popular "Economics Job Market Rumors" showcased an underbelly of meanness and misogyny running through the field.

The Fed's regional network did improve intellectual and background diversity to a degree. Officials and economists at the regional banks lived in their communities, and bank staff often came from local universities and not just elite colleges. That injected some range of perspectives into the conversation. Even so, the central bank remained at least somewhat monolithic—a majority of its top officials in 2020 had degrees from Ivy League universities.

"I get it, it's a signal," Gamble said in 2020, after he had left the regional branch and was getting started on an economics program at New York University. But he had a word for the sensation he felt when he googled someone he admired at the Fed and discovered that their academic credentials were so gold-plated that following in their footsteps seemed hopeless: "The Wikipedia letdown," he called it.

"It's a Fed issue, but it's related to a larger societal issue. I don't think the ceiling is made of glass. It has to be made of bricks."

In locking people out, economics and the Fed had managed to lock a certain set of beliefs in, often in ways that could influence policy-making even as the Fed moved toward greater responsiveness. Centrist liberal ideologies, dominant at many well-ranked universities, were also a common persuasion among monetary policy thinkers. The ideas that markets generally worked, that globalization had been good for the world, and that regulations should be used actively but should not be excessively onerous tended to be accepted as truth more easily than might have been the case if more people who had failed to benefit from those systems had wielded internal power.

Fed officials also relied heavily on the cold equations of economic models as they tried to understand the country around them, and when they turned to anecdotal evidence, it often came from businesses rather than their laborers. A widely available display of that pro-business, pro-markets, pro-expert worldview manifested in the way policy makers had sometimes interpreted the Beige Book.

The un-fabulously titled report was the Fed's regular survey of business contacts throughout the Fed's twelve districts, published eight times a year. Despite the lackluster name, it was at times an important input into how the regional presidents thought about the economy in the years following the Great Recession.

Contacts in the survey began to complain about worker short-ages as early as November 2011, when the national unemployment remained at 8.6 percent, more than twice the 3.5 percent it would reach before that business cycle ended. Millions of people who would eventually come back into the labor market remained sidelined at that point.

Despite that, "finding skilled workers continued to be a major concern," companies in the Richmond region reported. A North Carolina manufacturer said it was "having a tough time hiring good people."[25]

The complaints about labor shortages only intensified from there. As business contacts brought their gripes to regional presidents, some became concerned that monetary policy was too easy and that the labor market was growing too tight.

"Both statistically and anecdotally, we are now getting a consistent message from a variety of sources that the labor market, broadly considered—and not just in booming regional economies like Texas's—is tightening. The employment gap is closing faster than most forecasters foresaw," Richard Fisher said in a 2014 speech. Then the president of the Dallas Fed, he was a graduate of Harvard, Oxford, and Stanford who had spent his early career in banking and investing before winding his way into policy. He argued that the central bank should soon begin dialing back its economic help.[26]

He and his fellow worriers were wrong to fret. Workers continued to flow into jobs for months and years to come, and wages moved only gradually higher. By 2017, twenty million people were still actively searching for work, not looking because they had become discouraged, or working part-time when they would have preferred full-time hours.[27] The Fed lifted interest rates three times that year, with only Kashkari dissenting all three times on the basis that the job market had more room to heal.

By 2020, after years of labor market surprises, officials were thinking about how to cast a wider net. Regional Fed banks had always had community outreach agendas, but they spent the years leading up to the pandemic broadening who they talked to and how publicly they did it. In San Francisco, Mary Daly—one of the few central bankers with working-class roots and no Ivy League degrees, and someone

Gamble cited as a mentor—had recorded several seasons of a podcast called *Zip Code Economies* where she talked with workers and students from around her district. Eric Rosengren's Boston Fed ran a grant competition for small postindustrial cities in its district with the goal of helping them to coordinate and carry out revitalization efforts, an effort that pushed bank staff into their local communities on a regular basis. Powell, Clarida, and Brainard were clearly grappling with how to better talk to and represent labor at the Board level: The Fed Listens component of their signature policy review had moved forward despite complaints and eye-rolling from some regional presidents.

Kashkari had been among those who worried at first that it would be an exercise in showmanship, one that made it sound like the Fed wasn't already listening. The inaugural Fed Listens event in Chicago in June 2019—before the pandemic, when the labor market was widely assessed to be at or near full employment—had changed his mind. Brainard had moderated a panel with the chancellor of the City Colleges of Chicago, the chief executive of the National Skills Coalition, and the head of the Greater Kansas City AFL-CIO. It was titled "What Does Full Employment Look Like for Your Community or Constituency?" Juan Salgado, the chancellor, had pointed out that in one of the heavily minority communities his college served in Chicago, unemployment was at 35 percent and 47 percent of people were not in the labor force.[28]

"When I hear we're at full employment, that's not my reality. That's not our community's reality," Salgado said. "In a city that is vibrant and growing. And I don't want anybody to read into those statistics. These are people with incredible capabilities, and incredible talents, and incredible possibilities that can in fact stick in the labor market."

That comment became the topic of private conversations for the remainder of the conference, clearly having struck many of the academics and central bankers in attendance. Kashkari was shocked that *they* were surprised. It made him realize that even if he thought the Fed's regional branches were already listening, not every important decision maker and economist across the system was necessarily hearing and absorbing the same thing.

Central bankers across America were trying to think more deeply about who was being left out in the modern economy, whether that meant Black and Hispanic Americans, those with lower education levels, or people in left-behind geographies.

As policy makers intensified their focus on economic opportunity in summer 2020, they were also reflecting on what it meant for their own work. In a world with low inflation, did they have more room to push the economy toward a version of employment that could help to benefit groups who had long been neglected in the labor market? Could they set policy in a way that more quickly achieved the kind of job progress for marginalized populations that had taken hold in 2019? Officials continued to point out that their tools were too blunt to help specific groups of workers, but as a summer of painfully high joblessness wore on, they kept an increasingly careful eye on racial and educational unemployment rates to help them take stock of the labor market's strength.

"A tight labor market really does a lot of good things for minorities and people at the lower end of the income spectrum generally," Powell said at his July news conference, asked whether the Fed could explicitly target the racial unemployment gap—something the Biden presidential campaign had been pushing as it swung into full gear. He noted that following the financial crisis, it had taken nearly a decade to get to the point where joblessness was low enough to help workers at the margin.

"That's not a good strategy," he said. "We're going to get back there as quickly as we can, because that's what we can do."

The pendulum at the central bank was swinging more fully away from carefully guarding against inflation by trying to guard against job market overheating, the dominant approach ever since Keynesian fine-tuning in the 1960s had ended in high inflation. In response to a new era of slow price increases, rampant inequality, and an active social conversation about who benefited from economic opportunity in America, the Fed was moving toward a more ambitious approach. It was about to embrace a broad—and inclusive—understanding of full employment.

Chapter 12

LOVE SONGS TO FULL EMPLOYMENT

While the Fed has access to all the latest statistics and an excellent staff to analyze them, it has not found the stone tablet.

—Alice Rivlin, then a Fed governor, in a 1997 speech[1]

S AM BELL HAD SPENT much of the pandemic on Twitter. It was not, to be honest, a huge deviation from his pre-coronavirus life. Bell, thirty-seven and floppy-haired, had founded a nonprofit called Employ America in 2019 with the explicit goal of pressuring the Fed to focus more intently on its employment mandate. Part research organization, part advocacy group, and part buddy project, Employ America started as a three-person band of millennials who wrote online think pieces, fed lawmakers questions for Powell's Capitol Hill hearings, and tweeted about Fed governor nominees to try to influence who ended up with a seat at the policy-making table. Improbably, it was pretty successful. Bell had helped to kill the chances of two particularly unusual Trump Fed nominees—pizza mogul Herman Cain and conservative columnist Stephen Moore—by spending hours hunched over his computer in his D.C. row house unit digging up dish on the nominees and dripping it out over social media.

"The soundtrack to our children's short lives has been 'Wheels on the Bus' and Stephen Moore interviews," Kate Kelly, Bell's wife, told *The New York Times* in 2019.[2]

By August 2020, Bell was still dedicating much of his attention and Twitter feed to opposing Judy Shelton, the latest Trump nominee. She struck many Fed insiders as an unreasonable choice for the job. A longtime Fed critic and a fan of returning to a gold standard or some other form of "hard" money, Shelton had regularly heaped praise on President Trump. Her critics worried that she would champion bad policies while undermining the Fed's prized independence from politics. Bell was slowly dribbling out quotes from long-forgotten interviews she had given, building up a running and unflattering thread.

Skanda Amarnath, Employ America's New York–based co-founder, was a twenty-eight-year-old former hedge fund analyst who had once worked at the New York Fed. He was a fan favorite among influencers in the financial press, like Bloomberg's Joe Weisenthal, and had big ideas about how the nuts and bolts of monetary policy might be improved. Kim Stiens was managing hiring and funding. Money for the project came initially from Open Philanthropy, a charity backed by funding from Dustin Moskovitz, a founder of Facebook, and his wife, Cari Tuna.

The trio were working from an established foundation. Organizing groups on the left had become interested in the Fed in the wake of the Great Recession, as it became clear how phenomenally unequal the rebound was proving. Fed Up, Employ America's predecessor, had started to push the central bank to focus on "fuller" employment following the financial crisis. Many in the economic and central banking industry knew the movement simply as "the green shirts," because it sent community organizers dressed in shamrock tees bearing slogans like "Whose Recovery?" to protest outside the Eccles Building, at Fed congressional testimonies, and at the central bank's biggest annual research confab. Many attendees regarded the group with a mixture of skepticism and bemusement, but a few top Fed officials had taken the time to hear out their argument. It was unclear whether Fed Up changed any minds, but by exerting pressure from the left, it almost certainly gave Fed officials more room to talk about what that concept of full employment meant and how it might be interpreted more expansively.

Before the 2020 pandemic, Bell had felt that the conversation was moving in a positive direction—driven in some small way by advocates from Employ America and Fed Up, and in a large way by thirty years in which low unemployment did not spur higher inflation as expected. After the Fed had cut interest rates three times in 2019, officials had seemed content to leave them lower for some time, even though unemployment stood at a half-century low of 3.5 percent. That was a stark departure from what popular economic models would have suggested.

"We've learned, because we've been watching what's been happening, that unemployment can be lower than many had expected without raising inflationary or other concerns," Powell had told lawmakers in early February 2020.[3]

Then the coronavirus rocketed onto the scene in March, and suddenly America was anything but employed. Joblessness peaked just shy of 15 percent by the end of April, far higher than the 10 percent top during the 2007–2009 downturn. While many of those layoffs were expected to be temporary, ushered in by business closures that had been forced by state and local lockdowns meant to contain the virus's deadly spread, economists anticipated that at least some would last. Employers typically took advantage of recessions as an excuse to fire employees whom they had been considering getting rid of in the first place, and that so many layoffs had been forced practically overnight seemed likely to exacerbate that pattern. As of midsummer, the official jobless rate remained at 10.2 percent—and that understated the true share of Americans out of work, since many weren't even applying to jobs out of fear of the pandemic or because they were waiting to see if their old positions would come back.

The jobs crisis had come at an interesting time, from a policy perspective. The Fed had been nearly done with its almost two-year-long framework review, meant to examine how to deal with downturns and their aftermath, when the crisis hit. It had temporarily dropped the effort thanks to its all-consuming push to keep markets and the economy from crashing.

But by late summer, the Fed's various emergency programs were fully functional. The corporate facility was buying already-issued bonds based on an index the Fed itself had designed. The primary corporate program was open for business, though nobody was using it because private markets were working so well, rescued by a sweeping government economic response and the mere promise of a Fed backstop. The municipal bond market program had loaned money to Illinois and the Metropolitan Transportation Authority of New York, which runs the city's subway system. The Main Street program was lightly used, but it was at least available. The Fed's many programs to support market plumbing—from its commercial paper buying program to its money market and securitized debt relief programs—had succeeded at restoring order across the financial world. In fact, markets were functioning so seamlessly that America's financial market crisis in March seemed like nothing more than a distant memory to most people, a forgotten footnote in the pandemic fugue.

When it came to Fed monetary policy, the situation was about as under control as it was going to get. Rates were still at near zero, and after a period of breakneck buying, central bankers had stabilized their bond purchase program at $120 billion in Treasury debt and mortgage-backed securities each month to keep financial conditions easy.[4] With so much support in place, a full recovery had become a waiting game, one that hinged in large part on the pandemic's trajectory and on the elected government's actions. Congress had injected more money into the Paycheck Protection Program for small businesses, but it continued to debate whether it ought to pass additional fiscal policy relief for the pandemic-smacked economy. Negotiations were moving haltingly, as Democrats demanded a $3 trillion package and Republicans rejected that price tag.[5] At the Fed, though, officials had the capacity to turn their attention back to the policy review.

Powell and his colleagues had decided that the chair would roll out the results on August 27, at a venue sure to attract attention: the Federal Reserve Bank of Kansas City's annual Jackson Hole monetary policy conference. The invitation-only event had long been the preeminent conference in central banking and had been held in Jackson, Wyoming, since 1982. Winning an invite was the ultimate sign that you were a macroeconomic insider. Each August, the leading economic minds descended on Jackson Lake Lodge, where they took in sweeping views of the Teton Mountains and debated full employment over barbecue dinners and Huckleberry Old Fashioneds. (It is an interesting aside that besides offering a striking panorama of the Mountain West, Jackson was home to the widest wealth gap in America thanks to its sizable billionaire class.)

In 2020, the pandemic would fundamentally change the annual gathering. Because economists could not gather for the conference, the Kansas City branch had decided to stream it live online, opening it to the public for the first time. Whether the symbolism was intentional or not, Powell had chosen to unveil his central bank's plan for its future at a symposium that had long epitomized central banking's elitism and secrecy at the very moment that its exclusionary walls broke down.

Despite the warm and fuzzy staging, Employ America did not have high hopes for the review's outcome. Amarnath, who was getting married that weekend at his parents' house in central New Jersey, had spent the morning of the big speech parked on the carpet in front of the family's living room television (all of the furniture had been moved for the celebration) refining a *Medium* post that he planned to publish once Powell's remarks were released. It was going to be scathing. Analysts broadly expected the Fed to announce that it was going to shoot for a 2 percent inflation rate on average, over time, instead of as an absolute goal. The effect would be longer periods of low interest rates, as the Fed allowed for temporarily faster price gains. Amarnath's post was prepared to fault the Fed for making its way through a long review and coming out the other side still narrowly focused on inflation instead of thinking about its goals through a more employment-focused lens.

The Fed had created those low expectations. Vice-chair Richard Clarida, who had led the review, had gone around for most of the prior year promising that the changes would constitute an "evolution, not revolution" in the way the Fed carried out its duties. That undersold things. Powell knew that the announcement he was about to make would mark one of the most meaningful moments of his chairmanship.

The crisis response had pushed the Fed into financial markets in which it had never trodden. Powell's vocal advocacy for a more aggressive congressional spending response to the coronavirus crisis had crept close to violating the "don't tell us how to do our job and we won't tell you how to do yours" principle of American central banking. But revamping the way the Fed thought about and set monetary policy, and then formalizing that in a sort of constitutional document, would put the Fed's priorities on display to the world. Like Volcker choosing to focus carefully on inflation because it was the problem of the era decades earlier, the 2020 Fed was prepared to shape a new age of central banking in which policy makers focused intently on employment. Nobody could guess how fateful the timing of the overhaul would prove.

Powell had read the newspapers before breakfast on the morning of Jackson Hole—already a scorcher in Washington when he rose before dawn—so he knew what was expected from him.

"Officials have signaled they are ready to adopt a new approach of making up for periods of low inflation by seeking subsequent periods of higher inflation, and Mr. Powell's speech offers a natural venue to explain what the Fed is preparing to change and why," Nick Timiraos at *The Wall Street Journal* had written.[6]

"When the Federal Reserve announced a broad review of its monetary policy in November 2018, no one could have predicted that it would wrap up in the middle of a devastating recession and public health crisis," Rachel Siegel at *The Washington Post* had observed.[7]

"Officials have promised the coming tweaks will be more 'evolution' than 'revolution.' Yet they will represent the culmination of not just the review, but also a years-long process in which economists have been forced to fundamentally rethink the relationship between unemployment and prices," according to *The New York Times* story previewing the speech.[8]

Powell reviewed his text and got himself set up in the staged, book-lined set at the Eccles Building. Given the heat of the day and the typically casual vibe at the Jackson Hole event—usually the one conference at which macroeconomists can pretend to be cowboys—he decided to forsake his signature purple tie as the staff positioned him in front of the camera, his crisp white shirt buttoned up underneath a suit jacket.

Michelle Smith, his chief of staff, asked him if he was ready.

The chairman nodded.

The press had gotten the speech in advance, as was customary, and the headlines crossed the Bloomberg, Reuters, and Dow Jones newswires just after 9:00 A.M. As Fed officials had expected might be the case, they varied wildly. But the basic message had gotten across: The Fed was going to aim for 2 percent inflation on average rather than as a target, much as expected. Even as Powell began to deliver his remarks, former Fed officials were speaking to reporters to make sure they hadn't missed the other highlight.

"Our revised statement says that our policy decision will be informed by our 'assessments of the shortfalls of employment from its maximum level' rather than by 'deviations from its maximum level' as in our previous statement," Powell read on the webcast, and the communications crew emphasized. The change seemed innocuous, even pedantic, as big moments in central banking often do.

In fact, it marked something revolutionary. Now the Fed was effectively saying that it would not raise interest rates based purely on a suspicion that the labor market had heated up too much. Officials now cared only about "shortfalls"—too little employment would be a reason to leave rates low. They were giving up on trying to understand what constituted "too much" employment, hoping that the low-inflation era would again give America the chance to embrace all the benefits very low joblessness could offer.

"Our revised statement emphasizes that maximum employment is a broad-based and inclusive goal," Powell explained. "This change reflects our appreciation for the benefits of a strong labor market, particularly for many in low- and moderate-income communities."

Some members of the committee had worried that the new language went too far, tying the Fed to low rates in a way that policy makers might come to regret. But over dozens of phone calls, and by reinforcing that the Fed would still keep a careful eye out for financial bubbles, Powell and Clarida had managed to keep the whole committee on board.

In the framework text released in tandem with the speech, the policy-setting Federal Open Market Committee noted that "sustainably achieving maximum employment and price stability depends on a stable financial system." Policy decisions would weigh "the balance of risks, including risks to the financial system that could impede the attainment of the Committee's goals."

In central New Jersey, Amarnath was pleasantly surprised. Bell had guessed the Fed might do some sort of tweak to make it clear that full employment was hard to assess, but Amarnath hadn't been so sure. The Fed was effectively saying it could not reliably estimate how low unemployment could fall without pushing up prices, and that it would no longer try to do so while setting policy. That was huge. It was rejecting the consensus that had ruled policy since economists had embraced economist Milton Friedman's ideas—which stressed that central banks should not push for excessively low unemployment levels because doing so risked higher inflation—following the 1970s stagflation.

"Photoshop request," Amarnath said to Bell in a Twitter DM. "Powell and Friedman's photos on Iverson and Ty Lue."

Bell replied with the requested image. It was an iconic basketball photo in which Allen Iverson, a player for the Philadelphia 76ers, steps over Los Angeles Lakers player Ty Lue after scoring a shot—an extreme expression of disrespect and domination. Now it showed the Fed chair stepping over the champion of the "natural" unemployment rate. The meme's point? Friedman's approach was over, defeated by one high-stepping Jerome H. Powell.

Still, the pair didn't give the framework revamp unambiguously high marks.

"Skanda, what do you think of them adding this?" Bell asked Amarnath in the chat, highlighting the new financial stability language. "Is this like a permission slip to go hawkish?"

"It is an escape clause," Amarnath replied. He meant that officials could point to financial stability risks and use them as an excuse to raise rates if they felt that they needed to lift borrowing costs before inflation had moved substantially higher.

Amarnath still published his *Medium* piece, painting the continued devotion to an inflation-focused framework for setting policy as a disappointment. But on a webcast discussion with David Beckworth, host of a macroeconomic policy podcast and an economist at George Mason University's Mercatus Center, and Julia Coronado, a former Fed economist and founder of a macroeconomic consultancy, Amarnath and Bell seemed grudgingly happy, and about as content as activists who make it their job to critique the Fed could be expected to sound.

"This is the flipping of the order of operations here—the goal is now maximum employment, that takes precedence," Coronado said. She attributed the change to Powell. "I think he took Janet Yellen's lessons deep into his soul, he went out to the people and heard them—his fingerprints are all over this."

"Skanda and I have been going back and forth about—how satisfied should we be about this," Bell said. "Most of Powell's speeches now are love songs to full employment," but "if you're not actually targeting a labor market outcome, is that enough?"

"I'll say a big 'maybe,'" Beckworth replied.[9]

The Fed's new framework did nothing to prevent policy makers from raising interest rates to cool the economy if inflation jumped: It just said that falling unemployment alone would not be a sufficient reason to change policy so long as inflation remained below 2 percent. On the day of the Fed's September 2020 meeting, though, officials went a step further.

When the Federal Open Market Committee released its statement at 2:00 P.M. on September 16, the usually slow-to-change policy statement had undergone a major overhaul. The Fed pledged to tolerate periods of higher inflation to offset periods of weak ones, as expected. But the Fed's policy makers also said that they expected to keep interest rates at rock bottom "until labor market conditions have reached levels consistent with the Committee's assessments of maximum employment and inflation has risen to 2 percent and is on track to moderately exceed 2 percent for some time."[10] That tweak was profound. The wording implied that officials were not going to lift interest rates until they had achieved full employment, even if price increases began to pick up.

The pledge to keep interest rates at zero was so strong that it drew a dissent from Dallas Fed president Robert Kaplan, a former Harvard Business School professor who was worried that the central bank was hamstringing itself. The Fed was trying to prove that it would follow through on its framework and reassure its doubters. Pundits had been asking how it would achieve 2 percent inflation on average when it had failed to get inflation up to 2 percent for a decade. But Kaplan worried that the new language would make it hard to react if the economy surprised officials.

"If you make that kind of commitment, it's important for Fed credibility to keep it," Kaplan told *The Wall Street Journal* after his no vote. "There are costs to keeping rates at zero for a prolonged period of time. And I'm also conscious of the fact the world's changing."[11]

Neel Kashkari had dissented in the other direction. He would have liked an even firmer promise. He thought the central bank should have pledged that it would only raise rates if it had in fact reached 2 percent inflation for a sustained period, not just because it was on track.

"This new language still relies on the Committee to assess whether we are at maximum employment and whether inflation is expected to climb," Kashkari said in a statement explaining his dissent. "Those are difficult judgments to make in real time."[12]

Kashkari had spent the years before the 2020 pandemic crisis arguing that economists should stop declaring that the economy was at or near full employment with so much confidence. The Minneapolis Fed chief had adopted the awkward habit of publicly asking business leaders if they were paying more to lure workers when they complained about labor market shortages. The answer was usually a lot of blustering that boiled down to no.

If a hint of coming inflation spooked his colleagues in the future, Kashkari worried that the policy statement left them too much room to repeat the mistakes of the prior business cycle. But Kashkari's fellow policy makers worried that if they committed the Fed too absolutely, and the world changed in ways that they could not then predict, the central bank would not be prepared to respond. Once inflation pressures began to build, they might feed on themselves, making prices hard to control.

"At the time, I called such theories ghost stories, because there was no evidence they were true but they also couldn't be ruled out," Kashkari complained in his dissent that September. "I believe that characterization is still appropriate today."[13]

Unfortunately for Kashkari—and for Powell's Fed as a whole—it would be less than a year before that particular ghost story started to come true. Given the context in which it was enacted—one of tepid price gains and a chronically lukewarm economy—the Fed's policy revamp and its dramatic implementation made sense. Within a year, that context would shift.

Yet the pandemic would hold a few more near-term challenges for the central bank even before that sweeping economic change surfaced.

Chapter 13

A FED RESTRAINED

How far should a central bank—shielded from political
pressures—go in indirectly financing budget deficits
and influencing the distribution of credit broadly in the
economy?

—*Paul Volcker on the central question of*
central banking, Keeping at It

B Y EARLY AUTUMN 2020, it had become clear that Florida was
having a terrible pandemic, economically. The state's regular deluge of tourists, the lifeblood of its businesses, had slowed to a
trickle. Hotels, malls, and even Disney World were filing mass layoff notices with the government. The state's best hope for reprieve
was a vaccine, and there was some reason for hope: Breakthroughs
suggested that one would become slowly available starting in 2021.
But many Florida businesses had begun to seek out a more short-
term solution to the cash flow problems they were facing. They,
more than any other companies in the country, had begun to tap
the Federal Reserve's small- and midsize business loan program,
Main Street. Of the 1,800 loans the Main Street program would
eventually make, by far the biggest share—about 350—came from
the Sunshine State.[1]

That owed partly to local desperation, but also partly to City
National Bank of Florida, which had made an active effort to offer
the loans, advertising how they worked and suggesting the program
to clients. Customers who decided to go for it saw in Main Street

loans a way to live on borrowed time: The money would need to be paid back over five years—with principal payments starting after the loan's second year[2]—but by then, tourists from South America, Europe, and Asia might once again crowd streets and bars. The program might be a bridge to the other side.

Josh Wallack, a nightclub owner, made exactly that calculus. He and his father owned and operated Mango's Tropical Cafe in two locations, one on the main tourist drag in Orlando, the other in Miami's South Beach. The clubs usually pulled in $50 million in revenue a year, but they had closed practically overnight as coronavirus unfolded. The Wallacks took out a Paycheck Protection Program loan, but it wasn't enough to get them past the shock. They had laid off most of their 415 employees but still employed staff to keep up the buildings. Maintenance and mortgage costs on the two massive locations added up, with nobody paying for salsa dancing lessons or ordering passion fruit mojitos. When City National, the family's banker for the prior fifty years, suggested Main Street, Wallack looked over the terms and agreed that his business was a good fit. He took out a $10 million loan in August 2020.

"It was do or die at that point," he would later recall. "It opened up avenues for us to not have to act out of panic." Even so, he could see why the program had gotten such limited uptake.

Main Street borrowers couldn't have big debt loads to begin with and had to be in good financial shape more broadly. Few banks were advertising it like City National Bank of Florida had done. While Wallack's banker seemed to see the program as a service to clients, one that might earn it some fees along the way, its counterparts hadn't made a similar calculus. Many banks had complained from the start that the program was unworkable: Because they had to retain a slice of the loans, they would be on the hook if they loaned to risky companies. If a company was not risky and they wanted to lend to it anyway, why would they bother with the extra paperwork and rules of the Main Street program?

Bill Nelson, a former Fed staff official who by then worked for a bank lobbyist, had sent Randy Quarles a six-point email extremely early in the planning process—on March 25—detailing why the Fed's Main Street plan would fail. "Banks will not want to get involved in anything that smells of bailout or be exposed to put-back risk. Consequently, the facilities that we discussed yesterday probably won't work."

Without buy-in from their bankers, relatively few borrowers understood the program. Even those who did often saw it as an unattractive option. It would leave them more indebted in a worst-case scenario where the economy didn't reopen, or saddled with a loan that came with limits on executive pay and other strings attached if it did.

The program's rules and pricing were part of the problem, because a risk-averse Treasury had kept them stringent. Officials from the Fed Board, the Boston Fed (which was running the program), and the Treasury had spent months bickering about its terms and conditions over an endless stream of planning phone calls. Try as they might, nobody—not Brainard, not Boston's Rosengren, not the Fed staff, and not his own staff—could convince Mnuchin to go bigger, taking on more risk to make Main Street more attractive.

The program had gotten off the ground slowly amid all of the back-and-forth, launching only in July, and had been repeatedly revised even after it started.[3] Following months of design tweaks and long hours of work by the Treasury and Fed teams, the best option the group had come up with and agreed to by late summer and early fall would mainly work for healthy businesses without too much debt looking for big loans and expecting life to return to normal quickly once the pandemic ended—businesses like Mango's.

The clubs weren't just viable; they had been thriving. The company was around thirty years old and the two venues were local nightlife landmarks. The Wallacks owned their buildings, so while there were mortgages to keep up with and utilities to pay, there was no crushing rent burden building up month after month during the closure. Companies that were newer, more indebted, or less profitable were much less primed to benefit.

By the end of October, the Main Street program had used less than 1 percent of its $600 billion capacity, and while that owed partly to the reality that the economy was holding up better than just about anyone had expected, the headlines reviewing it were scorching.[4] Academics, politicians, and even the occasional unnamed Fed official took to sniping at Mnuchin in veiled and unveiled statements to the press.

"Many officials within the Fed wanted to create a program that businesses would actually use, but some at Treasury saw the program as more of an absolute backstop for firms that were out of options. Steven Mnuchin, the Treasury secretary, has resisted taking on too much risk," *The New York Times* wrote in early July.[5] "Some Fed officials privately have voiced frustration that painstaking negotiations wasted precious weeks in launching the program," *The Wall Street Journal* disclosed a few days later.[6] "Trouble on Main Street," NPR's *Planet Money* witheringly titled one article.[7]

"By any measure, the Main Street program has been a failure," Bharat Ramamurti, a former Elizabeth Warren staffer and a member of the Congressional Oversight Commission established to oversee the CARES Act programs, groused at the body's first-ever hearing in August 2020.[8]

The Fed's other programs were functioning more successfully. The new corporate facilities had worked as true backstops: Their very presence had a soothing effect. Bloomberg had titled them "the non-bailout," declaring that the Fed had "saved Boeing without paying a dime" and calling the corporate credit programs a "game changer" for the embattled airplane manufacturer.[9]* Even the municipal bond-buying program, which occasionally drew progressive ire for being insufficiently generous, seemed to have helped to soothe troubled state and local debt markets.[10]

But Main Street, perhaps the purest encapsulation of the Fed's effort to push its emergency credit support beyond the Wall Street banks and financial institutions that they were designed to help, had underlined both the central bank's potential to help and practical barriers to doing so. The program showed that the Fed could funnel credit to smaller companies in times of trouble. But it also demonstrated that risk aversion and political realities could curb the reach of such efforts, even in 2020, when the Fed and the Treasury had had access to essentially limitless funding.

---

* Boeing, which had been pushing for government money during CARES deliberations, had instead been able to raise $25 billion from private markets as they unstuck in the wake of the Fed's March 23 and April 9 announcements.

Mnuchin's conservativism when it came to Main Street was more than an instance of short-lived inside drama. It was a symptom of a political conversation bubbling up by the second half of 2020 about what role the Fed ought to be playing in America.

The Congressional Oversight Commission, which had been established to monitor the Fed programs and had four members, had become the beating heart of that debate in the months since CARES had passed and the various lending programs had gotten up and running. Besides Ramamurti, it included Senator Patrick Toomey, the Pennsylvania Republican; Republican Representative French Hill from Arkansas; and Democrat Representative Donna Shalala from Florida. It was supposed to have a chairperson, but that job would ultimately go unfilled. Toomey and Ramamurti jointly stepped into the leadership void—bringing with them sharply divergent concerns that defined the boundaries of a fight that would, however improbably, come to captivate Washington.

On the left, Ramamurti wanted a more populist and a more active Fed. He was distressed by how poorly Main Street was performing for smaller businesses, even as he worried that easier terms would be too much of a booster shot for big corporations if Congress didn't attach more strings to the program's terms. He wanted the Fed's state and local loan program to offer super-cheap loans to a wide variety of state and local governments, filling a void left by the CARES Act, since by mid-2020 it seemed likely that the federal government had undershot in its support for state and local governments. Like many progressive Democrats, Ramamurti increasingly saw the Fed's powers as something that could be leveraged to achieve social goals that the central bank had historically ignored. In the 2007–2009 recession, the Fed had bailed out Bear Stearns and AIG—why not New Jersey and Illinois in the 2020 crisis? Ramamurti had spent oversight hearings pushing for stricter limits on business loans and corporate programs, but also for a more expansive reading of the Fed's role as lender of last resort.

In a letter co-authored with Representative Ayanna Pressley, one of the members of the squad of first-time Democratic Congress members, Ramamurti had criticized what he saw as misplaced ambitions.

"You have both acknowledged that the COVID-19 pandemic has had an outsized impact on Black and Brown communities and women, and the Federal Reserve recently proclaimed that its full employment mandate—which applies to the CARES Act programs—is a 'broad-based and inclusive goal,'" the pair wrote. "And yet, your design of these programs appears to be widening racial and gender gaps rather than closing them."[11]

Senator Toomey, on the other hand, viewed the Democratic agenda with worried skepticism. He wanted to make sure the Fed remained focused on its mission of controlling inflation, and he did not want it to grow into an ever-bigger, ever-more-influential body that could determine where money flowed. Central bankers were unelected. They should not be trying to fix all of society's problems, he thought. Social policy, deciding who got cheap credit—those were tasks for elected officials and markets.

Before his political life started, Toomey had been a derivatives trader. He was a longtime champion of the sort of exotic financial products that had helped make him rich, and an ardent defender of light regulation, even at moments when other Republicans agreed that more regulation was needed. Not long after bundles of mortgage-backed derivatives went bad in 2008 and nearly brought the entire financial system to its knees, setting off a crippling recession in the process, Toomey warned against excessive controls on Wall Street. "I was seeing pretty close up which economies were succeeding and which ones weren't, and there is an unmistakable correlation," Toomey said during a 2010 interview with the newspaper *The Morning Call*. "Those that are heavily regulated and centrally controlled underperform. And those like Hong Kong, where there is regulation but it is sensible, they thrive."[12] Toomey was heavily backed by Wall Street donors.

Toomey had supported using the Fed's lender-of-last-resort function to back up broad markets when crisis struck. He had been the one to get up at a Senate lunch to tell his fellow lawmakers that they needed to go bigger when Mnuchin was asking for $200 billion to bolster the emergency lending programs, based on what he was hearing from his Wall Street contacts. But he saw the Fed as a first line of defense. By summer, he had concluded that the medicine had worked. Markets were functioning normally with the backstop, panic selling had stopped, and, as businesses and households seemed to hold up decently and economies tiptoed toward reopening, it seemed unlikely that the carnage was going to resume. As the financial meltdown became a memory, if a recent and painful one, he had started to voice concerns about the distortions the corporate bond programs were creating in the business debt market. He had at one point introduced language into a Republican bill that would have ensured that the programs backed by Congress's $454 billion appropriation from March had to close in January. By autumn, it was inescapable that he wanted them gone.

Powell and his colleagues had spent most of the year trying to navigate the contrasting partisan opinions—the push for the Fed to do more for the little guy coming from Democrats, and the insistence that it should avoid overstepping boundaries on the political right. Mnuchin, too, was stuck in the middle. While the Republicans were his obvious constituency, the Treasury secretary needed to maintain what goodwill he could with the Democrats if he hoped to get further stimulus packages through Congress.

Passing more legislation was an increasingly pressing priority. By the weeks leading up to the November 3 election, Fed and Treasury officials were beginning to believe that markets might be solidly out of the woods. Households, by contrast, remained anything but secure.

Congress had failed over and over to approve more spending to help workers and companies to weather what promised to be a scary and dangerous winter. Lawmakers had passed their relief legislation that March with an eye on helping America to take a short-term hit, not a yearlong clawback from the abyss that was regularly disrupted by additional waves of infection. Political consensus for more had been hard to achieve. Democrats had suggested a package in May with a $3 trillion price tag and eighteen hundred pages of text full of provisions Republicans balked at as unrelated, including immigration measures. Mitch McConnell, the Senate majority leader, had released a statement calling it an "expensive, unserious wish list."[13]

Republicans had put forth their own $1 trillion proposal in July, most notably leaving out additional funding for state and local governments. After months of acrimonious negotiating, no compromise had passed. Trump in August used a creative legal reading to unilaterally expand expiring enhanced unemployment benefits, but that was clearly a bandage and not a cure: It would pay only $300, half the prior benefit, for up to six weeks.[14]

Mnuchin continued to work his way through the Capitol in the months leading up to the November election, trying to get to some—any—solution. Part of the challenge was that the economy was beating expectations, taking some political pressure off lawmakers. The job market had lost some 20 million positions right away as lockdowns sent workers home, but the turnaround began more swiftly and strongly than just about anyone had anticipated. The economy added back 2.5 million jobs in May 2020, a month in which Wall Street had expected it to lose 8 million.[15] Likewise, the wave of bankruptcies economists had been predicting for months had failed to materialize. A cocktail of massive federal spending and phased state and local reopenings, combined with functioning markets and a boom in stocks, had kept the economic and financial damage in check. Still, millions of people remained out of work, food pantry lines were proof that some were slipping through cracks in the relief net, and many American families were living in a weird limbo of not knowing whether Congress would support them economically as the pandemic continued to upend their entire livelihoods.

The public, to the extent that it paid attention to the Fed, had embraced the institution's crisis response. The same could not be said for Congress's. "Powell's success runs counter to the populist political narrative of our era: The Fed's wonky technocracy has succeeded while the theoretically more politically accountable arms of our government have failed," Josh Barro wrote for *New York* magazine.[16] Opinion polling showed that people were less satisfied with their lives than they had been in nearly a decade, almost rivaling Great Recession–era lows.[17]

Then came the 2020 presidential vote, and something subtle but fundamental shifted.

Washington was tense in the days leading up to election Tuesday, prepared for anything after a summer of Black Lives Matter protests and counterprotests and riots that had seen curfews imposed and left local businesses boarded up with graffitied plywood. President Trump had already broadcast that he planned to legally challenge election results as early votes pointed to a Biden victory. Results were inconclusive on Election Day, but it looked bad for Trump from the outset. By Wednesday, it seemed likely that Joe Biden, the former vice president and Democrat, had won the presidential race.

By November 5, Biden's campaign was saying that it was a matter of when—not if—the race would be called in his favor.[18] Democrats had also clearly won the House, though they seemed unlikely to take the Senate. Suddenly, it looked like America would have a Democratic president but a divided government after four years in which Donald Trump redefined the Republican Party.

That Thursday also offered a clear hint that a serious change might be under way in Republican thinking around coronavirus relief efforts amid the changing political winds.

Toomey had given an exclusive interview to *Politico*'s Victoria Guida. In it, he fretted about an idea that had begun to percolate on the left as they faced the prospect of a divided Congress. If Republicans in the Senate wouldn't agree to pass legislation including state and local relief, the Fed could fill the void by making its lending program for states much more attractive. The plan seemed plausible. If Democrats took the White House, they could try to install a Treasury secretary who could sweeten the Fed program terms dramatically. The Fed, with its unlimited balance sheet and that largely untouched $454 billion in backstop, could step in to provide relief where political compromise would not, knowing that its credit risk was covered by the funding.

"If someone wants to make the case that we need the government to give money to people or businesses because they're struggling, by all means you can make that case," Toomey had said of the Democratic idea, according to Guida. "But that's not a Fed exercise."[19]

By the following week, news outlets had called the election for Biden. And, to *The New York Times,* Toomey's office had begun to push his argument just a hair further: Not only would it be inappropriate for Democrats to rely on the Fed to provide loans to favored constituencies, but it would be illegal. Congress, the senator argued, had intended for the Fed's programs to sunset on December 31, 2020.[20]

That was not what the law said. It clearly prevented Mnuchin from making additional direct loans after December 31, but it allowed outstanding loans to remain outstanding. Anyone with a basic understanding of the Fed's emergency lending powers knew that Treasury had already made tens of billions of dollars in loans to back up the legal vehicles that supported the Fed programs. The central bank could use that money to back up new loans to Main Street borrowers or purchases through the corporate bond programs without the Treasury having to earmark an additional penny. In fact, up until that point, Fed officials had been proceeding publicly as though the programs would likely be extended past the end of the year. Mnuchin's colleagues at the Treasury Department had likewise made it clear to reporters that they were mulling extending some, but not all, of the Fed facilities.[21] They might keep the corporate and Main Street programs going while killing the hot-button municipal program, for instance. As Toomey made his argument, though, that began to change.

With one short letter on Thursday, November 19, officially directed to "Dear Chair Powell" but also released to the world via Mnuchin's Twitter feed at 4:30 that afternoon, the Treasury made it clear just how far along the effort to kill the Fed programs had quietly advanced.[22]

"I was personally involved in drafting the relevant part of the legislation and believe the Congressional intent as outlined in Section 4029 was to have the authority to originate new loans or purchase new assets (either directly or indirectly) expire on December 31, 2020," Mnuchin wrote, supporting the Toomey argument wholeheartedly.

"As such, I am requesting that the Federal Reserve return the unused funds to the Treasury. This will allow Congress to re-appropriate $455 billion, consisting of $429 billion in excess Treasury funds for the Federal Reserve facilities and $26 billion in unused Treasury direct loan funds," he continued.

A ripple of shock rushed through the Fed's ranks. Phones buzzed. Emails swooshed. Most Fed officials hadn't known that a conversation over cutting off some of the programs was happening at all until

The New York Times and *The Wall Street Journal* reported the news in quick succession in early November. The fact that the decision had already been made was a near total surprise.

At the New York Fed, people who were deeply involved in the facilities found out that the Fed was ending the programs when they saw Mnuchin's tweet or, not long after, from their legislative affairs official on a conference call.

"What does this letter mean?" someone on the call asked.

"Why didn't we hear about this first?" several wondered.

Powell had spoken to the Treasury secretary earlier that day, so he had a heads-up that the release was coming. He and his colleagues at the Board decided to go to the highly unusual length of releasing a statement in response to Mnuchin's letter, because policy makers wanted to make clear that the Treasury's decision said nothing about their dedication to continue supporting the economy. Fed officials had spent the entire crisis trying not to air its conflicts with the Treasury Department publicly, which made the terse, to-the-point missive remarkable.

"The Federal Reserve would prefer that the full suite of emergency facilities established during the coronavirus pandemic continue," the central bank said in an email sent to reporters, arguing that they continued to have an important role to play "as a backstop for our still-strained and vulnerable economy."

Mnuchin's contention that he wanted to pull the funding back so that it could be "reappropriated" was an exercise in legislative smoke and mirrors. The pot of money Congress had handed the Fed had not cost the nation anything: It would be used only if a bunch of Fed loans went sour, but that was not expected to happen. The Congressional Budget Office hadn't counted it as an expense when it was adding up how much the legislation cost.[23] If it was "repurposed" toward actual spending instead of Fed lending, it was effectively the same as spending new money.

Meanwhile, some officials and analysts worried that the repercussions of what Mnuchin was doing could be severe. It could be that investors would take it in stride, of course, soothed by a vaccine on the horizon and massive central bank bond purchases. But Mnuchin's move to not just end the programs but also claw back the insurance money meant that the corporate bond programs would be difficult to restart at scale. The regulatory and structural vulnerabilities that had nearly led to a full-blown financial crisis nine months earlier had not been reformed in the time since. Now, not only would there be no backstop in place if a new virus variant or a vaccine failure sent markets tanking, but it might be politically untenable to get the money to restart one.

If it was potentially risky, not necessarily legally required, and not practically useful as a deficit reducer, why was Mnuchin—who surely understood the risk, and who seemed to care so desperately about doing a good job—cutting off the Fed programs?

The Treasury secretary, in a series of interviews over the following days and weeks, answered over and over that he believed it was his legal duty. Congress had intended the programs to be short-lived. A more uncharitable explanation of Mnuchin's actions spread like wildfire in Washington. Democrats claimed that Mnuchin had bowed to President Trump's will and was trying to tank the economy on the way out the door. The Treasury secretary had, in fact, spoken to Trump several times in the days leading up to his surprise announcement, his calendars would later show. He had also waited until just after the election results became clear to make the announcement, timing that was lost on no one.

"Secretary Mnuchin is engaged in economic sabotage, and trying to tie the Biden administration's hands," Senator Ron Wyden, a Democrat from Oregon, said in a November 24 statement reported by Bloomberg.[24]

Yet people close to Mnuchin panned the idea that he was engaging in economic sabotage. The man cared enormously about his own legacy and had taken pride in the Fed response, keeping the original term sheets for the CARES facilities out in his office.[25] Plus, there were more flattering ways to understand what the Treasury secretary had done. People who knew him said Mnuchin genuinely did not want the Fed's programs to become more lasting: He was worried that they would distort markets and prove difficult to shutter down the road. And though the "repurposing" ploy was a gimmick, that was difficult to understand. The idea that a huge pot of money could be redirected might make it easier for Republican senators who remained deficit shy to get behind a big spending package.

"I spent the last four months trying to work with Congress to get additional legislation passed," Mnuchin himself would at one point argue during a House Financial Services hearing. "These programs were not being used, and I've worked every day to try to get Congress to pass more legislation."[26]

The markets *might* need Fed help again if things got worse, but it seemed possible that they would be fine. In fact, Mnuchin had left a little bit of money in the programs so that they could restart at a smaller scale if push came to shove. Millions of out-of-work Americans *were* going to spend a crushing winter making hard choices between trying to return to work before it was safe to do so and going without. The need for government spending was more intense than the need for continued Fed support.

Whatever motivated Mnuchin's maneuver, politics or practicality, the play did not win him many fans. Over the weeks that followed his November 19 letter asking the Fed to return the pot of money, Democrats regularly brought the move up in anger.

"I know there's been this Jedi mind trick going on here, but we know what our intentions are, and we can read," Ayanna Pressley, the House Democrat, said at an early December hearing in which Mnuchin and Powell testified before a congressional committee on CARES.

Katie Porter, from California, went a step further, pointing out that Mnuchin did not have the authority to claw back the money dedicated by CARES until 2026, a date that had been specifically set out in the law.

"Is today the year 2026, yes or no?" Porter asked, speaking her question into a Web camera from her house, a vase of orange and red tulips behind her left shoulder creating a misleadingly cheery backdrop.

Mnuchin, sitting on a plexiglass-fronted witness stand on Capitol Hill, leaned into his microphone with a sour expression on his face.

"Of course it's not 2026. How ridiculous to ask me that question and waste our time," he chided.

"Well, Secretary Mnuchin, I think it's ridiculous that you're play-acting to be a lawyer when you have no legal degree," Porter volleyed back.

"I have plenty of lawyers at the Department of Treasury who advise me, so I'm more than happy to follow up" and "explain all the legal provisions," Mnuchin rebutted.

Porter pointed out that while Mnuchin lacked a law degree, Powell had one. And Powell had made it clear that he didn't think the programs needed to be ended.

"You've gotten into a disagreement with someone who's actually a lawyer," Porter pressed on.

"Are you a lawyer?" Mnuchin interrupted, his voice rising, his cool visibly shattered.

"And you're not listening to Congress, which actually wrote the law," Porter concluded. (Porter didn't mention it, but she had a law degree from Harvard University.)[27]

The conflict only escalated as the end of the year neared. Beefing up the Main Street and municipal facilities had been a point of conversation among wonkier Democrats before the Treasury's letter calling time on the Fed programs. In the wake of it, those plans became gospel among many progressives. Prominent members of the political left wanted those billions back, and if they got the money, they had designs for it.

A December 17 Congressional Research Service publication found that the Fed could have continued making loans under the law.[28] Upon its release, Ramamurti, the Warren ally on the Fed and Treasury oversight commission, swiftly tweeted that "the Biden administration could restart these lending programs next year."[29] Fed Up tweeted that the new Treasury secretary "could make use of the CARES Act Fed facilities to help the economy."[30]

Democrats were attuned to the Fed-related cash because it seemed unlikely that they would be able to pass additional help for state and local governments, having won the House but probably not the Senate (Georgia runoff elections were scheduled for the following month, and Republicans were expected to win). Many conservatives were still opposed to more state and local relief. It was not clear that the Fed would agree to sweeten the municipal program—in fact, all signs suggested that it wouldn't.[31] But the push coming from Democrats would certainly ramp up pressure on the central bank to expand its powers and its reading of its authorities and do more for local government borrowers, a sticky political position for the central bank.[32]

Senator Toomey, true believer in a limited Fed that he was, was having none of it. That is why, in the waning days of 2020, after ten months that had inflicted more human pain and suffering on the United States than it had seen in generations, Congress spent the final days of its legislative year talking about an esoteric set of rules governing the Fed.

Congress was hotly debating the desperately needed relief package by mid-December, and this one seemed like it finally had the potential to pass. The $900 billion spending plan contained onetime payments for households, an extension of small business relief, and an extension of more generous unemployment insurance programs.

Toomey, however, insisted that he would not vote for the package unless it also prevented the Fed from reclaiming the money Mnuchin had clawed back and precluded it from setting up "similar" facilities going forward. He convinced his fellow Republicans to join his cause. Toomey's provision, which surfaced in earnest on Thursday, December 17, had the potential to tank the entire bill.[33]

Speaking on a call with reporters that day, Toomey had called the Fed-related language "the most important thing" to him. The journalists on the line were silent for a moment after he uttered the words, as though they were unsure of what they had heard. Unemployment remained at 6.7 percent, nearly twice its prepandemic level. Families were struggling, and coronavirus cases were climbing again. Someone asked a clarifying question. The Fed language seemed like an odd top priority.

"It would be a terrible idea to morph these programs into something else," Toomey explained. Under some Democrats' plans, he warned, "the Fed wouldn't be the lender of last resort, it would be the lender of first resort."

A flurry of speeches, phone calls, and negotiations ensued. Democrats blasted Toomey for inserting the language as a wrench in the discussions at the eleventh hour, while Republicans stood firm behind him, even when they did not seem to understand what the provision did or why it mattered. Democrats were most worried about language in the Toomey provision that barred "similar" programs going forward. What constituted similarity? Would any program meant to help midsize businesses or keep the corporate bond market from crashing meet that standard?

The possibility that Congress would curb the Fed's powers so absolutely drew alarm beyond the political sphere. Ben Bernanke, the former Fed chair responsible for the 2008 financial crisis programs, on Saturday issued a statement warning that it was "vital that the Federal Reserve's ability to respond promptly to damaging disruptions in credit markets not be circumscribed." He said that "the relief act should ensure, at least, that the Federal Reserve's emergency lending authorities, as they stood before the passage of the CARES Act, remain fully intact and available to respond to future crises."[34]

Politicians were blunter. "It's a way for them to say to Joe Biden: 'We are tying your hands. No matter what comes down the pike, you can't do this,'" Nancy Pelosi, the House Speaker, said on a call with her fellow Democrats that day. Mnuchin spent that weekend speaking with Powell more than he had in months—four times each on Thursday, Friday, and Saturday[35]—to relay developments. But Senate staff negotiators had determined that Mnuchin had every intention of following Toomey's lead on the language. The Pennsylvanian was the man to convince, and he was determined.

Democrats arranged to have Chuck Schumer, their top official in the Senate, sit down with Toomey and Mitt Romney, a Utah Republican who seemed more amenable to compromise, during proceedings on the Senate floor that Saturday, a chilly and overcast day about a week before Christmas. As a crowd of Republicans gathered around them, it was clear that the conversation had morphed into an all-out negotiation. Toomey, Romney, and Schumer—together with a handful of other lawmakers—decided to move the conversation to Schumer's office.

The New York senator had a fire going as lawmakers took their seats to hash out a plan, surrounded by staff members. Schumer at one point accused Toomey of trying to sabotage the incoming administration, and voices were raised amid intense debating. After half an hour, though, the Republicans left the office on a hopeful note, having agreed to send revised language.

When the language came at 6:30 P.M., it was barely different. Schumer sent it back, insisting on changing the prohibition on "similar" facilities to one on the "same" facilities. He had been talking regularly with Powell, with former Fed officials like Yellen and Bernanke, and with his staff. He knew that the broader language could turn into an expansive curb on the Fed's powers.

Toomey's reply was swift. "No." He did not want to narrow the language.

As negotiations came down to a final wire late that Saturday night, Mnuchin ping-ponged between calls with Powell and Toomey. He spoke with Toomey at 8:45 P.M., Powell at 8:50 and 8:55, Toomey at 9:15, Powell at 9:20 and 9:40, and Toomey at 9:42, his calendars would later show. Afterward, none of the parties involved would say exactly what happened during those conversations, just that Mnuchin and Toomey had come to some sort of agreement.

Within an hour of the final call, Toomey's office began calling around to reporters to inform them that a solution had been reached. The law would prevent the Fed from setting up the exact "same" facilities in the future, but as long as the programs were changed somewhat, the Fed's ability to help the markets they had rescued in 2020 would remain intact.

"This agreement will preserve Fed independence and prevent Democrats from hijacking these programs for political and social policy purposes," Steve Kelly, Toomey's spokesperson, told reporters in a statement.[36] It wasn't clear what had changed Toomey's mind—the hours of negotiations with Democrats, the intercession of his Republican colleagues who were eager for a deal, or the headlines blaring across Fox News, showing his picture and declaring that "a new hold up" threatened to keep a deal at bay. Whatever it was, Democrats, Fed officials, and concerned onlookers expressed relief in private and in the press.

The Fed would remain the powerful crisis-fighter it had been in 2020 if another disaster rocked finance, threatening a meltdown that would erase wealth, roil companies, and cost livelihoods. More important for the immediate future, the fact that a deal had been struck meant that the first full-scale follow-up to the March relief package would pass into law, keeping the nearly four million people trapped in long-term unemployment afloat. It would give businesses extra money to bridge the gap at a time when restaurants were operating at partial capacity or with outdoor dining only across much of the country, and many salons and other service providers had yet to reopen at all. The Fed's support might have been huge—even unlimited—but it was too blunt to get into the corners of the economy most in need. Congress and the White House could do that, and, after months of delay, they were.

"I think this will take us through the recovery," Mnuchin had told CNBC in the hours leading up to the final vote.

As the holiday season started and the coronavirus raged on, Powell had again finished a year in crisis mode. But it was unlike 2018, when the dilemma was an unfolding trade war and a market meltdown he himself had precipitated. It was also unlike 2019, when he had been dealing with a president who painted him as an enemy and had needed to navigate the final step in a short rate-cutting cycle, a maneuver that had seemed important and delicate at the time. The year 2020 had brought immense tragedy, an economic challenge unlike anything Powell's predecessors had dealt with, and a flexing of the Fed's powers. By the end of December, it had also forced society to grapple with what role the Fed should play more actively than it had in years, and perhaps since Marriner Eccles's days, as some Democrats pushed it to stretch further and powerful Republicans insisted that its role should remain limited.

The central bank had carved out a middle path: It had gone farther than ever before to extend its help to companies and municipalities, but it had tried to remain as neutral as it could about who won and who lost because of its actions by setting broad and at times strict criteria, working with the politically accountable Treasury every step of the way. The decision-making and line-drawing had not been easy, and it had often been contentious. Debate over what position the Fed ought to play in modern America—especially in times of crisis— seemed destined to rise again in the future.

But as that sad and socially distanced winter break approached, the

Fed was emerging from the drama of late 2020 relatively unscathed. The public health situation remained precarious, but America's economy had held up through its first pandemic year, one many still hoped would be its last. The waves of evictions that policy makers had so feared had never materialized, and the job market was on the mend. Mnuchin's decision to kill the Fed lending programs had not disrupted markets, perhaps because investors were looking toward a brighter future. In Washington and across America, tenuous peace seemed to be settling in. The Fed's rates were set firmly at zero, and it had pledged in its final statement of the year to continue buying bonds at a pace of $120 billion per month until it saw "substantial further progress" in the economy.[37] Congress's compromise meant that more economic help was coming to households. Healthcare breakthroughs offered a brighter future for the world in 2021. Vaccines had worked in trials and were expected to become widely available in the first half of the new year. Powell, as was becoming his pattern, was closing out a rough year on an optimistic note.

"Recent news on vaccines has been very positive," he had said at his year-end news conference. "I think many people have the expectation that by the second half of next year, the economy should be performing strongly."[38]

Chapter 14

THE CREEPING CRISES

Change is difficult, but it is inescapable.

—*Randal K. Quarles, October 5, 2021*

RANDY QUARLES HAD WRAPPED up December 2020 scrambling to resolve a problem of his own, one that promised to bedevil the Fed long after that first pandemic year had faded into memory.

His policy question, if you took a sufficiently long view, traced back to Springdale, Pennsylvania, in the early 1900s. There, at around the time Marriner Eccles was taking over the family business out in Utah, a woman named Rachel Carson was born to an insurance salesman and teacher. She would grow up to write *Silent Spring*, a book on how the pesticide DDT was damaging nature that would light the environmental movement afire and convince the public that allowing blind pursuit of profit, unfettered by government oversight, could ravage the world we all share.[1] By 2020, environmentalists had evolved their focus from chemical poisoning to a larger issue: The carbon that cars, factories, and air conditioners were constantly spewing into the atmosphere had degraded the Earth's natural defenses. Glaciers were melting, sea levels rising, and natural disasters growing more severe. And as Carson's successors traced the environmental crisis, concerned citizens and elected officials had come to believe that people like Quarles had a role to play in preparing the world for the fallout.

Over the twentieth century and into the twenty-first, central banks had developed into the gatekeepers of capitalism. They set the tone for many types of financial regulation and they researched financial stability. They cooperated internationally, and those links often went deeper and were less delicate than typical diplomatic ties. Global central banking conferences tended to be reunions of old friends who had worked through graduate programs together and co-authored papers. The institutions were an obvious place for a conversation about what role finance was playing in global warming, how banks and markets might be put at risk by climate change, and how the world ought to respond.

The focus on climate change among large global monetary policy authorities had begun taking hold especially visibly at the Bank of England around 2015. Governor Mark Carney had given a speech that year warning that climate change would eventually beget global financial crises.[2]

"The challenges currently posed by climate change pale in significance compared with what might come," he had remarked, speaking to the insurer Lloyd's. "So why isn't more being done to address it?"

Carney went on to answer his own question, pointing to what he called "the tragedy of the horizon." His idea was an extension of the well-known "tragedy of the commons": the observation that people may fail to make individual changes that would benefit everyone because they can personally gain from using nature's resources to their full extent. Bob might know that overfishing his local lake will be bad news for his community, but if he's making a living by frying up fresh-caught bass for tourists, that knowledge may prove insufficient to change his behavior. Carney's "tragedy of the horizon" point suggested that the people and institutions that might be able to help prevent or mitigate climate change—be they politicians, businesses, or central bankers—typically make decisions based on relatively near-term analysis and incentives. Climate change might impact the world most intensely ten, fifty, or one hundred years from now, but the people making the choices that drive it are tasked with weighing pros and cons for the next two to three years. Carney, who was then the head of the global Financial Stability Board, had been asked by the Group of Twenty finance ministers to think about how financial institutions might account for climate risks. He'd found a lot to worry about, he told the insurers that day.

Banks and insurers would face steep costs as floods became more frequent, wildfires razed communities they had insured, and sea level rise left structures that had once seemed like a safe financing bet looking considerably riskier. Then there were the liability risks. Coal and gas companies might face lawsuits for the environmental damage they caused today. Finally, there were transition risks. Anytime something massive and systemic changed what sort of financial bets paid off, where costs and opportunities lay, instability was a possible outcome. Decarbonization would likely be no exception.

"Work done here at Lloyd's of London estimated that the 20-centimeter rise in sea-level at the tip of Manhattan since the 1950s, when all other factors are held constant, increased insured losses from Superstorm Sandy by 30 percent in New York alone," Carney had said, referencing the massive flooding and destruction that swept parts of the East Coast in 2012.

"While there is still time to act, the window of opportunity is finite and shrinking," he had ominously concluded.

Those comments were spoken at a moment of climate activism on a global stage, and two months before the so-called Paris Agreement was adopted at a United Nations convention in December 2015 with the long-term goal of keeping the rise in global average temperatures contained to reduce the impacts of global warming.[3] They also came as America was about to lurch away from accepting the basic premises behind Carney's statements. With Donald J. Trump's election to the White House in 2016, skepticism of climate change and man's role in it would temporarily strengthen its foothold in United States policy.

Financial regulators around the world had shared Carney's concerns and followed up on them, but in part because of the political backdrop, America's central bank veered away in the years that followed. In December 2017, Carney, Bank of France governor François Villeroy de Galhau, and the Dutch central bank's Frank Elderson announced the creation of the Network for Greening the Financial System, a global convening body that would share research and best practices and carry out analysis related to climate financial risks. Among the founding central banks and financial authorities—from the Netherlands, China, Germany, France, Mexico, Singapore, Sweden, and the United Kingdom—the United States was notably absent.[4]

In fact, as the Trump administration began the process to with-draw from the Paris Agreement and embraced carbon-heavy industries, Fed leaders ranged between careful and silent on the matter of climate. The United States' divergence from the global trend was thrown into sharp relief as the Fed's central banking counterparts pushed forward with efforts to curb carbon- and environment-tied financial risks. Before the pandemic struck, the Bank of England had begun to design what were often called climate stress tests, scenario analyses that banks could use to see how resilient they would be in the case of extreme weather events and how exposed they were to industries that might come under stress as the world shifted toward a lower-carbon future.

Trump himself was not the only reason for the Fed's reluctance; as with so many things in American culture at that time, the president personified a deeper divide running through society. Climate change was a partisan issue in America. Democrats typically accepted its reality and pushed for regulations to protect against it. Many Republicans questioned whether human activity was contributing to extreme weather events as they became more frequent, and even those who accepted the premise of man-created climate change often believed that regulations meant to curb climate risk needed to be carefully tailored to avoid unnecessarily burdening companies. Mitch McConnell had said in September that he believed in man-made climate change, but that "the question is how do you address it." According to the Kentucky senator, "the way to do this consistent with American values and American capitalism is through technology and innovation . . . not to shut down your economy, throw people out of work."[5]

Powell was environmentally conscious himself. His last job in private equity had been at the Global Environment Fund, which his brother-in-law had founded,[6] and which invested in sustainable energy sources. He drove a Tesla and had been involved with conservation-focused nonprofits. But if the central bank he led tiptoed into the liberal waters of climate discussions, it would open itself to attack from Republicans. Plus, many on the political left did want central bankers to do more than just assess climate risks. They wanted the Fed to make sure that environmental bad actors struggled to get financing.

That seemed to Powell to move beyond the Fed's jobs—safety, soundness, liquidity protection—and into the realm of deciding who had access to credit. It would risk politicizing the Fed, putting its independence at risk. The Fed could not be the answer to every problem in society, and if it tried to be, it might lose its freedom to do the important jobs it had at hand.

"Climate change is an important issue but not principally for the Fed," Powell told the Joint Economic Committee in November 2019. "We're not going to be the ones to decide society's response. That is for elected officials, not us."[7]

Staff grumbling about the Fed's slow-burn approach to climate change had grown louder as the years dragged on. Climate, some Fed researchers pointed out, was an existential question of our time and regulators had a clear role to play in making sure that the financial system was prepared. Some of that angst had bubbled to the surface through the regional central banks, whose status as "private" institutions had long left them capable of engaging on issues that their politically appointed and more closely watched counterparts in Washington struggled to address. The Federal Reserve Bank of San Francisco hosted the system's first-ever conference on climate in 2019. Despite the Board's hands-off stance, Brainard—by then the lone Democrat—spoke at the event. It was so oversubscribed that economists within the Fed system who wanted to attend were turned away. Media were not invited at all.

In a speech with the unsubtle title of "Why Climate Change Matters for Monetary Policy and Financial Stability," Brainard had insisted that "to support a strong economy and a stable financial system, the Federal Reserve needs to analyze and adapt to important changes to the economy and financial system. This is no less true for climate change than it was for globalization or the information technology revolution."[8] She was not suggesting that the Fed prevent banks from lending to fossil fuel companies. She was suggesting that the Fed had a responsibility to get on top of what kind of risks already-inevitable global warming would pose.

As the Fed wrestled over how active a role it should play in climate discussions, Quarles found himself at the center of things, as both vice-chair for supervision and Carney's successor as head of the global Financial Stability Board. He tended to believe that the private sector should be left to police itself, to the extent possible and prudent, and he echoed Powell's cautious approach in public remarks. By 2020, though, his was an increasingly uncomfortable position.

Staff members, many Fed officials, and even regulators across the rest of the government—including some at the Commodity Futures Trading Commission—had begun to push the Fed to join the network on greening the financial system that the other central banks had launched, by then commonly referred to as NGFS. It had blossomed from the time of its founding and claimed practically every other major central bank in the world among its members. Becoming a member was an important symbolic move.

Joining would risk triggering a political land mine in Trump's Washington, though, and the Fed tried to strike a middle ground—it had asked to "observe," the way that the World Bank and other global multilateral bodies did. It didn't make sense for an individual central bank, and the Network had not agreed to list the Fed among its observers, though it did allow Fed officials to informally participate in forums and information exchanges. Democrats regularly prodded Quarles to make a more concrete move.

"Do you have any updates on that?" Brian Schatz, a senator from Hawaii, asked Quarles about his progress toward joining the NGFS in late 2019. Quarles, looking serious in wire-rimmed glasses, was testifying before the Senate Banking Committee and answered guardedly.

"We have attended meetings, sort of auditing the class before formally registering," he told the senator, explaining that the Fed was "exploring" joining.[9]

But with the 2020 election, political attention to climate change was reinvigorated. The shift created an opening for the Fed to add its name to the global consortium. Quarles, himself a Trump appointee, was the person in the position to make the change. Given his personal politics, few expected that he would.

That is why his testimony before the Senate Banking Committee on November 10 shocked Fed-watchers and climate activists alike. Senator Schatz reupped his question, and Quarles responded bluntly and definitively.

"That's really up to the NGFS, we have requested membership, I would suspect that it will be granted," Quarles informed the Hawaiian.

That was news to the senator, and to the press. Washington news outlets rarely wrote up sleepy financial stability hearings, but Quarles's surprise announcement touched off a volley of headlines. In a sign of just how political the issue had become, *Newsweek* took Quarles's statement as a sign that the Fed was acknowledging Biden's still unofficial victory.* "Federal Reserve Appears to Acknowledge Joe Biden Election Win," the outlet titled its story.[10]

The Fed had yet to actually file its application at the time of Quarles's statement, but it rushed through the process in the weeks that followed. The official announcement came on December 15.[11]

It was a victory for climate-concerned economists and policy wonks, but it was unclear both how durable the decision would prove to the political cycle and what it would mean for the Fed's actual policy and supervisory approach. Could the Fed adjust the rule book when a simple election—a switch from Trump to Biden, or from Biden to some other politician—could change the national tone around dealing with climate risk?

"Now that they have joined this international effort, I will expect them to take further concrete steps towards managing climate risks," Schatz responded to the news.[12]

Quarles had surprised many by proving himself less of a partisan ideologue than many on the left painted him to be. Perhaps he was emulating Uncle Marriner's flexible thinking. Still, it was clear that the step he had taken toward better assessing climate risk in the financial system would be the Fed's first—not its last.

Lael Brainard entered 2021 thinking about another world-changing, and certainly Fed-changing, issue. What might the future of money look like?

It promised to be a weird year for Brainard. As Biden had neared

---

* While press accounts at the time frequently said that the Fed had been unable to join NGFS during the Trump administration because America was no longer in the Paris Agreement—which is why the decision to join it was equivalent to acknowledging Biden had won and the nation would rejoin the agreement— that was never a rule and would not have prevented the Fed from joining, had it wanted to do so.

election that fall, she had been widely seen as a candidate to be his Treasury secretary. She was a Democrat, she had more experience than just about anyone, and she had been a good soldier at the Fed through the Trump administration, opposing deregulation with a vigor that the most progressive Democrats applauded. Ironically, though, her habit of compromising had hurt her chances.

A headline in the progressive magazine *The American Prospect* declared her "liberalish," which basically encapsulated how the leftmost wing of the Democratic Party saw her.[13] Brainard had negotiated with China while at Treasury and the White House, and some progressives argued that she should have been more aggressive in those deliberations. Other critics pointed out that the Fed's corporate bond-buying program had helped to prop up fossil fuel companies, which some progressive Democrats had argued it should freeze out. Brainard had done nothing to stop it, they contended. "We cannot afford a Treasury Secretary who doesn't pursue every avenue to fight climate change," one blistering commentary published that autumn had insisted.[14] Brainard had always been destined to have her reputation colored by the 2020 crisis response. She had.

By the end of November 2020, it still looked like the administration would be working with a divided Congress—runoff elections in Georgia seemed likely to keep the Senate in Republican hands—so it was essential to nominate someone who could garner complete Democratic and some Republican support. Brainard seemed unlikely to fit that bill, and she hadn't gotten the job. Janet Yellen, the former Fed chair, had been named to the post, a nomination that would make her both the nation's first female Fed chair and its first woman Treasury secretary.[*]

It was clear, though, that other high-profile jobs would open at the Fed before long—Powell would need to be renominated or replaced. Clarida's term would expire in early 2022, and Quarles's term as vice-chair for supervision would end in 2021, though he could remain on as a governor should he choose. Brainard stuck around the central bank. As she waited to learn whether her years of loyalty would

---

[*] The artist Dessa greeted the news of Yellen's appointment with a rap called "Who's Yellen Now?," which included lyrics like: "She's five foot nothing, but hand to god, she can pop a collar, she can rock a power bob."

be rewarded with a higher post, she busied herself with the biggest upheaval money had faced since the end of the gold standard more than half a century earlier.

Bitcoin had roared onto the financial scene in 2008, and for years it was treated as something of a joke by the financial cognoscenti and by economists in academia and within the Fed system. In the years leading up to 2020, though, it had become clear that people were investing in it as an asset class, at a minimum, and that the technology behind it—distributed ledger—had security characteristics that might have broader uses. The global attention to cryptocurrencies suggested that people saw a benefit in them that they were not finding elsewhere, whether that was privacy, ease of transfer and convertibility, fad appeal, potential for illicit use and tax evasion, or something else entirely.

Central banks around the world had begun moving forward with development of their own digital money. The Swedish Sveriges Riksbank had pushed especially far in researching its e-krona, and the Bahamian central bank had developed and newly launched a digital "Sand Dollar." The euro area seemed likely to issue a digital euro, which its citizens would probably be able to hold in limited denominations in digital wallets. Digital central bank money was different from crypto in that it was backed by the full faith and credit of a national government—it was fiat currency. While many transactions already occurred in digital format, either in online commerce or when a shopper swiped a credit card, that digital money was backed by the banking system. Digital currency would be instead backed by the central bank, the electronic version of physical cash.

When it came to researching and considering developing such a technology, the Fed was lagging its peers. That irked Brainard.

America's central bank had good reasons to slow-walk the digital currency question, she knew. Chief among them, any digital dollar would need to be infallible on the first try. While messing up the rollout of a digital currency for a small country was unlikely to result in global upheaval, any missteps for the world's dominant one could prove catastrophic. But there was also a simpler force working against digital currency at the Fed: Brainard's colleagues just didn't like the idea all that much.

Quarles sometimes painted the digital dollar as a solution in search of a problem that didn't exist. Banks already issued money in digital form. Technically a Fed version would be safer, but because the Federal Deposit Insurance Corporation had insured bank deposits up to a point ever since the Great Depression, there was no real chance that the value of your digital money at Wells Fargo or Bank of America would just disappear. Market runs were still a regular feature of modern American finance; old-fashioned bank runs were not.

In a June 2021 speech, Quarles had compared the idea of Fed-issued digital money to parachute pants, the poorly informed fashion phenomenon of his youth. After explaining that he had been reflecting on the United States' enthusiasm for novelty, he said that "especially when coupled with an equally American susceptibility to boosterism and the fear of missing out, it has also sometimes led to a mass suspension of our critical thinking and to occasionally impetuous, deluded crazes or fads." A central bank digital currency, he said, could become an "appealing target for cyberattacks," "facilitate illicit activity," or prove "expensive and difficult for the Federal Reserve to manage." To sum it up, he concluded, "even if other central banks issue successful CBDCs, we cannot assume that the Federal Reserve should issue a CBDC."[15]

Brainard, as was so often the case, found Quarles's commentary colorful but firmly disagreed.

She could see the risks, but she also saw opportunities. While the Fed was in the process of developing an instant payment system, FedNow, a central bank digital currency might also help with rapid transactions and cross-border money transfers. Perhaps most critical, Brainard couldn't help but see the global geopolitical dimension of the question. The future of money would look different from its past, and Brainard thought it essential that the Fed stay at the vanguard of an evolving technology. Understanding the change, harnessing it, might prove essential to remaining the dominant currency, to monitoring growing risks, or to understanding private-sector innovation around the world. American central bankers could not simply sit back and watch as the digital renminbi, the digital euro, and corporate offerings became viable alternatives for cross-border transactions. America did not need to rush into issuing a digital dollar, but Brainard thought that it needed to thoroughly investigate the possibility and the technology.

"It is vital for the United States to be at the table in the development of cross-border standards," she urged in a May 2021 speech, delivered by webcast on account of the still-raging pandemic.[16]

By that point in 2021, Brainard's colleagues were coming around to her point of view. A wake-up call had come two years earlier, in 2019, when news broke that Facebook was researching its own digital coin, what would come to be known as Libra and later Diem. Facing strong backlash, the tech firm had slowed and ultimately changed the project,[17] but the experience had forced central bankers to realize how quickly they could find themselves competing with a private currency issuer with a huge platform. Brainard had given a speech in August 2020—just weeks before Powell's Jackson Hole appearance—discussing the Fed's newly invigorated research into a digital dollar.[18] She outlined research into distributed ledger technology happening across the system, as well as a collaboration between the Federal Reserve Bank of Boston and the Massachusetts Institute of Technology to examine technological options. One goal was to "give us hands-on experience to understand the opportunities and limitations of possible technologies for digital forms of central bank money," Brainard said.

She made it clear that creating a digital dollar would be a serious process, one that would probably require buy-in from Congress, since it wasn't clear if the Federal Reserve Act allowed it to issue a digital currency. She was outlining first, careful steps.

The urgency to keep up with digital innovation only intensified as the months passed, though. Internet-famous "meme" stocks took off in 2021, and so did cryptocurrencies, with everyday investors and major banks alike piling on. Stablecoins, private-sector digital tokens that were backed by a bundle of currencies or other assets, were growing exponentially as that happened, in large part because people used them to transact in and out of the new crop of crypto offerings. They were barely regulated because no regime existed yet to oversee them. Many were structured like money market mutual funds, which had so recently crashed. They frightened regulators, and they were a sign that the masses and market forces would decide whether the future of money was digital. The Fed wanted to move slowly and contemplatively, but the world was not giving it that option.

In May 2021, Powell—who had long sounded closer to Quarles than to Brainard in his comments on the matter—released a surprise announcement.

"Today we are in the midst of a technological revolution that is fundamentally changing our world," he began, speaking in a prerecorded video. Cryptocurrencies and stablecoins had quickly grown and evolved, he noted, and "as stablecoins' use increases, so must our attention to the appropriate regulatory and oversight framework."

It wasn't just regulation that the Fed was preparing to adjust. The central bank was taking comments on whether it should issue a digital currency. It was hardly a conclusive step, but it was a sign that the Fed was taking the future of money more seriously. America's central bank, as ever, was changing to keep up with the world around it.

As the Fed tried to find its place in modern America, the risk that politicians would take note of its broadening role—and try to either leverage or erode it—had grown. While the central bank had managed to dodge both the Democratic push to sweeten its municipal loan program and the Republican push to curb its emergency lending powers during the last-minute lawmaking at the end of 2020, another political event in those waning days of the Trump administration had struck a more lasting warning signal.

When it became clear that President Trump would lose the White House, the Senate had taken up the nomination of Judy Shelton to be a governor at the Fed. Shelton was an economic commentator with a doctorate in business who had a long track record of advocating for a return to a gold-backed money system. That made her an unusual pick for the central bank's board. Mainstream economists widely dismissed her ideas about gold as impractical at best and destabilizing at worst. Democrats derided them as quackery.

"Giving her authority over the dollar would be like putting a medieval barber in charge of the CDC," Ron Wyden, the Oregon senator, had quipped.[19]

Yet Shelton's beliefs were not the only or even the main problem with her candidacy. What concerned careful Fed-watchers about Judy Shelton was her lack of political separation from the White House. She had spent years arguing for more restrictive monetary policy, only to abruptly shift course as Trump came onto the scene and pushed for easy money. She had at times openly questioned the idea of Fed independence. "I don't see any reference to independence in the legislation that has defined the role of the Federal Reserve for the United States," she had said during an interview at an event in Washington in 2019. Instead, the law "demands that the Board of Governors of the Federal Reserve work hand in hand with Congress and the president to meet certain strategic economic goals for the U.S."[20] In fact, she had at times defended President Trump's bullying of the central bank. "I think it's in some ways healthier that criticism from the White House is out in the open. At least we know how the president feels," she said at one point.[21]

Shelton's disregard for Fed independence posed two potential threats, should she be confirmed. First, it might give Trump a loyal representative in the room for Fed discussions, one who could relay what the central bank was thinking and who could use public remarks to try to box Fed officials into or out of key decisions. The president had lost the election, but there was no hint that he was about to disappear from America's political scene. Plus, while Shelton's governor seat would expire in early 2024, that she had been confirmed to the Fed once might make it easier to put her back on the Fed as chair if Trump were to win election again later that year. Fed chairs in recent decades had uniformly been former central bank governors.

Initially, Shelton had run into plenty of opposition on Capitol Hill, including from Republicans. Senator John Kennedy, a Republican from Louisiana, had ventured early on that one wouldn't want to appoint a Fed member with "a fatal attraction to nutty ideas." But he had as of November decided that he would support her. Other early doubters including Pennsylvanian Patrick Toomey had come around to Shelton's side. While Mitt Romney from Utah and Susan Collins from Maine still pledged to vote against her, Lamar Alexander—who also opposed the nomination—announced that he would be out of town the day of her scheduled nomination vote. Given all that shuffling, the math broke down in such a way that she should have had enough votes to clear the Senate. A preliminary vote on her confirmation had been set for Tuesday, November 17, 2020, and headed into the day, it looked like she would narrowly pass the vote and sail toward final confirmation.

Chance intervened. That morning, Senator Charles Grassley, Republican of Iowa, announced that he had been exposed to the coronavirus and would miss the vote. Senator Rick Scott, Republican of Florida, was also in quarantine. The loss of two "yes" votes tipped the scales: In a dramatic last-minute hustle, newly elected Vice President Elect Kamala Harris rushed to Washington to cast the vote that would scupper Shelton's chances. A freshly elected Democratic senator was slated to take office the following week, meaning that Shelton would likely not have another shot at confirmation.

Still, the dramatic last-minute confirmation dance pointed out something critical about the modern Fed. It was not obvious that Shelton would have been a lackey for Trump if confirmed to the Fed, let alone if she were elevated to chair. She had sounded fuzzy on the matter of independence, but many appointees say things while campaigning for a job that they then soften once actually confirmed. Yet the fact that lawmakers spent late 2020 on the brink of appointing her illustrated that a president exasperated by the Fed might be able to get a loyalist onto its powerful Board. That was a risk worth noting.

The central bank had proven itself to be immensely powerful over the course of 2020. The new areas it was carefully exploring, including climate policy and digital currency, had the potential to make it even more influential. Yet as its responsibilities grew, its structure was largely unchanged. Much of the Fed's authority remained concentrated in the Fed Board in Washington, which answered to Congress, and which could choose to heed or ignore the White House. But if the Fed were to go awry, Congress could immediately punish it only by dragging officials up to Capitol Hill to testify and giving them a browbeating. Actual changes to the Fed would require passing legislation through both chambers that would then require a presidential signature to become law. That substantial freedom could isolate central bankers from partisan influence and allow them to set good, future-oriented policy, assuming central bankers themselves believed in independence and the Fed's broader mission. Powell's resistance to the White House's pressure campaign in 2018 and 2019 had made that clear.

But the Fed's autonomy, hard-won during Marriner Eccles's time, was a double-edged sword. If the dominant party in the Senate were to confirm central bankers who were highly partisan and who hoped to achieve political agendas, it could spell trouble. The same design that isolated the Fed from outside intervention and empowered it to make tough policy decisions for the good of the country's long-term future could instead allow it to become a potent political actor, one with few immediate checks and a limitless balance sheet at its disposal.

Half a century earlier, Arthur Burns had demonstrated that a politically loyal Fed chair might set bad policy to goose the economy in the near term for the White House's benefit, spurring inflation. In the modern era, politicization would carry an even bigger threat. The central bank had shown in 2020 that its emergency lending powers could be used to funnel money to just about anyone in times of crisis, given the Treasury's sign-off. And even outside acute crises and without Treasury involvement, mass bond purchases had become a regular part of the central bank tool kit. Those security purchases could help a government to finance itself cheaply, and they could influence the value of the dollar in the global market, making them a potent weapon in a trade war.

Much like the Supreme Court had sweeping authorities that could be wielded in partisan directions, the Fed's control over money could be used to achieve an agenda if its officials so chose.

That marriage of massive power and limited accountability explained why the Fed's top officials insisted on interpreting the central bank's role relatively narrowly, even as a changing world pulled it in new directions. Just as Democrats did not want the Fed to set rates based on Trump's opinions or offer backdoor bailouts to big corporations, Republicans did not want the central bank to set regulations in a way that made it impossible for oil and gas companies to get loans. It was key for the Fed to stay above the fray across political power cycles.

"We're not the forum where all the great issues of the day are to be hashed out, debated, and addressed," Powell had said when asked about climate in 2020. "Because we have a narrow remit, and because we stick to it, Congress has given us a precious grant of independence from direct political control."

Shelton's near appointment underscored that America could take for granted that lawmakers would always see perfect independence from politics as an essential trait in Fed officials. The years around the pandemic had both underlined the value of the Fed's autonomy—a freedom that allowed it to raise rates in 2018, cut them in 2019, and save markets in 2020 while maintaining the public's trust—and hinted at its potential fragility.

The new economic era that was quietly gearing up as 2021 got under way would reinforce why the Fed had been given the freedom to make potentially painful choices.

Chapter 15

A YEAR OF UNCOMFORTABLE QUESTIONS

The Federal Reserve's very effectiveness in setting monetary policy depends on the public's assured confidence that we act only in its interest.

—*Janet L. Yellen, in her 2017 final speech as Fed chair*

B Y APRIL 2021, THE Federal Reserve's new problem had begun to surface at Hertz and Enterprise kiosks across the country. Americans were beginning to travel again. As they did, car rental prices were jumping off the charts.

Before long, price increases also showed up on used car lots. Then furniture showrooms. Next, grocery store bills began to climb. Almost unbelievably, given the trends that had prevailed over the prior two decades, America and the world had found themselves in the middle of an inflationary burst.

Consumer demand had surged back, and supply was struggling to keep up. Factories had been closing intermittently for months thanks to coronavirus outbreaks in Taiwan, in Vietnam, in China, and around the world. Everything from semiconductor chips to bicycle tire tubes and cabinet handles had suddenly become hard to source. Shipping costs had shot up as global ports and container ships became overburdened by unusually high demand for goods like couches, cars, and televisions—a situation that had been made worse when a ship called the *Ever Given* became lodged in the Suez Canal, jamming a major trade route for days. As companies paid more for imported parts transported by sea or were forced to ship them by air, an expensive option, they began to charge more for fishing rods and ladies' dresses.

They could pull it off. Repeated relief checks from the government and expanded unemployment insurance had left many consumers with more cash on hand than usual, and a winter of dormancy had left them ready for a spending spree. They would accept higher prices.

Inflation had shown up just in time for—and at least partly because of policies passed by—the new presidential administration and Congress in Washington.* Joe Biden had taken office in late January 2021, completing a dramatic transfer of power. After months in which everyone had assumed that the administration would be working with a divided Congress, January 5 runoff elections in Georgia had surprised political commentators by swinging the Senate into Democratic control. The victory gave the new president the support he needed to pass ambitious legislation.† Biden had moved swiftly to fulfill promises made during the Georgia electioneering, during which candidates had pledged a fresh round of stimulus checks.

Biden's administration and the Democrat-controlled Congress passed a $1.9 trillion package that included $1,400 stimulus checks and money for states and kept pumped-up unemployment insurance in place, adding to the December 2020 aid package and March 2020 CARES Act passed under the Trump administration. The money pouring into the economy provided welcome relief to many families and was greeted happily by those who didn't strictly need it. Who doesn't like it when the government sends them a check?

Some Democrats were pleased that the administration had not

---

* It is worth noting that Trump also had been supportive of another round of large checks.

† Just as that transition was coming into sight, Trump supporters had violently broken into the Capitol building. Ballots were being counted as part of a postelection formality, and they attempted to disrupt it. The January 6 riots had shocked the nation, underlining the deep divides festering in American society and the potential danger lurking within them. They also may have finally cracked Mnuchin's loyalty to the president: ABC News's Jonathan Karl reported in *Betrayal: The Final Act of the Trump Show* that the Treasury secretary and other cabinet members had discussed using the Twenty-fifth Amendment to remove Trump from office because of the events.

curbed its ambitions out of fear of expanding the deficit. Economists and policy makers had begun thinking about government spending differently in an era of very low rates. In a world where it did not cost the government all that much to keep up with interest payments, the logic increasingly went, it didn't make sense to limit needed policy help just to balance the budget.[1]

Yet even as the latest installment of legislation made its way through the House and Senate, some prominent commentators fretted that it was an overly large mistake. The economy was healing, and the law was going to spend money inefficiently on the short-lived sugar high of stimulus. Many families had already amassed savings from the two relief packages passed under Trump's White House. Prices might jump as too many dollars chased too few goods, while the program would leave little room for future spending on more transformative infrastructure proposals.

"There is a chance that macroeconomic stimulus on a scale closer to World War II levels than normal recession levels will set off inflationary pressures of a kind we have not seen in a generation," Lawrence Summers, the former Treasury secretary and Harvard professor, critiqued in a February 4, 2021, column in *The Washington Post*. The Fed's new framework played a role in those worries, he thought, because it made it less likely that the central bank would react swiftly to a jump in prices.

"Given the commitments the Fed has made, administration officials' dismissal of even the possibility of inflation, and the difficulties in mobilizing congressional support for tax increases or spending cuts, there is the risk of inflation expectations rising sharply," he continued, urging that the Biden plan be enacted "in a way that neither threatens future inflation and financial stability nor our ability to build back better through public investment."[2]

Summers's arguments were widely heard and nearly as widely countered.

"This is balancing risks. And in our view, the risks of doing too little are far greater than the risks of doing too much," Jared Bernstein, a White House economic official, said at a briefing in February, as the legislation was passing.[3] During a press briefing in June, as prices began to rise, National Economic Council deputy director Sameera Fazili said, "We fully expect these bottlenecks to be temporary in nature and to resolve themselves over the next few weeks."[4] In August, as inflation lasted, press secretary Jen Psaki said, "We continue to be at a projection where it is going to come back to normal rates next year."[5]

But by autumn 2021, Summers could point to plenty of data points suggesting that his warnings had been prescient. Inflation was becoming harder to dismiss as temporary. Prices had jumped higher both overall and when stripping out volatile products like food and fuel to take stock of how strong price pressures were at their core. Wages were climbing swiftly, especially for lower-paid workers, as employers struggled to rehire enough waitstaff, factory hands, and shop assistants to meet their customers' vast appetite to buy. Government relief was far from the only driver of the gaping imbalances. Waves of coronavirus continued to disrupt factories across the globe, and people were still spending heavily on goods instead of services, exacerbating product shortages. As corporations faced rising costs and passed them along to consumers, they discovered that they could actually charge even more—swelling their profits—without losing customers.

Even so, the fact that households had so much money in their checking accounts to spend on a new living room set or a nice vacation was clearly contributing to both the surge in demand and companies' newfound pricing power. Very low rates were encouraging more families to attempt to buy a car or try for a house, which they might then have to remodel and furnish in an added boost to consumption, so the Fed's policies were also visibly playing a role. And the issue was clearly in part global in nature, because prices were beginning to shoot higher across many economies.

Consumer confidence and President Biden's approval ratings plummeted as prices rose. Inflation was a kitchen table topic for the first time in decades. Fiscal policy certainly had not repeated its sin of 2008, when it had offered too little help and left the central bank trying to stimulate the economy on its own. It remained to be seen whether it had repeated the missteps of the late 1960s and the 1970s—overheating the economy. As was the case back then, the answer was likely to hinge partly on how the Fed responded.

—

By the end of 2021, the situation was becoming deeply uncomfortable for the central bank. How the inflation revival turned out was sure to serve as a referendum on both the policy packages officials had enacted since the pandemic and the central bank's new policy-setting framework. Plus, central bankers suddenly, unexpectedly, had to decide how quickly to withdraw support from the economy.

Powell and the majority of his colleagues had spent much of 2021 predicting that price gains would calm down as pandemic weirdness worked itself out, labeling the inflation "transitory." The chair had used his speech at that year's Jackson Hole conference to list reasons why inflation was likely to fade on its own eventually. Breakneck price increases in big items like cars seemed unlikely to last, he pointed out. More fundamentally, economies around the globe had been stuck with weak inflation for the past decade or more, and the demographic and economic trends driving that had not abruptly reversed.[6]

Meanwhile, he noted, there was "considerable remaining ground to reach maximum employment." The implication was that it would be a bad idea to stage a knee-jerk policy response to inflation that might soon fade, stalling the economy just as it was healing. The Fed had internalized the lessons of the prior decade.

Yet even as Powell conveyed a sense of watchful calm, some Fed officials had begun to worry out loud that inflation would ease too little and too slowly. They were listening to businesses in their districts talk about rising costs that seemed likely to last for some time, and they were hearing workers and unions talk about wage wins that would have been unthinkable during most of the prior decade. They feared that the central bank was about to find itself in a situation where inflation would prove painful to contain.

The evidence was spotty, but in theory, if consumers came to expect much faster price increases and demanded pay hikes, it could set off an upward spiral in wages and prices that made it difficult for the central bank to get inflation back down to its 2 percent goal. It seemed increasingly unwise to have policy rates at rock bottom while buying huge amounts of government debt each month. Nearly repeating his line from 2015, James Bullard from the St. Louis Fed had begun warning that "it is time to end these emergency measures."

"It will be a challenge to keep inflation expectations in check," he told Bloomberg Television in July. The St. Louis Fed president wasn't alone in his push to begin normalizing policy. Other officials including Dallas Fed president Robert Kaplan and the Kansas City Fed's Esther George had soon started to warn about a potentially serious inflation problem.

By autumn 2021, the inflation hawk crowd—wrong for so much of the prior decade—had been joined by even their most full-employment-focused colleagues. Price increases were reaccelerating after a late summer lull. Rent prices were jumping, which was hard to explain away as a pandemic supply issue. Higher housing costs would keep inflation higher for months to come. Labor shortages were rampant, as many workers lingered on the economy's sidelines even as businesses and schools fully reopened, and as older workers retired. Wages had begun to pick up sharply across a widening range of occupations. The Fed had been trying to avoid pulling support away too quickly. Increasingly, the danger seemed to be that it would remove it too late.

The Fed signaled in September 2021 that it might soon dial back its bond purchases, and in November, Powell pivoted firmly.[7] Late that month, he acknowledged that the high inflation was surprising him and that the Fed was going to need to more swiftly withdraw help from the economy. At that point, the Fed was still buying $120 billion in bonds each month, pouring gasoline onto the fire by keeping mortgage rates low and bolstering a housing market that increasingly looked like it might be overheating. Asked if inflation was transitory during a congressional testimony on November 30, Powell instead listed reasons why it might last.

"I think it's probably a good time to retire that word," he said, explaining that it had been widely misunderstood as "short-lived." America's experience with inflation certainly wasn't that, it was proving.[8] Backing away from super-easy policy would take time, though.

Ben Bernanke had pushed global markets into a painful tantrum when he had signaled in 2013 that the Fed's bond purchases would begin to slow down. Nobody wanted to repeat that experience in 2021, and they had learned that the best way to avoid such volatility was to ease investors into a policy change by slowly and clearly signaling it over weeks and months. Plus, officials believed that they needed to maintain credibility. The Fed had promised to set policy in a certain way—buying bonds until it saw substantial further progress in the economy—and it needed to follow through if it wanted markets to believe similar pledges in the future.

When it came to rates, Fed officials had pledged in September 2020 not to raise them until the economy had returned to full employment, and policy makers had been saying for months that the labor market was not there yet. By fall, they had begun to amend those statements, a hint that rate increases might be coming sooner than previously forecast.

"The temptation at the beginning of the recovery was to look at the data in February of 2020 and say, well, that's the goal," Powell said at his November press conference. "We have a completely different situation now where we have high inflation, and we have to balance that with what's going on in the employment market."[9]

The Fed's late retreat from easy monetary policy owed to more than the careful inertia built into its policy practices.* Fed officials were hesitant to react to the changing backdrop in 2021 in part because they had become used to understanding themselves as the central players in the U.S. economy. It was a role they had begun to take on during Volcker's war on inflation and had cemented as they played the leading part in pulling the recovery along following the 2008 crisis.

The new framework itself—the one Powell had unveiled in August 2020 declaring full employment a "broad-based and inclusive goal" and changing the Fed's inflation target to an average over time— promised nothing that should have prevented the Fed from reducing its support as prices took off. The way the Fed had chosen to implement it was a different story. When the Fed pre-committed in September 2020 that it would not lift interest rates until the labor market had healed, it had assumed that insufficient demand would remain the problem of the era. It had not anticipated the spring 2021 spending package or the supply chain crisis plaguing the globe, and

---

* The Fed would ultimately buy bonds until March 2022, and it would be late summer 2022 before it had lifted rates to a point where they were no longer expected to stoke the economy.

so it had not anticipated the inflation that resulted when hot demand and widespread shortages had collided. In short, policy makers hadn't accounted for the chance that forces outside the Fed's control would speed up inflation in a lasting way before employment had fully recovered.

Would it have helped if the Fed had been faster to recognize that inflation was real? That was a question that was already beginning to haunt central bankers by late 2021. Cutting bond purchases and pushing rates up a few months earlier would not have slowed demand rapidly enough to counter the supply chain snarls that had already taken hold, and more expensive money clearly wouldn't have helped beleaguered auto companies suffering through a semiconductor chip shortage to build more cars. But a quicker reaction might have begun to slow demand and shift behavior in key parts of the economy, particularly housing, in ways that would have made inflation less likely to stick around. The central bank's reticence probably had not drastically shifted the course of economic history, but it certainly had not helped the situation. As Powell and his colleagues approached 2022, it seemed likely that they were going to have to be more aggressive in withdrawing policy support because they had been slow to start the fight against rising prices.

Fed policy was still potent. The need to counteract inflation was likely to make it central once more. But for a brief and fateful period, America's central bank had shared the economic spotlight.

In Minneapolis, Neel Kashkari was partly proud of what the recovery response had accomplished and partly worried about the burgeoning inflation. He was back to working from his office, which he had lined with history books about Abraham Lincoln and Civil War general Ulysses S. Grant instead of the economics texts more typical of Fed presidents. From his stately desk, he had taken a conference call with large employers from around the Minneapolis district on a chilly week in late November 2021.

One anecdote had him particularly worried. The company, a large employer, said that its union had been emboldened by the recent inflation. It had typically asked for 3 percent raises over a three-to-five-year period. Now, it was asking for 10 percent annual pay hikes.

Wage increases that massive would likely prod the company to charge customers more to cover its costs, it went without saying. Kashkari had long positioned himself as a champion of workers, but even he was worried that the sweeping response to the pandemic and the moment of rapid inflation might be starting to change behavior in ways that would make quick price increases last.

Policy makers had avoided repeating the mistakes of 2008, as Kashkari had hoped they would. That didn't mean they hadn't made new ones. His reason for voting against the Fed's September 2020 policy guidance seemed misplaced, in hindsight. The Fed's problem in 2021 was not that it might choke off a labor market recovery prematurely because it was afraid of an inflationary boogeyman. He had called the idea that inflation might begin to perpetuate itself a "ghost story" in that dissent; it looked less ephemeral with each passing data point.

That was the eternal challenge of monetary policy. The moment you thought you had figured out what the economy might do next with any amount of confidence, it defied expectations.

As inflation picked up, the concerns people and companies voiced at the Fed's outreach sessions had begun to shift. Rising living costs and supply uncertainty had replaced jobs as the predominant concern. At a Fed Listens event the New York Fed held in November 2021, small businesses and labor groups pointed to rising food insecurity and climbing house prices as issues in their communities. Workers had typically pushed the Fed to focus on employment throughout its long history—and labor movements had seen easy money as helpful to their cause well before the Fed's 1913 founding—but a strong job market without relatively stable prices felt like a hollow victory. What did it help if your wages were climbing if they could not keep up with your rent and grocery bills? Consumer confidence began to plummet. Inflation shot to the top of America's list of worries in Gallup surveys. For many people, the economy felt even worse than it had at moments of high unemployment. While joblessness affects a segment of the population acutely, inflation eroded the paychecks and savings of just about everyone. (Within months, as Russia's war in Ukraine began and exacerbated the inflation by pushing food and fuel prices sharply higher, lines would once again form at food pantries and soup kitchens as poor people in particular found that they could not keep up with the rising costs of everyday necessities.)[10]

For all of the very real problems rising prices were causing, though, Powell and his colleagues believed that the economy could have been faring so much worse had the sell-off of March 2020 turned into a financial crisis à la 2008 or 1930. By late 2021, the unemployment rate was poised to return to precrisis levels. Job openings outnumbered applicants. Wages were not keeping up with prices, but they were rising, and anecdotes suggested that employees were gaining more of an upper hand in negotiations around benefits.

East Hartford, where Powell had visited in late 2019, was among the places where the economy remained imperfect but felt full of opportunity.

Jasmine Ayala—the high school graduate whom the Fed chair had talked with at Fed Listens—was still working the night shift at Pratt & Whitney, a job she'd maintained throughout the pandemic. She used the money she earned on tuition and spent her days in class, studying criminology, and had also gotten her real estate license on the side. She was so busy that she rarely sold houses, but when she did, it was a welcome windfall.

The pandemic had roiled her early adulthood, but it hadn't derailed it. She and her friends were getting jobs, forging careers, taking advantage of a moment when labor seemed to have an advantage. The onset of the coronavirus had been a scary moment for her community, she said, but not a devastating one.

That neighborhoods on the margin like East Hartford could emerge from a near-complete economic shutdown shaken but relatively unscathed—people were still struggling, but were also occasionally triumphing—was a credit to the policy that had come out of Washington in the preceding year. The sweeping rescue Powell's Fed, Congress, and the Treasury had provided ensured that many companies had retained access to credit markets, allowing them to keep employing people and producing goods and services. Checks and unemployment benefits had kept households financially comfortable enough to spend. The combination ensured that people like Jasmine and her friends would not find themselves without a hopeful future. Unlike the people who had graduated high school in 2009 amid promises that the recession would end soon, only to battle years of tepid economic conditions that enabled low wages and exploitative employers, Ayala's generation faced a situation in which managers were eager to hire them and desperate to retain them.

The Fed had moved faster to stem damage in financial markets than it had in the prior downturn, in part because the crisis was so different and in part because memories of the earlier catastrophe remained fresh. The prior experience had given the central bank the tools and motivation to respond. The government's spending had helped to keep households whole.

That did not mean that the 2020 packages worked perfectly, even outside the obvious flaw of rapid inflation. When it came to Congress's direct, Fed-unrelated spending programs, the money had been widely spread to families and small and large businesses, but it had often been inefficiently distributed in the name of speed or political goals rather than in response to actual needs. Audits would find that a huge amount of money had been taken fraudulently. And no matter how good the government response was, neither Congress's relief nor the Fed's had been enough to tide over businesses with models totally upended by a pandemic that seemed poised to burn out over years rather than months. Bankruptcy data overall remained surprisingly tame, but vacant windows in city downtowns made it clear that some companies had succumbed.

Samantha Stephens at OatMeals, the shop in New York's West Village, had finally faced reality in late December 2020: She was going to have to close shop. The company was bleeding money. Nobody was going out to breakfast in Lower Manhattan. Office catering orders were a distant memory. New York University students, once a steady source of demand, were only trickling back.

Stephens had ultimately gotten the disaster relief and forgivable Paycheck Protection Program loans she applied for in March, and they had helped for a time. Quaker Oats had donated $20,000 when it noticed that she had a crowdfunding page. But with her lease up in January and sales at 25 percent of their pre-Covid level, she could not hang on. She was going to sink further into personal debt to try to save a sinking ship. She warned her two remaining employees and tried to help them look for new jobs. She found a storage space for her restaurant equipment, and she began looking for a job herself, applying to food editing gigs and renewing her contract as a Quaker content provider.

"It has not been an easy ride—I've loved it, I'm sad, but I have to accept the reality of the situation," she said in early January 2021, three weeks before the store was to close, talking on her mobile phone as she walked home through a damp New York City dusk after locking up shop for the day.

She believed it was the right choice, financially. That didn't make it easy, personally. It was when she was telling a regular customer that she was closing that the enormity of her loss hit Stephens. This had been her dream—and it had, with hard work and creativity, come true. Now that dream was ending.

"I just boo-hooed in front of my employees," she said. The pandemic era would leave economic scars, despite all the government's efforts, including the empty storefront where OatMeals had once stood.

The pandemic was imparting another legacy, beyond the surprising return of rapid inflation and a reshuffling in American commerce. Some parts of markets looked worryingly bubbly in the wake of the no-holds-barred relief packages. A sensational example had surfaced early in 2021.

"I like the stock," Keith Gill, the YouTube investor known as Roaring Kitty on his YouTube channel, had told lawmakers on the House Financial Services Committee virtual hearing in February. He usually wore a bandana wrapped around his forehead, but he had ditched the headwear and donned a tie for his Webex with Congress.

Gill, along with investors across America, had piled money into the stock of video game store GameStop over the prior months, sending its price on a precipitous rise that eventually gave way to a roller-coaster decline. It and other meme assets—stocks of Bitcoin and the movie theater chain AMC—had drawn lawmaker attention, as had the explosion in small-time trading on the Robinhood app and other platforms. Ordinary investors were carrying out complex transactions involving options, trading on borrowed money, and even staging crowdsourced rebellions against hedge funds. In GameStop's case, a plan had coalesced on the forum Reddit and small-time investors had shut down a bet that Wall Street funds had taken against the stock.

In a memorandum for the congressional hearing titled "Game Stopped?" the committee argued that the episode was raising "important questions" about "whether technology and social media have outpaced regulation in a manner that leaves investors and the markets exposed to unnecessary risks."[11]

Meme stocks making national headlines in 2021 did, at some level, trace back to the Fed, as participants in the phenomenon would tell you. "Ty Jpow" (translated: Thank you, Jay Powell) posts were frequent on WallStreetBets, the Reddit discussion board at the center of the phenomenon. Memes abounded in which people took real CNBC footage of Fed press conferences and superimposed, in place of what Powell had said, the chyron "Powell: F*** Your Puts." (Translated from Wall Street–ese: Powell's policies were making it a bad idea to take out put options, which give investors protection if a stock they hold goes down. Stocks, so long as Powell was at it, would never go down.) Easy money had helped to push stock prices up by keeping interest rates on safe debt extremely low and prodding investors into riskier assets in hopes of higher returns. By 2021, seemingly the entire internet was conscious of that reality.

Stock market frothiness was one vulnerability the Fed's low rates and big bond buying in response to the pandemic had exacerbated. It was far from the only one.

"Equity prices continued to increase, supported by strong earnings expectations, still-low Treasury yields, and high risk appetite," the Fed staff told officials at their November 2021 policy meeting. Money market mutual funds also remained vulnerable to the sort of runs that had necessitated Fed intervention twice in twelve years. Hedge fund debt, the culprit behind some of the March 2020 carnage, had again swelled to "noteworthy" levels, especially among the top firms, the Fed staff explained. Corporations had decreased their debt somewhat in the wake of the pandemic, but business loan piles remained large and ominous.

The early-pandemic meltdown had been nobody's fault. That didn't mean that the rescue from it had not created—or at least reinforced—a precedent in which financial market players knew the Fed was waiting in the wings to help if things turned ugly. Without changes to regulation, there was a real possibility that the same rescues would be needed again in a future crisis. The Securities and Exchange Commission and Janet Yellen's Treasury had begun to investigate ways to make the system more resilient, with particular focus on the money market funds. It remained to be seen if those reforms would prove any more successful than the sweeping but provenly incomplete post-2008 attempt.

Congress's 2020 and 2021 response had also left the government with more than $28 trillion in debt, compared to about $23 trillion before the pandemic. While recent history had shown that carrying a heavy national debt load was not necessarily the disaster politicians and pundits often claimed—Japan had been much more indebted, as a share of its GDP, for decades without any great crisis—America's burden had been amassed at least partly on the assumption that interest rates would remain low for years to come. If inflation remained higher and the Fed had to raise borrowing costs sharply to contain it, it would make it more expensive for the government to issue or renew bonds, costing America more in interest payments and potentially crowding out other types of spending if deficit-shy lawmakers balked at the rising outlays. The advice Powell had given Nancy Pelosi—go big—might suddenly seem less well informed as the low rate era ended.

By late 2021, Randal Quarles was worried about the aftermath of the Fed's pandemic-era efforts for political and institutional reasons as much as for the increasingly obvious economic ones. Quarles was facing down his last days in office. Biden's presidential victory had all but ensured that he would not be reappointed when his four-year term as vice-chair for supervision ended in October 2021. While Quarles had flirted with the possibility of staying on as a governor, he had in November announced that he would step down when his term as the global Financial Stability Board head ended the following month. As he contemplated the challenges that his successor would confront, he had come to fear that in trying to save the country, the Fed had sold its soul.

From Marriner Eccles's days, the central bank had mostly seen itself as a broad-based lender of last resort in times of financial trouble. Its job was to keep finance functioning, providing a last-ditch source of expensive funds to a wide variety of institutions if nothing else was available. The bank bailouts in 2008 had been a deviation from that principle, but Congress had viewed them as an aberration and had moved swiftly to make sure that they could not be repeated. The 2020 crisis had seen the Fed take on a much more activist role as it moved from backstopping markets to supporting the flow of credit within them—and instead of curbing those powers, it seemed possible that lawmakers would embrace them and push them further.

Quarles worried that now politicians would see the central bank as a conduit for funneling help to favored constituencies without debate and compromise. The Fed could become a new, immensely powerful, unelected but nevertheless political arm.

"There will inevitably be those whose plans are grand, and whose patience with democratic accountability low, who will begin to ask why the Fed can't fund repairs of the country's aging infrastructure, or finance the building of a border wall, or purchase trillions of dollars of green energy bonds, or underwrite the colonization of Mars," Quarles warned in a speech he delivered just before leaving the Fed.

While his concerns echoed the ones Toomey and Mnuchin had cited in ending the programs at the end of 2020, Quarles clearly did not think that shutting down those facilities rapidly had done enough to seal the Pandora's box that the corporate bond market rescues, Main Street, the municipal loan program, and the broader crisis response had opened. (There was reason to suspect that they might be used again. The Fed had continued perfecting the municipal program in the months after it was shut down, so that if it were to be taken off the shelf again, it would be able to buy bonds according to an index formula, as the corporate bond program had done. The team had already started the work and figured they might as well finish it. Even so, there would have been no point in perfecting a program that nobody thought would ever be revived.)

Political pressures, Quarles warned, could "turn us from a technocratic, nonpolitical institution with a crucial but focused mandate and great autonomy in the pursuit of that mandate, into the most politically entangled organization in the country."

—

Powell's trial by inflation and the questions bubbling up in the aftermath of the Fed's pandemic response came at a tough moment for the chair. His four-year gig at the top of the institution was nearing an end. He would need to be renominated to the job by President Biden if he hoped to remain in office, and whether that would happen was unclear.

Powell's chances, and the Fed's institutional rapport, had taken a hit that autumn. Just as the renomination process was kicking off, *Wall Street Journal* reporter Michael Derby broke a reputation-bruising story. Recently filed financial disclosures showed that Robert Kaplan, the Dallas Fed president who had been heavily involved in designing the central bank's emergency programs, had traded millions of dollars of individual stocks in 2020. As other Fed reporters began to dig further into the disclosures, it came to light that he had also traded in futures, essentially taking a bet on which direction the stock market would move during a year when the Fed's actions had played a heavy role in determining its course.

Bloomberg noticed that Eric Rosengren, the Boston Fed president, had also been trading in real estate securities in 2020, even as the Fed's actions had an enormous impact on that market. Then the outlet pointed out that Richard Clarida, the Fed's vice-chair, had rebalanced his portfolio toward stocks the day before Powell's February 2020 announcement signaling that the Fed would respond to coronavirus risks.*

The trades had terrible optics: It seemed at least possible that officials had taken advantage of their privileged positions for their own financial gain. Kaplan and Rosengren first pledged to move into broad-based investments, like mutual funds. Then, as outrage built, both resigned. Rosengren cited his health, while Kaplan said in his statement that "the recent focus on my financial disclosure risks becoming a distraction."[12]

---

* *The New York Times* would later break the news that Clarida had sold out of the same stock fund just days before buying into it, based on corrected government filings, raising serious questions about how the move had qualified as a "planned rebalance," which was the original explanation for the move. A later Fed watchdog report would clear him of wrongdoing, but would not address why the trades had happened.

The Fed's ethics watchdog launched an investigation into both presidents and Clarida, and Powell swiftly switched into damage control mode. "No one on the F.O.M.C. is happy to be in this situation, to be having these questions raised," he had said at his September post-meeting news conference. "This is an important moment for the Fed, and I'm determined that we will rise to the moment."

The Fed faced intense and immediate blowback in the public and from Capitol Hill for not policing officials more effectively. Elizabeth Warren pressed for more information about what had happened and why it had been allowed to occur, sending a scathing letter on October 21, when *The New York Times* reported that the Board had warned officials to avoid trading in early 2020. Officials had clearly been alert to possible optics and practical problems but had resumed transactions anyway. That same day, the Fed announced a new ethics regime that would ban its policy makers from actively trading in all but the most boring investments.[13] By Fed standards, the speed of the review had been astonishing.

Despite the swift repair effort, that Fed officials had felt comfortable doing something so obviously questionable reflected badly on the institution's culture. For many, it served to underscore the Fed's image as elite and maybe even self-interested. The scandal temporarily seemed like it might threaten both Powell's and Brainard's chances, since both could have been in positions to stop or at least dissuade such activity.

Joseph Stiglitz, a Nobel Prize–winning liberal economist, wrote an opinion piece citing the scandal as a reason that Powell needed to go.

"Powell's seeming insensitivity to conflicts of interest has long worried me, including in the management of some of the Fed's pandemic-response programs," Stiglitz wrote. "With four years of Trump having already weakened trust in U.S. institutions, there is a real risk that confidence in the Fed's integrity will be undermined even further."[14]

Aside from opposition based on the scandal, many of the arguments against reappointing Powell coalesced around a central point: He was not proactive enough in using the Fed's powers. He had done a lot to further labor's interests at the Fed, even his most strident opponents would grudgingly acknowledge, but he had not dissented against Randy Quarles's campaign to lighten financial regulation.

"Renominating you means gambling that, for the next five years, a Republican majority at the Federal Reserve, with a Republican chair who has regularly voted to deregulate Wall Street, won't drive this economy over a financial cliff again," Elizabeth Warren, the powerful Massachusetts senator, told Powell as he testified before the Senate in September.

Powell had supported big fiscal spending in 2020, but he had been slow to use the Fed's powers to curb climate change, progressives pointed out. And while he had been swift in rescuing markets that the central bank had never aided before, the programs that were servicing small companies and localities instead of Wall Street had not accomplished as much as some Democrats had hoped they would. As Quarles fretted about the lines that the central bank had crossed, some Democrats were arguing that the barriers could have been breached with more conviction.

The debate over Powell, ultimately, was a fight about what the Fed was supposed to be. Was America's central bank meant to be the quiet economic puppet master it had become since Marriner Eccles's days, one that tried to set broad policies with an eye on the entire economy and tried to stay out of the private sector's way to the extent possible? Or would it better serve the public as a powerful arm of government that could use its authorities to help advance goals like decarbonization and cheap financing for state and local governments? Should the Fed take its cues narrowly from the law and tradition, or should it fill in the cracks of the democratic process by stepping up to help when politicians struggled to pass economic policies?

It was a philosophical divide between the hands-off economic enablement that people like Quarles had long stood for and the more hands-on pursuit of common goals that many progressives, and to a more muted extent Brainard,[*] hoped to see.

Powell, as was so often the case, fit somewhere in between.

---

[*] Brainard was left of center on many central banking issues. For instance, she had been a fan of trying to make the municipal program as generous as the corporate bond program but had hardly been gunning for the spending-style program some progressives wanted. Likewise, she wanted to make sure banks knew their climate risk but did not publicly urge using climate stress tests as a tool to stop banks from lending to oil and gas companies.

EPILOGUE

None of us has the luxury of choosing our challenges;
fate and history provide them for us.

—*Jerome H. Powell, April 9, 2020, speech*

PRESIDENT JOE BIDEN CITED America's striking progress in bouncing back from the pandemic shutdowns when, on a sunny but brisk Monday just before Thanksgiving in 2021, he announced that he would be keeping Powell at the helm of the Fed for another four years, pending the Senate's blessing.

"We have made enormous progress in bringing our economy back to life and getting Americans back to work," the White House said in its statement unveiling the decision. That outcome was "a testament to decisive action by Chair Powell and the Federal Reserve to cushion the impact of the pandemic and get America's economy back on track."

Deliberations about the reappointment had dragged on for long months, leaving pundits wondering if Biden would choose Powell, Brainard, or someone else entirely for the job.

The decision, in some ways, completed the end of the early pandemic era in economic policy. Steven Mnuchin was long gone from government and back to building his fortune in finance. He had started a $2.5 billion investment fund in mid-2021, promptly raising money from the Saudi sovereign wealth fund—a deal so close to home relative to his government work that it looked like a possible payoff. It caused some ethics experts to suggest that top officials in U.S. government should have mandatory cooling-off periods before they jumped back into private work related to their public experience.[1]

It had been clear since the 2020 election that Fed vice-chair Richard Clarida, also a Trump appointee, would not win a second term when his governor seat expired in early 2022. Between that and Quarles's November announcement that he would be retiring from the Fed, Biden had a chance to remake the Fed's leadership team in Washington, appointing all three of its top leaders and at least three new governors.

In fact, Quarles's decision to leave had probably helped Powell's chances (a reality that influenced the vice-chair's thinking as he decided whether to resign). "This sets off a domino effect, in which Biden will be able to name a majority of Fed governors even if he keeps Powell as chair," Robert Kuttner at the progressive *American Prospect* wrote following the announcement.[2]

When Biden announced Powell's selection, he also announced that he would promote Brainard to take Clarida's place as vice-chair, elevating her to second-in-command. Trump had chosen Powell in 2017 as a way for the White House to keep Yellen's approach without keeping a Democrat in the role. That Biden had not pulled a similar maneuver by replacing Powell with his close—but Democratic—ally Brainard reinforced the Fed's separation from the partisan political process. The tradition of retaining competent Fed chairs across administrations was alive again. Fed independence had rested on shaky ground over the prior few years, but at least for the moment, it was again taking priority.

Biden's decision wasn't as much of a political stretch as it could have been. The president had promised to make the Fed look more like America, and he would go on to name other nominees to the central bank—including economists Lisa Cook and Philip Jefferson, both of whom are Black—who would make its leadership team more diverse than it had ever been. Powell and Brainard had together built a reputation for prioritizing workers, another of the administration's goals for the central bank.

"Powell and Brainard share the Administration's focus on ensuring that economic growth broadly benefits all workers," the White House explained in its release, calling the Fed's framework review a "landmark" reevaluation of its priorities. But that worker-centric

stance was in for a test, one that promised to make having an apolitical and independent leader at the Fed essential. Inflation hung over
the selection the way it hung over everything in Washington by that
point. It was the single biggest worry on voters' and thus politicians'
minds. To the extent that Powell came off as centrist, it was the kind
of neutrality that allowed him to get things done, and he possessed an
ideological nimbleness that would make him willing to lift rates and
hurt the job market to slow the economy and restore price stability.
With costs increasing at the fastest pace in decades, it seemed likely
that pragmatism would be an essential virtue.

As a team, Powell and Brainard in some ways resembled Eccles,
their long-ago predecessor. Both worked across ideological lines for
expediency's sake at a time of stark societal divide. Both were economically privileged themselves but felt strongly that the nation's success depended on making sure that opportunity was widely shared.
The pair had been fierce in helping the economy in its moment of
crisis, and they had celebrated the benefits of full employment, but
they were both reorienting to fight high inflation as 2022 dawned.

In short, the Fed's top officials recognized that the world around
them was variable and that good policy required intellectual
flexibility—even if rigidity dominated the airwaves and opinion
pages.

They were unlike Eccles in other obvious ways. Where Powell
and Brainard were relatively smooth operators, Eccles had been a
social gnat. (His own biographer and friend, Sidney Hyman, once
explained, "As a man born to have no peace himself, and to allow little peace to other people, he was not an easy person to be around.")[3]
More substantively, Eccles had believed that unemployment, inflation, and bank regulation should be the central bank's narrow remit.
The Fed had been forced by history to take on a more expansive role
in the modern era: Thanks to the rise of shadow banking and broad
financialization, an unfolding climate calamity, and the dawn of new
technologies, the Fed's leaders would need to battle a different set of
problems than the ones its mighty post-Depression chairman once
faced.

Powell, Brainard, and their colleagues had spent 2020 and 2021
demonstrating that the Fed's powers could be wielded to address

more of society's challenges than anyone had previously imagined. There were few groups the Fed could not help in moments of disaster.

Yet the pandemic era had also underlined that central bank policy was not an ideal fix for every problem society faced. The Main Street midsize business program had struggled to help a broad array of borrowers. By trying to continue stoking the economy to foster a rapid and widely shared labor market rebound, it seemed at least possible that the Fed's massive bond purchases and reluctant move away from super-low rates had helped to feed into the pickup in inflation. That mistake would force officials to act more rapidly, and potentially disruptively, to contain prices down the road. As 2021 had demonstrated, the Fed's traditional jobs—full employment and price stability—remained a challenge that could not be taken for granted.

How Powell and Brainard chose to reestablish the Fed's boundaries in the wake of the pandemic crisis would surely shape the institution's future and, through it, the nation's. How they interpreted and reinterpreted their new framework would determine when inflation could be brought under control and how much harm the labor market would suffer in the process. Powell had pushed the Fed to rethink policy for a low-rate, low-inflation era, only to have those conditions rapidly shift. Now the central bank would need to determine whether high inflation was a temporary phase or a new regime, one that would require another Fed evolution.

Marriner Eccles died in 1977, but his voice carried into the twenty-first century through the speeches and writings he left behind. The postscript to his memoir offered perhaps his most pointed advice to his successors as they stared down an uncertain future. Eccles had hoped America's central bank would be poised to stimulate demand in bad times but also prepared to restrain the economy when necessary. He wanted the Fed to know its power but also its limits.

The central bank's "actions are seldom popular," Eccles wrote. "If it is to succeed in its mission, it will need great internal strength in its composition, great courage in its action, and a sustained public and congressional understanding of the role it should play in our society of democratic capitalism."

ACKNOWLEDGMENTS

Thank you for reading my book. I hope that you've had as much fun learning about the adventures of Jerome Powell and crew as I've had observing and writing about them.

I will be forever indebted to Steve Merelman, who read and commented on nearly every line of *Limitless*. David Black, my agent, provided excellent coaching and writing feedback from the very start. Andrew Miller, Todd Portnowitz, and the whole team at Knopf are top-notch editors. Jim Tankersley, Ben Casselman, Jason Furman, Deborah Solomon, Kaleb Nygaard, Peter Conti-Brown, George Selgin, Tori McClemens, Tim Teresczuk, Jeremy Kress, Lev Menand, and many others who may prefer not to be named read sections or helped me fact-check passages and gave me useful and welcome feedback. Neil Irwin served as a tireless mentor and guide as I navigated the pitching and writing process. Matt Boesler offered valuable reading recommendations on occasionally obscure topics. Victoria Guida and Brian Cheung provided constant moral support.

This book would not have been possible without the help of the many public officials and historians across the Federal Reserve System, at academic institutions, and at think tanks who served as sources and sounding boards.

Limitless is an outgrowth of my time as a Fed journalist, and while I owe many mentors for making these years of reporting possible, I'll name just a few. Chris Roush helped me into business journalism; Tom Keene steered me toward economics; Craig Torres took a twenty-three-year-old reporter who didn't know anything about the Fed along to meetings with Powell and Lael Brainard; Deborah Solomon, Elisabeth Bumiller, and Ellen Pollock brought me to *The New York Times* and convinced me that there is no such thing as a story too big or a project too daunting.

I'm grateful to the many friends and family members (Mom, Dad, Salina, Liz, my Steamboat pals) who have listened to endless anecdotes about book writing over the past few years. Above all, I'm thankful for Peter Newland, my husband, who was my counselor and cheerleader throughout the many months that I spent working on this book. I am immensely lucky to have him as a partner.

BIBLIOGRAPHY

Abrams, Burton A. 2006. "How Richard Nixon Pressured Arthur Burns: Evidence from the Nixon Tapes." *Journal of Economic Perspectives* 20 (4):177–88.

Ahamed, Liaquat. 2009. *Lord of Finance: The Bankers Who Broke the World.* New York: Penguin Press.

Andalfatto, D., and L. Li. 2014. "Quantitative Easing in Japan: Past and Present." *Economic Synopses* 1. https://doi.org/10.20955/es.2014.1.

Anderson, Caitlin E. n.d. *1837: The Hard Times.* https://www.library.hbs.edu/hc/crises/1837.html.

Andrews, Edmund L. 2008. "Greenspan Concedes Error on Regulation." *New York Times,* October 23.

Anson, Mike, David Bholat, Miao Kang, and Ryland Thomas. 2017. "The Bank of England as Lender of Last Resort: New Historical Evidence from Daily Transactional Data." Bank of England Staff Working Paper No. 691, November 10.

Appelbaum, Binyamin. 2011. "Bernanke Defends Fed's Role in Running Economy." *New York Times,* April 27.

———. 2013. "Yellen's Exclusive Interview, with Yellen." *New York Times,* October 9.

———. 2015a. "Fed's Janet Yellen, in Testimony, Counsels Patience on Interest Rate Increase." *New York Times,* February 24.

———. 2015b. "House Republicans Intensify Attacks on Federal Reserve." *New York Times,* February 25.

Arnall, Daniel. 2011. "Bernanke Holds First Press Conference in Fed's History." ABC, April 27.

The Asia Group. 2021. "Press Release: Dr. Kurt M. Campbell to Join the Biden-Harris Administration." January 13. https://theasiagroup.com/press-release-dr-kurt-m-campbell-to-join-the-biden-harris-administration/.

Auerbach, Robert. 2006. "The Painful History of Fed Transparency." Market-Watch, May 8.

Bagehot, Walter. 1873. *Lombard Street: A Description of the Money Market.* New York: Scribner, Armstrong & Co.

Baier, Justin. 2020. "The Day Coronavirus Nearly Broke the Financial Markets." *Wall Street Journal,* May 20.

Baklanova, Viktoria, Isaac Kuznits, and Trevor Tatum. 2021. "Primer: Money Market Funds and the Repo Market." U.S. Securities and Exchange Commission, February 18. https://www.sec.gov/files/mmfs-and-the-repo-market-021721.pdf.

Barro, Josh. 2020. "The World's Best Bureaucrat." *New York* magazine, October 27.

Barth, Daniel, and Jay Kahn. 2020. "Basis Trades and Treasury Market Illiquidity." Brief Series, Office of Financial Research, July 16. https://www.financial research.gov/briefs/files/OFRBr_2020_01_Basis-Trades.pdf.

Basak, Sonali. 2020. "Before Fed Acted, Leverage Burned Hedge Funds in Treasury Market." Bloomberg, March 19.

Beckworth, David, Sam Bell, Julia Coronado, and Skanda Amarnath. 2020. "Employ America's Webcast Panel on the Federal Reserve's Updated Framework and Its Implications for Monetary Policy." *The Bridge* (Mercatus original podcast), September 2.

Belvedere, Matthew J. 2020. "5 Things to Know Before the Stock Market Opens Friday." CNBC, February 28.

Bentz, Alyssa. 2019. "Surviving and Thriving in the Great Depression." Wells Fargo, March 13. https://www.wellsfargohistory.com/surviving-and -thriving-in-the-great-depression/.

Bernanke, Ben S. 2002. "On Milton Friedman's Ninetieth Birthday." Federal Reserve Board, November 8. https://www.federalreserve.gov/boarddocs /speeches/2002/20021108/.

———. 2015. *The Courage to Act.* New York: W. W. Norton.

———. 2022. *21st Century Monetary Policy: The Federal Reserve from the Great Inflation to COVID-19.* New York: W. W. Norton.

Bernanke, Ben, and Harold James. 1991. "The Gold Standard, Deflation, and Financial Crisis in the Great Depression: An International Comparison." In R. Glenn Hubbard, ed., *Financial Markets and Financial Crises,* 33–68. Chicago: University of Chicago Press.

Bernanke, Ben, and Janet Yellen. 2020. "The Federal Reserve Must Reduce Long-Term Damage from Coronavirus." *Financial Times,* March 18.

Bertrand, Marianne, and Sendhil Mullainathan. 2003. "Are Emily and Greg More Employable Than Lakisha and Jamal? A Field Experiment on Labor Market Discrimination." National Bureau of Economic Research. NBER Working Paper Series, July. https://www.nber.org/papers/w9873.

Bhutta, Neil, Andrew C. Change, Lisa J. Dettling, and Joanne W. Hsu. 2020. "Disparities in Wealth by Race and Ethnicity in the 2019 Survey of Consumer Finances." Federal Reserve, September 28. https://www.federalreserve .gov/econres/notes/feds-notes/disparities-in-wealth-by-race-and-ethnicity-in -the-2019-survey-of-consumer-finances-20200928.htm.

Biden, Joe. 2020. "Joe Biden COVID-19 Remarks Transcript November 5." Rev, November 5. https://www.rev.com/blog/transcripts/joe-biden-covid-19 -remarks-transcript-november-5.

Binder, Sarah, and Mark Spindel. 2017. *The Myth of Independence: How Congress Governs the Federal Reserve.* Princeton, N.J.: Princeton University Press.

Blanchard, Olivier. 2019. "Public Debt and Low Interest Rates." *American Economic Review* 109, no. 4 (April): 1197–229.

Bloomberg News. 2020. "Italy Closes Most Stores; U.S. Eyes Europe Ban: Virus Update." Bloomberg, March 10.

Bloomberg View. 2013. "The Legacy of Ben Bernanke." December 19.

Blumenfeld, Laura. 2009. "The $700 Billion Man." *Washington Post,* December 6.

Board Meeting. 2019. "Open Board Meeting on October 10, 2019." Federal Reserve, October 10. https://www.federalreserve.gov/aboutthefed/board meetings/20191010open.htm.

Board of Governors. n.d. "Charles S. Hamlin." Federal Reserve History. https:// www.federalreservehistory.org/people/charles-s-hamlin.

Board of Governors of the Federal Reserve System. 2021. "Nonfinancial Corporate Business; Debt Securities; Liability, Level." FRED, September 23. https://fred.stlouisfed.org/series/NCBDBIQ027S.

Boeis, David. 2015. "Opening Brief in *Starr International Company Inc. v. United States.*" United States Court of Appeals for the Federal Circuit, August 25. https://ypfsresourcelibrary.blob.core.windows.net/fcic/YPFS/US_Court_of _Appeals_for_the_Federal_Circuit_SICO_Plaintiffs_Appeal_20150825.pdf.

Bordo, Michael. 2018. "The Imbalances of the Bretton Woods System 1965 to 1973: U.S. Inflation, the Elephant in the Room." Hoover Institution Working Papers, August 2. https://www.hoover.org/sites/default/files/research /docs/18115-bordo-2.pdf.

Bostic, Raphael. 2020. "A Moral and Economic Imperative to End Racism." Federal Reserve Bank of Atlanta, June 12. https://www.atlantafed .org/about/atlantafed/officers/executive_office/bostic-raphael/message -from-the-president/2020/06/12/bostic-a-moral-and-economic-imperative -to-end-racism.

Bradner, Eric. 2020. "Biden Blasts Trump for Mocking Face Masks." CNN, May 26.

Brainard, Lael. 2009. "Lael Brainard, Nominee for Under Secretary for International Affairs Opening Statement as Prepared for Delivery U.S. Senate Committee on Finance." U.S. Department of the Treasury, Press Center, November 20. https://www.treasury.gov/press-center/press-releases/Pages /20091120956403728.aspx.

———. 2016. "The Use of Distributed Ledger Technologies in Payment, Clearing, and Settlement." Board of Governors of the Federal Reserve System, April 14. https://www.federalreserve.gov/newsevents/speech/brainard 20160414a.htm.

———. 2018. "Read the Commencement Address by Dr. Lael Brainard." Claremont McKenna College, April 13. https://www.cmc.edu/news/read-the -commencement-address-by-dr-lael-brainard.

———. 2019. "Why Climate Change Matters for Monetary Policy and Financial Stability." Federal Reserve, November 8. https://www.federalreserve.gov /newsevents/speech/brainard20191108a.htm.

———. 2020. "An Update on Digital Currencies." Federal Reserve, August 13. https://www.federalreserve.gov/newsevents/speech/brainard20200813a.htm.

———. 2021. "Private Money and Central Bank Money as Payments Go Digital: An Update on CBDCs." Federal Reserve, May 24. https://www.federal reserve.gov/newsevents/speech/brainard20210524a.htm.

Breckenfelder, Johannes, and Victoria Ivashina. 2021. "Bank Balance Sheet Constraints and Bond Liquidity." European Central Bank Working Paper no. 2021/2589, September 24. https://ssrn.com/abstract=3929823.

The British Museum and BBC. 2014. "Gold Coin of Croesus." bbc.co.uk /ahistoryoftheworld/objects.

Brookings. 2020. "Webinar: Federal Reserve Chair Jerome Powell on COVID-19 and the Economy." Brookings, April 9. https://www.brookings .edu/events/webinar-federal-reserve-chair-jerome-powell-on-covid-19-and -the-economy/.

Brown, Courtenay. 2020. "Trump Says Fed Chairman Is Doing a 'Good Job' amid Coronavirus Crisis." Axios, March 24.

Bureau of Labor Statistics. 2021. "CPI Inflation Calculator." https://www.bls .gov/data/inflation_calculator.htm.

Burgess, W. Randolph. 1964. "Reflections on the Early Development of Monetary Policy." Federal Reserve Bank of New York, *Monthly Review,* November. https://fraser.stlouisfed.org/files/docs/meltzer/burref64.pdf.

Burkeman, Oliver, and Julian Borger. 2001. "The Ex-Presidents' Club." *The Guardian,* October 31.

Burr, Thomas. 2020. "Sen. Mitt Romney Proposes Immediate $1,000 Payment to Every Adult American Because of Coronavirus Outbreak." *The Salt Lake Tribune,* March 16.

Campbell, Sophia, and David Wessel. 2021. "How Well Did the Fed's Intervention in the Municipal Bond Market Work?" Brookings, August 31.

Carlyle. 2002. "The Carlyle Group Completes Rexnord Acquisition." November 24. https://www.carlyle.com/media-room/news-release-archive/carlyle-group-completes-rexnord-acquisition.

Carney, Jordain. 2019. "McConnell: 'I Do' Believe in Human-Caused Climate Change." *The Hill,* March 26.

Carney, Jordain, and Juliegrace Brufke. 2020. "This Week: Congress Set for Bipartisan Coronavirus Talks as Clock Ticks." *The Hill,* July 27.

Carney, Mark. 2015. "Mark Carney: Breaking the Tragedy of the Horizon—Climate Change and Financial Stability." Bank for International Settlements, September 29. https://www.bis.org/review/r151009a.pdf.

———. 2019. "The Growing Challenges for Monetary Policy in the Current International Monetary and Financial System." Bank of England, August 23. https://www.bankofengland.co.uk/-/media/boe/files/speech/2019/the-growing-challenges-for-monetary-policy-speech-by-mark-carney.pdf.

Casselman, Ben. 2020. "What to Make of the Rebound in the U.S. Jobs Report." *New York Times,* June 5.

Caygle, Heather, Andrew Desiderio, and John Bresnahan. 2020. "Dems Press Ahead on Coronavirus Package as Senate Waits for Trump." *Politico,* March 10.

CDC COVID-19 Response Team. 2020. *Evidence for Limited Early Spread of COVID-19 Within the United States, January–February 2020.* Centers for Disease Control and Prevention Morbidity and Mortality Weekly Report, June 5. https://www.cdc.gov/mmwr/volumes/69/wr/mm6922e1.htm?s_cid=mm6922e1_w.

Censky, Annalyn. 2011. "Bernanke Chides Occupy Wall Street 'Misconceptions.'" CNN Money, November 3.

Chappatta, Brian. 2020. "Fallen Angels Are Coming and the Fed Can't Save Them." Bloomberg, March 24.

Chernow, Ron. 1990. *The House of Morgan.* New York: Grove Press.

Cheung, Brian. 2021. "Fed Chairman Jerome Powell Retires the Word 'Transitory' in Describing Inflation." *Yahoo!Finance,* November 30.

Choi, Mark, Linda Goldberg, Robert Lerman, and Fabiola Ravazzolo. 2021. *The Fed's Central Bank Swap Lines and FIMA Repo Facility.* Federal Reserve Bank of New York, September. https://www.newyorkfed.org/medialibrary/media/research/staff_reports/sr983.pdf.

Clements, Michael. 2020. "Agencies Have Not Found Leveraged Lending to Significantly Threaten Stability but Remain Cautious Amid Pandemic." Government Accountability Office, December 16. gao.gov/assets/gao-21-167-highlights.pdf.

CNBC. 2020. "Full Interview with Treasury Secretary Steven Mnuchin on Coronavirus Stimulus." April 8. https://www.youtube.com/watch?v=UIV1J SfPvos.

CNBC Squawk Box. 2020. "CNBC Transcript: Treasury Secretary Steven Mnuchin Speaks with CNBC's Jim Cramer on CNBC's 'Squawk Box' Today." CNBC, March 23.

Cochrane, Emily, and Jeanna Smialek. 2020a. "Closing In on Stimulus Deal, Lawmakers Clash over Fed's Role." *New York Times,* December 17.

———. 2020b. "Lawmakers Resolve Fed Dispute as They Race to Close Stimulus Deal." *New York Times,* December 19.

Cohen, Patricia, and Tiffany Hsu. 2020. "$300 Unemployment Benefit: Who Will Get It and When?" *New York Times,* September 17.

Cohn, Gary, and Glenn Hutchins. 2020. "The Fed's New Mission to Save the Economy." *Wall Street Journal,* April 6.

Collins, Andrew, and John Walsh. 2014. "Fractional Reserve Banking in the Roman Republic and Empire." *Ancient Society* 44:179–212.

Committee, Federal Reserve Bank Organization. 1914. "Decision of the Reserve Bank Organization Committee Determining the Federal Reserve Districts and the Location of Federal Reserve Banks Under Federal Reserve Act Approved December 23, 1913." Fraser, St. Louis Fed, April 10. https://fraser.stlouisfed.org/title/decision-reserve-bank-organization-committee-determining-federal-reserve-districts-location-federal-reserve-banks-federal-reserve-act-approved-december-23-1913-603?start_page=16.

Condon, Christopher. 2012. "Money Funds Seen Failing in Crisis as SEC Bows to Lobby." Bloomberg. August 1.

Congressional Record. 1922. "Congressional Record—Senate." Govinfo.gov, January 7. https://www.govinfo.gov/content/pkg/GPO-CRECB-1922-pt2-v62/pdf/GPO-CRECB-1922-pt2-v62-4.pdf.

———. 1953. Washington, D.C.: United States Government Printing Office.

Conti-Brown, Peter. 2016. *The Power and Independence of the Federal Reserve.* Princeton, N.J.: Princeton University Press.

Cook, Nancy, and Matthew Choi. 2020. "Trump Rallies His Base to Treat Coronavirus as a 'Hoax.'" *Politico,* February 28.

Cooper, John Milton. 2021. "Woodrow Wilson." *Encyclopaedia Britannica,* January 30.

"Coronavirus: Armed Protesters Enter Michigan Statehouse." 2020. BBC News, May 1.

"Coronavirus, a Pavia 8 pazienti ricoverati al San Matteo: anche una coppia di medici." 2020. *Il Messaggero,* February 22. https://www.ilmessaggero.it/italia

/coronavirus_pavia_medici_contagiati_pieve_porto_morone_chignolo_po
_cosa_sta_succedendo_22_febbraio_2020-5068178.html.

Costa, Pedro Nicolaci da. 2020. "Trump's Simmering Ire at Federal Reserve Chair Jerome Powell Defies Economic Logic." *Forbes,* January 17.

Cowley, Stacy, and Anupreeta Das. 2020. "A Bank in Midtown Is Cleaned Out of $100 Bills." *New York Times,* March 14.

Cox, Jeff. 2015. "Bernanke's Legacy: A Fed That Did Too Much?" CNBC, October 5.

———. 2016. "Surprise Fed Speech Throws Markets for a Loop." CNBC, September 9.

———. 2020. "Fed's Kashkari Says, 'We Need to Err on the Side of Being Generous' with Rescue Programs." CNBC, April 2.

Crane, Jonah. 2016. "Remarks by Deputy Assistant Secretary Jonah Crane at a Meeting of the Financial Stability Oversight Council." U.S. Department of the Treasury, press release, November 16.

Crowley, Kevin. 2020. "Exxon Swells Debt Burden While Global Crude Markets Burn." Bloomberg Terminal, March 17.

C-Span. 1983. "Volcker Re-Confirmation Hearing." July 14.

———. 2017. "Treasury Secretary Confirmation Hearing." January 19.

———. 2019a. "Federal Reserve Chair Jerome Powell Testifies Before Two Congressional Committees." July 10.

———. 2019b. "Oversight of Financial Regulators." December 5.

———. 2020a. "Monetary Policy and the Economy." February 11.

———. 2020b. "President Trump Signs Coronavirus Economic Relief Bill." March 27.

Daly, Mary C., Bart Hobijn, and Joseph H. Pedtke. 2017. "Disappointing Facts about the Black-White Wage Gap." Federal Reserve Bank of San Francisco, September 5. https://www.frbsf.org/economic-research/wp-content/uploads/sites/4/el2017-26.pdf.

Dangremond, Sam. 2017a. "Treasury Secretary Steven Mnuchin Weds Louise Linton." *Town and Country,* June 25. https://www.townandcountrymag.com/the-scene/weddings/a10210066/steven-mnuchin-louise-linton-wedding/.

———. 2017b. "See Inside Treasury Secretary Steven Mnuchin's $12.6 Million Washington Home." *Town and Country,* July 18. https://www.townandcountrymag.com/leisure/real-estate/g10325252/steven-mnuchin-washington-house/.

Davies, Phil. 2013. "The Federal Reserve's Role During WWI." Federal Reserve, November 22. https://www.federalreservehistory.org/essays/feds-role-during-wwi.

De Blasio, Bill. 2020. "Statement from Mayor de Blasio on Bars, Restaurants,

and Entertainment Venues." City of New York, March 15. https://www1
.nyc.gov/office-of-the-mayor/news/152-20/statement-mayor-de-blasio-bars
-restaurants-entertainment-venues.

Decker, Ryan A., Robert J. Kurtzman, Byron F. Lutz, and Christopher J.
Nekarda. 2020. "Across the Universe: Policy Support for Employment and
Revenue in the Pandemic Recession." Finance and Economics Discussion
Series 2020–099, November 30. Washington, D.C.: Board of Governors of
the Federal Reserve System. https://doi.org/10.17016/FEDS.2020.099.

Derby, Michael S. 2020. "Transcript: WSJ Interview with Dallas Fed President
Robert Kaplan." *Wall Street Journal,* September 21.

Dexheimer, Elizabeth, and Jesse Hamilton. 2015. "CIT's $3.4 Billion OneWest
Deal Approved by Regulators." Bloomberg, July 21.

"Distributional Financial Accounts." 2021. Federal Reserve, December 20. https://
www.federalreserve.gov/releases/z1/dataviz/dfa/distribute/table/#quarter:
128;series:Home%20mortgages;demographic:networth;population:all;units:
levels.

Dmitrieva, Katia. 2019. "Federal Reserve Leaves Action on Climate Change to
Politicians." Bloomberg, November 13.

Dodd, Chris. 2010. "Dodd Statement on Implementation of Dodd–Frank
Act." U.S. Senate Committee on Banking, Housing, and Urban Affairs,
September 30.

Domm, Patty. 2020. "A Global Rush into the US Dollar Is Driving Extreme
Market Moves and a Temporary Shortage." CNBC, March 19.

Dwoskin, Elizabeth, and Damien Paletta. 2019. "Facebook Privately Pitched Its
Cryptocurrency Plan Last Month to Regulators. They Were Left Even More
Scared." *Washington Post,* July 16.

Eccles, Marriner S. 1933. "Investigation of Economic Problems." Fraser St. Louis
Fed, February. https://fraser.stlouisfed.org/files/docs/meltzer/ecctes33.pdf.

———. 1966. *Beckoning Frontiers.* New York: Alfred A. Knopf.

Ecenbarger, William. 1991. "Depressing Times: Recession Recalls the Bad Old
Days of the 1930s." *The Baltimore Sun,* September 22.

The Economic Club of Washington, D.C. 2021. "The Honorable Jerome H. Powell." YouTube, April 14. https://www.youtube.com/watch?v=uApyYqklsR8.

Editors of *Encyclopaedia Britannica.* 2013. "Greenback Movement." *Encyclopaedia Britannica,* July 29.

———. 2017. "Bank War." *Encyclopaedia Britannica,* September 15.

———. 2021. "Nicholas Biddle." *Encyclopaedia Britannica,* February 23.

Elwell, Craig K. 2011. *Brief History of the Gold Standard in the United States.*
Congressional Research Service, June 23. https://sgp.fas.org/crs/misc
/R41887.pdf.

European Commission. n.d. "Paris Agreement." https://ec.europa.eu/clima

/eu-action/international-action-climate-change/climate-negotiations/paris
-agreement_en.

Fed Listens Panel. 2019. "What Does Full Employment Look Like for Your
Community or Constituency?" Chicago Fed, June 4. https://www.chicago
fed.org/conference-sessions/panel-1.

Fed Up Campaign. 2020. "Fed Up Campaign Twitter." Twitter, December 17.
https://twitter.com/Fed_Up_Campaign/status/1339705619553644547.

Federal Open Market Committee. 2020. "Federal Reserve September 2020
Statement." Federal Reserve, September 16. https://www.federalreserve.gov
/monetarypolicy/files/monetary20200916a1.pdf.

Federal Reserve. 1965. "Federal Reserve Bank of St. Louis FRASER." Federal
Reserve, December. https://fraser.stlouisfed.org/files/docs/publications/FRB
/1960s/frb_121965.pdf.

———. 1996. "Meeting of the Federal Open Market Committee July 2–3,
1996." Federal Reserve, July 2–3. https://www.federalreserve.gov/monetary
policy/files/FOMC19960703meeting.pdf.

———. 2005. "Meeting of the Federal Open Market Committee on June 29–30,
2005." Federal Reserve, June 29–30. https://www.federalreserve.gov
/monetarypolicy/files/FOMC20050630meeting.pdf.

———. 2008. "Federal Reserve Announces It Will Initiate a Program to Purchase the Direct Obligations of Housing-Related Government-Sponsored
Enterprises and Mortgage-Backed Securities Backed by Fannie Mae, Freddie
Mac, and Ginnie Mae." Federal Reserve, November 25. https://www.federal
reserve.gov/newsevents/pressreleases/monetary20081125b.htm.

———. 2011. "The Beige Book." Federal Reserve, November 30. https://www
.federalreserve.gov/fomc/beigebook/2011/20111130/default.htm.

———. 2012. "Fed October Meeting Transcript." Federal Reserve, October 22–23. https://www.federalreserve.gov/monetarypolicy/files/FOMC
20121024meeting.pdf.

———. 2014. "Meeting of the Federal Open Market Committee on December 16–17, 2014." Federal Reserve, December 16–17. https://www.federal
reserve.gov/monetarypolicy/files/FOMC20141217meeting.pdf.

———. 2015. "Meeting of the Federal Open Market Committee on September 16–17, 2015." Federal Reserve, September 16–17. https://www.federal
reserve.gov/monetarypolicy/files/FOMC20150917meeting.pdf.

———. 2019. *106th Annual Report*. Federal Reserve. https://www.federal
reserve.gov/publications/files/2019-annual-report.pdf.

———. 2020a. "Minutes of the Federal Open Market Committee January 28–29, 2020." Federal Reserve, January 29. https://www.federalreserve
.gov/monetarypolicy/files/fomcminutes20200129.pdf.

———. 2020b. "Chair Jerome Powell, March 2020 Calendar." Federal

Reserve, March. https://www.federalreserve.gov/foia/files/chair-powell-calen
dar-032020.pdf.

———. 2020c. "Federal Reserve Issues FOMC Statement." Federal Reserve,
March 3. https://www.federalreserve.gov/newsevents/pressreleases/monetary
20200303a.htm.

———. 2020d. "Federal Reserve Announces Establishment of a Temporary
FIMA Repo Facility to Help Support the Smooth Functioning of Financial
Markets." Federal Reserve, March 31. https://www.federalreserve.gov/news
events/pressreleases/monetary20200331a.htm.

———. 2020e. "Federal Reserve Will Establish a Facility to Facilitate Lending
to Small Businesses via the Small Business Administration's Paycheck Protection Program (PPP) by Providing Term Financing Backed by PPP Loans."
Federal Reserve, April 6. https://www.federalreserve.gov/newsevents/press
releases/monetary20200406a.htm.

———. 2020f. "Federal Reserve Board Announces It Is Expanding the Scope
and Eligibility for the Main Street Lending Program." Federal Reserve,
April 30. https://www.federalreserve.gov/newsevents/pressreleases/monetary
20200430a.htm.

———. 2020g. "Federal Reserve Board Expands Its Main Street Lending Program to Allow More Small and Medium-Sized Businesses to Be Able to
Receive Support." Federal Reserve, June 8. https://www.federalreserve.gov
/newsevents/pressreleases/monetary20200608a.htm.

———. 2020h. "Federal Reserve Board Adjusts Terms of Main Street Lending Program to Better Target Support to Smaller Businesses That Employ
Millions of Workers and Are Facing Continued Revenue Shortfalls Due to
the Pandemic." Federal Reserve, October 30. https://www.federalreserve.gov
/newsevents/pressreleases/monetary20201030a.htm.

———. 2020i. "Federal Reserve Board Announces It Has Formally Joined the
Network of Central Banks and Supervisors for Greening the Financial System, or NGFS, as a Member." Federal Reserve, December 15. https://www
.federalreserve.gov/newsevents/pressreleases/bcreg20201215a.htm.

———. 2020j. "Main Street Lending Program FAQ's." Federal Reserve, December 29. https://www.federalreserve.gov/monetarypolicy/mainstreetlending
.htm.

———. 2021a. "Z.1 Financial Accounts." Federal Reserve, October. https://
www.federalreserve.gov/releases/z1/dataviz/dfa/distribute/chart/.

———. 2021b. "Periodic Report: Update on Outstanding Lending Facilities
Authorized by the Board Under Section 13(3) of the Federal Reserve Act."
Federal Reserve, October 13. https://www.federalreserve.gov/publications
/reports-to-congress-in-response-to-covid-19.htm.

Federal Reserve Bank of New York. 2020a. "Statement Regarding Treasury Reserve Management Purchases and Repurchase Operations." March 12. https://www.newyorkfed.org/markets/opolicy/operating_policy_200312a.

———. 2020b. "Statement Regarding Treasury Reserve Management and Reinvestment Purchases." March 13. https://www.newyorkfed.org/markets/opolicy/operating_policy_200313.

———. 2020c. "Central Bank Swap Arrangements." March 19. https://www.newyorkfed.org/markets/international-market-operations/central-bank-swap-arrangements.

———. 2021. "Lorie K. Logan." August. https://www.newyorkfed.org/about thefed/orgchart/logan.

Federal Reserve Bank of St. Louis FRASER. n.d. "Timeline: Treasury-Federal Reserve Accord of 1951." https://fraser.stlouisfed.org/timeline/treasury-fed-accord#26.

———. 1966. "Fifty-Third Annual Report of the Board of Governors of the Federal Reserve System." https://fraser.stlouisfed.org/title/annual-report-board-governors-federal-reserve-system-117/1966-2421.

Federal Reserve Bank of St. Louis FRED. 2021. "Unemployment Rate." https://fred.stlouisfed.org/series/UNRATE.

Federal Reserve Z.1 n.d. "DFA: Distributional Financial Accounts." Federal Reserve. https://www.federalreserve.gov/releases/z1/dataviz/dfa/compare/chart/.

Ferguson, Niall. 2008. *The Ascent of Money.* New York: The Penguin Press.

Ferré-Sadurní, Luis. 2020. "New York City Schools, Restaurants and Bars Are Shut Down over Coronavirus." *New York Times,* March 15.

Feuer, Alan. 2009. "For Playing Solitaire or Saving the Economy." *New York Times,* March 18.

"Financial Panic of 1873." n.d. Treasury.gov. https://home.treasury.gov/about/history/freedmans-bank-building/financial-panic-of-1873.

"Financial Services Forum Statement on Share Buybacks." 2020. Financial Services Forum, March 15. https://fsforum.com/news/financial-services-forum-statement-on-share-buybacks.

Financial Stability Board. 2019. *Vulnerabilities Associated with Leveraged Loans and Collateralised Loan Obligations,* December 19. https://www.fsb.org/wp-content/uploads/P191219.pdf.

———. 2020a. *Holistic Review of the March Market Turmoil,* November 17. https://www.fsb.org/wp-content/uploads/P171120-2.pdf.

———. 2020b. *Global Monitoring Report on Non-Bank Financial Intermediation,* December 16. https://www.fsb.org/wp-content/uploads/P161220.pdf.

Fisher, Richard. 2014. "Monetary Policy and the Maginot Line." Federal

Reserve Bank of Dallas, July 16. https://www.dallasfed.org/news/speeches /fisher/2014/fs140716.cfm.

Flaherty, Michael, and Emily Stephenson. 2014. "Fed Eyes Audit Push as Key Political Challenge in 2015." Reuters, December 18.

Flitter, Emily, David McCabe, and Stacy Cowley. 2020. "Small Business Aid Program Stretches Agency to Its Limits." *New York Times,* April 7.

Flowers, Andrew, and Harry Enten. 2015. "The Fed Has Never Been More Polarizing." FiveThirtyEight, February 24.

Foreign Policy Staff. 2012. "The Most Powerful Women You've Never Heard Of." *Foreign Policy,* April 23.

Fox, Michelle. 2018. "Jeff Gundlach and His Deputy Think Fed's Powell Made a Mistake by Tightening on 'Autopilot.'" CNBC, December 19.

Freidel, Frank, and Hugh Sidey. 2006. "Andrew Jackson, the 7th President of the United States." https://www.whitehouse.gov/about-the-white-house/presi dents/andrew-jackson/.

Frost, Robert. 1964. "50 Years Marked by Reserve Bank." *New York Times,* November 16.

FSC Majority Staff. 2021. "Game Stopped? Who Wins and Loses When Short Sellers, Social Media, and Retail Investors Collide?" House Financial Services Committee, February 18. https://financialservices.house.gov/uploadedfiles /hhrg-117-ba00-20210218-sd002.pdf.

———. 2022. "Where Have All the Houses Gone? Private Equity, Single Family Rentals, and America's Neighborhoods." House Financial Services Committee, June 28. https://financialservices.house.gov/uploadedfiles /hhrg-117-ba09-20220628-sd002.pdf.

Furman, Jason. 2020. "The Case for a Big Coronavirus Stimulus." *Wall Street Journal,* March 5.

George Leonard Obituary. 2018. *Washington Post,* November 21.

Georgieva, Kristalina, and Lesetja Kganyago. 2020. "Joint Statement by the Chair of International Monetary and Financial Committee and the Man-aging Director of the International Monetary Fund." International Mon-etary Fund, March 27. https://www.imf.org/en/News/Articles/2020/03/27 /pr20114-joint-statement-by-the-chair-of-imfc-and-the-managing-director -of-the-imf.

Ghizoni, Sandra Kollen. 2013. "Reserve Bank Organization Committee." Fed-eral Reserve History, November 22. https://www.federalreservehistory.org /essays/reserve-bank-organization-committee.

Glass, Carter. 1927. *An Adventure in Constructive Finance.* Garden City, N.Y.: Doubleday, Page.

Goley, Mary Anne. 2002. "Architecture of the Eccles Building." Federal Reserve

Board, May 23. https://web.archive.org/web/20020612085850/http://www
.federalreserve.gov/generalinfo/virtualtour/architecture.cfm.

Gopinath, Gita. 2015. "The International Price System." National Bureau of
Economic Research. NBER Working Paper Series, October. https://www
.nber.org/system/files/working_papers/w21646/w21646.pdf.

Gopinath, Gita, and Jeremy C. Stein. 2018. "Banking, Trade, and the Making
of a Dominant Currency." Harvard and NBER, March 28. https://scholar
.harvard.edu/files/gopinath/files/dominantcurrency.pdf.

Graeber, David. 2011. *Debt: The First 5,000 Years.* Brooklyn, N.Y.: Melville
House.

Greenhouse, Steven. 1992. "BUSINESS PEOPLE; New Duties Familiar to
Treasury Nominee." *New York Times,* April 14.

———. 1993a. "Greenspan and Panel Clash Over Fed's Status." *New York
Times,* October 14.

———. 1993b. "Greenspan Supports Fed's Secrecy." *New York Times,*
October 20.

Greenspan, Alan. 2001. "Remarks by Chairman Alan Greenspan." Federal
Reserve Board, October 11. https://www.federalreserve.gov/boarddocs
/speeches/2001/20011011/default.htm.

Greider, William. 1987. *Secrets of the Temple: How the Federal Reserve Runs the
Country.* New York: Simon & Schuster.

Guida, Victoria. 2020. "Toomey Calls for Fed Special Loan Programs to End,
Setting Up Clash with Democrats." *Politico,* November 5.

Haberman, Maggie, and Mikayla Bouchard. 2017. "Mnuchin's Wife Mocks
Oregon Woman over Lifestyle and Wealth." *New York Times,* August 22.

Hale Shapiro, Adam, and Daniel Wilson. 2021. "Taking the Fed at Its Word:
A New Approach to Estimating Central Bank Objectives Using Text Analysis." Federal Reserve Bank of San Francisco. Working Paper Series, January.
https://www.frbsf.org/economic-research/files/wp2019-02.pdf.

Hammond, Bray. 1957. *Banks and Politics in America from the Revolution to the
Civil War.* Princeton, N.J.: Princeton University Press.

Harrington, Shannon D., and Craig Torres. 2020. "Fed May Target Commercial Paper Purchases, BofA Says." Bloomberg, March 15.

Hetzel, Robert L. 2013. "Launch of the Bretton Woods System." Federal
Reserve History, November 22. www.federalreservehistory.org/essays/bretton
-woods-launched.

Hetzel, Robert L., and Ralph F. Leach. 2001. "The Treasury-Fed Accord: A
New Narrative Account." Federal Reserve Bank of Richmond *Economic
Quarterly,* Winter. https://www.richmondfed.org/-/media/richmondfedorg
/publications/research/economic_quarterly/2001/winter/pdf/hetzel.pdf.

Hill, Andrew T. 2015a. "The First Bank of the United States." December 4. https://www.federalreservehistory.org/essays/first-bank-of-the-us.

———. 2015b. "The Second Bank of the United States." December 5. https://www.federalreservehistory.org/essays/second-bank-of-the-us.

Hilt, Eric, and Katharine Liang. n.d. *Andrew Jackson's Bank War and the Panic of 1837.* Preliminary and incomplete draft, Department of Economics, Harvard University. https://economics.harvard.edu/files/economics/files/panic_1837_harvard_final.pdf.

Hirsch, Lauren. 2020. "Federal Reserve Seeks Banks' Advice as It Gets into Direct Lending with Coronavirus Relief." CNBC, April 28.

Hirsch, Lauren, and Kevin Breuninger. 2020. "Trump Signs $8.3 Billion Emergency Coronavirus Spending Package." CNBC, March 6.

Ho, Dale E. 2016. "Virginia Needs to Fix Its Racist Voting Law." *New York Times,* July 19.

Holston, Kathryn, Thomas Laubach, and John Williams. 2017. "Measuring the Natural Rate of Interest: International Trends and Determinants Journal of International Economics." *Journal of International Economics* 108, supplement 1:S39–S75.

Hunt, Kasie, Leigh Ann Caldwell, Julie Tsirkin, and Rebecca Shabad. 2020. "White House Eyeing $1 Trillion Coronavirus Stimulus Package." *NBC News,* March 17.

Hyman, Sidney. 1976. *Marriner S. Eccles, Private Entrepreneur and Public Servant.* Stanford, Calif.: Graduate School of Business, Stanford University.

Iden, V. Gilmore. 1914. "The Federal Reserve Act of 1913: History and Digest." FRASER, Federal Reserve Bank of St. Louis. https://fraser.stlouisfed.org/title/federal-reserve-act-1913-962.

Imbert, Fred. 2020. "Even the World's Biggest Hedge Fund Was Caught Flat-footed by the Coronavirus Market Sell-off." CNBC, March 15.

Imbert, Fred, and Thomas Franck. 2020. "Dow Plunges 10% amid Coronavirus Fears for Its Worst Day Since the 1987 Market Crash." CNBC, March 11.

Investment Company Institute. 2020. "Experiences of US Money Market Funds During the COVID-19 Crisis." Report of the COVID-19 Market Impact Working Group, October. www.ici.org/pdf/20_rpt_covid3.pdf.

Irwin, Neil. 2013. *The Alchemists.* New York: The Penguin Press.

Itkowitz, Colby, and *Call* Washington Bureau. 2010. "Election Profile: Pat Toomey." *Morning Call,* September 25.

Iwayemi, Joshua Timi, Miranda Litwak, Jeff Hauser, and Pete Sikora. 2020. "Biden's Treasury Could Fight Climate Change, but Would Lael Brainard's?" Common Dreams, October 15.

Jeffrey Leonard Obituary. 2018. *Washington Post,* October 17.

Jencks, C., and M. Phillips. 1998. *The Black–White Test Score Gap.* Brookings Institution Press.

Jensen, Michael C. 1977. "Marriner S. Eccles Is Dead at 87." *New York Times,* December 20.

Jones, Jeffrey M. 2020. "U.S. Satisfaction at 13%, Lowest in Nine Years." *Gallup News,* August 4.

JPMorgan Chase. 2020. "JPMorgan Chase on Supporting Customers and Clients." March 15. https://www.jpmorganchase.com/ir/news/2020/supporting-customers-clients-031520.

Kahn, Suzanne, Mark Huelsman, and Jen Mishory. 2019. *Bridging Progressive Policy Debates: How Student Debt and the Racial Wealth Gap Reinforce Each Other.* Roosevelt Institute, September 9. https://rooseveltinstitute.org/publications/bridging-progressive-policy-debates-student-debt-racial-wealth-gap-reinforce-each-other/.

Kansas City Public Library. 2018. "Prohibition and Vice." The Pendergast Years: Kansas City in the Jazz Age & Great Depression. https://pendergastkc.org/topics/vice.

Kashkari, Neel. 2020a. "Neel Kashkari: Big US Banks Should Raise $200bn in Capital Now." *Financial Times,* April 16.

———. 2020b. "It was as if they were saying . . ." Twitter, May 27. https://twitter.com/neelkashkari/status/1265653755732688896?lang=en.

———. 2020c. "Why I Dissented: Neel Kashkari." Federal Reserve Bank of Minneapolis, September 18. https://www.minneapolisfed.org/article/2020/why-i-dissented.

"Katie Porter Criticizes Mnuchin for 'Play-acting' as a Lawyer." 2020. *Washington Post* YouTube channel, December 2. https://www.youtube.com/watch?v=Gs5Jy4Yeo3I.

Kelly, Kate. 2021. "At Saudi Investment Conference, Trump Allies Remain Front and Center." *New York Times,* October 31.

Kelly, Kate, Andrew Ross Sorkin, and Jeanna Smialek. 2020. "As Market Convulses, Big Banks Plan to Borrow Funds from Fed." *New York Times,* March 16.

Kiley, Michael T., and John M. Roberts. 2017. "Monetary Policy in a Low Interest Rate World." Brookings Institution, March 23. https://www.brookings.edu/bpea-articles/monetary-policy-in-a-low-interest-rate-world/.

Kornblut, Anne E. 2008. "At Sidwell Friends School, Obamas Will Encounter Parents from Clinton Campaign." *Washington Post,* December 12.

Krugman, Paul. 2001. "Reckonings; Et Tu, Alan?" *New York Times,* January 28.

Kuttner, Robert. 2020. "Liberalish: The Complex Odyssey of Lael Brainard." *American Prospect,* September 23.

————. 2021. "Biden's Appointments to the Fed: The Endgame." *American Prospect,* November 8.

Labonte, Marc. 2020. *Federal Reserve: Emergency Lending.* Congressional Research Service, March 27. https://fas.org/sgp/crs/misc/R44185.pdf.

Labor Reformer. 1873. "SPECIE PAYMENTS." *New York Times,* October 25.

Lane, Sylvan. 2017. "Senate Confirms Trump's First Fed Nominee." *The Hill,* October 5.

Lawder, David. 2014. "U.S. House Passes Fed Audit Bill; Measure Seen Doomed in Senate." Reuters, September 17.

Leicht, Eric, and Duane Wall. 2017. "GAO Determines Leveraged Lending Guidance Is a 'Rule' Under Congressional Review Act." White & Case, October 31.

Leonard, Christopher. 2022. *The Lords of Easy Money.* New York: Simon & Schuster.

Levy, Mickey D. 2018. "The Fed's Economic Forecasts, Uncertainties and Monetary Policy Uncertainty." Shadow Fed, March 9. https://www.shadowfed .org/wp-content/uploads/2018/03/LevySOMC-March2018.pdf.

Li, Yun. 2020. "Plunging Stocks Triggered a Key Market 'Circuit Breaker'— Here's What That Means." CNBC, March 15.

Liedtke, Michael. 2007. "Rash of Subprime Defaults May Hurt Overall Economy." *Seattle Times,* March 13.

Liesman, Steve, and Fred Imbert. 2018. "San Francisco Fed President John Williams Being Considered by Trump for Vice-chair." CNBC, January 19.

Lindsey, David E. 2003. *A Modern History of FOMC Communication: 1975–2002.* Federal Reserve, June 24. https://www.federalreserve.gov/monetary policy/files/FOMC20030624memo01.pdf.

Logan, Lorie K. 2020. "Treasury Market Liquidity and Early Lessons from the Pandemic Shock." Federal Reserve Bank of New York, October 23.

Long, Heather. 2019. "Trump's Fed Nominee Judy Shelton Recently Questioned the Need for an Independent Central Bank." *Washington Post,* November 21.

Lowenstein, Roger. 2015. *America's Bank.* New York: Penguin Books.

Lowery, Annie. 2013. "Lael Brainard to Step Down from Treasury Post." *New York Times,* November 5.

Markets Desk. 2020. "Statement Regarding Treasury Securities, Agency Mortgage-Backed Securities, and Agency Commercial Mortgage-Backed Securities Operations." Federal Reserve Bank of New York, June 10. https:// www.newyorkfed.org/markets/opolicy/operating_policy_200610.

Marshall, William F. 2020. "COVID-19 Infections by Race: What's Behind the Health Disparities?" Mayo Clinic, August 13. https://www .mayoclinic.org/diseases-conditions/coronavirus/expert-answers/coronavirus -infection-by-race/faq-20488802.

Martin-Buck, Frank. 2019. "LEVERAGED LENDING AND CORPORATE BORROWING: Increased Reliance on Capital Markets, with Important Bank Links." *FDIC Quarterly* 13 (4):41–50.

Massachusetts Historical Society. 2008. "United States Continental Paper Currency." https://www.masshist.org/collection-guides/view/fao0005.

Matthews, Steve, Cheyenne Hopkins, and Jeff Kearns. 2015. "Yellen Says 'Audit the Fed' Would Politicize Monetary Policy." Bloomberg, February 24.

McClintock, Pamela. 2017. "From 'Avatar' to 'Borat' and 'The Devil Wears Prada': A Look at All the Films Trump's Treasury Pick Steven Mnuchin Helped Finance." *Hollywood Reporter,* January 19.

McConnell, Mitch. 2020. "House Democrats' Expensive, Unserious Wish List." Mitch McConnell, Republican Leader, May 14. https://www.republicanleader.senate.gov/newsroom/research/house-democrats-expensive-unserious-wish-list.

McKie, Robin. 2012. "Rachel Carson and the Legacy of *Silent Spring*." *Guardian,* May 27.

McNeil, Jr., Donald G. 2020. "Coronavirus Has Become a Pandemic, W.H.O. Says." *New York Times,* March 11.

Mehrling, Perry. 2000. "An interview with Paul A. Volcker" (April 18). In Paul A. Samuelson and William A. Barnett, *Inside the Economist's Mind*, 165–91. Malden, MA: Blackwell Publishing, 2007.

Meltzer, Allan. 2003. *A History of the Federal Reserve, Volume 1: 1913–1951.* Chicago and London: University of Chicago Press.

Mervosh, Sarah. 2019. "How Much Wealthier Are White School Districts Than Nonwhite Ones? $23 Billion, Report Says." *New York Times,* February 27.

Mnuchin, Steven. 2020a. Interview by Maria Bartiromo. Fox Business Interview, March 19.

———. 2020b. Interview by Maria Bartiromo. *Mornings with Maria: Treasury Secretary Steven Mnuchin,* April 7. https://www.facebook.com/watch/?v=2952465214813191.

———. 2020c. "Letter from Secretary Steven T. Mnuchin on the Status of Facilities Authorized Under Section 13(3) of the Federal Reserve Act." Treasury Department, November 19. https://home.treasury.gov/news/press-releases/sm1190.

———. 2020d. "Secretary Mnuchin's Calendar, December 2020." Treasury Department, December. https://home.treasury.gov/system/files/236/December-2020-Final.pdf.

Mohsin, Saleha. 2020a. "U.S. Plans to Keep Markets Open as Virus Spreads, Mnuchin Says." Bloomberg, March 13.

———. 2020b. "Mnuchin Plans to Put $455 Billion Beyond Yellen's Easy Reach." Bloomberg, November 24.

Moran, Danielle. 2020. "Worst Muni Rout Since 1984 Deepens Even with Treasury Gain." Bloomberg, March 19.

Network of Central Banks and Supervisors for Greening the Financial System. 2017. "Joint Statement by the Founding Members of the Central Banks and Supervisors Network for Greening the Financial System—One Planet Summit." December 12.

Newman, Andy. 2020. "Drastic 'Shelter in Place' May Be Next for N.Y.C. to Combat Coronavirus." *New York Times,* March 17.

New York Athletic Club. 2021. "Membership." https://www.nyac.org /membership.

New York Times. 1921. "Makes New Attack on Reserve Bank." December 17.

———. 1938. "Charles S. Hamlin Dies in Washington." April 25.

———. 1953. "New Reserve Bank for Buffalo." August 7.

———. 1985. "Elissa Leonard Wed to Jerome Powell." September 15.

———. 2013. "Many Cities Seek to Be Bank Centers." December 23.

New York Times Editorial Board. 1913. "An Important Omission." *New York Times,* December 25.

Nicholas, Peter. 2017. "President Trump Says Jerome Powell Is His Choice to Lead Federal Reserve." *Wall Street Journal,* November 2.

Niquette, Mark. 2018. "Mulvaney Says Trump Now Realizes He Can't Fire Fed Chairman." Bloomberg, December 23.

Novet, Jordan. 2020. "Bill Gates: Countries That Shut Down for Coronavirus Could Bounce Back in Weeks." CNBC, March 18.

Novick, Barbara, et al. 2020. "Lessons from COVID-19: U.S. Municipal Bond Market." BlackRock, July. https://www.blackrock.com/corporate/literature /whitepaper/viewpoint-lessons-from-covid-19-us-municipal-bond-market -july-2020.pdf.

OCC. 2022. "1863–1865 Founding of the National Banking System." Office of the Comptroller of the Currency. https://www.occ.gov/about/who-we-are /history/1863–1865/index-occ-history-1863–1865.html.

Open Secrets. 2019. "Donor Lookup: Barbara Novick." https://www.opensecrets .org/donor-lookup/results?name=barbara+novick&order=desc&sort=D.

Orphanides, Athanasios, and John Williams. 2011. "Monetary Policy Mistakes and the Evolution of Inflation Expectations." National Bureau of Economic Research. NBER Working Paper Series, May. https://www.nber.org/papers /w17080.

Page, Jeremy, Wenxin Fan, and Natasha Khan. 2020. "How It All Started: China's Early Coronavirus Missteps." *Wall Street Journal,* March 6.

Pelley, Scott. 2020. "Coronavirus and the Economy: Best and Worst-Case Scenarios from Minneapolis Fed President." *CBS News,* March 22.

Phillips, Matt. 2020. "Stocks Take Dive Not Seen Since 2011 over Virus Crisis." *New York Times,* February 28.

Phillips, Matt, Peter Eavis, and David Enrich. 2020. "Economy Faces 'Tornado-Like Headwind' as Financial Markets Spiral." *New York Times,* March 9.

Podleski, Genevieve, and David C. Wheelock. 2021. "Carter Glass." Federal Reserve History, September 13. https://www.federalreservehistory.org/people/carter-glass.

Powell, Jerome. 2011. "More on Stanley Druckenmiller and the Risk of Death." *Wall Street Journal,* May 25.

———. 2017. "Treasury Markets and the TMPG." Federal Reserve, October 5. https://www.federalreserve.gov/newsevents/speech/files/powell20171005a.pdf.

———. 2018. "Monetary Policy in a Changing Economy." Federal Reserve, August 24. https://www.federalreserve.gov/newsevents/speech/powell20180824a.htm.

———. 2019a. "Monetary Policy: Normalization and the Road Ahead." Federal Reserve, March 8. https://www.federalreserve.gov/newsevents/speech/powell20190308a.htm.

———. 2019b. "Business Debt and Our Dynamic Financial System." Federal Reserve, May 20. https://www.federalreserve.gov/newsevents/speech/powell20190520a.htm.

———. 2020a. Interview by Savannah Guthrie. *Today* show, March 26.

———. 2020b. "Fed Chair Jerome Powell Press Conference Transcript December 16: Market Update." Rev, December 16. https://www.rev.com/blog/transcripts/fed-chair-jerome-powell-press-conference-transcript-december-16-market-update.

———. 2021a. "Monetary Policy in the Time of COVID." Federal Reserve, August 27. https://www.federalreserve.gov/newsevents/speech/powell20210827a.htm.

———. 2021b. "Transcript of Chair Powell's Press Conference November 3, 2021." Federal Reserve, November 3. https://www.federalreserve.gov/mediacenter/files/FOMCpresconf20211103.pdf.

"Press Release." 1994. Federal Reserve, February 4. https://www.federalreserve.gov/fomc/19940204default.htm#:~:text=FRB%3A%20Press%20Release%20%2D%2D%20FOMC%20statement%20%2D%2D%20February%204%2C%201994&text=Chairman%20Alan%20Greenspan%20announced%20today,term%20money%20market%20interest%20rates.

Pressley, Ayanna, and Bharat Ramamurti. 2020. "Pressley, Ramamurti Urge Fed, Treasury to Make Emergency Lending Facilities More Equitable." U.S. Congresswoman Ayanna Pressley, October 30. https://pressley.house.gov/media

/press-releases/pressley-ramamurti-urge-fed-treasury-make-emergency
-lending-facilities-more.

Quarles, Randal [K.]. 2005. "Remarks by United States Treasury Assistant Secretary Quarles Harvard Symposium on Building the Financial System of the
21st Century: An Agenda for Europe and the United States Eltville, Germany."
U.S. Department of the Treasury, August 20. https://home.treasury.gov
/news/press-releases/js2463.

———. 2006. "Remarks of Treasury Under Secretary for Domestic Finance
Randal Quarles to the Money Marketeers New York, NY." U.S. Department
of the Treasury, May 10. https://www.treasury.gov/press-center/press-releases
/Pages/js4248.aspx.

———. 2010. "Herding Cats: Collective-Action Clauses in Sovereign Debt—
the Genesis of the Project to Change Market Practice in 2001 Through
2003." Duke Law. https://scholarship.law.duke.edu/cgi/viewcontent.cgi
?article=1584&context=lcp.

———. 2017. "Statement of Randal Quarles, Nominee to Be a Member and
Vice Chairman of Supervision of the Board of Governors of the Federal
Reserve System, Before the Committee on Banking, Housing, and Urban
Affairs, United States Senate, July 27, 2017." Senate Banking Committee.
https://www.banking.senate.gov/imo/media/doc/Quarles%20Testimony
%207-27-17.pdf.

———. 2021. "Parachute Pants and Central Bank Money." Federal Reserve,
June 28. https://www.federalreserve.gov/newsevents/speech/quarles202106
28a.htm.

Quarles, Randal K., and Lawrence Goodman. 2016. "Focusing on Bank Size,
Missing the Real Problem." *Wall Street Journal,* March 31.

Ramamurti, Bharat. 2020. "In case you missed it yesterday . . ." Twitter, December 18. https://twitter.com/BharatRamamurti/status/1339944124162727936
?ref_src=twsrc%5Etfw.

Rappeport, Alan, Emily Cochrane, and Nicholas Fandos. 2020. "'Go Big' on
Coronavirus Stimulus, Trump Says, Pitching Checks for Americans." *New
York Times,* March 17.

Rappeport, Alan, and Jeanna Smialek. 2020a. "Clash over Municipal Loan Program Delays Stimulus Report." *New York Times,* October 9.

———. 2020b. "Legacy on the Line, Mnuchin Gambles by Ending Fed Programs." *New York Times,* December 9.

"READ: White House Guidelines for 'Opening Up America Again.'" 2020.
CNN Politics, April 16.

Rennison, Joe. 2021. "How the Fed's Fine Intentions Feed US Wealth Inequality." *Financial Times.* July 26.

Reuters. 2014. "The Bernanke Legacy." *Wall Street Journal,* January 28.

Reuters Staff. 2020a. "Mnuchin Warns Senators of 20% U.S. Unemployment Without Coronavirus Rescue." Reuters, March 17.

———. 2020b. "Fed's Kashkari Aims for Beige Book That Looks Beyond Business." Reuters, October 7.

Richardson, Gary. 2013. "The Great Depression." Federal Reserve History, November 22. https://www.federalreservehistory.org/essays/great-depression.

Richardson, Gary, Alejandro Komai, and Michael Gou. 2013a. "Banking Act of 1935." Federal Reserve History, November 22. https://www.federalreserve history.org/essays/banking-act-of-1935.

———. 2013b. "Gold Reserve Act of 1934." Federal Reserve History, November 22. https://www.federalreservehistory.org/essays/gold_reserve_act.

———. 2013c. "Roosevelt's Gold Program." Federal Reserve History, November 22. https://www.federalreservehistory.org/essays/roosevelts_gold _program.

Richardson, Gary, Daniel Park, Alejandro Komai, and Michael Gou. 2013. "McFadden Act of 1927." Federal Reserve History, November 22. https:// www.federalreservehistory.org/essays/mcfadden-act.

Richardson, Gary, and Jessie Romero. 2015. "The Meeting at Jekyll Island." Federal Reserve History, December 4. https://www.federalreservehistory.org /essays/jekyll-island-conference.

Richardson, Gary, and Tim Sablik. 2015. "Banking Panics of the Gilded Age." Federal Reserve History, December 4. https://www.federalreservehistory.org /essays/banking-panics-of-the-gilded-age.

Riley, Russell, John Gilmour, Jim Pfiffner, and Stacie Pettyjohn. 2002. "Alice Rivlin Oral History, Transcript." UVA Miller Center, December 13. https://millercenter.org/the-presidency/presidential-oral-histories/alice -rivlin-oral-history.

Robb, Gregg. 2019. "Powell Says Fed 'Paddling Against the Current' of Public Mistrust in Institutions." MarketWatch, February 6.

Roche, Darragh. 2020. "Federal Reserve Appears to Acknowledge Joe Biden Election Win." *Newsweek,* November 11.

Rosalsky, Greg. 2020. "Trouble on Main Street." NPR, October 13.

Rucker, Philip, Josh Dawsey, and Damian Paletta. 2018. "Trump Slams Fed Chair, Questions Climate Change and Threatens to Cancel Putin Meeting in Wide-ranging Interview with *The Post.*" *Washington Post,* November 27.

Sanders, Bernie. 2016. "Sanders Supports Audit the Fed Bill." Press release, January 12.

Sastry, Parintha. 2018. "The Political Origins of Section 13(3) of the Federal Reserve Act." Federal Reserve Bank of New York, September. https://www .newyorkfed.org/medialibrary/media/research/epr/2018/epr_2018_political -origins_sastry.pdf.

Schmidt, Rob. 2017. "Warsh vs. Quarles Feud Has Been Renewed by Trump Fed Search." Bloomberg, October 25.

Schroeder, Peter. 2017. "Trump: We Will Do a 'Big Number' to Dodd-Frank." *The Hill,* January 30.

Schroeder, Pete, and Trevor Hunnicutt. 2019. "Fed Chief Calls for Facebook to Halt Libra Project Until Concerns Addressed." Reuters, July 9.

Schumer, Chuck. 2020. "Schumer Floor Remarks Blasting Pres. Trump's Dangerous Incompetence & Lack of Plan to Deal with the Coronavirus; Outlines Five Steps Trump Admin. Must Take Immediately." Senate Democrats, February 25.

Scigliuzzo, Davide, and Julie Johnsson. 2020. "The Non-Bailout: How the Fed Saved Boeing Without Paying a Dime." Bloomberg, May 2.

Selgin, George. 2017. "The 'Bagging Rule'—or Why We Shouldn't Arrest (All) the Bankers." Alt-M Blog, September 6. https://www.alt-m.org/2017/09/06/the-bagging-rule-or-why-we-shouldnt-arrest-all-the-bankers/.

Semega, Jessica, and Melissa Kollar. 2022. "Increase in Income Inequality Driven by Real Declines in Income at the Bottom." U.S. Census Bureau, September 13.

Shalal, Andrea. 2020. "Exclusive: U.S. Sees No Material Impact from Virus on U.S.-China Trade Deal—for Now." Reuters, February 24.

Siegel, Rachel. 2020. "Powell to Describe Fed's New Approach to Full Employment and Stable Prices." *Washington Post,* August 26.

SIFMA. 2020. *2020 Capital Markets Fact Book,* July 28. https://www.sifma.org/resources/research/fact-book/.

———. 2021. *2021 Capital Markets Fact Book,* September. https://www.sifma.org/wp-content/uploads/2021/06/US-Fact-Book-2020-SIFMA.pdf.

Silbey, Joel. n.d. "Martin Van Buren: Domestic Affairs." Miller Center, the University of Virginia.

Smialek, Jeanna. 2019a. "Trump Isn't Alone. These Millennials on the Left Want Low Interest Rates, Too." *New York Times,* June 12.

———. 2019b. "The New York Fed Chief Is Facing His Biggest Test. Here's His Response." *New York Times,* September 29.

———. 2019c. "Meet the Man Loosening Bank Regulation, One Detail at a Time." *New York Times,* November 29.

———. 2020a. "How the Fed Chairman Is Shielding It from Trump." *New York Times,* January 28.

———. 2020b. "Trump Called Powell an 'Enemy.' 'Ugh' Was a Response Inside the Fed." *New York Times,* January 30.

———. 2020c. "As Congress Prepares to Vet Judy Shelton, Worries About the Fed's Future Mount." *New York Times,* February 12.

————. 2020d. "Judy Shelton, Trump's Fed Nominee, Faces Bipartisan Skepticism." *New York Times,* February 13.

————. 2020e. "Fed Moves to Keep Credit Flowing and Money Markets Calm Amid Coronavirus Turmoil." *New York Times,* March 9.

————. 2020f. "The Fed Goes All In with Unlimited Bond-Buying Plan." *New York Times,* March 23.

————. 2020g. "Why State and Local Debt Is Fraught Territory for the Fed." *New York Times,* April 1.

————. 2020h. "Fed Gives Banks a Break to Keep Markets Calm, Asking for Little in Return." *New York Times,* April 15.

————. 2020i. "Fed Makes Initial Purchases in Its First Corporate Debt Buying Program." *New York Times,* May 12.

————. 2020j. "Minneapolis Fed President Says Systemic Racism Hurts the Economy." *New York Times,* June 17.

————. 2020k. "A Coffee Chain Reveals Flaws in the Fed's Plan to Save Main Street." *New York Times,* July 9.

————. 2020l. "Oversight Member Blasts the Fed's Efforts to Rescue Main Street." *New York Times,* August 7.

————. 2020m. "The Fed's Evolution Is Coming to a Computer Screen Near You." *New York Times,* August 26.

————. 2020n. "Fed Pledges Low Rates for Years, and Until Inflation Picks Up." *New York Times,* September 16.

————. 2020o. "The Fed's $4 Trillion Lifeline Never Materialized. Here's Why." *New York Times,* October 21.

————. 2020p. "Fed Joins Climate Network, to Applause from the Left." *New York Times,* December 15.

————. 2021a. "Why Are There So Few Black Economists at the Fed?" *New York Times,* February 2.

————. 2021b. "Top U.S. Officials Consulted with BlackRock as Markets Melted Down." *New York Times,* June 24.

————. 2021c. "Federal Reserve Signals a Shift Away from Pandemic Support." *New York Times,* September 22.

————. 2021d. "Fed Officials Under Fire for 2020 Securities Trading Will Resign." *New York Times,* September 27.

————. 2021e. "Fed Unveils Stricter Trading Rules amid Fallout from Ethics Scandal." *New York Times,* October 21.

Smialek, Jeanna, and Alan Rappeport. 2020a. "Fear of Risk Could Diminish the Economic Rescue by the Treasury and Fed." *New York Times,* May 18.

————. 2020b. "Federal Reserve's Emergency Loan Programs at Center of Political Fight." *New York Times,* November 9.

Smialek, Jeanna, and Emily Flitter. 2020. "Federal Reserve Moves to Pump Up Small Business Lending." *New York Times,* April 6.

Smialek, Jeanna, Kate Kelly, and Peter Eavis. 2020. "Fed Unveils Emergency Lending Programs as Companies Struggle to Raise Cash." *New York Times,* March 17.

Smialek, Jeanna, and Patricia Laya. 2017. "The New Face of American Unemployment." Bloomberg, February 7.

Smith, Brian. 2020. "IG ANALYSIS US: Exxon, Verizon, PepsiCo Lead Biggest Day of 2020." Bloomberg Terminal, March 17.

Smith, Molly. 2020. "Exxon, Verizon Capitalize on Credit Calm to Restart Debt Sales." Bloomberg, March 17.

Soto, Jesús Huerta de. 2002 (Spanish) and 2006 (English). *Money, Bank Credit and Economic Cycles.* Madrid and Auburn, Ala.: Unión Editorial and Ludwig von Mises Institute.

"SPECIE PAYMENTS." 1874. *New York Times,* December 9.

Spratt, Stephen. 2020. "How a Little Known Trade Upended the U.S. Treasury Market." Bloomberg.com. March 17.

Sprunt, Barbara. 2020. "The History Behind 'When the Looting Starts, the Shooting Starts.'" NPR, May 29.

Steelman, Aaron. 2013a. "Employment Act of 1946." Federal Reserve History, November 22. https://www.federalreservehistory.org/essays/employment -act-of-1946.

———. 2013b. "Full Employment and Balanced Growth Act of 1978 (Humphrey-Hawkins)." Federal Reserve History, November 22. https:// www.federalreservehistory.org/essays/humphrey_hawkins_act.

Stewart, James B., and Alan Rappeport. 2020. "Steven Mnuchin Tried to Save the Economy. Not Even His Family Is Happy." *New York Times,* August 30.

Stiglitz, Joseph. 2021. "Why the Federal Reserve Chair Jerome Powell Must Go." *Guardian,* November 10.

Summers, Lawrence H. 2013. IMF Fourteenth Annual Research Conference in Honor of Stanley Fischer, November 8.

———. 2021. "The Biden Stimulus Is Admirably Ambitious. But It Brings Some Big Risks, Too." *Washington Post,* February 4.

Sveriges Riksbank. n.d. "History." https://www.riksbank.se/en-gb/about-the -riksbank/history/.

Swagel, Phillip L. 2020. "CBO Letter to Senator Enzi." Preliminary Estimate of the Effects of H.R. 748, the CARES Act, Public Law 116–136, Revised, with Corrections to the Revenue Effect of the Employee Retention Credit and to the Modification of a Limitation on Losses for Taxpayers Other Than Corporations, April. https://www.cbo.gov/system/files/2020-04/hr748.pdf.

Sykes, Jay B. 2020. "Section 4029 of the Coronavirus Aid, Relief, and Economic Security (CARES) Act and the Extension of the Federal Reserve's Emergency-Lending Programs." Coronavirus.house.gov, December 17. https://coronavirus.house.gov/sites/democrats.coronavirus.house.gov/files /Memo%20re%20CARES%20Act%20Section%204029.pdf.

Tankersley, Jim, and Neil Irwin. 2019. "Trump's Fury vs. Shaky Markets: Jerome Powell's Balancing Act as Fed Chief." *New York Times,* April 13.

Tarullo, Daniel K. 2021. "The SEC Should—and Can—Pay More Attention to Financial Stability." Brookings Institution, May 13.

Thornton, Daniel L. 2004. "When Did the FOMC Begin Targeting the Federal Funds Rate? What the Verbatim Transcripts Tell Us." Federal Reserve Bank of St. Louis, August. https://research.stlouisfed.org/wp/more/2004-015.

———. 2006. "When Did the FOMC Begin Targeting the Federal Funds Rate? What the Verbatim Transcripts Tell Us." *Journal of Money, Credit and Banking* 38 (8):2039–71.

Timberlake, Richard H. 1999. "The Tale of Another Chairman." Federal Reserve Bank of Minneapolis.

Timiraos, Nick. 2020a. "Fed Unveils Major Expansion of Market Intervention." *Wall Street Journal,* March 23.

———. 2020b. "The Fed Transformed: Jay Powell Leads Central Bank into Uncharted Waters." *Wall Street Journal,* March 30.

———. 2020c. "Powell Headlines Virtual Jackson Hole Conference." *Wall Street Journal,* August 26.

———. 2020d. "This was an interesting exchange at yesterday's oversight hearing." Twitter, December 11, 10:40 a.m. https://twitter.com/NickTimiraos /status/1337421885982773250.

Timiraos, Nick, and Kate Davidson. 2020. "Fed, Treasury Disagreements Slowed Start of Main Street Lending Program." *Wall Street Journal,* July 12.

Timiraos, Nick, and Heather Gillers. 2020. "Federal Reserve Considering Additional Support for State, Local Government Finance." *Wall Street Journal,* March 27.

Todd, Tim. 2016. "A Corollary of Accountability: A History of FOMC Policy Communication." Federal Reserve Bank of Kansas City, August. https:// www.kansascityfed.org/documents/6512/acorollaryofaccountability.pdf.

Torres, Craig. 2016. "Fed Governor Donates to Clinton as Bank Guards Independence." Bloomberg, March 8.

"Transcript, Federal Open Market Committee Conference Call." 1993. Federal Reserve, October 15. https://www.federalreserve.gov/monetarypolicy/files /FOMC19931015confcall.pdf.

Treasury Department. 2020. "Secretary's Calendar." January to March. https://home.treasury.gov/system/files/236/STM-Jan-Mar-2020-Calendars -Scanned.pdf.

Truman, Harry S. 1951. Letter to Thomas McCabe on the International Situation and Its Implications on the Economy, Box 539, Folder 4, Item 21, Harry S. Truman Papers. Harry S. Truman Library. https://fraser.stlouisfed.org/archival/1346/item/72900.

University of Utah. 2020. "Navigating COVID-19: The Federal Reserve, Macroeconomic Forces, and Your Business." University of Utah, April 10. https://www.youtube.com/watch?v=YO9uX_IAcOw&feature=youtu.be.

U.S. Government Printing Office. 1990. "Nomination of Jerome H. Powell to Be Assistant Secretary, Domestic Finance, U.S. Department of the Treasury." September 11.

———. 1993. "The Federal Reserve Accountability Act of 1993: Hearing Before the Committee on Banking, Finance, and Urban Affairs, House of Representatives, One Hundred Third Congress, First Session, October 13, 1993." Fraser, Federal Reserve Bank of St. Louis, October. https://fraser.stlouisfed.org/title/federal-reserve-accountability-act-1993-1154/fulltext.

———. 1994. "The Federal Reserve Accountability Act of 1993: Hearing Before the Committee on Banking, Finance and Urban Affairs, House of Representatives, One Hundred Third Congress, First Session, October 13, 1993." Fraser, St. Louis Fed. https://fraser.stlouisfed.org/title/hr-28-federal-reserve-accountability-act-1993-1155.

Vazza, Diane, Nick Kraemer, and Evan Gunter. 2019. "The 'BBB' U.S. Bond Market Exceeds $3 Trillion." S&P Global, May 29. https://www.spglobal.com/en/research-insights/articles/the-bbb-u-s-bond-market-exceeds-3-trillion.

Vogel, Kenneth P. 2009. "15 D.C. Power Couples." *Politico,* June 15.

Volcker, Paul, and Christine Harper. 2018. *Keeping at It.* New York: PublicAffairs.

Wallach, Philip A., and Justus Myers. 2020. "The Federal Government's Coronavirus Response—Public Health Timeline." Brookings Institution, March 31.

"War Finance Corporation Act." 1918. Fraser, Federal Reserve Bank of St. Louis, April 5. https://fraser.stlouisfed.org/title/war-finance-corporation-act-1122.

Warekar, Tanay. 2020. "NYC's Restaurant Reopening Could Include Outdoor Seating on Closed Streets." *Eater New York,* April 28.

Warner, Bernhard. 2020. "Why the Fed's Stunning Move to Buy Corporate America's Junk Bonds Is So Significant." *Fortune,* April 9.

Warner, Mark. 2020. "Warner Statement on the Economic Response to the Coronavirus." Mark R. Warner, U.S. Senator, March 17. https://www.warner.senate.gov/public/index.cfm/2020/3/warner-statement-on-the-economic-response-to-the-coronavirus.

Warren, Elizabeth. 2020a. "Senator Warren Unveils Legislation to De-Fund President's Border Wall, Use Funds to Combat Coronavirus Outbreak." Elizabeth Warren, U.S. Senator, February 27. https://www.warren.senate.gov

/newsroom/press-releases/senator-warren-unveils-legislation-to-de-fund
-presidents-border-wall-use-funds-to-combat-coronavirus-outbreak.

———. 2020b. "Any taxpayer assistance that goes to giant corporations must
come with real strings attached to ensure the money is truly going to support
the workforce through this crisis." Twitter, March 19. https://twitter.com
/ewarren/status/1240784477879705600?lang=en.

Washingtonian Staff. 2008. "Luxury Homes: September 2008." *Washingtonian,*
September 1.

Weiland, Noah, Emily Cochrane, and Maggie Haberman. 2020. "White
House Asks Congress for Billions to Fight Coronavirus." *New York Times,*
February 24.

Weissert, Will, and Jonathan Lemire. 2020. "Face Masks Make a Political Statement in Era of Coronavirus." AP, May 7.

Werner, Erica, Mike DeBonis, and Paul Kane. 2020. "Senate Approves
$2.2 Trillion Coronavirus Bill Aimed at Slowing Economic Free Fall." *Wash-
ington Post,* March 25.

Wessel, David, and Anita Raghavan. 1994. "A Growing Glasnost at the Fed Is
Dispelling a Lot of Its Mystique." *Wall Street Journal,* February.

Wheelock, David. 2013. "The Fed's Formative Years." Federal Reserve
History, November 23. https://www.federalreservehistory.org/essays/feds
-formative-years.

White, Ben, and Aubree Eliza Weaver. 2017. "Morning Money." *Politico,*
October 26.

The White House. 2021a. "Press Briefing by Press Secretary Jen Psaki and
Council of Economic Advisers Member Jared Bernstein, February 5, 2021."
February 5.

———. 2021b. "Press Briefing by Press Secretary Jen Psaki, Deputy Director
of the National Economic Council Sameera Fazili, and Senior Director for
International Economics and Competitiveness Peter Harrell, June 8, 2021."
June 8.

———. 2021c. "Press Briefing by Press Secretary Jen Psaki, August 11, 2021."
August 11.

Whiteman, Charles H. 1978. "A New Investigation of the Impact of Wage
and Price Controls." *Federal Reserve Bank of Minneapolis Quarterly Review*
2 (2):2–8.

Wines, Michael. 2020. "'Looting' Comment from Trump Dates Back to Racial
Unrest of the 1960s." *New York Times,* May 29.

Woellert, Lorraine. 2017. "How Mnuchin Flipped the Ultimate Fixer-Upper—
His Bank." *Politico,* January 19.

World Health Organization. 2020. *Coronavirus Disease 2019 (COVID-19)*

Situation Report—55, March 15. https://www.who.int/docs/default-source /coronaviruse/situation-reports/20200315-sitrep-55-covid-19.pdf.

Ydstie, John. 2012. "Ryan's Mission for Fed: Focus on Prices, Not Unemployment." NPR, August 16.

Yellen, Janet. 2016. "Current Conditions and the Outlook for the U.S. Economy." Speech, World Affairs Council of Philadelphia, Philadelphia, Pennsylvania, June 6. https://www.federalreserve.gov/newsevents/speech /yellen20160606a.htm.

Zumbrun, Joshua. 2013. "The Secret Life of Marriner Eccles." *Wall Street Journal,* September 3.

NOTES

Chapter 1: The Before Times

1. This is based on Powell's calendars from when he was a Fed governor, which showed him visiting the Metropolitan Club ten times between January and September 2017. Prior to his joining the Fed and having public calendars, it is hard to tell with whom he met.
2. Powell 2011. Powell wrote in a 2011 *Wall Street Journal* letter to the editor that "any credible threat of a default would run unacceptable risks for the markets, the economy and our standing in the world."
3. Barro 2020; the Economic Club of Washington, D.C., 2021. While Powell doesn't talk about his father or career trajectory during this appearance, he does talk about the size of his family: four sisters and one brother. The six siblings remained close into adulthood. "They don't laugh at my jokes, but other people do, fortunately," Powell said of his siblings.
4. Greenhouse 1992.
5. *New York Times* 1985.
6. George Leonard Obituary 2018.
7. Powell 2017.
8. Greenhouse 1992.
9. Burkeman and Borger 2001. "For 14 years now, with almost no publicity, the company has been signing up an impressive list of former politicians—including the first President Bush and his secretary of state, James Baker; John Major; one-time World Bank treasurer Afsaneh Masheyekhi and several south-east Asian powerbrokers—and using their contacts and influence to promote the group," *The Guardian* reported of Carlyle in 2001, while Powell was at the firm. The firm's address in between Capitol Hill and the White House "reflects Carlyle's position at the very centre of the Washington establishment."

10. Carlyle 2002.
11. For instance, Chris Leonard details a huge deal Powell worked on in 2002—the takeover of Rexnord, an industrial conglomerate in Wisconsin—as one that resulted in an "immense" payoff for Powell and Carlyle but left Rexnord "crippled with debt." He argues that the company, aiming to become more attractive to an outside buyer and work off its debt load—or at least expand profits—ended up disassembling plants and moving production and jobs to Mexico. He implies that the sort of heavy debts Rexnord shouldered, and the type of financial engineering that allows companies to keep kicking their payoff down the road, have become even more common in the years since thanks to the Fed's bond-buying programs and low rates. Leonard 2022, 161–200.
12. Smialek 2020a.
13. Federal Reserve Bank of St. Louis FRED 2021.
14. Federal Reserve 2014.
15. Federal Reserve 2015.
16. Nicholas 2017.
17. Flowers and Enten 2015.
18. Bureau of Labor Statistics 2021.

Chapter 2: The Month Markets Melted

1. Imbert 2020; Basak 2020.
2. Federal Reserve 2021a.
3. Federal Reserve Bank of New York 2021.
4. Greider 1987. It is worth noting that Logan's job was half of the job that had initially been given this label. Responsibilities were, as of 2019, split between a System Open Market Account manager and a person given the title Head of the Markets Group.
5. Volcker and Harper 2018, 34.
6. Logan 2020. "Dealers noted that risk measures rose sharply, and many suggested that internal risk management processes developed to ensure compliance with regulations limited the nimbleness with which they could respond to rapidly evolving circumstances," Lorie Logan would later explain in a speech on the meltdown.

   U.S. Department of the Treasury 2021. Likewise, a later Treasury working report would point out that a key leverage ratio "has been cited as among the factors motivating banking organizations to dedicate capital to higher-margin businesses and limiting the amount and flexibility of bank and bank-affiliated broker-dealer balance sheets dedicated to low-margin businesses, such as many forms of Treasury market intermediation."

7. Federal Reserve 2008. The Fed's first quantitative easing program in the 2008 crash, often called QE1, was explicitly undertaken to "foster improved conditions in financial markets."
8. World Health Organization 2020.
9. Blumenfeld 2009.
10. Cowley and Das 2020. At one Bank of America branch, "so many people sought huge sums that the bank branch, at 52nd Street and Park Avenue, temporarily ran out of $100 bills to fulfill large withdrawals."
11. Pelley 2020.

Chapter 3: One Nation, Under Banks

1. Eccles 1966, 6.
2. Eccles 1966, 29.
3. Hyman 1976, 43.
4. Eccles 1966, 37.
5. The British Museum and BBC 2014.
6. Graeber 2011, 39.
7. Collins and Walsh 2014.
8. Soto 2002 (Spanish) and 2006 (English).
9. Selgin 2017. It is worth noting that this was not necessarily a sneaky decision on the part of the bankers: It was often legally implicit between the banker and the depositor that the deposits might be loaned out. For instance, George Selgin at the Cato Institute has written that in England, it was common to have "sealed deposits" in which gold was kept entirely on hand in a vault. Other, unsealed deposits were available for lending.
10. Bank runs were a problem in England at the time. The first true bank wasn't established in America until 1782 (Hammond 1957, 10). There had been a painful British bank run in 1772–1773.
11. Hammond 1957, 11. "As fast as specie was received, it was exported to pay for goods that could not be produced at home," Hammond writes of the colonial years. Trade languished at times for want of money to pay for things. "It was the dearth of specie, the only legal tender, that in 1786 drove the Shays rebels in Massachusetts to demand a medium with which they could protect their farms from tax sales," he wrote.
12. Massachusetts Historical Society 2008. Between 1775 and 1779, the Continental Congress issued what were called "continentals," but because states were issuing their own bills and debt to fund the war and as the English counterfeited some issues, the currency became devalued.
13. Hill 2015a.
14. Ferguson 2008, 46–48.

15. Hill 2015a.
16. Hammond 1957, 229. The Treasury had no "one respectable place to turn for quick loans," and "its funds were no longer available where it needed them, as the Bank's branch organization had made possible, but must be transported by such means as could be found," Hammond writes of the situation in his book on American banking. Attributing the fact to a lawmaker at the time, Hammond also notes that in "five years or so" the amount of paper currency in circulation had increased from around $90 million to $200 million, and that "banks had been too prodigal of their engagements, issuing more paper than they could possibly redeem." The government had lost control over money, which Congress was supposed to control, ceding it to the state banking system.
17. Hill 2015b.
18. Editors of *Encyclopaedia Britannica* 2021.
19. Freidel and Sidey 2006.
20. Freidel and Sidey 2006.
21. Editors of *Encyclopaedia Britannica* 2017.
22. OCC 2022.
23. Hilt and Liang n.d.
24. Anderson n.d. Ironically, the recovery from that crisis was tanked early on by the Bank of England, which was so central to the interconnected global economy at that point that London's decision to raise interest rates caused U.S. banks to raise rates to remain competitive, crushing lending and slowing demand on the American side of the Atlantic.
25. Silbey n.d.
26. Lowenstein 2015, 3.
27. Editors of *Encyclopaedia Britannica* 2013.
28. OCC 2022.
29. "SPECIE PAYMENTS" 1874.
30. "Financial Panic of 1873" n.d.
31. Labor Reformer 1873.
32. Elwell 2011.
33. For more detail, please see Lowenstein 2015, 18–19.
34. Sastry 2018.
35. Hammond 1957, 705. The New York Clearing House was put into place in 1853.
36. Richardson and Sablik 2015.
37. Bagehot's *Lombard Street* was originally published in periodical form in the 1860s (Bagehot 1873).
38. Lowenstein 2015, 51.
39. Lowenstein 2015, 57.

40. Feuer 2009; Irwin 2013.
41. Sveriges Riksbank n.d.
42. Bagehot 1873.
43. Lowenstein 2015, 88.
44. See additional discussion of this point in Lowenstein 2015, 108 and 109.
45. Lowenstein 2015, 110.
46. Richardson and Romero 2015.
47. Lowenstein 2015, 119.
48. Lowenstein 2015, 117 and 122.
49. Podleski and Wheelock 2021.
50. Cooper 2021.
51. Glass 1927, 67.
52. See, for instance, Ho 2016, where Glass is quoted arguing in favor of a voting law on the basis that it would further "complete supremacy of the white race in the affairs of government."
53. Chernow 1990, 157.
54. Glass 1927, 112–16.
55. Wheelock 2013.
56. Iden 1914.
57. Sastry 2018, 5.
58. Meltzer 2003, 65.
59. Wheelock 2013.
60. Conti-Brown 2016, 93.
61. Glass 1927, 31.
62. New York Times Editorial Board 1913.
63. *New York Times* 2013.
64. Wheelock 2013.
65. Kansas City Public Library 2018.
66. Binder and Spindel 2017.
67. Ghizoni 2013.
68. Committee, Federal Reserve Bank Organization 1914.
69. Board of Governors n.d.
70. *New York Times* 1938.
71. Davies 2013.
72. Meltzer 2003, 105.
73. Ahamed 2009.
74. Frost 1964.
75. Wheelock 2013.
76. Burgess 1964, 220.
77. Eccles 1966, 188.
78. *New York Times* 1921.

79. Burgess 1964, 220.
80. Richardson, Park et al. 2013.
81. Eccles 1966. This was not entirely true, but it captured the sentiment around America's central bank.
82. Wheelock 2013.
83. Richardson 2013.
84. Bernanke and James 1991.
85. Bernanke in a famous speech related that "Hamilton showed that the Fed's desire to slow outflows of U.S. gold to France—which under the leadership of Henri Poincaré had recently stabilized its economy, thereby attracting massive flows of gold from abroad—further tightened U.S. monetary policy. The next episode studied by Friedman and Schwartz, another tightening, occurred in September 1931, following the sterling crisis. In that month, a wave of speculative attacks on the pound forced Great Britain to leave the gold standard" (Bernanke 2002).
86. Ecenbarger 1991. According to a *Baltimore Sun* retrospective, "The New York City Welfare Council reported 29 such deaths in 1933; an additional 100 people, most of them children, died from malnutrition."
87. Jensen 1977.
88. Eccles 1933.
89. Conti-Brown 2016, 144.
90. Fed historian Peter Conti-Brown in particular says this (Richardson, Komai, and Gou 2013a). Eccles became a Fed official in 1934 and oversaw staff as they drafted the legislation.
91. Conti-Brown 2016, 157.
92. Bentz 2019.

Chapter 4: The Fed's Second Act

1. *New York Times* 1953. As a sign of this, a search of the *New York Times* archive from the time shows that most articles referencing the Fed reported its asset holdings, traced personnel movements at its regional branches, or talked about new regional office spaces. The central bank was not the closely watched source of daily headlines that it is now.
2. Eccles 1966, 422.
3. Hetzel and Leach 2001.
4. *Congressional Record* 1953.
5. Federal Reserve Bank of St. Louis FRASER n.d.
6. Eccles 1966, notes.
7. Timberlake 1999.
8. Truman 1951.

9. Eccles 1966. This is according to Eccles's own account of the matter. He summoned Felix Belair of *The New York Times* to the Shoreham Hotel, where he was staying, and arranged to have him distribute a statement.
10. Steelman 2013a.
11. Elwell 2011.
12. Richardson, Komai, and Gou 2013b, 2013c.
13. Zumbrun 2013.
14. Hetzel 2013.
15. Hetzel 2013.
16. Volcker and Harper 2018, 38.
17. Orphanides and Williams 2011.
18. Orphanides and Williams 2011.
19. Bordo 2018.
20. Federal Reserve 1965.
21. Meltzer 2003, 760.
22. Abrams 2006, 180.
23. Whiteman 1978.
24. Mehrling 2000.
25. Steelman 2013a.
26. Steelman 2013b.
27. C-Span 1983.
28. Greider 1987, 181.
29. Volcker and Harper 2018, 138.
30. Krugman 2001.
31. Powell 2018.
32. Thornton 2006.
33. Thornton 2004.
34. Greenspan 2001.

Chapter 5: The Temple Is Under New Management

1. U.S. Government Printing Office 1993.
2. My description of both men on this day relies on C-Span footage that is viewable at https://www.c-span.org/video/?51415-1/us-federal-reserve -policy.
3. Greenhouse 1993a.
4. Smialek 2021a.
5. Lindsey 2003.
6. Greenhouse 1993b.
7. Todd 2016.
8. Auerbach 2006; Government Printing Office 1994.

9. Lindsey 2003.
10. "Transcript, Federal Open Market Committee Conference Call" 1993.
11. Todd 2016, 36.
12. "Press Release" 1994. On the argument about taking power away from the regional banks with rate-increase releases, see page 34 in the February 1994 transcript.
13. Wessel and Raghavan 1994.
14. Federal Reserve 2005.
15. Andrews 2008.
16. Bernanke 2022, 136.
17. Anson et al. 2017.
18. Andalfatto and Li 2014.
19. Arnall 2011; Appelbaum 2011.
20. Levy 2018.
21. Powell 2019a.
22. Ydstie 2012.
23. Federal Reserve 1996.
24. Hale Shapiro and Wilson 2021.
25. Bernanke 2015, 77. Bernanke explains that the statement, "though convoluted, focused attention on too-low inflation and, most importantly, conveyed that substantially lower inflation would be 'unwelcome'—in stark contrast to the past 40 years, when declining inflation was invariably viewed as good."
26. Federal Reserve Z.1 n.d.
27. Censky 2011.
28. Lawder 2014.
29. Bloomberg View 2013.
30. Reuters 2014.
31. Cox 2015.
32. Appelbaum 2013.
33. Yellen 2016.
34. Flaherty and Stephenson 2014.
35. Sanders 2016.
36. Matthews, Hopkins, and Kearns 2015.
37. Condon 2012.
38. Quarles 2017.

Chapter 6: A Polarized Fed

1. Page, Fan, and Khan 2020.
2. Rucker, Dawsey, and Paletta 2018.

3. Fox 2018. The DoubleLine executive was Jeffrey Sherman.

4. Niquette 2018.

5. Tankersley and Irwin 2019. "Mr. Powell spent the holidays holed up at a family gathering in South Florida watching financial market swings, negative corporate news, and shaky economic data—and plotted a way to correct the mistakes. He scratched out bullet points on a notepad and waited for an opportunity to publicly pivot," *The New York Times* reported.

6. Smialek 2020b.

7. Kiley and Roberts 2017.

8. Federal Reserve 2012.

9. Summers 2013. An excerpt from the speech is worth reading: "But imagine a situation where natural and equilibrium interest rates have fallen significantly below zero. Then, conventional macroeconomic thinking leaves us in a very serious problem, because we all seem to agree that whereas you can keep the federal funds rate at a low level forever, it's much harder to do extraordinary measures beyond that forever; but, the underlying problem may be there forever. . . . Now, this may all be madness, and I may not have this right at all."

10. Holston, Laubach, and Williams 2017.

11. Dodd 2010.

12. Schmidt 2017.

13. Schmidt 2017.

14. White and Weaver 2017.

15. Costa 2020.

16. Quarles 2010.

17. Quarles 2005.

18. Quarles 2006.

19. Smialek 2019c.

20. Lane 2017.

21. Federal Reserve 2019. See trends in common equity tier one capital, charted throughout the report. The changes were relatively small but noticeable.

22. Quarles and Goodman 2016. The Fed should "adopt a monetary policy rule, such as the Taylor rule, that would normalize interest rates and reduce the incentive for big banks and even smaller institutions to take dangerous risks," the pair wrote. A standard Taylor rule, which would set the policy rate based on how much growth is either falling shy of or exceeding its potential and the current rate of inflation, would have called for notably higher interest rates between 2010 and 2020.

23. Brainard 2018.

24. Brainard 2009.
25. Vogel 2009.
26. Washingtonian Staff 2008.
27. Kornblut 2008.
28. The Asia Group 2021. According to a news release when Campbell joined the Biden administration, "Dr. Kurt M. Campbell is a Co-Founder of The Asia Group, and one of the six partners that manages the firm. Over the past eight years, The Asia Group's team of nearly fifty professionals has successfully built the premier strategic advisory firm focused on helping companies seize opportunities and overcome challenges in the Indo-Pacific region."
29. Foreign Policy Staff 2012.
30. Lowery 2013.
31. Torres 2016. The donations were legal and consistent with the Fed's rules, but the donations created a reception issue, as Torres reported in his story.
32. Brainard 2016.
33. Cox 2016.
34. Board Meeting 2019.
35. Liesman and Imbert 2018.
36. Federal Reserve 2019.
37. The mid-2000s New York Fed president (later Treasury secretary) Tim Geithner had been well versed in markets, but was not what most people referred to as a "markets guy," having worked in diplomacy and public policy before arriving at the Fed. His successor, William Dudley, was a former Goldman Sachs economist, but the New York Fed was steadily stripped of power during his tenure between 2009 and 2018—Tarullo, the governor who unofficially performed the vice-chair for bank supervision role during the Yellen years, pulled important bank supervisory authorities toward the Fed Board.
38. Robb 2019.

Chapter 7: March Madness

1. Cook and Choi 2020. "The Democrats are politicizing the coronavirus," Trump said. "One of my people came up to me and said, 'Mr. President, they tried to beat you on Russia, Russia, Russia.' That did not work out too well. They could not do it. They tried the impeachment hoax." And he then labeled the coronavirus "their new hoax."
2. "Coronavirus, a Pavia 8 pazienti ricoverati al San Matteo: anche una coppia di medici" 2020.
3. Thanks to Alan Rappeport for this detail.

4. CDC COVID-19 Response Team 2020.
5. Belvedere 2020.
6. Weiland, Cochrane, and Haberman 2020.
7. Wallach and Myers 2020.
8. Schumer 2020.
9. Warren 2020a.
10. Phillips 2020.
11. Goley 2002.
12. New York Athletic Club 2021; U.S. Government Printing Office 1990.
13. Stewart and Rappeport 2020.
14. Dangremond 2017a; McClintock 2017.
15. Haberman and Bouchard 2017.
16. Federal Reserve 2020g.
17. Bloomberg News 2020
18. Trump 2020.
19. Phillips, Eavis, and Enrich 2020.
20. McNeil, Jr., 2020.
21. Imbert and Franck 2020.
22. SIFMA 2020, 2021.
23. Baklanova, Kuznits, and Tatum 2021.
24. Smialek 2020e.
25. Investment Company Institute 2020. See Figure 3.6.
26. Breckenfelder and Ivashina 2021.
27. Financial Stability Board 2020a. "Large-scale unwinding of these trades, of almost US$90 billion during March, was likely one of the contributors to a short period of extreme illiquidity in government bond markets," the report wrote of the Treasury basis trade.
28. Federal Reserve Bank of New York 2020a.
29. Federal Reserve Bank of New York 2020b.
30. Ferré-Sadurní 2020.
31. De Blasio 2020.
32. Harrington and Torres 2020.
33. Li 2020.
34. Baier 2020. Baier notes that on March 17, UBS Group AG closed two exchange-traded notes tied to mortgage real estate investment trusts, and that a few days later, a mortgage trust run by a hedge fund had warned its lenders that it wouldn't be able to meet future margin calls.
35. Novick 2020. Please see Exhibit 2. Municipal bond issuance ground to a standstill midway through March.
36. "Financial Services Forum Statement on Share Buybacks" 2020.
37. JPMorgan Chase 2020.

38. Kelly, Ross Sorkin, and Smialek 2020.
39. Kelly, Ross Sorkin, and Smialek 2020.
40. Smialek, Kelly, and Eavis 2020.
41. *Congressional Record* 1922.
42. "War Finance Corporation Act" 1918. The War Finance Corporation, for instance, ran from 1918 to 1939 and was meant to provide credit support to industries essential to World War I, at a time when government borrowing was attracting away private capital.
43. Sastry 2018.
44. Sastry 2018.
45. Boeis 2015.
46. Federal Reserve Bank of St. Louis FRASER 1966.
47. Sastry 2018. "My provision allows the Fed more power to provide liquidity, by enabling it to make fully secured loans to securities firms in instances similar to the 1987 stock market crash," Senator Chris Dodd, who introduced it, said of the change.
48. Labonte 2020.
49. Sastry 2018.
50. Smialek, Kelly, and Eavis 2020.
51. Hirsch and Breuninger 2020.
52. See Furman 2020 and Burr 2020.
53. Rappeport, Cochrane, and Fandos 2020.
54. See Harker in Smialek, Eavis, and Kelly 2020.

Chapter 8: A Corporate House of Cards

1. B. Smith 2020.
2. Crowley 2020; M. Smith 2020.
3. As a group, the companies had issued at expensive rates compared to where corresponding bonds were trading in the secondary market.
4. Moran 2020.
5. Chappatta 2020.
6. Chappatta 2020.
7. The table can be seen in Decker et al. 2020, published later that year.
8. Financial Stability Board 2020b.
9. Tarullo 2021.
10. Clements 2020.
11. Open Secrets 2019. For instance, BlackRock's influential lobbyist, Barbara Novick, in 2019 gave to Democratic House Financial Services Chairwoman Maxine Waters, prominent Democratic Senate Banking Committee member Mark Warner, Republican Kevin Brady on the House

Financial Services Committee, and, over the years, to Republicans Mike Crapo and Paul Ryan. She also donated, via BlackRock's PAC, through the Investment Company Institute, which in turn funneled money to other PACS and to Republican and Democratic candidates alike.

12. Barth and Kahn 2020. This paper provides an excellent description of the mechanics of basis trades. It also finds that they were probably not a decisive contributor in March 2020; that finding is debated elsewhere.

13. Crane 2016.

14. Spratt 2020.

15. Board of Governors of the Federal Reserve System 2021. This excludes financial companies.

16. Vazza, Kraemer, and Gunter 2019.

17. Martin-Buck 2019.

18. Liedtke 2007.

19. Financial Stability Board 2019.

20. Federal Reserve 2020a.

21. Powell 2019b.

22. Leicht and Wall 2017.

23. Powell 2019b. About 70 percent of leveraged loan holdings at the end of 2018 were in so-called collateralized loan obligations, and another 20 percent were in mutual funds.

24. Bernanke and Yellen 2020.

25. It is worth noting that these programs were not typically leveraged as much at 10:1 in practice.

26. Shalal 2020.

27. Stewart and Rappeport 2020.

28. Caygle, Desiderio, and Bresnahan 2020.

29. Treasury Department 2020.

30. Reuters Staff 2020a.

31. Hunt et al. 2020.

32. M. Warner 2020.

33. Novet 2020.

34. Trump 2020.

35. Newman 2020.

36. Mnuchin 2020a.

37. Warren 2020b.

Chapter 9: The Day the Fed Changed

1. Timiraos 2020b.

2. Smialek 2020f.

3. The Fed had extended loans to businesses between 1932 and 1935 through 13(3)—in fact, that had been the statute's initial use case—but it had been lightly used during those years. The Fed had also extended commercial and industrial loans under 13-B, but that section was repealed in 1958.

4. Brown 2020.

5. Powell 2020a.

6. CNBC Squawk Box 2020.

7. Werner, DeBonis, and Kane 2020.

8. That extra oomph came at no expense to the nation's budget deficit: The Congressional Budget Office would go on to score the Fed programs as costless. Whatever loans the Fed extended would eventually be repaid, so the money would only be spent if the rescue programs took massive, unexpected losses.

9. Woellert 2017.

10. Mohsin 2020a.

11. Dexheimer and Hamilton 2015.

12. C-Span 2017.

13. C-Span 2020b.

14. Georgieva and Kganyago 2020.

15. M. Carney 2019.

16. Gopinath 2015.

17. Gopinath and Stein 2018.

18. M. Carney 2019.

19. Federal Reserve Bank of New York 2020c.

20. Domm 2020.

21. Federal Reserve 2020d.

22. Choi et al. 2021.

23. Cohn and Hutchins 2020.

24. Smialek 2021e.

25. Cox 2020.

Chapter 10: Racing Across Red Lines

1. Flitter, McCabe, and Cowley 2020.

2. Smialek and Flitter 2020.

3. Mnuchin 2020b.

4. Federal Reserve 2020e.

5. CNBC 2020.

6. Smialek 2020g.

7. Timiraos and Gillers 2020.

8. C-Span 2019a.
9. Nobody I managed to talk with remembers for sure whether Powell actually drove himself on this specific day, so I'm taking some artistic license. It is the case that he drove himself throughout much of this period, so it's likely that was also true on April 9.
10. Smialek 2020o. While Mnuchin had $454 billion to use for the Fed programs, he did not earmark all of it: The Treasury allocated $195 billion to the programs.
11. B. Warner 2020; Domm 2020.
12. Brookings 2020.
13. Dangremond 2017b.
14. Smialek and Rappeport 2020a.
15. Hirsch 2020.
16. Smialek 2020h.
17. Smialek 2020h.
18. Kashkari 2020a.
19. University of Utah 2020; Smialek, Kelly, and Eavis 2020.
20. Financial Stability Board 2020a. Quarles had previously argued that nonbank risks should be more closely monitored than they were, which was the general perception in the regulatory community leading up to the crisis. His tone shifted considerably after the 2020 meltdown, however, becoming more full-throated. When the Financial Stability Board released a 2019 report on interconnections and risks at nonbanks, for instance, Quarles had commented in it that "Non-bank financing is a valuable alternative to bank financing for many firms and households," and that they "may" pose risks to the financial system, while emphasizing the benefits of the FSB's monitoring and information sharing. In a year, he went from emphasizing benefits and suggesting only a possibility of danger to saying bluntly that more regulation should be considered.

Chapter 11: Culture Wars and Capital

1. Weissert and Lemire 2020.
2. Bradner 2020.
3. "READ: White House Guidelines for 'Opening Up America Again'" 2020.
4. Warekar 2020.
5. "Coronavirus: Armed Protesters Enter Michigan Statehouse" 2020.
6. Marshall 2020.
7. Sprunt 2020. The president later said that he did not know the phrase's

charged history. It had been originally uttered in 1967 by a Miami police chief with a track record of racist and discriminatory behavior.

8. Wines 2020.

9. Kashkari 2020b.

10. Appelbaum 2015b.

11. Bostic 2020.

12. Smialek 2020j.

13. While I've chosen to focus on Black–white divides in this chapter, many of the disadvantages applied to various minority groups, including Hispanic people.

14. Daly, Hobijn, and Pedtke 2017. The quoted data point is for the first quarter of 2020, based on Bureau of Labor Statistics data, and it does not control for worker characteristics. Research by Federal Reserve Bank of San Francisco president Mary Daly and her colleagues in 2017 found that for men, industry, type of job, physical location, age, and occupation explained about half of the earnings gap. Half could not be explained by any of those easily measured economic differences, meaning that forces "such as discrimination, differences in school quality, or differences in career opportunities" probably accounted for the divide.

15. Bhutta et al. 2020.

16. Mervosh 2019; Jencks and Phillips 1998.

17. Kahn, Huelsman, and Mishory 2019.

18. Bertrand and Mullainathan 2003.

19. Semega and Kollar 2022. For instance, see the Gini index measures that the Census Bureau produces. Gini is a statistical measure of income inequality—0 representing perfect equality, and 1 perfect inequality. It has been climbing for years.

20. Federal Reserve 2021a.

21. "Distributional Financial Accounts" 2021. Federal Reserve distributional accounts showed that by the end of 2020, the top 1 percent by wealth held $18.6 trillion in corporate equities and mutual funds, roughly half of their total wealth. By comparison, the bottom 50 percent of wealth holders held $0.22 trillion in those securities, about 6 percent of their total wealth.

22. FSC Majority Staff 2022. While housing industry groups regularly pointed out that institutional investors still owned only a relatively small slice of the single family housing market, their footprint had been growing in the wake of the 2008 crisis, particularly in America's Sunbelt. A congressional inquiry into the phenomenon in 2022 offered good background reading.

23. Rennison 2021.

24. Smialek 2021a.
25. Federal Reserve 2011.
26. Fisher 2014.
27. Smialek and Laya 2017.
28. Fed Listens Panel 2019.

Chapter 12: Love Songs to Full Employment

1. Riley et al. 2002.
2. Smialek 2019a.
3. C-Span 2020a.
4. Markets Desk 2020.
5. Carney and Brufke 2020.
6. Timiraos 2020c.
7. Siegel 2020.
8. Smialek 2020m.
9. Beckworth et al. 2020.
10. Federal Open Market Committee 2020.
11. Derby 2020. Kaplan also worried that years of rates at zero would blow up financial bubbles. The March 2020 meltdown had proved that low rates can drive risk-taking, to his mind, and he thought a Fed funds rate even slightly above zero might help to forestall some of that.
12. Smialek 2020n.
13. Kashkari 2020c.

Chapter 13: A Fed Restrained

1. Federal Reserve 2021b.
2. Federal Reserve 2020j.
3. Boston Fed staff and Fed Board officials had spent all spring and summer joining regular phone calls, often as early as 7:00 A.M., stretching for ways to improve it. The minimum loan size was regularly adjusted: At the end of October 2020, the Main Street program's minimum loan size would be dropped to $100,000, making it more tenable for some small businesses. It had originally been $500,000, and had been dropped to $250,000 in an earlier update in June 2020. Other major tweaks made it available to nonprofits (that happened in September), increased the loan terms from four to five years (June), delayed principal payments for two years rather than one (June), and clarified how bank supervisors should think about the loans (September).
4. Federal Reserve 2020h.

5. Smialek 2020k.
6. Timiraos and Davidson 2020.
7. Rosalsky 2020.
8. Smialek 2020l.
9. Scigliuzzo and Johnsson 2020.
10. Campbell and Wessel 2021. "Despite low take up of the Municipal Liquidity Facility, research suggests the availability of the program was quite effective at easing investors' concerns and stabilizing muni bond yields," researchers at the Brookings Institution would later write of the program.
11. Pressley and Ramamurti 2020.
12. Itkowitz and *Call* Washington Bureau 2010.
13. McConnell 2020.
14. Cohen and Hsu 2020.
15. Casselman 2020.
16. Barro 2020.
17. Jones 2020.
18. Biden 2020.
19. Guida 2020.
20. Smialek and Rappeport 2020b.
21. Timiraos 2020d.
22. Mnuchin 2020c.
23. Swagel 2020.
24. Mohsin 2020b.
25. Rappeport and Smialek 2020b.
26. Rappeport and Smialek 2020b.
27. "Katie Porter Criticizes Mnuchin for 'Play-acting' as a Lawyer" 2020.
28. Sykes 2020.
29. Ramamurti 2020.
30. Fed Up Campaign 2020.
31. "Our mandate is to serve as a backstop lender to accomplish these objectives—not as a first stop that replaces private capital," Kent Hiteshew, who ran the municipal bond program, had said at a congressional hearing in September.
32. Rappeport and Smialek 2020a.
33. Cochrane and Smialek 2020a.
34. Cochrane and Smialek 2020b.
35. Mnuchin 2020d.
36. Cochrane and Smialek 2020b.
37. Federal Reserve 2020c.
38. Powell 2020b.

Chapter 14: The Creeping Crises

1. McKie 2012.
2. M. Carney 2015.
3. European Commission n.d.
4. Network of Central Banks and Supervisors for Greening the Financial System 2017.
5. J. Carney 2019.
6. Jeffrey Leonard Obituary 2018.
7. Dmitrieva 2019.
8. Brainard 2019.
9. C-Span 2019b.
10. Roche 2020.
11. Federal Reserve 2020i.
12. Smialek 2020p.
13. Kuttner 2020.
14. Iwayemi et al. 2020.
15. Quarles 2021.
16. Brainard 2021.
17. Schroeder and Hunnicutt 2019.
18. Brainard 2020.
19. Smialek 2020d.
20. Smialek 2020c.
21. Long 2019.

Chapter 15: A Year of Uncomfortable Questions

1. Blanchard 2019. Olivier Blanchard, then an economist at the Peterson Institute for International Economics, had prominently made this argument (theoretically, not in relation to the Biden package). A more extreme version of it came in modern monetary theory, which argued that the meaningful constraints on spending were the real ones: how much the economy could produce without generating inflation. Stephanie Kelton's book on the topic, *The Deficit Myth,* became a surprise bestseller when it was published in 2020.
2. Summers 2021.
3. The White House 2021a.
4. The White House 2021b.
5. The White House 2021c.
6. Powell 2021a.
7. Smialek 2021c.

8. Cheung 2021.
9. Powell 2021b.
10. By July 2022, local media were reporting increased soup kitchen usage in many cities across America.
11. FSC Majority Staff 2021.
12. Smialek 2021d.
13. Smialek 2021e.
14. Stiglitz 2021.

Epilogue

1. Kelly 2021.
2. Kuttner 2021.
3. Hyman 1976.

INDEX

community outreach events of,
233; digital currency and role of
Fed, position on, 270, 272–5; Fed
Listens outreach branding by, 132;
governor role of, 6, 122, 124–8;
influence of, 126–7; loyalty of and
higher position for, 271–2; Main
Street program role of, 212–14,
247; marriage and family of,
123–4; monetary policy ideology
of, 125–8, 297, 297*n*; opposition
to regulatory changes by, 122,
125–6, 127; pandemic rescue
program role of, 162, 168, 204,
206; political donation of, 124–5,
342*n*31; politics of, 122, 124–5,
127, 127*n*, 268, 270–1; reputation
of and respect for, 124–5, 126,
162, 214, 271–2; suspension of
bank payments, opinion about,
215; Treasury secretary candidacy
potential for, 271; trust between
and working relationship of
Powell, Quarles, and, 127–8; trust
between and working relationship
with Powell, 300; vice-chair
position of, 6, 299; wealth of, 133
Bretton Woods meeting and
monetary system, 75–6
Buffet, Warren, 16, 24
Bullard, James B. "Jim," 18–19, 141,
284–5
Burgess, W. Randolph, 61
Burns, Arthur, 78, 81, 87, 278
Bush, George H. W., 16, 83, 117,
333*n*9
Bush, George W., 92, 117, 119
businesses/Main Street, 211–12;
economic impact of pandemic on,
40–1, 137–8, 139, 166–8, 202–4,

218–19, 252; rescue programs
during pandemic, 3, 4–5, 6, 7,
35–7, 40–1, 163–5, 177–80,
183–4, 187, 188–9, 189*n*, 191–2,
199, 201, 204–7, 204*n*, 206*n*,
212–14, 237–8, 245–9, 289–91,
301, 346*n*3, 346*n*8, 349*n*3;
support for by Fed, 6, 40–1

Campbell, Kurt, 123–4, 342*n*28
CARES Act and programs, 192, 195,
196, 199, 207, 211, 248, 248*n*,
256–8, 260, 281, 347*n*10
Carlyle Group, The, 17, 117, 333*n*9,
334*n*11
Carney, Mark, 142, 196, 265–6, 268
Carson, Rachel, 264
Carter, Jimmy, 81, 81*n*
Chevy Chase, Maryland, 17–18, 18*n*
China: economic effects of pandemic
in, 134–5; illness of merchant
from Wuhan market, 105, 111;
NGFS role of, 266; reports about
coronavirus in, 134; trade war
with, 107–8, 109
City National Bank of Florida,
245–6
Civil War, 48–9, 53
Clarida, Richard: candidacy for
Fed Board appointment, 14;
career in private sector of, 14,
170, 170*n*; communication role
and trial balloons of, 131, 135–6;
community outreach event role
of, 131–2; community outreach
events of, 233; early thinking
on impact of pandemic, 135–6;
expiration of term of, 271, 299;
guitar playing by, 131; meeting
before Asian markets open during

A NOTE ABOUT THE AUTHOR

JEANNA SMIALEK has been the Federal Reserve reporter at *The New York Times* since April 2019, having previously covered economics for Bloomberg since 2013 from Washington, D.C., New York, and, briefly, Frankfurt. She is a regular contributor to *Marketplace* radio. A Pittsburgh native, Smialek studied journalism and global affairs at the University of North Carolina at Chapel Hill and received her master's in business administration from New York University. She resides in Alexandria, Virginia.

A NOTE ON THE TYPE

This book was set in Adobe Garamond. Designed for the Adobe Corporation by Robert Slimbach, the fonts are based on types first cut by Claude Garamond (ca. 1480–1561).

Composed by North Market Street Graphics
Lancaster, Pennsylvania

Printed and bound by Berryville Graphics
Berryville, Virginia

Designed by Michael Collica